Community Besieged
The Anglophone Minority and the Politics of Quebec

Until the Quiet Revolution of the 1960s English-speaking Quebeckers seldom thought of themselves as a minority and the Quebec government had little influence on their lives. Over the last generation their situation has been totally transformed, as Quebec governments have sought to promote the French language, to reform education and social policy, and to influence the Quebec economy. Quebec's dissatisfaction with its status in Confederation and the growth of the sovereignty movement have also placed the interests of the English minority at risk. While many English-speaking Quebecers have responded by migrating to other provinces, most have stayed in Quebec and tried to adapt to their new circumstances.

In *Community Besieged* Garth Stevenson describes the unusual circumstances that allowed English-speaking Quebeckers to live in virtual isolation from their francophone neighbours for almost a century after Confederation. He describes their relations with Maurice Duplessis and the Union Nationale and their ambivalent response to the Quiet Revolution. New political issues – language policy, educational reform, sovereignty, and the constitution – undermined the old system of elite accommodation in Quebec, causing conflicts between anglophones and francophones and creating a new sense of anglophone identity that transcends religious differences. The changing relations of Quebec anglophones with the major political parties, as well as the role of newer entities such as Alliance Quebec and the Equality Party, are also examined. Stevenson concludes with a look at the future of anglophones in Quebec.

Based in part on interviews with more than sixty English-speaking Quebeckers who have played prominent parts in Quebec's political life, *Community Besieged* is a comprehensive and up-to-date description of the political life of this unique minority at both the federal and provincial level.

GARTH STEVENSON is professor of political science, Brock University.

Community Besieged

The Anglophone Minority and the Politics of Quebec

GARTH STEVENSON

McGill-Queen's University Press
Montreal & Kingston · London · Ithaca

ISBN 0-7735-1839-8

Legal deposit second quarter 1999
Bibliothèque nationale du Québec

Printed in Canada on acid-free paper

This book has been published with the help of a grant
from the Humanities and Social Sciences Federation of
Canada, using funds provided by the Social Sciences
and Humanities Research Council of Canada.

McGill-Queen's University Press acknowledges the
financial support of the Government of Canada
through the Book Publishing Industry Development
Program for its activities. We also acknowledge the
support of the Canada Council for the Arts for our
publishing program.

Canadian Cataloguing in Publication Data

Stevenson, Garth, 1943–
    Community besieged: the anglophone minority and
    the politics of Quebec
    Includes bibliographical references and index.
    ISBN 0-7735-1839-8
    1. Canadians, English-speaking – Quebec (Province) –
    History. 2. Quebec (Province) – Politics and
    government – 1960–   I. Title.

FC2950.5.S74 1999   971.4′004112   C99-900191-4
F1055.E53S74 1999

Typeset in New Baskerville 10/12
by Caractéra inc., Quebec City

Contents

Tables

Acknowledgments

Writing a book that is based on extensive research over a period of almost four years is facilitated by the assistance and cooperation of numerous persons, and I am happy to acknowledge their contribution to this work. In particular, I would like to thank the many present or former English-speaking Quebeckers who agreed to be interviewed, and whose names are listed in the appendix to this book. Several of them also supplied me with documents that would not otherwise have been easily available, if at all.

The Social Sciences and Humanities Research Council of Canada funded the research under grant no. 410-94-0335. My parents, Andrew and Ruth Stevenson, supplied me with free room and board during numerous field trips to Montreal. My two valued research assistants, Christine Czapnik and Nancy Stefureak (now Nancy Chambers), read newspapers on microfilm and parliamentary debates while working towards their master's degrees in the Department of Politics at Brock University. They helped to guide this project through some difficult times and I am happy to report that both received their degrees before the book was completed. Roger DuPuis, a graduate student who entered the department after Christine and Nancy had left, compiled the bibliography and the index. My colleague, Jacqueline Krikorian, read the first draft of the entire manuscript and suggested many improvements. She also checked the endnotes for both accuracy and style, both of which are significantly improved as a result of her efforts. Two anonymous referees who read the manuscript also made useful suggestions which have been implemented, at least in part. Finally, I would like to thank my editor, Philip Cercone of McGill-Queen's University Press, for his faith in this project and for guiding it through to completion.

Community Besieged

1 Intercultural Politics and the Case of Quebec

In his 1979 presidential address to the Canadian Political Science Association, Kenneth D. McRae argued that "Western political thought in general has shown little understanding or respect for the cultural diversity of mankind and has made scant allowance for it as a possible concern of government."[1] McRae was speaking primarily of the classics of normative political philosophy in the European tradition, but until quite recently his comment would have been equally applicable to the modern academic discipline of political science. Political science was born in the United States at a time when faith in the efficacy of the American "melting pot" was at its height and when the only foreign governments considered worth studying were those of Great Britain, Germany, and France. As a result, the discipline initially took for granted the paradigm of the homogeneous "nation-state," whose citizens spoke a common language and for the most part shared common origins. There seemed to be no reason to discard the paradigm until the second half of the twentieth century, when the collapse of western Europe's colonial empires created a large number of new states that were culturally and ethnically diverse. Even then, cultural diversity was considered to be little more than a consequence of the artificial boundaries imposed by the colonial powers and an unhappy complication added to the numerous travails of "development." Those polities afflicted by such woes were consigned to the "third world," an expression that conveyed the sense of an anomalous and somewhat marginal category. The homogeneous nation-state was still considered the norm, rather than the exception. Serious politics, according to this view, was about the management of the economy and the distribution of economic benefits among groups defined by economic function, occupation, or class. Language, ethnicity, religion, and other ascriptive characteristics of populations might complicate the picture in some places, but in the more stable and successful polities they appeared to do so to such a limited extent that they could virtually be ignored.

In some smaller European countries, although not in the major ones, matters did not appear to be quite that simple, even as early as the 1960s. A few scholars noted the paradox that these political systems were deeply divided by social cleavages that were not primarily economic in nature, but that they still managed to escape the instability, ineffectiveness, and wholesale violations of liberal rights and freedoms that characterized the postcolonial states. The theory of consociational democracy, which is discussed in more detail below, was invented to explain the paradox. Yet the homogeneous polity was still considered the norm and the divided polity, whether stable and successful or not, the exception. Perhaps most political scientists implicitly agreed with John Stuart Mill that "Free institutions are next to impossible in a country made up of different nationalities."[2] Hardly any endorsed Lord Acton's contrary view that "The combination of different nations in one State is as necessary a condition of civilised life as the combination of men in society."[3]

As the twentieth century approaches its end, the ubiquitous phenomena of ethnicity, language, and culture, as well as their impact on the operation of political systems, can no longer be ignored. With the end of the cold war the distinctions between first, second, and third worlds lost whatever semblance of meaning it once had. In the former first world, even the most stable and long-established states are enduring the centrifugal forces of disaffected nationalities and other minorities, as well as the conflicts between established populations and newer immigrants who differ from them in language and culture. In the former second world, the once-mighty Soviet Union has disintegrated into fifteen successor states, most of which have internal ethnic and minority problems of their own. In the former third world, economic progress, such as it is, has brought no relief from cultural conflicts. It is difficult to find a "nation-state" anywhere on the planet that is free of cultural conflict, or that corresponds to the old paradigm of one ethnic group, one language, and one culture. The issues of ethnic, linguistic and cultural diversity have moved from the sidelines to the centre of the political stage.

In the circumstances, an examination of one instance where two communities speaking different languages have coexisted peacefully on the same territory for more than a century and a half may be of interest, not only in the country where it has taken place, but even elsewhere. It may be of particular interest insofar as a long period of stability, during which the numerically smaller group was so complacent and secure as to be hardly aware of its minority status, was followed by a period of uncertainty and conflict, caused mainly by social changes within the numerically larger community but also by external circumstances. In the process the old stable relationship between the two linguistic communities broke down. As a result, the smaller community has had to experiment with new ways of defending its interests in the political arena, which it has done with varying degrees of success. Nonetheless, a remarkable degree of civility and peaceful coexistence has been maintained, at least in comparison with other parts of the world. Both communities, the majority and the minority, deserve some credit for that achievement. While the story is not yet over, and some uncertainties remain regarding the outcome, it appears that the peaceful coexistence of the two communities in the territory which they share will continue for the foreseeable future.

It is probably superfluous to explain that these two linguistic communities are the French-speaking majority and the English-speaking minority in the province of Quebec. Since "French-speaking" and "English-speaking" are unwieldy terms, and since they do not automatically convey the sense that the language referred to is the individual's primary language, it has become customary in Quebec to call them francophones and anglophones, terms that will be generally employed in this book. Persons of other mother tongues, who are mainly immigrants or the children of immigrants, are known in Quebec as allophones. While in former times they were largely shunned or ignored by the two established communities, in recent years they have been courted by both sides as possible allies in the peaceful struggle for space and power.

When Canadians think of their country as an example of cultural coexistence, or for that matter of cultural conflict, they usually focus on Canada as a whole and on the relationship between "French-speaking Canadians, centred in Quebec ... and English-speaking Canadians, concentrated outside Quebec."[4] In the vast literature that historians and political scientists have devoted to this topic, the relationship is usually reduced for all practical purposes to that between French Quebec and the rest of the country, or even between French Quebec and the federal government in Ottawa. This relationship is manifested within federal institutions like the cabinet, Parliament and public service, within political parties, and through intergovernmental relations between the two levels of government. Its examination forms a large part of the substance of academic courses and textbooks on Canadian politics.

The Canada-Quebec relationship will no doubt be studied for as long as it continues to exist. The relationship within Quebec, between that province's francophone majority and its anglophone minority, has received much less attention but is at least equally interesting, and perhaps more directly comparable to most of the instances of coexistence between ethnic, linguistic and cultural groups within a political system. Such relationships usually involve groups that mingle on the same territory, or that are geographically segregated only to a limited extent. Most cannot be conducted or managed through mechanisms of intergovernmental relations, as the Canada-Quebec relationship is, at least in part, because the overwhelming majority of the world's polities are unitary rather than federal in their formal structures. Even in those that are federal, the boundaries of the provinces or states rarely coincide even approximately with cultural or linguistic boundaries. The reasons why federal institutions were adopted have in most cases little to do with cultural diversity. Canada is one of the few exceptions. The classic, and still unrivalled, defence of the federal concept by James Madison, Alexander Hamilton, and John Jay makes no mention of cultural diversity or its political implications.[5]

Rather than federalism, the most successful instances of managing such relationships involve the use of another device which has been called consociationalism, or consociational democracy. One may go further and suggest that federalism, corporatism, and consociationalism are three distinct ways of managing three distinct kinds of conflicts, which is not to deny that a political system may include federalist, corporatist and consociational features in various combinations. The three concepts are analytically distinct, even if they may occur together. Federalism is a device for managing conflicts of region or geographical space. Corporatism is a device for managing conflicts of economic function or class. Consociationalism is a device for managing conflicts of ethnicity, language, religion or culture.[6]

In Canada corporatist tendencies have been weak, except perhaps in Quebec where they were encouraged by the Catholic Church after the publication of the papal encyclical *Rerum Novarum* in 1891.[7] As a result federal institutions, which were copied from the United States although modified by conservative and monarchical aspects of the Canadian political culture, have largely borne the burden of managing all three types of conflicts. Class conflict between prairie farmers and eastern capitalists, and cultural conflict between French Catholic Quebec and the English-speaking Protestant majority, were mediated through Parliament and cabinet or through intergovernmental relations, not always with great success.

Outside of Quebec there were relatively few places where anglophones and francophones lived in close enough proximity to be frequently reminded of one another's existence. Even in New Brunswick, where the minority group comprises a relatively large share of the population, the almost unpopulated interior separates the Acadian north shore from the Loyalist south and west. Quebec, however, was a special case that required special treatment. Within Quebec, where large numbers of anglophone and francophone Canadians interacted and mingled on the same territory, social harmony was preserved, until recently, through effective consociational arrangements. Besides enabling Quebec itself to prosper, these arrangements removed from the federal government much of the burden of facilitating the peaceful coexistence of the two linguistic communities.

The consociational arrangements in Quebec were subjected to severe stresses and strains by social, economic and political developments that began with the so-called Quiet Revolution of the 1960s. Eventually the arrangements ceased to be viable, and collapsed. The theme of this book is how the anglophone minority in Quebec responded to these developments and how it adapted to its new circumstances. Before discussing these matters, however, it is necessary to examine the concept of consociationalism and how it applies to the case of Quebec.

THE CONCEPT OF CONSOCIATIONAL DEMOCRACY

The concept of consociational democracy was developed in the 1960s by Arend Lijphart, who applied it to the study of Dutch politics in his book *The Politics of Accommodation*. Lijphart began by stating the paradox that the political system in the Netherlands was both democratic and stable despite "an extraordinary degree of social cleavage." He described Dutch society as follows: "Deep religious and class divisions separate distinct, isolated, and self-contained population groups. Social communication across class and religious boundary lines is minimal. Each group has its own ideology and its own political organizations: political parties, labor unions, employers' associations, farmers' groups, newspapers, radio and television organizations, and schools – from kindergarten to university."[8]

Furthermore, Lijphart noted that there was little in the way of national consensus, common loyalties, or attachment to national symbols to transcend the deep divisions between the ideological blocs.

Social cleavages were mutually reinforcing rather than cross-cutting, violating what some political scientists had alleged to be a necessary condition for stable democracy. Nonetheless, the kingdom of the Netherlands had survived as a united, stable, and successful democracy for several generations and its continued survival was not in question. Lijphart's exploration of how the Dutch version of liberal democracy actually worked led him to develop a new concept which he called consociational democracy, in contrast to the usual type of majoritarian liberal democracy. He defined consociational democracy as "government by elite cartel designed to turn a democracy with a fragmented political culture into a stable democracy."[9]

More specifically, Lijphart observed that each of the subcultures in the Netherlands had a recognized elite, including politicians, leaders of voluntary organizations, and so forth, who enjoyed the trust and confidence of the people whom they represented. Institutional mechanisms were available for elite bargaining and accommodation. Overarching cooperation at this level compensated for the lack of national sentiment and of cross-cutting affiliations at the mass level, since the elites were dedicated to ensuring the survival of the nation.

Lijphart identified seven "rules of the game" that seemed to characterize the behaviour of Dutch elites and that facilitated elite accommodation and stability: be businesslike, pragmatic and result-oriented, don't try to change the fundamental convictions of other groups, make decisions through summit diplomacy, practice proportionality rather than majoritarianism in the distribution of benefits among groups, depoliticize issues wherever possible, shield pragmatic compromises and concessions from public scrutiny, and allow the executive to govern with minimal interference from the legislature and from the voters.[10]

Lijphart also discovered that the political culture of the Netherlands was deferential. Rank-and-file members of the different subcultures seemed content to leave the task of governing the country in the hands of their respective elites rather than seeking open ideological debate and a high level of mass participation. In these circumstances the lack of social interaction between subcultures at the mass level and the lack of overarching national sentiment were not detrimental to stable democracy, as most students of comparative politics would have predicted. The mutual isolation of the subcultures lessened the risk of friction and conflict that might have resulted from greater contact between them, and was thus advantageous.[11] Contact was virtually confined to elites who observed the "rules of the game," were experienced in the art of accommodation, and were highly committed to the peaceful resolution or avoidance of disputes.

Although devised to describe and explain a particular political system, the concept of consociationalism is more broadly applicable both as a description of other political systems that share some of the characteristics of the Netherlands and possibly as a prescription for other societies that have been less successful in dealing with cultural diversity. Both applications require the definition of those essential features without which a consociational democracy cannot be said to exist. According to Lijphart, these "basic principles" are four in number: an executive government in which the political leaders of all significant segments participate, the delegation of extensive decision-making autonomy to the segments, proportionality in the allocation of benefits among the segments, and the ability of any segment to veto decisions that would threaten its vital interests.[12]

In the decade that followed the publication of *The Politics of Accommodation,* a substantial literature on consociationalism was produced by a number of political scientists including Lijphart himself, Hans Daalder, Gerhard Lehmbruch, Val Lorwin, Eric Nordlinger, and others. The model was applied with apparent success to certain other countries, including Austria, Belgium, and Switzerland. Summarizing the conclusions of this literature, it is possible to identify the main conditions for, and characteristics of, a consociational democracy. The countries which seem to fit the model are small to medium in size and are, or have been, menaced by more powerful neighbours. They are deeply divided along lines of religion, ideology, culture, language, or some combination thereof. Their political cultures are characterized by considerable deference to elites and institutions, rather than by populism. The elites representing the subcultures are determined to avoid instability and violence. They are also determined to avoid secession or partition of the country, possibly because it would either damage the economy or encourage interference by neighbouring states, and so they make use of procedures for accommodating the interests of their followers and devising consensual solutions to problems. These procedures over time become institutionalized, and usually include multiparty coalition governments, proportional representation to prevent any one group from dominating the legislature and to ensure that all groups will be adequately represented at all times, and application of the proportionality principle to other institutions such as the public service and the courts. Subcultures are treated with equal respect, even if they are not strictly equal in size. The "rules of the game" identified by Lijphart are consistently and conscientiously observed.

As the literature on consociational democracy proliferated, a number of other variables were identified that seemed to contribute to its existence. Nordlinger, for example, counted no less than fourteen necessary conditions.[13] On the other hand, Adriano Pappalardo examined a long list of variables and concluded that only two were really essential for successful consociational democracy: a stable pattern of social segmentation and strong subcultural elites supported by deferential followers. Those that he rejected as unimportant included small size, an external threat, a neutral or passive foreign policy, cross-cutting cleavages, overarching loyalty to the nation-state among elites, and historical traditions of elite accommodation.[14]

While the contributors to the literature seem to be broadly in agreement regarding most of the fundamentals, there are differences in how they understand the relationship among the three main variables of social segmentation, elite accommodation, and consociational democracy itself. Lijphart seemed to argue that "overarching cooperation at the elite level" is learned behaviour, devised "with the deliberate aim of counteracting disintegrative tendencies in the system."[15] Daalder, on the other hand, suggested that elite accommodation is an independent variable that existed prior to the rise of liberal democracy and the emergence of potential threats to unity and stability, arguing that "accommodationist styles developed in the Netherlands in the sixteenth, seventeenth, and eighteenth centuries."[16] Lorwin emphasized social and cultural segmentation as the defining characteristic of a consociational society, whether or not effective elite accommodation takes place. He claimed that "Not building effective elite co-operation into the definition makes one more likely to examine the conditions which induce, and those which inhibit or frustrate, such co-operation."[17]

Consociational democracy, which is essentially egalitarian and consensual, is not the only way in which a deeply divided society can achieve stable government. Ian Lustick developed a model which he called "control," to describe a non-egalitarian and non-consensual alternative; South Africa under apartheid was cited as an example. In a control system the dominant group controls the authoritative allocation of resources and gives its own interests priority over those of one or more subordinate groups. There is little bargaining between groups, except possibly in situations where the system is breaking down. The regime is an instrument in the hands of the dominant group rather than an impartial umpire or a forum for intergroup negotiations. The official ideology emphasizes the specific needs of the dominant group, rather than the desirability of intergroup accommodation. Lustick suggests that control systems occur as frequently as consociational democracies, if not more so.[18]

Another alternative to consociational democracy is suggested by Martin N. Marger, who presents a typology of three types of multi-ethnic society.[19] The first, or colonial, type is identical to Lustick's control model. The second type, which Marger calls "corporate pluralistic," is similar to the consociational model. The third type, of which Brazil, Israel, and the United States are cited as examples, is assimilationist. In contrast to the first and second types, there is little segregation or institutional separation among groups. Instead, the dominant group encourages other groups to assimilate to its way of life and cultural values, although members of minority groups may continue to interact much more with each other than with other citizens. Official ideology does not proclaim the superiority of the dominant group, as it does in the colonial system. Marger makes the interesting suggestion that intergroup conflict may be greater in this system than in either of the others. In the colonial system the subordinate groups are unable to challenge the status quo, while in the corporate pluralist type "conflict is held in check by a relative balance of political and economic power." In the assimilationist system conflict for position and power is largely unrestrained, although the dominant group enjoys significant advantages over other groups.[20]

Proponents of the consociational model view it as the best alternative for a multi-ethnic society since it is both egalitarian, in the sense that no group is dominant over other groups, and relatively peaceful. In other words it appears to minimize both conflict and injustice. On the other hand, there are possible reasons for scepticism. Since consociationalism requires particular circumstances for it to arise, the model cannot be easily or automatically exported to societies that suffer from intergroup conflict or injustice. Furthermore, consociationalism can be a precarious and short-lived achievement even in societies where it has been established. Finally, it may be suggested that consociationalism requires populations that are relatively passive and deferential to their elites, and thus falls short of the democratic ideal. Although some may argue that this is not an excessive price to pay for the advantages of consociationalism, others would disagree.

APPLICATIONS OF THE MODEL TO CANADA AND QUEBEC

Given the Canadian preoccupation with social segmentation and "national unity," it was predictable that the concept of consociational democracy would attract the attention of Canadian political scientists soon after it appeared. Apart from its usefulness as a tool for analyzing Canadian politics, the concept offered reassurance that a democratic state could be viable without either cultural homogeneity or ideological solidarity based on a founding myth like that of the American

Declaration of Independence. A conference on the theme of "Integration and Disintegration in the Canadian Political System," held in Quebec City in 1970, featured a paper on consociational democracy presented by Lijphart and later published in the *Canadian Journal of Political Science.*[21]

S.J.R. Noel presented a paper at the same conference which attempted to apply the consociational model to Canadian federal-provincial relations.[22] It argued, not very plausibly, that the ten provinces were distinct subcultures, an assumption that the sociologist John Porter had earlier and rightly dismissed as "Some of the hallowed nonsense that goes into the theory of Canadian federalism."[23] Noel's paper went on to suggest that federal-provincial conferences – then much in vogue – were the Canadian equivalent of the coalition governments within which elite accommodation took place in the European consociational democracies.

Kenneth McRae, who is perhaps Canada's leading student of the politics of culturally divided societies, edited a book of essays on consociational democracy which appeared in 1974. Some of the essays dealt with the consociational democracies of western Europe, while others tried to apply the model to the Canadian case. McRae however argued, with some regret, that Canada was not in fact a consociational democracy, mainly because the anglophone majority was wedded to majoritarian principles and thus disinclined to make the necessary consociational compromises with the francophone minority.[24] McRae doubted whether consociational patterns of elite accommodation really existed in Canada, except perhaps at the provincial level in Quebec. The closest approach to an institutionalized pattern of elite accommodation in Canada as a whole had existed prior to 1867, when Canada East and Canada West, the future Quebec and Ontario, comprised a single province and were equally represented in its parliament. McRae concluded that "the quest to accommodate linguistic diversity in Canada may be viewed as a series of lost opportunities."[25]

Another prominent Canadian political scientist, Donald V. Smiley, questioned the applicability of the consociational concept to Canada in 1977. Perhaps influenced by his western Canadian background, Smiley was not convinced "that the relations between English and French dominate Canadian politics as do subcultural relations between ethnic groups in such nations as Belgium and Switzerland."[26] He also suggested, like McRae, that "the dominant traditions and practices of the Canadian political system work against French-English consociationalism."[27] He did note that politics at the provincial level in Quebec had been characterized by a high degree of consociationalism "until recently." However, this was likely to change since Quebec nationalists were beginning to reject consociationalism and to act in a majoritarian manner.

Despite the hints by both McRae and Smiley that Quebec would be a more appropriate case to examine with the aid of the consociational model than Canada as a whole, few political scientists showed any inclination to take up the challenge. As Smiley suggested, the electoral victory of the Parti Québécois in 1976 seemed to have ended the era of consociationalism in Quebec politics. Most of the political scientists who wrote extensively about Quebec politics were sympathetic to Quebec nationalism and not favourably inclined towards the anglophone minority in the province or towards the tradition of elite accommodation. Pierre Fournier's Marxist analysis of elite accommodation between government and business, based largely on interviews conducted in 1973, downplayed the importance of the cultural cleavage and made no reference to the consociational literature.[28] In *Quebec: Social Change and Political Crisis*, perhaps the most widely-read English-language book about Quebec politics, Kenneth McRoberts mentioned consociationalism only to note its non-existence at the federal level.[29] Political scientists writing in French ignored the subject almost completely.

An American political scientist, Milton J. Esman, has applied the consociational model to Quebec in one chapter of his book *Ethnic Politics*.[30] Esman asserts that "During the century preceding the Quiet Revolution, ethnic pluralism in Quebec was regulated by consociational arrangements."[31] Although arguing that the Quiet Revolution of the 1960s began to undermine these arrangements, he suggests that the real turning point came in 1974 when the Bourassa government adopted legislation making French the official language and restricting the use of English in public institutions. Since 1974, according to Esman, "terms of coexistence are not negotiated, they are dictated by nationalist elites in firm control of Quebec's political institutions."[32]

The only book-length attempts to apply the consociational model to Quebec politics have been unpublished master's theses. In 1980 Brendan P. O'Donnell used the consociational model with some success to examine accommodation between anglophone and francophone elites in the first five years after Confederation.[33] A more contemporary, and much more theoretical, thesis by Christopher C. Cooper was presented at the University of Alberta in 1987.[34] Cooper applied the three versions of consociational theory associated with Lijphart, Daalder, and Lorwin to an examination of Quebec society and politics between 1936 and 1977. He concluded that all three versions fit the Quebec case reasonably well. Consociational elite accommodation between anglophones and francophones had been effective at the beginning of the period studied but had gradually deteriorated under the impact of increasing Quebec nationalism and the decline of the anglophone economic elite. However, he predicted that the increasing commitment of francophone elites to economic growth, greater political activism among the anglophones, and the return of the Quebec Liberals to office in 1985 would contribute to a rapprochement between the two communities and a revival of consociationalism.

One published work that applies the consociational model to the study of a Canadian province should also be mentioned, although it deals with New Brunswick rather than Quebec. Edmund Aunger's book *In Search of Political Stability*, based on his doctoral dissertation at the University of California, compares New Brunswick with Northern Ireland. He concludes that New Brunswick is a successful case of elite accommodation between two cultural communities while Northern Ireland, obviously, is not. He notes that New Brunswick is successful even though it lacks three of Lijphart's conditions for effective conso-ciational democracy: an external threat, a multiple balance of power among subcultures, and a penchant for coalition governments. On the other hand, the stability of New Brunswick is possibly aided by the fact that many anglophones are Catholics, so that religion is to some extent a cross-cutting cleavage.[35]

There are few parts of North America where ethnic, religious, and cultural segmentation have been as obvious as they have been in Quebec since its acquisition by the British Empire in the eighteenth century. From the "conquest," until responsible government was established in 1848, the situation closely approximated Lustick's control model or Marger's colonial system, with the British as the dominant group. Although British rule in Quebec was never as harsh as that of the dominant group in white-ruled South Africa or in most colonies of the European empires, there was little question that they enjoyed effective control. Even after responsible government established a consociational regime that gave real political power to some franco-phone elites, the situation was complicated by the forced union between mainly francophone Canada East and mainly anglophone Canada West that existed from 1841 until 1867.

In 1867, however, Quebec became a self-governing province within a Canadian federation. After that date, as Esman has suggested, and until recently, Quebec seemed to have most of the characteristics that are associated with consociational democracy in the literature. The social and cultural segmentation between "English" and "French" was as great as before, but both language groups were elitist rather than populist: relations between the two took the form of elite bargaining and search for consensus rather than the dictation by one group to the other. The overarching elites generally recognized the need to accommodate the different interests and preferences of the two language communities and devoted conscious efforts to doing so. Quebec's population, about one million at the time of Confederation and about seven million today, has always been relatively small. The heavily populated central core of its territory, roughly a triangle with its corners at Hull, Quebec City, and Lac Memphremagog, is comparable in physical size to the smaller democracies of western Europe. Its anglophone and francophone elites have at times shared the perception of an external threat either from the United States or from populist forces in other parts of Canada.

Until the 1970s, Lijphart's seven "rules of the game" were generally followed by Quebec premiers, cabinet ministers, and other influential persons. Even the more nationalist governments tended to be pragmatic and businesslike in their approach. The fundamental convictions of the anglophone minority were accepted and respected, although not always admired, by the francophone majority. Proportionality was usually maintained, with the relatively small anglophone group receiving at least its fair share of most benefits. (Jobs in the public service are an exception to this rule, but anglophones have traditionally not been much interested in them.) Fundamental decisions affecting the interests of the minority were usually made after private negotiation with its representatives. Important matters were traditionally depoliticized where possible, as Ralph Heintzman has argued in his study of Quebec's political culture before the Quiet Revolution.[36] Executive dominance in policy-making is a characteristic that Quebec shares with other political systems whose institutions are based on the Westminster model. There has been little criticism of it in Quebec, in contrast to certain other Canadian provinces.

The most obvious difference between Quebec and the European consociational democracies is the fact that Quebec is a province within a federation rather than a sovereign state. This may have complicated somewhat the operation of consociational democracy, but did not impede it except insofar as a few instances of federal policies imposed on Quebec (the execution of Louis Riel in 1885, conscription in 1917 and 1944, and constitutional reform in 1982) caused a deterioration in relations between Quebec's two language communities. Most of the matters that directly affect relations between the two communities on a day-to-day basis, such as education, municipal government, health and social services, fall under provincial jurisdiction in Canada. During the years when consociational democracy flourished in Quebec the provincial level of government was the primary forum of elite accommodation, although the federal level was sometimes relevant as well.

As Esman argues, Quebec ceased to be truly consociational some time after the Quiet Revolution. How, when, and why consociational arrangements broke down are discussed in some detail in the middle chapters of this book. Quebec has entered a post-consociational phase, but it is still not a unilingual or homogeneous society. How then should it be characterized today? Some disgruntled Quebec anglophones might argue that Lustick's control model or Marger's colonial type is now applicable, with the francophone majority as the dominant group. However, it would be grossly unfair and misleading to classify present-day Quebec in this way. The anglophone minority in Quebec may suffer some inconvenience and loss of status, but they are not exploited, controlled or dominated by their francophone compatriots, whatever some of the rhetoric heard in English-speaking Montreal might suggest. It would be more accurate to state that Quebec is attempting to become what Marger calls an assimilationist society, like the United States but with French rather than English as the common language. This attempt may or may not be successful. Meanwhile it is causing increased intergroup conflict, as Marger's model predicts.

CONSOCIATIONALISM AND THE ANGLOPHONE MINORITY

This book is not a comprehensive treatment of Quebec politics using the consociational model, in the sense that Lijphart's *The Politics of Accommodation* is a comprehensive treatment of politics in the Netherlands. It is a study of the anglophone minority in Quebec politics. Its purpose is to explore how the anglophone minority, which benefitted from an effective system of consociational elite accommodation for about a century after Confederation, adapted to changes in its circumstances after the Quiet Revolution. The most significant of those changes were the transfer of education and other "social" responsibilities from the Catholic Church to the bureaucratic state, the politicization of language, and the rise of a major political party dedicated to the goal of making Quebec a sovereign state. Because of these changes, along with the end of (anglophone) Montreal's historic role as the headquarters of the commercial empire of the St Lawrence, consociational democracy in Quebec has been replaced by majoritarian democracy. As a result the anglophone minority has had to discover, by a process of trial and error that is still continuing, new ways of defending its collective interests within the society of Quebec.

A few words regarding the definition of the anglophone minority in Quebec are probably appropriate. Anglophones in Quebec are not an ethnic group sharing common origins and a common culture, like the Acadians of New Brunswick, the Flemish in Belgium, or the francophone Swiss. Even in 1867 they included, at the very least, British Protestant and Irish Catholic elements that were quite distinct, as well as Irish Protestants (by no means all of whom came from the six counties that were later separated from Ireland) who shared some characteristics of both groups. Today the anglophones of Quebec include people with a variety of ethnic, religious, and racial origins, some of them recently arrived in the province and some with roots there that extend back for many generations. In fact the anglophone community of Quebec is as heterogeneous as the total population of other provinces that have received significant immigration in recent years, such as Ontario or British Columbia. The only attribute that all Quebec anglophones share is something that most other North Americans take for granted: the English language. In Quebec it cannot be taken for granted, because it sets them apart from most of their fellow-citizens.

The language-related categories in the Canadian census are of some help in defining and measuring this population, but they have not been consistent over time and are not without ambiguity. Until 1921 the census had no question related to language, although it collected data on ethnic origins. For these early years, the size of the anglophone community in Quebec can be estimated approximately by combining the numbers who stated their ethnic origin to be English, Scottish, or Irish. The census of 1921 added a question on "mother tongue," which is still used. Mother tongue is defined as the language first learned in childhood and still understood. This category greatly understates the size of the anglophone population in Quebec, since many persons have for all practical purposes abandoned the mother tongue which they learned from immigrant parents or learned in another country before coming to Canada themselves. Until recently such persons tended to adopt English rather than French as their new language, even in Quebec. The francophone majority did not discourage them from doing so, since it was wary of outsiders and confident that its high birth rate would maintain its numerical dominance without the necessity of seeking reinforcements from the immigrant communities.

The 1971 census added a new category, "language spoken at home," which better reflects present reality than that of a "mother tongue" which may have been learned sixty, seventy or eighty years ago and abandoned since. The difference between the number declaring

English as a mother tongue and those who speak it at home represents the net transfer to the anglophone community of persons who originally had other languages.

Even "language spoken at home," however, may not accurately measure the size of the anglophone community for some relevant purposes. Some persons who speak a non-official language at home may be more fluent in English than in French and may thus prefer to use English rather than French in their dealings with public or parapublic authorities. They may also prefer English newspapers, magazines, radio and television to their French equivalents. Persons of this kind are also, for some purposes at least, a part of the anglophone community in Quebec. On the other hand there are some francophones who speak English at home with anglophone spouses and children, but retain their francophone identity. Since 1991, but not before that, the census has recognized these facts with another category: "first official language spoken." This indicates, roughly, the official language that the person would probably prefer to use in his or her dealings with the federal state and its agencies.

As an added complication, the census since 1986 allows multiple responses, not only for ethnic origin but for mother tongue, language spoken at home, and even first official language spoken since that category was introduced. While most people in the Western hemisphere are of mixed ethnic origin, whether they admit it or not, multiple language categories seem somewhat more questionable. However, they are realistic in Quebec insofar as many persons have an anglophone father and a francophone mother, or vice versa. This situation is becoming more common since religious inhibitions against "mixed" marriages have diminished, anglophones have gained fluency in French, and the traditional disparity in economic status between anglophones and francophones has disappeared. Depending on how the persons with multiple responses in the language categories are allocated, the size of the anglophone community can be made to seem larger or smaller. Table 1.1 suggests some of the possibilities.

Different ways of estimating the size of the community may have political implications. Francophones may minimize the apparent size of the anglophone population in order to suggest that there is less need for English-language services in education, health, or municipal government, or less need for affirmative action to correct the under-representation of anglophones in the public service. Alternatively, they may maximize its size in order to suggest that the primacy of the French language or the numerical predominance of francophones in Montreal is threatened by the anglophone presence. Anglophones can also vary estimates of the size of their community for similar purposes.

Table 1.1
Size of the Anglophone Community in 1991, Using Different Criteria

1	Mother tongue, English only	601,405
2	Mother tongue, English or English and other	738,640
3	Home language, English only	716,155
4	Home language, English or English and other	800,275
5	First official language spoken, English only	832,050
6	First official language spoken, English only or English and French	976,560
7	"Official Language Minority"[1]	904,305

Source: Calculated from data in Canada, *Census,* 1991–96.

[1] The official language minority is defined as the number whose first official language spoken is the minority official language in the province, plus half of those whose first official language spoken is both English and French.

At least Canada has so far avoided the situation of Nigeria in 1975, when the data from the census conducted two years earlier were officially abandoned because they "will not command general acceptance throughout the country."[37]

While the boundaries of the anglophone community in Quebec can thus not be defined with precision, its existence as a demographic reality, reinforced by a variety of public and private institutions that provide for its needs and that tend to distinguish it from the francophone majority, has been one of the most durable, and distinctive, aspects of life in the province. The present book examines the community's participation in the politics of Quebec and Canada and its efforts to adapt to the changes that have overtaken it in recent years.

Chapter 2 describes the origins and development of the community and of the system of consociational democracy that survived almost unchallenged from Confederation until the Quiet Revolution of the 1960s. While Quebec anglophones did not generally support Confederation, they were given constitutional guarantees that reassured them to some extent, and were subsequently able to strengthen their position as a distinct and nearly autonomous minority. Social and institutional segregation and an effective system of elite accommodation at the provincial level maintained this situation with remarkably little change for a century, despite enormous economic and social changes in Quebec. Although anglophones were generally hostile to the Quebec government after the Second World War, that government in no way threatened their privileges. So secure was the situation of anglophones in Quebec that they could devote most of their political energy and attention to the federal level of government.

Chapter 3 describes the response of Quebec anglophones to the Quiet Revolution of the 1960s. Since it was presided over by the

Quebec Liberal Party, to which they gave overwhelming support, and since it was expected to make Quebec less nationalistic and more similar to other parts of North America, the Quiet Revolution was generally welcomed and supported by anglophones. However, in the long run it weakened their position by creating a modern bureaucratic state at the provincial level. The new bureaucratic state naturally aspired to govern the entire population in the manner of other states, rather than delegating many of its functions to religious communities and private institutions that served distinct groups of the population. This threatened the mutual isolation of the anglophone and franco-phone subcultures and also made it more difficult to depoliticize sensitive issues. Nationalism did not disappear as expected but began to assume more threatening forms, including a movement for an independent sovereign Quebec. Simultaneously with these develop-ments, changes in the political economy of Canada and in federal politics were almost equally dramatic. These external changes under-mined the importance of the Montreal-based anglophone economic elite, and thus weakened the Quebec anglophone community as a whole.

Chapter 4 describes how and why the status of the English and French languages in Quebec, which had been largely unchanged and largely taken for granted for a century, became a major political issue between 1968 and 1976. This development coincided with the increasing polarization of Quebec society between supporters of sovereignty and federalism. Anglophones became an unpopular and insecure minority, forcing them to devote more of their attention to provincial than to federal politics for the first time. They felt particularly betrayed when a Quebec Liberal government with strong anglophone representation introduced legislation that reduced the public role of the English language to some extent and made French the official language of the province. Many anglophones abandoned the Liberal Party in the 1976 election and voted for the Union Nationale, but they found themselves in more dire straits when the Parti Québécois won a major-ity of seats in the National Assembly.

Chapter 5 considers the response of the anglophone community to the election of a Parti Québécois government in 1976 and its relations with that government over the next nine years. The government's first major initiative was the adoption of a new language law, the Charter of the French Language, or Bill 101, which further restricted the status and privileges of the anglophone community. Many anglophones responded by leaving the province, with the consequence that the size of the community declined in absolute terms for the first time in its history. Those who remained recognized that consociational elite accommodation in the old style was no longer possible and that other means of political action were necessary, at least for as long as the Parti Québécois remained in office. A number of groups and associations were formed, culminating in the emergence of an inclusive federally-funded anglophone lobby group known as Alliance Quebec. Alliance Quebec opened a dialogue with the government and was able to secure some concessions in language legislation through lobbying, while other victories were won through litigation.

Chapter 6 begins with the return of the Liberals to office in 1985 and the restoration of significant anglophone representation in the cabinet. The new government, as anticipated, made some concessions to anglophone interests but one of its major promises – to allow the public display of commercial signs in English as well as French – was abandoned, despite a judicial ruling that the prohibition of bilingual signs violated a constitutional right to freedom of expression. These events provoked the resignation of three anglophone ministers from the government and the formation of a new protest party which won a majority of anglophone votes, and four seats, in the election of 1989. However, the new party soon lost its momentum and disintegrated, partly because of controversies involving the Canadian constitution and partly because the resurgence of the sovereignty movement drove anglophone voters back into the arms of the Liberals.

Chapter 7 describes an anglophone community in disarray following the 1994 election, which restored the Parti Québécois to office, and the referendum a year later, in which political sovereignty for Quebec was rejected by a very narrow majority of the voters. Consociational elite accommodation was permanently defunct, but neither interest group lobbying nor protest voting had really provided acceptable substitutes for it. Many anglophones blamed their community's own leadership for its predicament and espoused extreme remedies, including the idea of partitioning Quebec to remove the predominantly anglophone areas from the province. The Quebec government attempted to reopen a dialogue with its anglophone minority but found them too divided and disgruntled to respond to its overtures.

Chapter 8 examines the relations of Quebec anglophones with the federal level of government since 1968, a period during which the provincial level has occupied a larger share of their attention. It suggests that the federal level was of limited, although not entirely negligible, help to the anglophones in their struggles to maintain a viable community in the province. Despite the strong anglophone support for the federal Liberal Party, that party was no more supportive of their interests than the Progressive Conservatives, who held office from 1984 to 1993. The chapter includes an examination of the Quebec anglophone outlook on the controversies over the Canadian constitution, suggesting that anglophones were torn between their desire for restrictions on provincial powers and their reluctance to provoke a resurgence of pro-sovereignty sentiment among their francophone compatriots.

Chapter 9 considers the future of relations between language groups in Quebec. Francophone political elites argue that French should be the common language of the province and that minorities should accept this fact, just as minorities in the United States and in most Canadian provinces accept the predominance of English. Where does Quebec's anglophone minority fit into this scenario? The chapter examines the options available to Quebec anglophones in their "peaceful struggle for space and power"[38] within Quebec. It suggests that measures to strengthen their civil society and to welcome immigrants into their community may be as important as participation in elections, parties, and interest groups, if not more so. The book concludes with a prognosis for the future of the anglophone community in Quebec, suggesting that its future may not be as bleak as is often believed.

2 Consociationalism Established: 1867–1960

As was noted in the previous chapter, Hans Daalder has suggested that a pre-democratic tradition of elite accommodation may have paved the way for consociational democracy in the Netherlands. This seems also to be true in the case of Quebec. The roots of intercultural elite accommodation in Quebec can be traced back to the relationships developed between British officials and military officers and French clergy in the aftermath of the British conquest. The colonial regime was neither consociational nor democratic, since the French were clearly subordinated to British control and had little political or economic power. Nonetheless, the very small size of the British minority in the colony, and the precariousness of British rule before, during, and after the American Revolution, led the conquerors to make some concessions.

When French officers, officials, and merchants returned to France after the conquest, to be replaced in Canada by their British counterparts, the clergy filled the vacuum of leadership that these departures created. The British, although officially hostile to Catholicism, soon recognized the convenience of making an arrangement with the clerical elite, perhaps in part because some aristocratic British governors found the French clergy more congenial than the English-speaking entrepreneurs who entered the colony after the conquest. Through a process of trial and error the colonizers developed the technique of indirect rule that their successors would later use in India and Africa, leaving local institutions, customs and elites in place to manage the indigenous population while they devoted their attention to business

and military defence. The Quebec Act, adopted by the British Parliament in 1774, guaranteed the continuation of French civil law and
the special privileges of the Catholic Church. The clergy in return
preached submission to British rule which, as time went on, they
contrasted favourably with the alleged horrors of the American and
French revolutions. During two American invasions, in 1775 and
1812, and throughout the long war between the British Empire and
revolutionary France, French Canadians remained loyal to King
George.

English-speaking settlers had begun to arrive in what is now the
province of Quebec as soon as, and even before, the formal transfer
of Canada to British rule in 1763. Fur traders, farmers and merchants,
demobilized soldiers and United Empire Loyalists, English, Irish, Scots
and Americans, they settled in many parts of the province, particularly
in the two main cities of Montreal and Quebec and in outlying regions
that had not been extensively settled by French-speaking Canadians
before the conquest. The most important rural concentration developed in the hilly area south of the St Lawrence and east of the
Richelieu known as the Eastern Townships. Other important concentrations of English-speaking settlement were in the southwestern
corner of the province between New York State and the St Lawrence,
along the south shore of the Gaspé peninsula, and in the Ottawa
Valley.[1]

The partition of Canada into Upper Canada and Lower Canada by
the Constitution Act of 1791, which also established representative
assemblies in both sections, laid the foundations for what are now the
provinces of Ontario and Quebec respectively. The purpose of the
partition was to provide the United Empire Loyalists of the western
section with a colony of their own that would be English-speaking,
mainly Protestant, and governed by English common law. The Upper
Canada thus established would be, as it still is more than two centuries
later, a magnet for immigrants. Given the recent loss of the thirteen
colonies further south, it represented the largest supply of unoccupied
arable land for British subjects who wished to move to North America
without leaving the British Empire.

Yet if the partition was meant to separate English-speaking Protestants from French-speaking Catholics, this purpose was not entirely
achieved. As noted above, a substantial English-speaking population
already existed in predominantly French-speaking Lower Canada, and
no effort was made to discourage further arrivals from the British Isles
or the United States. Lord Durham noted this anomaly almost half a
century after the partition in his report on the affairs of British North
America, which describes Lower Canada with the now-celebrated

expression "two nations warring in the bosom of a single state."[2] Durham argued that conquered territories can be dealt with in two ways, either by preserving the existing society if the territory is thickly populated or by opening it to new settlement if it is not.[3] Neither policy was consistently followed in the Canadian case and the imperial government had made matters worse by the "unwise course" of dividing Canada into two parts. Durham thought it inadvisable to constitute the French of Lower Canada into a majority living under French institutions, but even this policy had not been pursued consistently. The imperial government had encouraged "the emigration of English into the very Province which was said to be assigned to the French."[4] Rather than solving a minority problem, the partition had created one.

The Act of Union, adopted by the imperial parliament in 1840, followed Durham's advice by reuniting the two colonies. This instantly reduced the French Canadians to the status of a minority, given the large number of anglophones in Lower Canada. To make matters doubly certain, Canada West (Upper Canada) was given equal representation with Canada East (Lower Canada) in the colonial parliament, despite its smaller population. After 1851, when the census revealed that Canada West's population had surpassed that of Canada East, this provision worked to the disadvantage of the western section and became a source of discontent there. In Canada East, on the other hand, the English-speaking inhabitants shared in the benefits of their section's over-representation.

Responsible government, which Durham had proposed, came to Canada by 1849 under the administration of Durham's son-in-law, Lord Elgin, who was appointed governor general in 1847. Durham's other recommendation, the assimilation of the French, was tacitly abandoned by imperial policy-makers at about the same time, a fact symbolized when Elgin read part of the speech from the throne in French.[5] English-speaking inhabitants of Canada East may have been disappointed by this, but they were far more seriously affronted when Elgin signed a bill to compensate French Canadians whose property had been damaged or lost by British troops during the suppression of the rebellion in 1837–38. A serious riot ensued which culminated in the burning of the Parliament buildings in Montreal, which was then a predominantly English-speaking city. As a result Montreal lost, and never regained, its status as the capital of Canada. Reinforcing the unhappiness over the imperial government's adoption of free trade, which benefitted the United States at the expense of the British colonies, this episode contributed to the annexation manifesto which was signed in 1849 by a number of English-speaking Montrealers, including a future prime minister of Canada, John J. Abbott.[6]

Once this crisis had passed, however, the English-speaking inhabitants of Canada East seem to have had little cause for dissatisfaction, although their newspapers continued to stir up francophobic sentiments.[7] Immigration kept their share of Canada East's population stable at about one-quarter of the total from 1844 through 1861, a reciprocity treaty with the United States provided the economic benefits of annexation without the political costs, and the building of the Grand Trunk Railway, with its operating headquarters in Montreal, reinforced that city's position as the Canadian metropolis. Protestants controlled their own system of public education as well as two post-secondary institutions, McGill University and Bishop's College. Irish Catholics were taught in English-language schools within the Catholic system, and from 1860 onwards there was almost always an Irish representative on the Catholic school commission of Montreal.[8]

Responsible government and the parity of representation between East and West gave the anglophones of Canada East the best of both worlds. On sectional issues they and their French-Canadian neighbours could prevent Canada West from acting as a majority while on ethnic issues they and Canada West could decisively outvote the French Canadians. Comprising about one-eighth of the total population in the United Province in 1851, they held the balance of power between the two larger groups, tending to share the conservatism of the French Canadians at the same time as they shared the language, and in most cases the religion, of the reform-minded farmers in the western section. A pattern of elite accommodation and government more or less by consensus among recognized spokesmen of the three groups began to emerge even before Lord Elgin's arrival and was solidified in the 1850s, when the United Province reached the high point of its success both economically and politically. [9]

QUEBEC ANGLOPHONES AND CONFEDERATION

Under the circumstances outlined above, the lack of enthusiasm for Confederation among the English-speaking inhabitants of Canada East is understandable. As Edward Blake pointed out some years after the event, Confederation for Ontario and for French-speaking Quebec was more like a divorce than a marriage. For George Brown and his followers in Canada West it meant representation by population at the federal level and freedom from French and Catholic influence at the provincial level. For George-Étienne Cartier's followers in Canada East, it meant responsible government in a province of Quebec that was overwhelmingly French and Catholic and that would have jurisdiction over education, social affairs, municipal institutions, and property and civil rights. Yet all of these gains for their various compatriots would be losses for the English-speaking inhabitants of Canada East. In the new federal state they would be a small minority at both levels of government. Admittedly they had lived in a predominantly French province before 1841, but at that time there had been no responsible government and the French majority had been in no position to impose its will on them. Even then they had favoured reversing the partition of 1791, until the Act of Union gave them their wish. With Confederation they would lose what the Act of Union had given them, except insofar as the federal government could be counted on to overrule the French majority on their behalf. Furthermore their share of the population, after remaining stable for nearly two decades, had begun to decline a few years before Confederation was achieved.[10]

Support for Confederation by the Bank of Montreal and other business interests did not mean that it was supported by the anglophone population of Canada East as a whole. Pierre Corbeil, whose doctoral dissertation is the most detailed study of the subject, concludes that most of them probably opposed it.[11] While their economic interests might benefit from Confederation, their interests as a cultural minority did not. The Protestant clergy, teachers, journalists and professionals, referred to by Corbeil as the cultural elite of the anglophone community, expressed considerable hostility to the project. Charles Dewey Day, the most prominent anglophone lawyer in Montreal, co-author of the Civil Code of Lower Canada, chancellor of McGill University, and a supporter of Confederation, privately admitted in 1864 that Confederation would weaken the anglophone minority in Canada East, even though it was justifiable on other grounds.[12] An editorial in the *Sherbrooke Gazette* charged that anglophone influence in the province would be "nearly extinguished" under the regime envisaged by the Quebec Resolutions, and the Montreal *Witness* challenged the Protestants of Lower Canada to mobilize themselves and make their opposition known before it was too late.[13] In the colonial parliament Christopher Dunkin of Brome County delivered the longest and most detailed speech against the Quebec resolutions, a critique of Canada's constitution that still seems remarkably *apropos* after 130 years. Among other criticisms, Dunkin predicted that conflicts between anglophones and francophones in Canada East would increase after Confederation.[14] The county council of Compton, petitioning the imperial parliament to entrench educational guarantees for Protestants in the British North America Act, claimed that "the great body of Protestants in Lower Canada are not in favour of the proposed Federal Union."[15]

Lower Canadian anglophones had no particular objection to the territorial enlargement of Canada. A legislative union like that between England and Scotland, which was John A. Macdonald's original preference, would have suited them perfectly. What they feared was the re-establishment of a provincial government for Quebec. From a modern perspective it is easy to forget what a radical innovation this was. Nowhere else in the British Empire before the twentieth century was responsible government conceded to an electorate that was predominantly of non-British ancestry. A similar proposal for Ireland, some twenty years later, was enough to split the Liberal Party and bring down Gladstone's government. Similarly the Americans did not grant statehood to Louisiana, New Mexico, Alaska or Hawaii until anglophone majorities were established in those territories.

However, a French-speaking and semi-autonomous province of Quebec was the only condition on which French Canadians would accept Confederation, and Confederation was essential for a variety of economic, strategic and political reasons. Not for the last time the interests of English-speaking Lower Canadians, as Day implicitly recognized, would have to be sacrificed for the larger interests at stake. The task of sweetening the pill fell to Alexander T. Galt of Sherbrooke, a political ally of Cartier and a leading father of Confederation. Besides writing most of the sections of the Constitution Act of 1867 that dealt with fiscal federalism, Galt was the principal author of the various guarantees and safeguards for Quebec anglophones that were written into the document.

These safeguards are to be found in several sections of the Constitution Act. Sections 22 and 23 provide that Quebec's twenty-four senators must represent and own property in twenty-four specific districts, unlike the senators from other provinces. The districts are those used to elect legislative councillors in the last years of the old United Province, and are described in Chapter 1, Schedule A of the consolidated statutes of 1859. Given the patterns of land ownership in 1867, this requirement almost guaranteed a substantial representation of anglophones since four districts (Bedford, Inkerman, Victoria and Wellington) were almost entirely English-speaking and five others had substantial English-speaking populations.

Section 72 provided that Quebec, unlike Ontario, would have an appointed Legislative Council of twenty-four members, who were also required to represent, and own property in, the same twenty-four districts. Again, the intent was to ensure a minimum quota of anglophones in the upper chamber. Section 80 entrenched twelve English-speaking constituencies for the election of members to the Legislative Assembly. Although Quebec could, and eventually did, increase the

total number of members in the house, the boundaries of the protected ridings could only be changed with the consent of a majority
of the representatives of those ridings – an interesting application of
John C. Calhoun's theory of concurrent majorities.

The most complex and contentious of the safeguards concerned
education, a subject that has continued to provoke conflict between
English-speaking and French-speaking Quebeckers right up to the
present day. After 1846 the Education Act for Canada East had provided for both Catholic and Protestant school boards in Quebec City
and Montreal. Elsewhere in the province the religious majority in each
county or district determined the religion of the public schools, but
the minority could establish a dissentient board to provide schools of
its own religious persuasion. In effect, these provisions guaranteed
Protestant schools wherever there was a demand for them, either
through Protestant boards in the two major cities, through public
boards in the Eastern Townships and other Protestant districts, or
through dissentient boards in the remainder of the province.

Section 93 entrenched these rights of the Protestant minority, or
any other rights that might be established "by law" before the date of
Confederation, in the constitution of the new dominion. A bill providing further protection to Protestant schools, including establishment of a college to train Protestant teachers, was introduced by the
government at Galt's behest in 1866. When it threatened to provoke
a countermeasure that would have given the same rights to Catholics
in Canada West it was withdrawn, and Galt resigned from the government.[16] At the London Conference later that year, which Galt attended
in spite of his resignation, Section 93 was extended to provide that
the minority could appeal to the dominion government for redress if
its educational rights were violated by the province, and also that
Parliament could adopt remedial legislation to rectify the situation.
Galt was privately promised by Cartier that a bill in support of Protestant education, similar to the one withdrawn in 1866, would be introduced by the provincial government of Quebec as soon as possible
after Confederation.[17]

It is significant, and would prove inconvenient in later times, that
the educational guarantees were based on religion rather than
language. The English-speaking (mainly Irish) Catholics of Canada
East received no guarantees at all, although they comprised more
than a quarter of the English-speaking population. This anomaly
resulted in part from the fact that religion, rather than language, was
widely viewed as the most fundamental distinction between Canada's
two solitudes. It also reflected the political weakness of the Catholic
Irish as persons with little property and as recent immigrants from a

country that was in reality an oppressed colony within the United Kingdom rather than being "British" in the full sense. The Fenian movement, whose apparent threat to the security of Canada was a major and perhaps decisive argument in favour of Confederation, did not add to their popularity or political influence. Their precarious position between the two dominant groups resembled that of the Italians and other allophone minorities in Quebec a century later.

The final guarantee was contained in Section 133, which provided that either the English or the French language could be used in the legislature and in the courts of Quebec, that both languages must be used in the records and journals of the legislature, and that the statutes of the province must be printed and published in English as well as in French. The same section entrenched a similar degree of bilingualism in the federal parliament and courts, where the French would be the minority.

These elaborate arrangements, incidentally, belie the notion frequently expressed by modern Quebec anglophones that concern for "collective rights" is a uniquely francophone aberration.[18] Nineteenth-century Quebec anglophones, both Protestant and Catholic, saw themselves as belonging to communities that had collective rights and were insistent that those rights be clearly defined and consistently respected. Recent attempts by Quebec anglophones to claim some kind of moral superiority over their francophone neighbours on the grounds that anglophones believe only in "individual rights" betray an ignorance of their own history, whether or not there is any reason to believe that individual rights deserve a higher level of legitimacy.

In addition to the guarantees outlined above, some English-speaking inhabitants of Canada East may also have found reassurance in Section 90 of the Constitution Act, although it was not drafted with them in mind. It provided that the federally-appointed lieutenant-governor of a province could refuse assent to any bill or reserve it for a final decision on its fate by the federal government. Furthermore, a provincial bill which did receive the lieutenant-governor's assent and become a law had to be sent to Ottawa where it could be disallowed by the federal government at any time within a year of its receipt. As it turned out, these provisions, consciously modelled after the procedures by which the imperial government maintained control of its colonies, would be used by the new dominion mainly to control its own empire west of the 95th meridian.[19] The few efforts to invoke them in support of Quebec's English-speaking minority were invariably unsuccessful.

THE FORMATIVE YEARS AND
THE PATTERN OF POLITICS

Like many other opponents of Confederation, most of the English-speaking Quebeckers were soon incorporated into the Macdonald-Cartier coalition. Federal patronage, the necessity of building provincial institutions overnight where none had existed since 1840, and the dual mandate, which allowed the same individual to hold a legislative seat at both levels, enabled the coalition to control the governments of the two central provinces, as well as the dominion government, for the first few years after Confederation.

In the first provincial election most of the English-speaking ridings returned followers of Cartier, apart from the southwestern county of Huntingdon which tended, then and later, to favour the anti-Catholic Scottish liberalism of George Brown and his *Globe* in nearby Ontario. Government candidates wisely did not emphasize their support for Confederation. In the province as a whole Cartier's party won fifty of the sixty-five seats. The first premier was expected to be Joseph Cauchon but he did not wish to carry out Cartier's promise to adopt legislation that would reinforce the autonomy of the Protestant educational system. As a result Christopher Dunkin, now the leading anglophone in provincial politics, refused to serve in a Cauchon government, ending Cauchon's hopes of being premier.[20] An acceptable substitute was found in the person of P.J.O. Chauveau, the former superintendant of public instruction for Canada East, who was known to appreciate Protestant sensitivities. Dunkin entered the cabinet as provincial treasurer, establishing a convention of anglophone treasurers in Quebec that lasted almost without interrruption until 1944. George Irvine of Megantic was named attorney-general, and so the two most important portfolios in the first government of Quebec were held by English-speaking Protestants.

The Chauveau government established the pattern of elite accommodation between anglophones and francophones in Quebec politics that lasted, despite some periods of difficulty, for a hundred years. Consociational elite accommodation was not new, but to some degree it was simplified by the fact that Ontario was now a separate province and did not have to be taken into account. The advantages were illustrated by the success of the promised education bill, introduced in 1869, that replaced the one that had been withdrawn three years earlier to avoid offending the sensitivities of Canada West. The terms of the bill were negotiated privately, with Dunkin and Irvine acting as spokesmen for the Protestant minority. It increased the membership of the Council of Public Instruction from fifteen, including four Protestants, to twenty-one, including seven Protestants, and divided the council into Protestant and Catholic committees which met and decided independently of one another. It also resolved a dispute over the sharing of tax revenue between the two denominational school boards in Montreal. There was no apparent opposition to the measure, and it received a third reading in the Legislative Assembly only eight days after it was introduced.[21] Charles Dewey Day was named the first chairman of the Protestant committee.

The Education Act of 1869 was an important milestone in the development of two distinct and almost unrelated societies, French Catholic and English Protestant, coexisting in the territory of Quebec. Segregation allayed Protestant fears of domination by the majority at the same time as it pleased ultramontane Catholics fearful of domination by the liberal state and the contaminating influences of liberalism. The process continued with the abolition of the ministry of public instruction in 1875, a concession to ultramontanism that was supported by most Protestants. The state now delegated all responsibility for education to private and religious bodies, a decision that was not to be reversed for ninety years. Whatever its other disadvantages, this arrangement apparently helped to maintain social peace between the two communities, as consociational theory would suggest. Although a few Protestants, including Galt, publicly opposed the abolition of the ministry of public instruction, most viewed it as a reinforcement of their autonomy, with practical advantages they preferred to the theoretical benefits of a separation between church and state.[22]

The ultramontane and anti-liberal tendency in the Catholic Church after 1870 was nonetheless a target of criticism by Quebec Protestants, and to some extent a source of genuine concern. After Cartier's departure for England in 1872, and his death the following year, an ultramontane faction gained considerable influence in the Conservative Party of Quebec. Since the Liberals favoured, more or less, the separation of church and state, this development gave party politics in Quebec an ideological intensity that was not paralleled, and not really understood, in other provinces. Protestants in Quebec could not ignore the controversy but it was not clear how, if at all, they could usefully involve themselves in it and how they should position themselves between the contending factions.

In 1875 Bishop Bourget of Montreal denounced the principle of separation between church and state and declared in effect that government policy in a Catholic province must follow the dictates of the Church. Galt, now retired from politics but still prominent, wrote to J.G. Robertson, who had succeeded Dunkin as treasurer of the province, urging the Conservative government to repudiate the bishop's views. When it predictably failed to do so, Galt published a pamphlet which reproduced his correspondence with Robertson and claimed that the party had fallen "under the baneful influence of foreign intrigue." According to Galt, this threatened the rights of the Protestant minority, whom he advised to throw their support to the liberal elements in the Catholic Church, and by implication to the Liberal Party.[23] Thomas White, a prominent Conservative, wrote another pamphlet in reply which questioned the sincerity of Galt's concern for minority rights, suggested that the difference between ultramontanes and other Catholics was only one of degree, and urged Quebec Protestants to preserve a strict neutrality in controversies within the Catholic Church.[24] In effect they should vote without regard to religious issues. This advice was given some credibility by the tendency to keep sensitive issues, such as education, out of politics and away from the direct intervention of the state. This tendency may have reflected a prevailing belief that politics were inherently corrupt, as Ralph Heintzman has argued.[25] However, its real merit was the fact that it suited the preferences of both ultramontane Catholics and English-speaking non-Catholics, although for different reasons.

A remarkable instance of how the separateness of the two religious communities was taken for granted occurred in 1912 when Dr Finnie, a Scottish-born Liberal member from Montreal, introduced a bill in the Legislative Assembly that would have provided compulsory education for Protestants only. Finnie assumed, with good reason at the time, that Quebec Catholics would not accept compulsory education for themselves, so he emphasized that his bill would not affect them. Four of the eight Protestants in the house voted for Finnie's bill but only two Catholic members, both from Montreal, did so.[26]

The prominence of religion in the political discourse of the late nineteenth century had the additional consequence of inhibiting any sense of community or solidarity among English-speaking Quebeckers as a group. Irish Catholics could hardly be expected to feel any solidarity with other anglophones whose utterances frequently offended their own religious beliefs. Instead they sought recognition as a third force who shared a language with the British Protestants and a religion with the French but who were clearly distinct from both. They had somewhat more success in gaining this recognition in post-Confederation Quebec than in the United Province before 1867, but it was still an uphill struggle. The Irish had neither the numbers of the French nor the economic resources of the British. There were only two constituencies, one in each of the major cities, where they were a majority and a few others, mainly in the Ottawa Valley, where they held the balance of power. Irish immigration to Quebec was insignificant after 1867 and many Irish Quebeckers apparently migrated to the United States. The number of Quebec residents claiming Irish ancestry hardly changed between the first and second dominion census. Thereafter it declined from 123,749 in 1881 to only 94,947 in 1921. By 1961 natural increase had brought it back to 129,326, almost exactly the level at the time of Confederation.[27]

Despite, or perhaps because of, these demographic trends, Irish politicians in Quebec complained that their community did not receive its fair share of patronage and that it was not always represented in the provincial cabinet. At times they argued, erroneously, that the Irish Catholics outnumbered the Protestants in Quebec, a claim that could only be supported by including every French Canadian who had the slightest trace of Irish ancestry.[28] Because of their shared religion Irish Catholics did intermarry frequently with the French Canadians. Some Quebec politicians with Irish names like Lawrence Cannon and Charles Fitzpatrick (or Daniel Johnson and Claude Ryan in a later generation) were francophones for all practical purposes, while some with French names were partly Irish. Even today, brief speeches paying tribute to Quebec's Irish heritage are made whenever the National Assembly meets on 17 March.

MINORITY REPRESENTATION IN PROVINCIAL INSTITUTIONS

While social and institutional segregation facilitated the *modus vivendi* between English-speaking and French-speaking Quebeckers, elite accommodation through political institutions was also necessary to maintain it. At the provincial level, the main institutions in which the different communities were represented and in which accommodation took place included the Legislative Council, the Legislative Assembly, and the cabinet. As we have seen, anglophone representation in two of these was more or less constitutionally guaranteed and in the third, which was arguably the most important, it was governed by rather rigid conventions from the outset. How did this representation of the English-speaking minority (or minorities, if the distinct nature of the Irish Catholic community receives due consideration) work out in practice?

Nine of the original legislative councillors were anglophones, but the number fell to seven over the next ten years and then declined gradually to five in 1935. During the Duplessis era there were only three or four, and there were four when the Legislative Council was abolished in 1969. The districts of Victoria (the west end of Montreal) and Inkerman (the Ottawa Valley) were always represented by anglophone Protestants in the Legislative Council until its abolition. Wellington (the city of Sherbrooke and its environs) remained an anglophone Protestant preserve until 1937 and Gulf (the Gaspé peninsula) until 1941. Stadacona (the west end of Quebec City) was considered the Irish Catholic seat in the Legislative Council, at least until 1934 when a francophone was appointed. Bedford, consisting of Brome, Missisquoi and Shefford counties, was represented by anglophone Protestants until 1904. These six districts provided thirty of the thirty-eight anglophones who sat in the Legislative Council from 1867 to 1969.

Although cabinets normally included one member of the upper house, the Legislative Council never fully lived up to expectations. Its abolition was discussed as early as 1878, and seriously considered by Premier Chapleau a few years later. The first bill to abolish the upper house was seconded in the Legislative Assembly by Alexander Cameron, the Liberal member for Huntingdon. Speaking in English, Cameron described the upper house as a waste of money and pointed out that Ontario did not have one and that Manitoba's had been recently abolished. A.R. Angers, the attorney-general, claimed that the Protestant minority wanted the Legislative Council to continue as a protection against public opinion that might be stirred up by demagogues. His amendment to retain the status quo was seconded by Levi Church from English-speaking Pontiac, who argued rather oddly that Quebec needed an upper house, unlike Ontario, because of its system of civil law. The Angers/Church amendment passed easily on division.[29] Despite the attorney-general's comments, Harry Blank, the Liberal member for St-Louis, was closer to the truth ninety years later when he stated in the Legislative Assembly that "the Council never passed or blocked any legislation in respect to the minorities."[30]

In the Legislative Assembly, as noted above, the existence of twelve supposedly anglophone ridings was constitutionally entrenched. Reading from west to east the ridings were Pontiac, Ottawa, Argenteuil, Huntingdon, Missisquoi, Brome, Shefford, Stanstead, the town of Sherbrooke, Compton, Richmond-Wolfe and Megantic. In fact, Shefford and Megantic had slight majorities of francophones by 1867, although the fathers of Confederation were probably not aware of this. The census of 1871 also revealed slight francophone majorities in Richmond-Wolfe and Ottawa County. The urban ridings of Quebec West, Montreal West, and Montreal Centre had anglophone majorities, with Irish voters predominating in the first two, but were not constitutionally protected. All three elected anglophones to the first house, as did nine of the protected ridings, including Megantic. Two of the anglophone members, Christopher Dunkin of Brome and Julius Scriver of Huntingdon, represented their ridings in the dominion House of Commons at the same time, as was permitted until 1873. Dunkin retired from politics before 1873 and Scriver chose to abandon his provincial seat and keep his federal one in that year.

In 1875 Galt admitted that the migration of francophones into the Eastern Townships would make most of the protected ridings irrelevant in the long run.[31] Sherbrooke was predominantly francophone by 1891, Compton and Missisquoi by 1901, Argenteuil and Stanstead by 1911, and even Huntingdon by 1941. By around the turn of the century Missisquoi, Ottawa, Sherbrooke and Stanstead had ceased to elect anglophones to the Legislative Assembly, a fact that reflected their changing linguistic composition. Other protected ridings continued to elect anglophone representatives more often than not, even after their electorates became mainly francophone. Huntingdon, Brome and Pontiac, the counties that remained anglophone longest, elected anglophones for as long as they were constitutionally protected. Quebec West elected Irish Catholics to the Assembly until 1935. Other ridings in and around Quebec City and in the Gaspé peninsula frequently were represented by anglophones, particularly Irish Catholics, after the turn of the century.

As anglophones became increasingly concentrated in Montreal that city and its suburbs became a stronghold of anglophone representation. Because the number of seats in the Legislative Assembly was not fixed, it was easy to increase Montreal Island's representation from the original five seats (including then-rural Hochelaga and Jacques-Cartier) to eight seats in 1890 and to twelve in 1912. The number of predominantly anglophone ridings on the island increased from the original two to three in 1890, five in 1912, six in 1923 and seven in 1939. After the First World War the rapidly growing metropolitan area was seriously under-represented, since its penchant for electing opposition members did not give governments any incentive to represent it more fairly. In the Duplessis era it had one-third of Quebec's population but only one-sixth of the seats.

Montreal always had a riding reserved for Irish candidates, known as Ste-Anne after 1912 and based on the municipal ward of the same name. St-Louis was regarded as the Jewish riding after it elected Peter Bercovitch, the first Jewish member of the Legislative Assembly, in 1916. Westmount became a riding in 1912, although most wealthy anglophone Montrealers still lived in the area near McGill University known as the Square Mile. Working-class Verdun in 1923 and middle-class Notre-Dame-de-Grâce in 1939 were added as additional anglophone ridings. Jacques-Cartier county, the western half of the island, was originally a rural francophone riding but was acquiring a more suburban, and more anglophone, character by the era of Duplessis. On the other hand, Verdun had become a mainly French-speaking city by the 1950s. At the same time Ste-Anne and St-Louis were losing their ethnic character as their original residents moved farther west. However, Frank Hanley represented Ste-Anne from 1948 until 1970. In St-Louis the tradition of a Jewish representative was restored, after a brief interlude, in 1960 by Harry Blank, who continued to represent the riding until 1985.

With gains in Montreal making up for losses in the Townships, and with anglophones sometimes able to win election in mainly francophone ridings, the number of English-speaking members in the Legislative Assembly declined slowly. Twelve were elected in 1867 and an all-time high of eighteen in 1878, when the Legislative Assembly still had sixty-five members. There were eighteen out of ninety elected in 1897, and the number did not fall below a dozen until 1931. Only eight were elected in 1956, the year of the last election won by Duplessis.

Until 1944 anglophone members of the Legislative Assembly were usually on the government side of the house. The only exceptions were in 1878–79, when the Liberal lieutenant-governor appointed a Liberal premier, Henri Joly, after dismissing the Conservative incumbent, and in 1887–91, when Honoré Mercier's Parti National unseated the Conservatives by appealing to resentment against the execution of Louis Riel. Anglophone voters probably recognized that supporting the government facilitated elite accommodation and their representation in cabinet.

Until 1920 there were generally seven or eight ministers in the cabinet, including two or three anglophones. After 1920 cabinets were larger, so that the proportion of anglophones was closer to their share of Quebec's population. More important than numbers, however, was the fact that a spokesman for the anglophone community traditionally held the most important portfolio in the government, that of provincial treasurer. The appointment to this office of an anglophone Protestant who was acceptable to the financial community of St James Street was apparently one of the secret commitments made in the bargaining prior to Confederation. On the rare occasions when no suitable anglophone Protestant could be found, the premier usually took the portfolio himself. Only one potential anglophone minister could be found in 1878 to serve in the Joly government, which had two francophone treasurers during its brief term. There was some difficulty in finding Protestants who were willing to hold office in Mercier's government, and an Irish Catholic, Joseph Shehyn, had to be appointed as treasurer.

That the Mercier government tried to force the province's creditors to convert their debentures from a 5 per cent rate of interest to 4 per cent probably reinforced the financial community's belief that only a Protestant treasurer could be trusted to protect their investments.[32] Since Quebec governments were forced to borrow frequently, the need to retain the confidence of potential lenders could not be disregarded. In 1897 the *Montreal Star* alleged that the office of provincial treasurer belonged "by right" to an English-speaking Protestant. As late as 1930 Premier Alexandre Taschereau referred to "the Quebec tradition" of confiding the treasury portfolio to an anglophone.[33]

Several anglophone ministers came from the Legislative Council, but treasurers could not sit in the Legislative Council since they were required to present their budgets in the Assembly. In 1930 Legislative Councillor Gordon Scott was appointed treasurer and resigned his council seat to contest a by-election. When he failed to win the by-election he resigned as treasurer but was reappointed to the council. In 1936 E.S. McDougall was appointed treasurer in the moribund Liberal government although he was not a member of either house, but his term of office – and the government's – lasted only a few weeks.

Five Irish Catholics held cabinet office in Quebec before the Quiet Revolution, for a total of fifty-one years. Another Catholic of non-French origin, Jonathan Wurtele, was provincial treasurer for a short interregnum in the 1880s when J.G. Robertson temporarily resigned in a dispute over the government's railway policy. No Jews were appointed to cabinet before 1970, although there was talk of appointing Peter Bercovitch as treasurer in 1936. Bercovitch complained, probably with good reason, that prejudice against his religion led to the appointment of McDougall instead.[34]

Most of the anglophone ministers before the Quiet Revolution, apart from the Irish Catholics, were from rural ridings. Of the fourteen anglophone treasurers who held a seat in the Assembly no less than four represented Brome county, five were from other ridings protected by Section 80, one was from a rural francophone riding, three were from Montreal and one was from Quebec City.

The last anglophone treasurer, J. Arthur Mathewson, represented the then-new riding of Notre-Dame-de-Grâce in the west end of Montreal. By the time of his appointment in 1939 about two-thirds of Quebec's anglophone population lived on Montreal Island. Mathewson, a fluently bilingual lawyer, veteran of Vimy Ridge, and former chairman of the Montreal Protestant School Board, perhaps typified the ideal qualities expected of a consociational representative but not always attained in practice. He was appointed with no previous experience in the Legislative Assembly, although he had been a city councillor in Montreal and co-chairman of the Liberal Party's convention in 1938.[35]

ANGLOPHONES AND THE PARTY SYSTEM

Generalizations about anglophone voting, particularly in the early days, must be made with caution. Even the most anglophone ridings contained significant numbers of francophone voters, and most constituency contests were decided by narrow margins. The ethnicity and religion of the candidate, and his status in the community, probably had as much influence on voting as his party label. However, some generalizations can be ventured, at least tentatively.

Despite their distaste for Confederation, most anglophones supported Cartier's party in the first provincial election. Nevertheless, the growing ultramontane tendency in the Conservative Party caused many English-speaking voters to defect to the Liberals in the 1870s. Protestant businessmen in Montreal supported two petitions for the disallowance of Quebec statutes that had economic as well as religious implications. The first, in 1873, authorized the city to purchase shares in a colonization railway promoted by the enterprising Laurentian priest, Father Antoine Labelle. The second, four years later, gave an order of nuns permission to manufacture and sell clothing in competition with commercial enterprises. The federal government refused in both cases to disallow the act.[36] The business community was also unfavourably impressed in 1882 when the Chapleau government imposed a corporation tax, which was later upheld by the Judicial Committee of the Privy Council in *Bank of Toronto v. Lambe*. Partly because of these episodes, some anglophone businessmen became provincial Liberals while continuing to support the Conservative Party and the National Policy in federal elections.[37]

The situation was greatly complicated by the emergence of Honoré Mercier, a crypto-separatist who had left the Conservative Party because of his opposition to Confederation in 1867. The devoutly religious Mercier was the antithesis of an old-style *rouge*, but he won the leadership of the Liberal Party and transformed it into the Parti National by incorporating Conservative nationalists offended by the execution of Louis Riel. One English-speaking Liberal, William Watts of Drummond, resigned his seat in response to these developments while another, Alexander Cameron of Huntingdon, publicly denounced Mercier and sat as an independent member. Cameron proclaimed that if forced to choose between good government and the rights of the English minority he would choose the latter.[38] George Washington Stephens, the Liberal member for Montreal Centre, also refused to vote for a resolution that supported Riel's rebellion.[39] Stephens remained a Liberal but was defeated in the election of 1886, as was every other Protestant candidate running for Mercier's party. Mercier finally found a Protestant for his cabinet two years later by running William Rhodes in a by-election in Megantic, which was now a predominantly francophone riding.

The Jesuits' Estates Act, although a reasonable response to a complicated problem, offended many Protestants in Quebec and elsewhere. The Protestants in both houses of the Quebec legislature privately opposed the bill, but were persuaded not to vote against it by L.O. Taillon, the leader of the Conservative opposition. In the end it passed without a roll call.[40] About six thousand Quebec Protestants signed petitions calling for its disallowance but the Macdonald government, as usual, refused to intervene in a religious controversy.[41] When the Equal Rights Association was formed in Toronto, with George Washington Stephens present on the platform, Mercier publicly warned Quebec Protestants not to join the "fanatics" of Ontario in an anti-Catholic crusade.[42] He also tried to lure Cameron back into the party, with temporary success. However in the 1892 election, which followed Mercier's dismissal by the lieutenant-governor, Cameron ran as a Conservative. Stephens ran as an anti-Mercier Liberal in Huntingdon, defeating Cameron by a narrow margin.

The death of Mercier in 1894 returned most English-speaking Quebeckers to the Liberal ranks but reciprocity in 1911 and conscription in 1917 shifted many anglophone voters in Montreal towards the Conservatives, even though neither was really a provincial issue. Rural Protestants, who were more interested in provincial issues and more favourable to free trade in any event, continued to support the Liberal government, as did most of the Irish Catholics and the Jews. Rural anglophones generally had an even greater tendency than rural francophones to support the incumbents, all other things being equal, and this made them strongly Liberal in the early decades of the twentieth century.[43] Urban anglophones were more detached from provincial politics and more independent. At the lowest point in its fortunes, between 1916 and 1923, the Conservative opposition had only three francophone members in the Legislative Assembly, along with two or three anglophones. Anglophone voters helped to keep the party alive during the long Liberal hegemony from 1897 to 1936.

SOCIAL AND ECONOMIC DEVELOPMENTS

The demographic, social and economic evolution of the English-speaking community in Quebec has been ably portrayed in Ronald Rudin's excellent history, *The Forgotten Quebecers: A History of English-Speaking Quebec 1759–1980*, to which the reader is referred for further details. There were a number of dramatic changes in Quebec society between the era of Confederation and the middle of the twentieth

Table 2.1
Growth of the Anglophone Population of Quebec, 1861–1971

Year	Anglophone Population	Percentage of Quebec Population
1861	263,344	24
1871	243,041	20
1881	260,538	19
1891	–	–
1901	289,680	18
1911	318,799	16
1921	356,943	15
1931	429,613	15
1941	468,996	14
1951	558,256	14
1961	697,402	13
1971	789,185	12

Source: Adapted from Rudin, The Forgotten Quebecers, 28.
Note: Up to and including 1921, the criterion used is British Isles ethnic origin. From 1931 onwards the criterion used is English mother tongue. Neither ethnic nor mother tongue data were recorded in the 1891 census.

century, but the pattern of consociational politics established in the era of Cartier, Chauveau, Dunkin, and Galt adapted to them and survived with remarkably little modification.

The anglophone population continued to grow in absolute terms, as shown in table 2.1, but less rapidly than the population of Quebec as a whole. The anglophone population actually declined outside of Montreal as many rural anglophones moved to the city, to other provinces or to the United States. The vacuum was filled by French Canadians moving from the overcrowded valley of the St Lawrence to outlying parts of the province.[44] As the discussion of the protected ridings suggested, these developments were already underway in 1867. Twenty years later they were obvious enough to cause some anxiety among anglophones, which was expressed with particular force by the Scottish-born editor of the Huntingdon Gleaner, Robert Sellar.

Sellar was a Scottish Clear Grit of a kind familiar in western Ontario, a believer in temperance, free trade, limited government, and the separation of church and state. Like others of his ilk in rural Quebec, he was decidedly confused when his party was taken over by Honoré Mercier, and this may have increased his penchant for imagining Catholic conspiracies. At around this time Sellar discovered that between 1871 and 1881 the Catholic population of Argenteuil, Brome, Compton, Huntingdon, Missisquoi and Stanstead counties had increased by more than half while their Protestant population had increased by only 1 per cent.[45] He began to comment on the implications of these facts in his newspaper, and also in a column which he wrote under a pseudonym for a Toronto daily. Eventually he published a book, *The Tragedy of Quebec*, in which he accused the Catholic Church of deliberately encouraging the expulsion of Protestants from those parts of Quebec where they had formerly predominated. By the time the last edition of the book appeared, in 1916, Sellar had abandoned hope for the Protestant cause in Quebec but expressed the hope that at least Manitoba, Saskatchewan and Alberta might be saved from "the thrall of the priest and the foreigner."[46]

Sellar was wrong about the Church, although its interest in "colonization" as a means of preserving the rural way of life made his theory at least faintly plausible. In fact the francophone "invasion" of the Townships was mainly directed towards the cities and small towns rather than the countryside. A sociologist writing about the Eastern Townships half a century after Sellar first sounded the alarm about clerical colonization stated more accurately that "The French invasion is a function of the development of modern capitalist society."[47] Under the impetus of John A. Macdonald's National Policy the province industrialized rapidly and the industries, usually launched by anglophone entrepreneurs, tended to be established in areas that had been mainly English-speaking. The surplus population of the French parishes was drawn in to the industrializing areas in search of jobs, usually as unskilled labour. At the same time, many of the English were moving out to seek better opportunities in Montreal and further afield.

The developments that worried Sellar and others of his persuasion did not so much spell the end of English-speaking (or even Protestant) Quebeckers as their transformation into a different kind of society – concentrated in Montreal and its suburbs, urban in their outlook, more interested in federal than in provincial politics, and conspicuously more affluent and educated than their French-Canadian neighbours. These developments in turn reinforced their social, cultural and even economic segregation and their determination to maintain it, a determination which the government and the French-speaking people of Quebec did not seriously oppose until long afterwards. While the sociologist quoted above noted, in 1939, the decline of English institutions and English community life in the Eastern Townships, their counterparts in Montreal were flourishing and would do so for many years more.

Montreal was already the economic centre of Canada in 1867, but the National Policy and the Canadian Pacific Railway did even more to improve its fortunes, and those of its anglophone elite, than the Reciprocity Treaty and the Grand Trunk had done a generation earlier.

In the half-century between the beginning of the National Policy and the beginning of the Great Depression, Montreal was the commercial, financial, industrial and transportation centre of the dominion and the buckle that joined the United Kingdom to the hinterlands of the Canadian West. While the city's francophone entrepreneurs were largely relegated to the sidelines, these fifty years were the heyday of the anglophone and mainly Protestant elite who lived in the Square Mile and reputedly controlled half the wealth in Canada. While they played little direct part in provincial politics, they financed, supported, and largely directed the institutions that were the backbone of English-speaking Quebec: the Protestant school system, the Montreal General and Royal Victoria hospitals, McGill University, the Montreal Symphony Orchestra, the Museum of Fine Arts, and the charities and social services that served the needs of less fortunate English-speaking Quebeckers. Their economic power was all that was needed to protect these institutions from any interference by the government of the province. Margaret Westley, in her brilliant study of the Square Mile, noted that the middle-class clientele of the anglophone institutions generally relinquished the right to make decisions about their own community to the anglophone elite, in return for the protection and financial support which the elite provided.[48]

Most Montreal anglophones, of course, lived in far different circumstances than the residents of the Square Mile. There was still an unskilled anglophone working class, predominantly Irish, down the hill between the railway tracks and the waterfront, although their counterparts in Quebec City dwindled rapidly after Confederation. The plight of the working class in this part of Montreal was the subject of a book published in 1897, *The City Below the Hill*. Its author, Herbert Ames, was a progressive-minded young Montreal businessman and later a Conservative member of parliament. He reported that Griffintown, the Irish ghetto between William Street and the Lachine canal, was the worst slum in the western half of the city, with only one family in four having indoor plumbing.[49] His book probably contributed to the formation of the Charities Organization Society in 1900 to serve the needs of Montreal's anglophone poor. Twenty years later it was replaced by the Montreal Council of Social Agencies whose "Red Feather" campaign, equivalent to the United Appeal in other parts of Canada, was a feature of anglophone life in Montreal until after the Quiet Revolution.[50]

The growing manufacturing industries of the city and the extensive repair shops of the railways created a need for skilled anglophone labour which was imported largely from England and Scotland, and which congregated in areas such as Côte St-Paul, Maisonneuve, Rosemont, Verdun, and Lachine, close to the industries that employed them. They and their families provided much of the clientele for Protestant schools and the other institutions of the anglophone community. By the 1930s, however, a sociologist who studied them noted that skilled jobs in Montreal were increasingly occupied by francophones, as the children of the anglophone working class moved into the middle class or out of the province.[51]

Growing white-collar employment in the financial, commercial, industrial and transportation sectors caused a great expansion of the anglophone middle class in the twentieth century. White-collar jobs in the large firms required fluency in English. A large firm, unnamed but almost certainly the Sun Life Company, informed the author of a sociological study published in 1935 that more than half of its male employees were British immigrants or the sons of British immigrants.[52] While British immigration was important, some middle-class anglophones were the upwardly mobile children of the working class while others came from rural Quebec or from eastern Ontario and the Maritime provinces, areas which had no large cities of their own. American-owned firms also brought some personnel from the United States.

Notre-Dame-de-Grâce, a rural parish annexed by the city in 1912 after some rather complicated machinations, developed into the principal stronghold of middle-class anglophones. NDG, as it was always called by its anglophone residents, became a provincial riding in 1939 and a federal one a decade later. Middle-class anglophones could also be found in other parts of western Montreal and in several of the suburban municipalities that began to develop after the First World War. Even more than working-class or rural anglophones, they were geographically and socially segregated from the French Canadians. Mary Peate, an Ontario-born Catholic child growing up in NDG in the 1930s, recalled the situation in her memoirs: "It seemed as if we'd moved back to an English-speaking province. Except for the occasional exchange with the French-speaking kids on the next street, and a few tradespeople, we seldom heard the French language spoken, even though we were living in the second largest French-speaking city in the world."[53]

Predictably, the French lessons taught by Irish nuns failed to give her any command of the language. The situation was certainly no better for Protestant children, whose schools were not permitted to employ Catholics as teachers. Apparently the authorities agreed with Dr Bigbee, the headmaster of a private school in Hugh MacLennan's *The Watch That Ends the Night*, when he asserted "Far better not having a Frenchman for French – the boys can never understand a word he says."[54] Although French was compulsory in all schools from grade 3 until the end of high school, few Montreal anglophones in the middle of the twentieth century could actually speak or even read it.

As they moved into the middle class, Protestant and Catholic anglophones increasingly lived in the same neighbourhoods and socialized together, although the educational system kept them apart and they were still far from being a cohesive anglophone community. Jews, however, the third major component of Quebec's English-speaking population, faced obstacles to social acceptance in the twentieth century even more severe than those encountered by Irish Catholics in the nineteenth. Although Quebec's Jewish population numbered only a few hundred persons at the time of Confederation, it grew rapidly after the turn of the century because of immigration from eastern Europe. By 1931 there were more than sixty thousand Jews in Quebec, mainly concentrated in Montreal where they comprised about 6 per cent of the population.

Unlike the Irish immigrants of an earlier time, the Jews did not speak English when they arrived, but most soon adopted it as their new language. This was partly their own choice and partly a choice imposed on them. In 1903, just as large-scale Jewish immigration to Quebec was getting underway, the legislature decreed that Jews must be considered as Protestants for educational purposes: since Protestant schools in Quebec at that time taught only in English, this ensured that second-generation Jews would be English-speaking. In 1928 the Judicial Committee of the Privy Council ruled in *Hirsch v. Protestant School Commissioners of Montreal* that the legislation of 1903 violated Section 93 of the 1867 Constitution Act. The Taschereau government considered the option of creating a third educational system for Jews but eventually chose a modified version of the status quo: Jewish children were still sent to Protestant schools but their parents could not be elected to the school boards, even though they paid taxes to them. Probably the Jews accepted this inequitable solution without complaining only because school board elections in Quebec were largely a formality. In the case of the Protestant boards new members were usually chosen by the existing members from among their friends and then declared elected by acclamation.[55]

The Jews gained fluency in English but not much else from their status as honorary "Protestants." The real Protestants excluded them from living in certain suburbs, discouraged them from working for the chartered banks, and imposed a discriminatory quota on Jewish applicants to study at McGill University. A socio-economic study of Montreal in 1938 reported that the larger law firms, defined as those with seven or more lawyers, had eighty-five lawyers of British ancestry, twenty of French ancestry, and no Jews.[56] Jews were also excluded from golf clubs, yacht clubs and fraternities. The anti-semitism of the French Canadians, while it became decidedly unpleasant in the 1930s, had far less real impact on the welfare of Jewish Montrealers than the discrimination practiced by the British Protestants. Perhaps for this reason the Jews seemed to prefer francophones as neighbours, even though they adopted the English language as their own.[57]

Montreal in the decades before the Quiet Revolution, when it contained about one-tenth of the total population of Canada, was an oddly segmented society. The British and French lived in almost completely separate worlds, with complete networks of autonomous and parallel institutions. There was a even a distinction between the Board of Trade, mainly anglophone and representing most of the large firms, and the Chambre de Commerce, representing mainly small, and mainly francophone, firms. The Jewish and Irish-Catholic networks were less complete, less autonomous, and less securely established, but also quite impressive. The Italians, the last group to arrive in significant numbers, were beginning to establish a network of their own when the Quiet Revolution, with its development of a more normal role for the state, brought the process of increasingly complicated segmentation to an end. It is possible that the curious doctrine of "multiculturalism," invented by Prime Minister Pierre Trudeau in 1971 and proclaimed soon afterwards to be a Canadian tradition, reflected not so much the theories of Lord Acton as its author's experience growing up in this peculiar environment.

In the municipal politics of Montreal a tradition of alternating anglophone and francophone mayors was violated in 1914 when Mederic Martin was elected in succession to another francophone. J.A. Mathewson, subsequently provincial treasurer, was the last anglophone to make a serious bid for the mayor's office, and his convincing defeat by Camilien Houde in 1930 really ended the tradition.[58] City Council minutes continued to be kept in both languages. (Between 1862 and 1883 they had been in English only.)[59] The declining influence of anglophones in Montreal's municipal affairs reflected their growing tendency to settle in anglophone-dominated suburbs outside the city limits, of which Westmount was the most celebrated but by no means the only example. Annexation of these suburbs by the city was, and apparently still is, politically unthinkable. Even within the city anglophone representation was artificially sustained between 1940 and 1960 by the corporatist practice of allowing interest groups to appoint one-third of the city councillors. About 40 percent of these appointees were anglophones, almost all of British or Irish ancestry.[60]

DUPLESSIS AND THE ANGLOPHONES

Maurice L. Duplessis, premier of Quebec from 1936 to 1939 and again from 1944 to 1959, remains one of the most controversial and important figures in Quebec's political history. His five election victories and eighteen years in office are records exceeded by no other premier of Quebec before or since. His long reign was not quite *la grande noirceur* denounced by the generation of liberals who opposed him in his last years, but it certainly contained episodes of which Quebec had no reason to be proud. In reality it was a watershed between two very different eras in Quebec's history and as such it had some affinities with what went before and some with what followed.

Long after it was over, an anglophone lawyer interviewed by Margaret Westley for her study of the Square Mile expressed regret that the anglophone establishment had assisted the rise of Duplessis. According to this man Duplessis had used the anglophones but then abandoned them. "By supporting him, the English assisted in their own demise. He led us down the garden path."[61] Richard Holden, from the same milieu but a later generation, had somewhat different memories: "I never felt Duplessis was this evil black force. He obviously didn't believe very much in open democratic government but as a Quebecker he was a very strong nationalist and I always felt that the Quebecois were under-recognized in Canada."[62]

Other anglophones, of course, prefer to emphasize the opposition to Duplessis from within their community and to suggest that it was unanimous from beginning to end. According to this view, with which Trudeau gently took issue in "Some Obstacles to Democracy in Quebec," the failings of the Duplessis government reflected the inadequate appreciation of liberal and democratic values on the part of francophone Catholics, an inadequacy for which the anglophone minority was in no way responsible.[63]

A diametrically opposed view was expressed by André Laurendeau in a guest editorial for *Maclean's* that appeared a few months before the death of Duplessis.[64] Laurendeau criticized the English-language dailies of Montreal for their failure to discuss the shortcomings of the Duplessis government. He concluded that the anglophone establishment preferred to keep Duplessis in power for the same reason that European colonists in Africa sometimes tolerated a puppet *roi-nègre* whose democratic credentials were equally dubious: he kept the natives quiet and was willing to cooperate with those who wielded the real power behind the scenes. Laurendeau's analogy was eventually adopted by left-wing nationalist militants and given a more general application as an alleged description of the political economy of

Quebec; there were echoes of it a decade later in the manifesto of the Front de Libération du Québec.

Maurice Duplessis became leader of the Conservative Party of Quebec in 1933, succeeding Camilien Houde, the past and future mayor of Montreal. Under Houde's leadership the party had elected eleven members in 1931, but Houde had lost his own seat. The caucus included three anglophones: Charles Ernest Gault in Montreal-St-George, Charles Smart in Westmount, and Martin Fisher in Huntingdon. Mainly English-speaking Verdun was also represented by a Conservative. Gault had represented his riding, which included the Square Mile, since 1907, and Smart had sat for Westmount since its creation as a riding in 1912. Fisher was a new arrival in 1931. The party retained a hard core of anglophone and mainly Protestant supporters in spite of Houde, a rambunctious populist who had received very few anglophone votes in his municipal campaign.

Most anglophone Conservatives seemed to prefer Duplessis to Houde, although some supported Duplessis' rival for the leadership, Onésime Gagnon, on the grounds that he was less of a nationalist. The only prominent anglophone who remained a Houde supporter to the end was the elderly and unilingual Gault, who had been improbably named as parliamentary leader by Houde after the latter's defeat in an effort to appease the anglophone community.[65] Gault was temporarily expelled from the caucus in December 1933 after he failed to endorse Duplessis as the new leader, but he ran and was elected again in 1935 as a Conservative and the party did not oppose him. Duplessis apparently did not wish to offend the anglophone elite. Smart, an admirer of Duplessis, won a substantial majority in NDG, which was still part of his Westmount riding, but outpolled the Liberal candidate by only eighty votes in Westmount proper. In upper Westmount, the most affluent part of the riding, the Liberal was actually ahead.[66] The Conservatives elected sixteen members including a fourth anglophone, P.A. Sherman of Compton, while their allies, the Action Liberale Nationale, elected twenty-six. The Liberals barely held office in a campaign that was notoriously corrupt, at least in Montreal. It was in this election that a Liberal impersonator cast the vote of the Anglican bishop of Montreal, John Farthing, who arrived at the poll to be told that he had already voted.[67]

In the election of 1936 the Conservatives and their allies organized themselves into a new party, the Union Nationale. Smart was not a candidate and Gault ran as an independent Conservative, coming second to Union Nationale candidate Gilbert Layton. The Union Nationale held the anglophone ridings inherited from the Conservatives and also picked up Brome and Montreal-St-Laurent. Even St-Louis, the

Jewish riding, fell to the Union Nationale in a by-election in 1938 when the Liberals unwisely nominated a francophone.

Duplessis formed a government after the 1936 election and named three anglophones, including an Irish Catholic, to his cabinet. Martin Fisher of Huntingdon became provincial treasurer, with the unofficial but equally important responsibility of serving as the chief spokesman for anglophone interests. Significantly, Duplessis gave Fisher the task of recommending reforms to Protestant education, although this had nothing to do with his portfolio.[68]

Although ostensibly heading a party of nationalism and reform, Duplessis was usually careful not to challenge the privileges enjoyed by the anglophone minority. On one occasion when he did so, albeit to a very slight extent, he quickly retreated. In 1937 his government introduced a bill entitled "a law respecting the interpretation of the laws of the province." It provided that in the event of any dispute over the interpretation of the Civil Code, the Municipal Code, the Code of Civil Procedure, or any other Quebec statute, the French text and not the English text would be considered authoritative.[69] Although quickly adopted by both houses of the legislature, it was not warmly received by the anglophone community. In the following year this first instance of language legislation was repealed on the ostensible grounds that it "may give rise to friction and problems difficult of solution, which it is expedient to avoid."[70]

The Duplessis government also redistributed constituency boundaries, combining the seriously underpopulated riding of St George with Westmount. The anglophone bourgeoisie were beginning to move out of the Square Mile and in 1936 fewer than three thousand votes had been cast in St George. There was no net loss of anglophone representation since NDG became a separate riding at the same time.

In 1939 the Union Nationale coalition of nationalists and anglophones, conservatives and reformers began to crumble. Duplessis asked for a dissolution and waged a campaign so nationalist in tone that it was interpreted as an effort to obstruct Canada's war effort against Nazi Germany. The federal Liberal ministers from Quebec, at the suggestion of Charles G. "Chubby" Power from Quebec South, intervened in the campaign by promising to resign if Duplessis were re-elected.[71] The Gazette, Montreal's Conservative English daily, turned against Duplessis. Gilbert Layton, the minister without portfolio running in what was now Westmount-St George, and W.R. Bullock, former member for Westmount and now the candidate in NDG, resigned from the Union Nationale in mid-campaign. New candidates were hastily found but the Liberals swept both ridings along with every other anglophone riding except Brome. The Union Nationale retained only fourteen seats in total. J.A. Mathewson, the triumphant Liberal in NDG and soon-to-be treasurer, rejoiced in his victory speech that Quebec was "above all, British."[72]

Results in the English-speaking ridings were little different five years later, with the Union Nationale candidate running behind the CCF in some cases, and even behind the Communist in St-Louis. *The Gazette* refused to endorse any party. The Liberals in anglophone ridings made support for the war effort the major issue. They also emphasized that they had implemented compulsory education and female suffrage but in Westmount-St George and NDG, as well as middle-class and ethnically-mixed Outremont, they soft-pedalled their nationalization of the Montreal Light, Heat and Power Company. Union Nationale candidates in anglophone ridings emphasized the government's conservative fiscal policy but anglophone voters were not impressed.[73] Jonathan Robinson in Brome was the only anglophone elected as a Union Nationale member.

Perhaps in part because he did not intend to increase the provincial debt, Duplessis abandoned the practice of naming an anglophone as provincial treasurer. Robinson, a Montreal lawyer despite his rural constituency, had hoped to receive this traditionally anglophone portfolio, which his father-in-law Andrew McMaster had held under Taschereau, but became minister of mines. When he died suddenly soon after the 1948 election the same portfolio was given to Daniel French of Compton, an elderly farmer who had just been elected for the first time. When French died in 1954 the mines portfolio passed to another farmer, William Cottingham of Argenteuil, establishing an anglophone tradition which Jean Lesage continued by giving the same portfolio to Paul Earl in 1960. Apart from Robinson, French and Cottingham, no anglophones served in the second Duplessis cabinet.

The minimal anglophone representation in the postwar Union Nationale government was an early indication of declining anglophone influence in provincial politics. The anglophone elite of Westmount, where most of them now lived, were losing their entrepreneurial drive and their economic power as American direct investment poured into the province. American capitalists dealt directly with Duplessis, who seemed to enjoy their company, and their Westmount counterparts soon learned to do the same. Robinson was personally close to Duplessis and reasonably close to the anglophone establishment, so he could play the traditional consociational role to some extent despite his relatively minor portfolio. On the other hand French had much less influence and Cottingham hardly any. (Significantly, Cottingham does not even appear in the index to Conrad Black's massive biography of Duplessis.) In 1958 Duplessis decreed that all his ministers, including Cottingham, must answer all parliamentary questions in French, even if the question had been asked in English.[74] Christopher Dunkin would not have been amused.

The anglophone business establishment continued, on balance, to approve of Duplessis in the postwar years. His anti-communism was appreciated even if it sometimes took bizarre forms, such as the accusation that Communist sabotage had caused the collapse of a poorly constructed bridge in Trois-Rivières. His parsimonious fiscal policies and hostility to organized labour were also welcome. Resistance to federal centralization and to the Keynesian welfare state was generally approved of, particularly when Duplessis made common cause with Premier George Drew of Ontario, although there were some misgivings about Duplessis' Quebec nationalism.[75]

The Gazette was reconciled to Duplessis soon after the war ended. It was traditionally a Conservative paper and its proprietor, John Bassett, was a close personal friend of the premier. The paper's news editor, Tracy S. Ludington, was both a friend of Duplessis and a part-time employee of the Union Nationale, which paid him to write English-language press releases and campaign literature. He also touted the Union Nationale as a commentator on the leading English radio station, CJAD, and in the NDG weekly newspaper, *The Monitor. The Montreal Star,* Liberal in federal politics, also supported Duplessis in the postwar years. Its proprietor was another of the premier's friends, J.W. McConnell.[76]

Despite the views expressed in their media and by their economic elites, most of the English-speaking voters on Montreal Island remained implacably hostile to Duplessis and the Union Nationale. In 1948, when the Union Nationale campaign emphasized the theme of provincial autonomy, the Liberals elected only eight members, but six of them were on the western half of the island. As Jack Jedwab has argued, "In a sense, Montreal's English ridings were responsible for the survival of the Liberal party in 1948."[77] In the 1950s Liberal leader Georges-Émile Lapalme, a dour Quebec nationalist with no great liking for anglophones, represented the riding of Outremont, which included Côte-des-Neiges and the Town of Mount Royal and was less than one-third francophone. There were very few other ridings where he would have had a realistic chance of being elected. Liberal majorities in the west end throughout the Duplessis years were so enormous that the Union Nationale usually ran only token campaigns.

At first sight there seems no obvious reason for this behaviour. The Duplessis government scrupulously respected the desire of English-speaking Quebeckers to control their own institutions, not to mention their dominant position in the economy. Duplessis himself had no hostility towards anglophones, got along well with them, and often did them favours. Few anglophones who actually met him were immune to his charm. In 1953, for example, he secured the passage of a private bill so that a newly arrived Rhodes scholar from British Columbia, John Turner, could practice law in Quebec without the usual three years of study for a degree in civil law. He also gracefully complimented the future prime minister on his ability to speak French, and then took him out to lunch. As Turner recalled, "I became a good friend of Duplessis."[78]

Ordinary anglophone Montrealers, however, were not impressed. They disliked the premier's nationalism, mild though it was by later standards, and resented his constant rhetorical attacks on the federal government. In a few instances the Union Nationale's defence of provincial autonomy caused them genuine inconvenience, as when Duplessis refused to participate in the Trans-Canada Highway project or when Quebec universities were forbidden to accept federal grants. The provincial income tax imposed in 1954, at a time when no other province had one, affected anglophones disproportionately because of their generally higher incomes. The refusal to give Montreal Island its fair share of seats in the Legislative Assembly was also a genuine grievance, although it was as much a consequence as a cause of anglophone hostility to the government.

More generally, though, English-speaking Montrealers wished to participate in the postwar economic boom and the transformation of North American society that resulted. A government that was trying to protect Quebec's way of life against that transformation could only be the object of resentment or ridicule, never of support. There were various petty grievances, some of them tenuously related to Duplessis himself but all vaguely attributed to him. Margarine could not be bought. Revealing bathing suits could not be worn. A divorce required the adoption of a private bill by the federal Parliament. Drive-in theatres were not allowed and children under sixteen could not go to movies at all, although occasionally a Disney feature received a special dispensation. In 1953 a film about Martin Luther failed to meet the approval of the provincial censors (all French-speaking Catholics) and had to be shown in the basements of Protestant churches. Paul Earl, the Liberal member for NDG, demanded that non-Catholics be represented on the board of censors, but to no avail.[79]

There was one exception to the solid sea of Liberal red in western Montreal. In 1948 Frank Hanley, a Montreal city councillor and an ally of Mayor Camilien Houde, ran as an independent supported by City Hall in the Ste-Anne constituency. The traditionally Irish riding was by this time about half francophone with a number of other minorities, but Hanley was bilingual, an indefatigible campaigner, and a natural politician who seemed to know everyone in the district. The Liberals, who normally had a stranglehold on Ste-Anne, were at a low point in their fortunes and Hanley won the riding, which he would hold for the next twenty-two years while retaining his municipal seat at the same time.

Hanley could have stepped from the pages of Edwin O'Connor's novel of Boston politics, *The Last Hurrah*. Eric Kierans recalled asking him, towards the end of his legislative career, whether he would be back in Quebec City on the following Monday. Hanley retorted: "Of course not, I have to do my funerals!"[80] He soon attracted the attention of Duplessis, whose policies he was willing to support if it would benefit the voters in his riding. Thereafter Duplessis ran a token Union Nationale candidate in Ste-Anne, who was instructed not to campaign too vigorously, and threw his support, as well as a substantial contribution towards campaign expenses, to Hanley. Just before the election of 1960, according to Hanley's recollection, the new Union Nationale premier, Antonio Barrette, asked him how much Duplessis had contributed to his campaign in 1956. "Thirty-five thousand dollars," was the reply. Barrette was shocked. "I was his minister of labour and all I got was twenty-five thousand!"[81]

In rural Quebec the English-speaking population gave substantial support to the Union Nationale. Like their francophone neighbours they recognized the benefit of being on the winning side when government spending and patronage were distributed in an overtly partisan fashion. They did not fully share the Montreal anglophones' instinctively centralist view of Canadian federalism, and the aspects of life in Quebec that offended the Montrealers did not greatly concern them. In fact the ridings with substantial anglophone populations seemed even more partial to the Union Nationale after the war than other parts of rural Quebec.[82] Although Jonathan Robinson in Brome was the only anglophone Union Nationale candidate elected in 1944, four years later the party added John Rennie in Huntingdon, Raymond Johnston in Pontiac, Daniel French in Compton, and William Cottingham in Argenteuil. Although Brome was lost to Glen Brown of the Liberals in 1956, the other ridings remained Union Nationale until after Duplessis' death. In the absence of Montreal members, they were relied upon to provide anglophone representatives for the cabinet, as noted above.

The years from 1944 to 1959, when Duplessis and the Union Nationale dominated Quebec politics, may be viewed in retrospect as a time of transition, or even a prelude to the Quiet Revolution that followed. This perspective raises the question, among others, of whether Duplessis' return to office in 1944 signals a stage in the decline of the consociational arrangements that had protected Quebec's anglophone minority. It is clear that the anglophone minority lacked significant representation in the government after Robinson's death in 1948, and even Robinson was not influential enough to be given the office of provincial treasurer, which marked a significant break with tradition. Admittedly the refusal of Montreal anglophones to elect Union Nationale candidates was not conducive to giving them adequate representation, but Duplessis could have parachuted a prominent Montreal anglophone into a rural riding after Robinson's death or even named an anglophone minister from the Legislative Council. Since he did neither of these things, it may be argued that the Duplessis government in its last decade was not a "grand coalition," Lijphart's term for an executive that includes the political leaders of all significant segments in a consociational democracy. Nonetheless, Duplessis made up for this by conducting his own form of elite accommodation outside the formal institutions of government. Instead of using ministers as intermediaries, he dealt directly with prominent anglophone business leaders and with the heads of anglophone institutions like McGill University, the Protestant school boards, and the major hospitals.

Duplessis must be given a higher rating, furthermore, in terms of the other defining criteria of a consociational regime. Segmental autonomy was scrupulously respected: he did not interfere with existing arrangements regarding education, health, social services, or municipal affairs. As had been true since Confederation, the provincial government continued to have little direct influence on the lives of anglophones. The economic power of anglophones was left undisturbed, to the chagrin of some Quebec nationalists. The rule of proportionality was also generally observed. Although it is well known that Duplessis discriminated against ridings that voted Liberal in allocating funds for roads and other purposes, he never discriminated on ethnic grounds. Similarly, anglophone universities and other institutions were treated at least as well as their francophone counterparts in the allocation of resources.

It is more difficult to answer the question of whether and, if so, how the anglophone community was able to veto decisions that might have threatened its vital interests. It has already been noted that the anglophone middle class of Montreal had many grievances against the government. On the other hand, none of the matters complained about really threatened any vital interest of the community as a whole, or of the economic elite that tended to assume the role of speaking and acting on the community's behalf. There were no further initiatives to promote the French language after 1938 and Duplessis actively opposed the nationalization of electric power, even though this had been part of the Union Nationale's original program. Even Duplessis' Ottawa-bashing, in contrast to that of his successors, did not go so far as to alarm the anglophone establishment; in fact, he involved the establishment with his autonomist position by appointing John P. Rowat, the chairman of the Protestant committee in the Council of Public Instruction, to the Royal Commission on Constitutional Problems, better known as the Tremblay Commission. Rowat signed the final report with no apparent reservations, and Duplessis later appointed him to the Legislative Council.

On balance, the evidence suggests that the essential features of Quebec's consociational regime survived the Duplessis years with relatively little modification. The neo-nationalism and anti-clericalism that developed in opposition to Duplessis' conservative policies would prove much more threatening to anglophone interests when they came to fruition after his death.

FEDERAL REPRESENTATION, VOTING, AND POLITICS

The federal government has been rather neglected so far in this account, but its importance should certainly not be disparaged. English-speaking Montrealers, although probably not the anglophones in rural Quebec, considered it more important and more interesting than the provincial level. A woman from the Square Mile explained to Margaret Westley how it was before the Second World War: "We had the same kind of attitude toward the provincial government that we now have to the city government, that it was just a group of people lining their own pockets and not too interested in good government. The real government was in Ottawa, at least for my generation."[83]

In fact this rather complacent and patronizing attitude reflected the consociational *modus vivendi* whereby the provincial government tacitly allowed the anglophones to run their own affairs without interference. Since they could take this for granted, English-speaking Quebeckers were free to ignore the provincial level of government and to concentrate their efforts on the federal. In later years, as subsequent chapters of this book will describe, they did not have the same luxury.

Nine of Quebec's first twenty-four senators were anglophones, and there were still seven as late as 1931, when anglophones were only 15 per cent of the population. Both of the senatorial districts in Montreal, Alma and Victoria, always had anglophone senators, as they do to the present day. Inkerman (the Ottawa Valley) and Wellington

(Sherbrooke and its environs) were also anglophone preserves until the 1960s. Other districts had anglophone senators only occasionally, and very rarely after 1945 when the anglophone quota fell to about four.

In the House of Commons anglophones were given no constitutional guarantees, but in the early years they were more than adequately represented. Some francophone politicians were apparently reluctant to go to Ottawa, where business was conducted mainly in English, so francophone ridings often sent an anglophone to the House of Commons and a francophone to the Legislative Assembly. The sixty-five federal members elected (or in some cases acclaimed) in 1867 included twenty-one anglophones, or nearly one-third of the total. In the third House of Commons, elected in 1874, the number reached an all-time high of twenty-three. Thereafter there was a gradual and steady decline, with eighteen anglophones elected in 1896, fourteen in 1921, and only nine in 1945. The Diefenbaker landslide of 1958 brought a temporary increase, with eleven anglophones elected in that year, but by that time Quebec sent a total of seventy-five members to the House of Commons.

As at the provincial level, there was a gradual shift of anglophone representation from the rural counties, especially those along the southern border of the province, to Montreal and its suburbs. Since the number of federal ridings remained fixed at sixty-five until the 1953 election, and since none were constitutionally protected, the process of combining thinly populated rural ridings proceeded rapidly so as to allow increasing representation for Montreal. Ottawa County disappeared by 1896, Huntingdon was combined with Chateauguay from 1917 onwards, and Brome was combined with Missisquoi in 1925, leaving Pontiac as the only predominantly anglophone riding off the island of Montreal. In 1949 Pontiac was merged into the new riding of Pontiac-Temiscamingue.

Nonetheless, some of these counties continued to send anglophone members to Ottawa for some time after they lost their anglophone majorities and even after they were combined with neighbouring counties. As late as the Second World War there were still anglophone members from Chateauguay-Huntingdon and Stanstead as well as Pontiac. The city of Sherbrooke elected only anglophones to Parliament until 1940, half a century after it had become predominantly francophone. Quebec West was recognized as an Irish riding until 1917, when it was merged into the new riding of Quebec South. Nevertheless it continued the tradition of Irish representation with "Chubby" Power, the son of the last member for Quebec West, holding Quebec South continuously from 1917 until he was appointed to the

Senate in 1955. His son Frank Power succeeded him but fell victim to the Diefenbaker landslide in 1958.

In Montreal the two predominantly anglophone ridings were increased to three in 1896, with one (Ste-Anne) still traditionally reserved for Irish Catholic candidates. Cartier was added as a Jewish riding in 1917, Mount Royal, including NDG and the western suburbs, in 1925, and Verdun in 1935. Population movements had produced non-francophone majorities in Jacques-Cartier (the West Island) and in Outremont by the Second World War and NDG finally received its own federal member in 1949, but thereafter the number of ridings that could be considered anglophone gradually declined. Outremont never elected an anglophone member of parliament and Verdun did so only after 1958 when it had ceased to be a predominantly English-speaking city.

Data on the religious affiliation of members of parliament are scant for the early years, but from 1904 onwards most members' biographies in the Parliamentary Guide contain this information. Protestants were always a majority of the Quebec anglophone members until 1940, although Irish Catholic and Jewish members were elected as noted above. Most of the Protestant members belonged to the Anglican Church, traditionally the largest Protestant denomination in Quebec. The declining number of Protestants in later years was partly the consequence of the decline of the Conservative Party, since Liberals were less likely to be Protestant.

From the outset English-speaking Quebeckers staked a claim to representation in the federal cabinet. John A. Macdonald originally intended to include Thomas D'Arcy McGee to represent the Irish Catholics of the province and Alexander T. Galt to represent the Protestants. However, Ontario insisted on having more representatives than Quebec, Quebec francophones demanded more representatives than Quebec anglophones, and the result was that McGee was not included.[84] Galt was given the Department of Finance but resigned in October 1867 after he was blamed for the failure of a bank. Macdonald's friend, the Montreal banker John Rose, succeeded to the portfolio and was elected in a by-election in Huntingdon, where he catered to anti-Confederation sentiments by emphasizing his preference for legislative union.[85] When Rose left the government two years later Christopher Dunkin replaced him as the spokesman for English-speaking Quebeckers.

The result of these developments was the convention that one Protestant from Quebec would serve in the cabinet. An Irish Catholic from Quebec was not considered essential but might be appointed in addition, as was done occasionally after 1896. The Liberal government formed in 1935 was the first to have no Protestant from Quebec, with "Chubby" Power apparently being deemed to represent Quebec anglophones of all religious persuasions. Charles Howard from Sherbrooke, a member of parliament with ten years experience, might have merited a cabinet appointment but did not receive one. The lack of Quebec Protestant representation continued until near the end of the war, when Brooke Claxton and Douglas Abbott, both from Montreal, were brought into the government. Both held senior portfolios until 1954, when Claxton returned to the private sector and Abbott was appointed to the Supreme Court of Canada.

Until 1917 most English-speaking ministers from Quebec represented one of the rural counties or the city of Sherbrooke. After 1917 most were from Montreal. The riding of St Lawrence-St George, which included the Square Mile, had seven members of parliament between 1917 and 1968, of whom five were appointed to the cabinet: C.C. Ballantyne, Herbert Marler, Charles Cahan, Brooke Claxton, and John Turner. Most ministers were lawyers or businessmen. Only one anglophone senator from Quebec, John J. Abbott, was ever appointed to cabinet and he held no portfolio, serving briefly as a caretaker prime minister after the death of Macdonald in 1891. Anglophone ministers from Quebec held a variety of portfolios and the closest thing to a tradition that emerged was, oddly enough, in Agriculture, which was held by Christopher Dunkin and then John Henry Pope in the Macdonald governments and by Sydney Fisher in the Laurier government.

Because the first line of defence for anglophone interests was at the provincial level, the federal spokesmen for the community rarely had to concern themselves with such matters as religion, language or education. The main significance of Ottawa lay in the economic realm, particularly after the National Policy of 1878. The Bank of Montreal served as the dominion's banker until a central bank was established in 1935, the transcontinental railways were centred in Montreal, and the protective tariff stimulated industrialization in both Montreal and the Eastern Townships. Anglophone Quebec representation in the dominion cabinet ensured the continuation of these policies and also protected Montreal against the rising influence of Toronto. These interests were shared by French-speaking Quebeckers in Montreal and the Townships, although not so much by those in other parts of the province. The speeches of English-speaking members from Quebec often emphasized the theme of *bonne entente* and sought to explain Quebec's viewpoint to the rest of the country. Although Julius Scriver of Huntingdon was one of the thirteen members to vote for a resolution demanding the disallowance of the Jesuits' Estates Act in 1889, the other Protestants from Quebec, both Liberal and Conservative, all voted against the resolution.

Until the Second World War Quebec's English-speaking voters leaned towards the Conservative side in most federal elections. Even more than Quebec francophones, they resisted the Liberal landslide of 1874, which was an expression of hostility to the Montreal-centred Pacific scandal. They did not support Laurier in 1891, when he favoured free trade with the United States, although they accepted him five years later when he did not. They also began to drift away from Laurier's Liberals in 1904, when Montreal-St-Antoine, Argenteuil, Huntingdon and Pontiac all elected Conservative members. Laurier's project of a direct railway from Quebec City to Winnipeg, built at the government's expense and bypassing Montreal and the Ottawa Valley, understandably won him few votes in those areas. Nationalists in eastern Quebec, and the Catholic clergy, favoured it as a means of opening the Abitibi region to colonization.

In 1917 a coalition between Conservatives and dissident Liberals was formed to impose conscription. This was anathema to francophone Quebec, but supporters of the coalition government were elected in Ste-Anne, St-Antoine, and St Lawrence-St George. Charles C. Ballantyne, a prominent businessman who lived in the Square Mile, entered the cabinet as a coalition Liberal when he was assured that Charles Smart, the provincial member for Westmount, would support his candidacy.[86] The nationalization of the Grand Trunk Railway, however, turned English-speaking Quebeckers against the coalition. It was feared that the Grand Trunk's headquarters and repair shops would be moved to Toronto since the Canadian Northern, which had already been nationalized, was based in that city. Even when that concern proved to be unfounded there was unhappiness about the creation of a government-owned compethitor to the Canadian Pacific. The latter railway was Montreal's largest employer, it was closely associated with the Bank of Montreal, its presidents had always lived in the Square Mile, its steamships linked Montreal with the United Kingdom, and its main line to the Maritimes ran through the English-speaking areas of southern Quebec. In 1921 the government lost even its English-speaking rump in Quebec and failed to elect a single member in the province.

By 1925, however, the Liberals were the incumbents and had little choice but to defend the government railway. The Conservative Party returned to its traditional alliance with the Canadian Pacific, and the English-speaking west end of Montreal returned to the Conservatives and remained with them for the next four elections. Cartier, the largely Jewish riding, repeatedly elected Sam Jacobs, a Liberal maverick who continued to oppose government ownership of railways.

After 1939, however, the notoriety of Duplessis and his Union Nationale spilled over into the federal arena. In the plebiscite of 27 April 1942 the eight Montreal Island ridings with non-francophone majorities voted solidly for conscription, while the rest of the province voted against it. Mount Royal had the third highest pro-conscription percentage in Canada.[87] (Pontiac, the last remaining anglophone rural riding, voted against conscription as it had in 1917.) In 1940, 1945, and 1949 the federal Liberals swept the province, including every riding on the island of Montreal. There were significant pockets of Conservative support among rural anglophones, corresponding to their provincial support for the Union Nationale, but they failed to elect any federal members of their party. In the postwar years, with Douglas Abbott in finance and Brooke Claxton in national defence, anglophone Montreal had its strongest representation in the federal cabinet since the departure of John Rose two years after Confederation. When Abbott went to the Supreme Court of Canada in 1954 his place in the House of Commons and in the cabinet was taken by his friend George Marler, previously the provincial member for the same riding and the nephew of an earlier federal member for Claxton's riding of St Lawrence-St George. (George Marler would later be appointed to the Legislative Council and the provincial cabinet by Jean Lesage, who had been his colleague in Ottawa.) Claxton encouraged the careers of Alan McNaughton, the federal member for Mount Royal from 1945 to 1965, and of Bud Drury, who would be Westmount's member of parliament after 1962.

The first breach in the Liberal fortress was made in 1953 when Bill Hamilton won NDG for the Progressive Conservatives. Hamilton was so right-wing that he accused the St Laurent government of "socialism" in his maiden speech.[88] Nonetheless, he had so little rapport with francophones that he could not plausibly be associated with the notoriety of the Union Nationale. He also attracted sympathy by campaigning vigorously despite a serious physical handicap: he had been crippled by polio. In 1957, with John Diefenbaker beginning to attract the attention of English-speaking Canadians, the Progressive Conservatives also elected John Pratt, the mayor of Dorval, in suburban Jacques-Cartier-Lasalle. Hamilton became Diefenbaker's postmaster-general. In the following year Progressive Conservatives won St Lawrence-St George, Verdun and St-Antoine-Westmount on Diefenbaker's coattails. The Diefenbaker forces received significant organizational and financial help from the Union Nationale, and won most of the rural and semi-rural counties held by that party at the provincial level. Heward Grafftey, one of several anglophones who came in on the tidal wave in rural Quebec, recalled that a $10,000 contribution to his campaign was delivered by Daniel Johnson. Five years earlier, the Tory candidate had won only one poll in the entire riding.[89]

For English-speaking Quebeckers, the federal election of 1958 seemed like a dramatic upheaval. The Tories won fifty seats in Quebec. The "Government Party," which had presided over the postwar economic boom and built a Keynesian welfare state, was reduced to its lowest level of support since Confederation. Far more significant changes, however, were about to occur in their own province. These changes would soon direct the attention and the energies of Quebec anglophones towards provincial politics and would eventually sweep away the consociational *modus vivendi* that had sheltered their way of life for almost a century.

3 Consociationalism Threatened: Anglophones and the Quiet Revolution, 1960–68

June 22, 1960 – the date of the election that ended sixteen years of uninterrupted rule by the Union Nationale – would be viewed in retrospect as the end of an era and the beginning of a revolution, but that was hardly how it seemed at the time. The election on the first day of summer was not unexpected because Maurice Duplessis had established a tradition of summer elections every four years.[1] Duplessis had died in the preceding September and his chosen successor, Paul Sauvé, had died even more unexpectedly in January, but the old leader's preferences were still respected by Antonio Barrette, who had become the third leader of the governing party. Although Barrette was a less impressive leader than Sauvé had been, few really expected the Liberals under their new leader Jean Lesage to defeat the long-entrenched Union Nationale machine. *The Montreal Star* and *The Gazette,* as usual, advised their readers to vote for the Union Nationale.

Life in Montreal was little different in that June from the June before, or the June before that. People swam and fished in Lac St-Louis or in the Rivière-des-Prairies, which English-speaking Montrealers more mundanely called the Back River. Tourists admired the wax figures of Christian martyrs in the Canadian Historical Museum on Queen Mary Road, or crossed the Mercier Bridge to buy souvenirs at Chief Poking Fire's Wigwam. Steam locomotives could still be seen and heard on the Canadian Pacific lines around the city, although they would all be retired by the end of the summer. Several transatlantic shipping companies – Cunard, Canadian Pacific, Anchor-Donaldson and the Home Lines – operated frequent passenger services to western Europe from the old port of Montreal. The Royals, the Triple-A affiliate of the recently relocated Los Angeles Dodgers, were playing what would be their last season at Delorimier Stadium. J.J. Joubert, a well-known local dairy, made its daily deliveries of fresh milk by horse and wagon. In the absence of an official Canadian flag the Union Jack flew proudly over Protestant schools, Westmount City Hall, and most of the principal office buildings. The blue and white provincial flag, adopted twelve years earlier by Duplessis, could be seen in the eastern part of the city and post offices displayed the red federal ensign, but English-speaking Montreal still saw itself as British.

Montreal was the largest city in Canada and, while it might also be the second-largest French-speaking city in the world, everyone knew that English was the working language in the financial offices on St James Street and in the new steel and glass office towers that were sprouting along Dorchester Boulevard. English-speaking Montrealers had little reason to speak French and few were capable of doing so. Women were even less likely to speak it than men, owing to their lesser participation in the labour force and the extreme degree of residential segregation. Anglophones who were bilingual when they were young tended to lose the facility as they grew older.[2] Some liked to boast that they had "never been east of Morgan's." Morgan's, which would be absorbed a few years later by the Hudson's Bay Company, was the most easterly of the four department stores on St Catherine Street West.

The result of the election, although surprising, was not particularly overwhelming. The Liberals had run on a fairly conventional platform and their narrow majority was based on a shift of about 6 per cent of the popular vote from one major party to the other. Their star candidates, Paul Gérin-Lajoie and René Lévesque, won by majorities of 149 and 129 votes respectively.[3] *Montréal-Matin*, a daily tabloid owned by the Union Nationale, was able to announce the outcome without overt misrepresentation in a memorably ambiguous headline: "*Une lutte serrée; M. Barrette tient son siège à Joliette.*"[4]

Mr Barrette had indeed retained his seat in the Legislative Assembly, but he would soon be gone, relegated to a footnote in history. French Canada, which Goldwin Smith had once compared to the body of an extinct animal preserved in the Siberian permafrost, was about to shake off the weight of its past.[5] In the process, although not immediately, the peculiar set of arrangements and relationships that had sheltered the English-speaking community of Quebec for two centuries would be called into question.

THE COMING OF THE QUIET REVOLUTION

There are many interpretations of, and explanations for, what would come to be called the Quiet Revolution, and it is probably neither possible nor necessary to discover a single cause that will explain so complex a phenomenon.[6] Industrialization, urbanization, and postwar prosperity had led to a gradually increasing incongruity between the material circumstances in which most French Canadians lived and the ideological vision espoused by their traditional elites. Television linked all of the French-speaking people of Quebec for the first time into a single network of electronic communication, and one that to a great extent escaped the censorship imposed on the printed media. The Roman Catholic Church, particularly in western Europe, was undergoing a process of intellectual and spiritual regeneration that was accelerated by the accession of John XXIII to the papacy in 1958. In Canada, the development of a merit-based public service and a Keynesian welfare state at the federal level, largely closed to those not fluent in English and with little sensitivity to Quebec's distinct way of life, exposed the inadequacy of the province's own political institutions and practices, as well as its vulnerability to decisions made outside its borders.

Above all, as Hubert Guindon was the first social scientist to appreciate, the institutional Church in Quebec was increasingly unable to continue both its spiritual vocation and the unusual burden of responsibility for health, education and social welfare which history had placed on its shoulders.[7] This burden was the product of several circumstances: the British colonial tradition of indirect rule combined with British control of the economy, the discrediting of secular French Canadian leadership by the defeat of the liberal rebellion in 1837, and finally the complex combination of consociational and federal arrangements that took shape in the age of Galt and Cartier. The Church acquired extensive responsibilities that it carried out reasonably well until the middle of the twentieth century.[8] But increasingly and inevitably its "bureaucratic empires," as Guindon has described the congeries of church-related institutions, outgrew the Church's own human and financial resources. They became dependent on the paid labour of lay personnel and on financial assistance from the state, beginning with the Taschereau government's Public Charities Act in 1921 and accelerating in the postwar years as Duplessis and the federal authorities competed against one another for the support of those who staffed the bureaucratic empires. Belying the popular image of the Duplessis era as a period of stagnation, per capita spending by the

Quebec government tripled in real terms between 1944 and 1959, while the proportion of that spending devoted to health, education and welfare increased from just over a third to almost half.[9] Yet there never seemed to be enough money. More and more government was involved in the Church's affairs and vice versa, to the detriment of the Church's independence, authority and legitimacy. More and more clerical energies were diverted from spiritual matters into administration, lobbying, fund-raising and government relations. The younger clergy and the lay personnel of the bureaucratic empires grew restless under the rule of Duplessis. Their hopes were raised by the arrival of Paul Sauvé, only to be dashed again by his untimely death.[10] Meanwhile other Quebeckers were asking a question previously deemed beyond the pale of respectable controversy. If the Church was no longer capable of performing its many tasks without assistance, how could it justify the rigid ideological control which it still exercised over the province?

The liberals and anti-clericals who discussed such matters in the last years of the Duplessis regime found their voice in Pierre Trudeau's cardboard-covered magazine *Cité Libre*, in Jacques Hébert's small publishing house Les Éditions de l'Homme, in the Faculty of Social Sciences at Laval University, and in the federal government's radio and television networks. Like the Paris mob who stormed the almost empty Bastille in 1789, they did not realize how weak their enemy was or how quickly clerical power would collapse after 1960.

Another group of Quiet Revolutionaries chose to confront a more formidable, but also declining, adversary: the English-speaking economic elite. In Quebec as elsewhere, the miseries of the 1930s had stimulated fresh thinking about the management and control of the economy. In a province where economic power and wealth were conspicuously enjoyed by an elite who shared neither the language nor the faith of the majority, this inevitably took the form of economic nationalism. Attacks on trusts and monopolies, support for francophone small businesses, public ownership of electric power utilities, co-operatives, price controls, farm credit, colonization, and the corporatist management of economic decision-making recommended by the Church in the encyclical *Quadragesimo Anno* were among the specific ideas on the subject that circulated in prewar Quebec.[11] Such ideas found their way into the original program of the Union Nationale (which was largely ignored by Duplessis) and later into that of the short-lived Bloc Populaire, a nationalist party that grew out of the anti-conscription movement during the war. Postwar growth and prosperity dulled the hard edge of resentment, but economic nationalism was kept alive, especially in the University of Montreal, the intellectual

daily newspaper *Le Devoir,* and the magazine *l'Action nationale.* While
the theory might be naive and the practice disappointing, the problem
of French-Canadian economic inferiority was real and demanded
some solution.

Over the years, and especially after 1968, the two schools of discontent which Michael Behiels has called the citélibrists and the neo-
nationalists would come to be recognized, and to recognize themselves, as opponents.[12] Originally the distinction between them,
though apparent to those who read between the lines, was much less
obvious and they seemed merely to be different aspects of a broad
process and project of modernization. English-speaking Quebeckers
were certainly not in a position to draw fine distinctions. Most had
only casual contacts, if any, with French-speaking neighbours. Their
printed and electronic media ignored intellectual developments in
French-speaking Quebec before 1960 and gave them little attention
afterwards although the *Montreal Star,* from 1961 until its demise, did
somewhat better in this regard than *The Gazette.* Even major events
like the riot that followed the suspension of hockey player Maurice
Richard in 1955 or the producers' strike at Radio-Canada in 1959
failed to disturb the complacency of English-speaking Quebeckers. If
noted at all, they were not felt to have any political implications,
although both in fact were symptoms of a deeply rooted resentment
against anglophone power. At McGill University in the early 1960s a
course on French-Canadian political thought was taught by a young
political scientist, Michael Oliver, whose brilliant dissertation on the
subject would not be published until thirty-five years after it was
written.[13] Most McGill students, however, saw little reason to study
"Pepsi Politics," as many of them irreverently referred to the course,
when other courses could teach them about Africa, Asia, or the Soviet
Union.

THE SILENT EROSION OF ANGLOPHONE POWER

Alexis de Tocqueville argued in his study of the French Revolution
that the aristocracy were only attacked and overthrown when their real
power and importance had already begun to wane from natural
causes.[14] Traditionally the existence of the aristocracy had been justified by its essential role in defending and administering the country,
but when it was no longer capable of performing these functions, and
no longer needed for these purposes, its inherited wealth and status
came to be viewed as illegitimate, immoral, and unnecessary. This

insight seems to provide the basis for a general theory of revolutions, including quiet revolutions.

It has already been suggested that clerical power, the primary target of the citélibrists, was much more fragile by 1960 than it appeared. The Church was no longer really capable of performing the various tasks which it had traditionally been assigned in Quebec, nor was it really necessary that it do so. These facts would be demonstrated by the ease with which clerical power was swept away over the decade that followed. Yet while much less obvious at the time than it seems with hindsight, the gradual erosion of clerical power was already contributing to the increasing boldness and relative impunity with which it was attacked.

Anglophone economic power, the primary target of the neo-nationalists, was also in decline by 1960, although the process was less advanced and the result less obvious than the wane of clerical power. Because clerical power was an easier target at the time, the first phase of the Quiet Revolution would be dominated by the citélibrists and their agenda. The neo-nationalists in the early 1960s were less conspicuous than the anti-clericals, and tended to attack their adversary more by implication than directly. After the Liberals received a second mandate in November 1962, running on the neo-nationalist slogan of "*Maîtres chez nous*," the neo-nationalists became more assertive. After 1968 they would move into the centre of the stage, as chapter 4 of this book describes.

In 1960 the power of the English-speaking economic elite in Quebec still superficially appeared strong. Later in the decade, the Royal Commission on Bilingualism and Biculturalism, using data from the census of 1961, would describe in detail the anglophone control of Quebec's economy. Only 15.4 per cent of the value added by manufacturing industries in Quebec came from firms controlled by French-speaking Canadians, with English-speaking Canadians and non-Canadians sharing the rest in roughly equal proportions.[15] Only 21.8 per cent of jobs in manufacturing, and only 47.3 per cent of those in the private sector as a whole, were in enterprises owned by French-speaking Canadians.[16] Among non-agricultural employees in Quebec, males of British origin earned, on the average, more than one and a half times as much as those of French origin, with those of Jewish, German and Ukrainian origin also earning more than the French. Men of British origin in Quebec had higher incomes on the average than men of British origin in any other province.[17] Men of French origin in Quebec earned almost 50 per cent more if they were bilingual than if they knew French only. On the other hand, men of

British origin in Quebec earned slightly *less* if they were bilingual than if they knew English only.[18]

Despite these facts, and despite the new office towers and other evidence of commercial vitality in west-central Montreal, the conditions that had produced the economic power of English-speaking Montreal were already disappearing. That power, and the importance of Montreal itself, rested on the mundane fact that the Lachine Rapids blocked the access of ocean shipping to the upper St Lawrence and the Great Lakes, making Montreal the linchpin of a trading system that linked western Europe with the Canadian, and at times North American, interior. Financial institutions had clustered in Montreal for the same reason, beginning with the Bank of Montreal, "Canada's First Bank," in 1817. Having become dominant in the age of water transport, Montreal had prolonged its hegemony by becoming the headquarters of the major railway systems: first the Grand Trunk, later the Canadian Pacific, and later still the Canadian National. With excellent transportation and a large supply of cheap labour close at hand, it had benefitted from Macdonald's National Policy. From then until the Second World War, Canada's economy had been based on British portfolio investment, British and European immigration, railway transport, import-substituting industry protected by high tariffs, and the export of bulky staples by water transport to transatlantic markets. In each of these aspects Montreal, and specifically its English-speaking economic elite, had been able to play the commanding role.

As these conditions began to change the Montreal elite, perhaps coincidentally, began to lose its original vitality. An early sign, even before the Second World War, was the success of Toronto in gaining control of the mineral resources in northwestern Quebec and northeastern Ontario. In 1928 the railway owned by the Ontario government ran a branch line across the Quebec border to Noranda, preempting a possible move by the Montreal-based Canadian Pacific. In the 1930s, when gold mining was the only flourishing sector of the economy, the Toronto Stock Exchange for the first time surpassed the Montreal Stock Exchange in volume of trading.

As Canada moved into a closer economic relationship with the United States, and as direct investment by American firms became the major source of capital for Canadian development, Toronto began to replace Montreal as the economic link between Canada and its external markets and sources of capital. Southern Ontario, shaped like a wedge driven into the industrial heartland of the United States, naturally became the centre of branch-plant manufacturing. Toronto was the logical place for corporate headquarters and for many of the branch plants, and eventually for banking, insurance, advertising and other services. The influence of the federal government, and Quebec's importance to the Liberal Party, helped to maintain Montreal as a centre of transportation and of defence-related industries, but in other sectors of economic activity it was falling behind. As their city and its economic role declined in importance, English-speaking Montrealers began to move away to Ontario, British Columbia, or the United States. Many were transferred by their employers, while others took the initiative in seeking better opportunities in places that were newer and growing faster.

The opening of the St Lawrence Seaway, just a few months before the death of Maurice Duplessis, both symbolized and contributed to Montreal's fate. Even trade with Great Britain and Europe could now bypass the city, as ocean-going ships proceeded directly to the Great Lakes, but in fact the Seaway was built for an entirely different purpose – the transport of Labrador iron ore to the steel mills around the Great Lakes. Although hailed as a great Canadian project, it was the product of American priorities, particularly those related to the strategic requirements of the cold war. Those Montrealers who feared the advent of the Seaway were more astute than those who saw it as evidence that the commercial empire of the St Lawrence retained its vitality.

Thus the Montreal economic elite in 1960, like the French aristocracy in 1789, was becoming an anachronism. Its conspicuous wealth was the legacy of earlier and, for it, happier times, rather than an accurate indication of its present or future importance. It no longer provided Quebec with real benefits that Americans, or potentially the francophones themselves, could not provide as effectively. Its privileges thus seemed anomalous and without purpose. It is possible that Duplessis understood the trend as early as 1944 when, as noted in the preceding chapter, he did not follow the tradition of appointing an anglophone as provincial treasurer. Perhaps the ease with which the wartime Liberal government had taken over the Montreal Light, Heat and Power Company after the death of its founder, Sir Herbert Holt, persuaded him that the anglophone elite need not be taken as seriously as before.

ANGLOPHONE VOTERS AND
THE QUIET REVOLUTION

Three general elections took place in Quebec in the 1960s. The first, in 1960, resulted in a Liberal government with a narrow majority. The second, in November 1962, saw the Liberals returned with a more comfortable majority, which was generally interpreted as a mandate to proceed with their plans to bring the privately-owned electric power utilities under state ownership. The third, in June 1966, was won by the Union Nationale with a narrow majority of seats. As in 1944, the defeated Liberals in 1966 won more popular votes than their victorious opponents, thanks to the overwhelming Liberal majorities in the predominantly English-speaking constituencies.

In 1960 more than one-sixth of Quebec's population had a mother tongue other than French, which in most cases was English. However, there were only seven constituencies out of ninety-five in which non-francophones were a majority of the electorate, even though the tendency of non-francophones to cluster in a few areas of the province might have been expected to produce a closer correspondence between their numbers and their representation in the Legislative Assembly. The main reason why it did not was the persistent under-representation of Montreal and its suburbs, which had been exacerbated by the rapid postwar population growth in the metropolitan region. Since most of the ridings that consistently elected Liberals in the Duplessis era were on the island of Montreal, Duplessis had been understandably reluctant to give the island more representation, even though by not doing so he penalized large numbers of Union Nationale supporters in the eastern part of Montreal.

NDG was the least francophone riding in the province, with less than one-fifth of its population of French ethnic origin. It was closely followed by Westmount and Outremont, both of which included considerably more territory than the municipalities for which they were named. Both were between 20 and 30 per cent French, with Westmount voters mainly of British origin and Outremont primarily Jewish. Suburban Jacques-Cartier and inner-city St-Louis were both between 40 and 50 per cent francophone, while Verdun and Ste-Anne had substantial English-speaking minorities. Four rural ridings – Argenteuil, Brome, Huntingdon and Pontiac – had anglophone minorities of 30 per cent or more.[19]

Of these eleven ridings at dissolution in 1960, three were held by English-speaking Union Nationale members and two by independents. The sole change in the 1960 election was a party-approved Liberal replacing an independent; in 1962 all incumbents were returned in each riding.

Thus the non-francophone vote remained essentially stable over a time when francophone voters shifted massively from the Union Nationale to the Liberals. Moreover, anglophones maintained the same voting patterns in the 1960s as during the Duplessis era, showing a strong preference for Liberals in the metropolitan region and a leaning towards the Union Nationale in rural areas.[20]

In 1960 there was actually a small shift of anglophone voters in Montreal towards the Union Nationale. Duplessis was dead, and the party soft-pedalled its traditional themes of provincial autonomy and resistance to "centralization," perhaps because its Progressive Conservative allies now held power in Ottawa. By reaching a federal-provincial agreement on university grants – the prototype for many subsequent schemes that substituted "tax points" for direct federal subsidies – the Sauvé government resolved one of the major problems that had prevented middle-class Montreal anglophones from supporting the party. For the first time since the war the Union Nationale ran a serious campaign in Westmount, with much of the volunteer labour supplied by Progressive Conservative supporters who had unexpectedly won the federal riding in the Diefenbaker landslide of 1958. Their candidate was Murray Hayes, the vice-chairman of the executive committee in the city of Montreal (an office traditionally reserved for anglophones), and he received almost 40 per cent of the vote.

One of the more interesting races was in St-Louis, which was traditionally supposed to be the Jewish riding although by 1960 most of the Jewish population had moved out to the suburbs or to more affluent parts of Montreal. The population that remained was almost half francophone with a variety of other ethnic groups. Furthermore, St-Louis had not actually had a Jewish representative in the Legislative Assembly since 1947, when Maurice Hartt gave up his provincial seat to run federally. In 1960 the Liberals decided to revive the tradition, partly to encourage financial support from the Jewish community and partly to get rid of Dave Rochon, a municipal politician and former Liberal who had sat as an independent since his expulsion from the caucus. The riding was not considered winnable, given the increasing number of francophone voters and the expectation that Rochon would run as an independent and split the Liberal vote. No prominent member of the Jewish community was much interested in running, but a young lawyer named Harry Blank, who lived outside the riding and had been active in Liberal politics, was persuaded to let his name stand. As he recalled later, "I figured if I ran and lost and the Liberals lost I would have my name in the papers and it would be good for business. If I ran and lost and the Liberals won, in those days patronage was a big deal and I'd be sitting in my glory ... We ran a campaign with professional organizers, but all the workers were people who had never been in politics before. They didn't live in the area although their parents might have lived there. So we ran our campaign and there were eighty-seven recounts, but finally I won by 108 votes."[21]

Paul Earl, the senior anglophone in the Legislative Assembly, was easily elected for the fourth time in NDG. Richard Hyde of Westmount and Glen Brown of Brome were also re-elected as Liberals. George O'Reilly, a soft-drink bottler and mayor of Verdun, ran for the Liberals and was elected in that constituency, although his majority was smaller than that of the francophone Liberal elected in 1956. Dr Charles Kirkland, a francophone despite his name and the former mayor of Ville St-Pierre, was re-elected in suburban Jacques-Cartier (known to English Montrealers of that era as "the Lakeshore") which he had represented as a Liberal since 1939. When he died in 1961 he was succeeded by his daughter Claire Kirkland-Casgrain, the first woman ever elected to the Legislative Assembly; she was re-elected in 1962. Frank Hanley had another easy victory in Ste-Anne. To no one's surprise the three rural English-speaking Union Nationale members – William Cottingham in Argenteuil, Henry Somerville in Huntingdon, and Raymond Johnston in Pontiac – were all re-elected.

The historic tendency of rural anglophones to support the governing party did not seem to operate to the advantage of the Liberals in 1962, possibly because the reform of the public service during the Lesage government's first term had eliminated most of the small-scale patronage traditionally used by governing parties to build support in rural areas. In purely francophone counties this disadvantage was counteracted to some extent by the nationalist appeal of "*maîtres chez nous,*" but English-speaking farmers had no interest in Quebec nationalism.

English-speaking Montrealers generally welcomed the reforms that marked the early stage of the Quiet Revolution, as will be discussed in more detail below. The new Union Nationale leader, Daniel Johnson, seemed more of a throwback to the Duplessis era than either Sauvé or Barrette, and his position on the nationalization of electricity was too ambiguous to attract the support of those who resented the Liberal proposal as an attack on anglophone economic power.[22] Thus the Union Nationale lost the little ground it had gained in 1960 in the west end ridings. Although the Liberals did well in all the major regions of Quebec their strongest support, somewhat ironically, was in English-speaking Montreal.

George O'Reilly was appointed to the Legislative Council in 1964 so that Claude Wagner could run in Verdun. Prior to the 1966 election the number of seats in the Legislative Assembly was increased by thirteen, with Montreal Island and Laval gaining most of the additional representation. Four new predominantly English-speaking ridings were created. D'Arcy-McGee included the mainly Jewish suburbs of Hampstead and Côte St-Luc and thus replaced Outremont as one of the three ridings with the smallest proportion of French voters. (Outremont itself retained a non-French majority, although a much narrower one than before the redistribution.) St-Laurent included the city of that name and the Cartierville district of Montreal. Marguerite-Bourgeoys included Montreal West, Lasalle, and Ville St-Pierre. Robert-Baldwin comprised the newer suburbs west of Dorval. With these excisions Jacques-Cartier, whose largest component was the industrial city of Lachine, became a predominantly French riding. Boundary changes caused the percentage of French Canadians to decline significantly in St-Louis.[23]

With these modifications in the map there were eight predominantly non-French ridings on Montreal Island instead of five. All were won by Liberals in 1966 with enormous majorities, except for Robert-Baldwin where the mayor of Pointe-Claire, Art Seguin, ran as an independent Liberal after failing to win the nomination and defeated the official candidate in the election, with the Union Nationale candidate in third place. Seguin, whose best polls were in the more anglophone parts of the riding, was admitted soon afterwards to the Liberal caucus. Daniel Johnson's graceless comment on election night that the Liberals owed their province-wide plurality of the popular vote to "the English and the Jews" was widely resented, although no one really questioned its accuracy.

While much of rural and small-town Quebec was swinging back to the Union Nationale in 1966, the only counties to move in the opposite direction were Argenteuil and Huntingdon. In Argenteuil William Cottingham's retirement resulted in a struggle for the succession with the consequence that there was an independent candidate to split the Union Nationale vote. In Huntingdon Ken Fraser, a Liberal farmer making his third attempt to win the riding, finally defeated Henry Somerville, the incumbent for fourteen years, in an extremely close race. Neither language nor party platforms had much bearing on the results, which seemed to have more to do with rivalry between the eastern and western ends of the county.[24] As a result of these developments Raymond Johnston from Pontiac was the only anglophone in the caucus of the victorious Union Nationale.

The irrepressible Frank Hanley continued to represent Ste-Anne in the Legislative Assembly throughout the 1960s. His influence at the municipal level was reduced when Jean Drapeau, whom he detested, was returned for a seemingly interminable tenure as mayor in October 1960. At the provincial level Hanley managed to adapt to the new regime, quietly supporting the Liberals on many issues when they were in office and reverting to his more customary support for the Union Nationale after 1966. He also flirted with Social Credit in 1962–63, when that party seemed to be a rising force in Quebec, but jumped ship long before the party began to disintegrate.

The Quiet Revolution, which changed so much else, thus saw little real or significant change in the voting behaviour of Quebec anglophones at the provincial level. Rural anglophones seemed to maintain their traditional preference for the incumbent party, except in 1962, although local issues and personalities also had some bearing on the outcomes. English-speaking Montrealers, whether Protestant, Catholic, or Jewish, continued to reject the Union Nationale as they had done since 1939 and to give massive support to the Liberals. This tendency was self-reinforcing since it ensured that there would be a significant number of anglophones in the Liberal caucus, and in the cabinet when the Liberals were in office. This in turn persuaded anglophone voters in Montreal, where nationalism and linguistic tensions were more conspicuous than in the rural counties, that the Liberals would protect them against more extreme forms of nationalism. This belief even persisted in 1962, when the Liberals temporarily persuaded francophone voters that they were more nationalist than their opponents.

CABINET REPRESENTATION AND ELITE ACCOMMODATION

As the previous chapter suggested, the provincial cabinet was traditionally the principal, although not the only, institution through which consociational elite accommodation operated to regulate the relationship between the English-speaking and French-speaking communities in Quebec. Beginning with Christopher Dunkin and George Irvine in the first cabinet formed in 1867, prominent representatives of the English-speaking community were brought into the government, with the senior or most prominent anglophone usually holding the office of provincial treasurer. Within the cabinet, these anglophone representatives could use their influence to prevent or discourage policy initiatives that would harm the interests of the community which they represented. More positively, they could use it to promote or encourage initiatives that would benefit the English-speaking community.

Under the Union Nationale government after 1944, as we have seen, this mechanism of elite accommodation had atrophied somewhat, partly for reasons beyond the control of Premier Duplessis and perhaps partly through a deliberate choice on his part. With the return of the Liberals to power in 1960 the opportunity for consociational elite accommodation through the cabinet was increased, although not as much as it would have been if Montreal Island had had its fair share of seats in the Legislative Assembly. Paul Earl, the veteran member for NDG, was appointed minister of mines, a portfolio that had been held exclusively by anglophones since the appointment of Jonathan Robinson in 1944. Earl was the proprietor of a small business and a well-respected member of Montreal's anglophone community, but he was handicapped by his inability to speak or even understand French, a fact that Georges-Émile Lapalme noted with some disdain in his memoirs.[25] As a courtesy to Earl, Premier Lesage often spoke English in cabinet meetings, but a more effective representative of anglophone interests was obviously needed. [26]

Anglophone influence in the government was significantly reinforced in October 1960, when George Marler was appointed to the Legislative Council and made a minister without portfolio. He was a nephew of Sir Herbert Marler, who had also been a minister without portfolio, in the federal government led by Mackenzie King in the 1920s. George Marler was a notary, a former vice-chairman of the executive committee of the city of Montreal, and had represented Westmount in the Legislative Assembly from 1942 until 1954. He served as interim leader of the Liberal Party in the interval between the disastrous 1948 election (when party leader Adelard Godbout lost his seat) and the election of Lapalme as leader in 1950. Conrad Black later wrote that Marler was "The logical leader in all respects except the most important, that of being a French Quebecker."[27] Despite this handicap, Marler spoke flawless French. Lapalme wrote in his memoirs that he heard Marler make only one grammatical mistake from 1950 to 1954: a possible failure to use the subjunctive.[28] From 1954 to 1957 Marler was federal minister of transport, but he lost his seat in Parliament in the Diefenbaker landslide of 1958 and was thus without political employment when he joined the Lesage government.

For at least the first two years after his appointment, Marler was one of the most influential members of the government. He was the leading spokesman for English-speaking Quebeckers, the liaison between the government and the business community, and Premier Lesage's right-hand man at the ministry of finance, which had replaced the old Treasury in 1951 and of which Lesage himself was nominally the minister.[29] Marler also led the Liberals in the Legislative Council, where the Union Nationale still held a majority of the seats and the passage of the government's legislation could not always be taken for granted.

Marler's influence was almost always exercised on the side of caution and conservatism, particularly in matters relating to the economy. He was thus a counterweight to left-wing Liberals like René Lévesque, and was probably valued by Lesage for this reason. He had been the only Liberal MLA to oppose the nationalization of the Montreal Light, Heat

and Power Company in 1944,[30] and he vigorously, although unsuccessfully, opposed the nationalization of the remaining privately-
owned electric utilities in 1962.[31] He also warned against increasing
the provincial debt, and favoured private funding of Sidbec, the steel
company that was a major project of the government's second term
in office.[32] Marler's influence declined after the 1962 election and the
nationalization of the electric companies in the following year. He had
lost his most important battle, and the policy which he had opposed
had been resoundingly endorsed by the anglophone voters of Montreal Island as well as by Quebeckers more generally. In October 1965
he quietly resigned from the cabinet but he retained his seat in the
Legislative Council until that body was abolished.

George Marler was the last of the old-style political representatives
of the anglophone business elite. Several persons interviewed for this
book cited him as the most influential anglophone spokesman since
the Second World War. His retirement from politics ended a tradition
that had begun with Alexander Galt in an era when Montreal was the
metropolis of British North America. Political spokesmen like Galt and
Marler had been respected by French-Canadian politicians because
they represented the power of capital, and by their English-speaking
clientele because they understood the mysteries of French-Canadian
politics and could protect the community from any encroachment on
its privileges. But by 1965 the declining power and economic importance of the Westmount establishment made Marler as much of an
anachronism as the Legislative Council in which he sat. St James Street
had become no more than a regional satellite of Toronto's Bay Street.
Its influence over the government of Quebec had been decisively
reduced in 1963 when the government successfully challenged the
traditional monopoly of the A.E. Ames-Bank of Montreal syndicate,
which had handled the province's debt from time immemorial. The
subsequent establishment, three months before Marler's resignation,
of the Caisse de dépôt et de placement reduced it to total irrelevance.

Meanwhile other changes had taken place in the English-speaking
membership of the government. In March 1961 the ministry of mines
was absorbed into a new ministry of natural resources headed by René
Lévesque. At the same time Paul Earl was shifted to another new
portfolio, the ministry of revenue. Like several of the government's
other administrative innovations, this was modelled after a counterpart
in the federal government, whose institutions Premier Lesage – a
former federal minister – greatly admired. The ministry of revenue
was responsible for the machinery of tax collection, but not for fiscal
policy, which remained with the ministry of finance. After 1961

revenue became the portfolio most frequently given to anglophone ministers, as mines had been between 1944 and 1961 and the Treasury had been before that.

Earl spent slightly more than two years in his new portfolio before he died suddenly while vacationing in Ireland. With Marler's influence waning the government needed another prominent anglophone representative, as well as a new minister of revenue and a candidate for Earl's old riding of NDG, which was probably the safest Liberal constituency in the province. Premier Lesage approached Eric Kierans, the president of the Montreal Stock Exchange and a former professor of commerce at McGill, during the annual meeting of the Learned Societies which happened to be in Quebec City that year. Speaking in English, the premier asked his prospective minister: "All my ministers are French! Do you know what that means?" While Kierans was still pondering what would be a tactful and politically correct response to this odd question, the premier supplied one. "It means they are all spenders. I need someone to collect the money!" Kierans decided that this was a leader he could work with.[33] Although somewhat worried about whether he spoke French adequately for the job, he soon agreed to run in NDG and to join the government. The by-election was little more than a formality once Lesage had persuaded the federal MP and political boss of NDG, Eddie Asselin, to accept the new candidate. Kierans became minister of revenue on 8 August 1963, just eleven weeks after the death of his predecessor. George Marler had reservations about the appointment although Kierans, in an interview years later, described Marler as "a first class person in every way."[34]

Eric Kierans became as influential in the Lesage government during its last three years as Marler had been in its earlier phase, but he was cut from a very different mould. He was a Catholic of mixed Irish and German lineage and had grown up in working-class St-Henri, a long way from the world that Marler represented. His first political involvement was during the federal election campaign of 1935. Lacking a job after graduating from Loyola College in the midst of the depression, he was paid five dollars a night to make speeches denouncing R.B. Bennett at Liberal rallies. Kierans would deliver the English speech while another person was hired to deliver a similar address in French.[35] During his years at McGill he was involved to some extent in the Liberal Party, but he only emerged as a public figure following his appointment as president of the Montreal Stock Exchange in 1960. As president he tried to revive the Exchange, which had been declining in importance relative to that of Toronto, by making it more open to francophones and Jews, groups that had been traditionally excluded from the inner circle of the Montreal financial elite. He began to publish the Exchange's newsletter in French as well as English and brought about its move to a new headquarters on Place Victoria.[36]

In 1962 Kierans made a well-publicized speech, in French, denouncing the economic theories of Social Credit, which had just won twenty-six Quebec seats in the federal election. The speech was appreciated by the Quebec Liberals, who were fearful that Social Credit might run candidates at the provincial level. The Quebec leader of Social Credit, Réal Caouette, subsequently blamed Kierans for the party's loss of several seats in the 1963 election. Meanwhile Kierans had become friendly with René Lévesque and had quietly assisted the government in its purchase of the electric power utilities and its successful borrowing of the necessary funds without total reliance on the A.E. Ames–Bank of Montreal syndicate. Lévesque, who was not instinctively sympathetic to the presidents of stock exchanges, subsequently praised Kierans as "the first highly placed Anglophone to associate with the mood of '60–63."[37] In June 1963, when he was already being sounded out by Lesage as a possible minister of revenue, Kierans attracted further attention by publicly criticizing the tax on foreign takeovers imposed in Walter Gordon's federal budget.

In contrast to Marler and Earl, Kierans as a minister reinforced the more nationalist and interventionist wing of the government, whose projects were often considered too radical or too risky by the cautious and essentially conservative Lesage. He became a particularly enthusiastic proponent of Sidbec, the proposed Quebec steel company, and argued strenuously that it should be a crown corporation rather than a mixed enterprise or a private venture supported by the government. Lesage was irate when Kierans made a public speech on economic policy which included a brief statement of his preference for a crown corporation. The government was still seeking private funding for the project and Lesage's preference for a private enterprise was widely known. The premier warned Kierans that ministers had resigned over lesser indiscretions but did not ask for his resignation, probably because other prominent ministers might have resigned as well.[38] In the end Sidbec became a crown corporation, although it did not begin operations until after the Lesage government had left office.

When Marler resigned in October 1965 there was a cabinet shuffle. Kierans became minister of health and René Lévesque the minister of family and social welfare, enabling the two friends to wage a joint campaign against the centralizers in Ottawa. Richard Hyde, the member for Westmount who had been speaker of the Legislative Assembly for almost four years, was brought into the cabinet as minister of revenue, replacing Marler as the second anglophone (and only

Protestant) in the government. Hyde's father had been the Liberal member for Westmount from 1939 until his appointment to the Legislative Council in 1942, making way for George Marler.

Kierans made headlines again in December 1965 when he denounced the federal government for secretly agreeing to "guidelines" imposed by the United States government that restricted the export of capital to Canada by American corporations and their Canadian subsidiaries. Ironically, American concerns about capital flows to Canada and their impact on the U.S. balance of payments had first been aroused by Quebec's borrowing from American sources to finance the purchase of the electric power companies. The governor of the Bank of Canada complained to Lesage about Kierans' intervention.[39] The episode further strained relations between the federal and provincial Liberal parties, which had formally separated into two distinct organizations in July 1964.

The unexpected defeat of the Quebec Liberals in June 1966 brought to office the Union Nationale, a party that had only one anglophone representative in the Legislative Assembly. Raymond Johnston of Pontiac, a local wood merchant and a Scottish-Irish Catholic, had represented Quebec's most anglophone county in the Legislative Assembly since 1948. Unfortunately, he could not speak French. Nonetheless, and to no one's great surprise, he was appointed minister of revenue. Johnston was a very inconspicuous minister for the next four years. Pontiac was so peripheral, socially and geographically, that it would have been an inappropriate political base for anyone wishing to be regarded as the spokesman for English-speaking Quebeckers. Premier Daniel Johnson relied on the informal methods of contact with anglophone community leaders that had been practiced by his mentor, Duplessis, although he was less successful in this endeavour than Duplessis had been. His successor, Jean-Jacques Bertrand, attempted to continue in the same way, but relations between the two language groups in Quebec deteriorated sharply after Johnson's death, as will be described in the next chapter.

Soon after the 1966 election, Eric Kierans was elected president of the Quebec Liberal Party, apparently because he was the only candidate acceptable both to Jean Lesage and to those who wanted to move the party in a more left-wing and more nationalist direction. While Kierans agreed with the latter group on many matters, he was still a federalist and could not endorse the sovereignty-association proposal which his friend René Lévesque unveiled in 1967. Nor could the party, which was still controlled by the more conservative group around Lesage. In October 1967 sovereignty-association was rejected by the party convention, with Kierans leading the fight against it. Lévesque resigned his membership and walked out of the convention. Kierans was technically the victor but his career in the Quebec Liberal Party was also at an end. He was blamed for the split in the party and could only continue as a politician by moving to the federal arena.

Just as Marler was the last of the old-style anglophone ministers, Kierans was the prototype of a new variety whose advent indicated the fragility of consociational arrangements in the era of the Quiet Revolution. The new type of anglophone representatives were academics or middle-class professionals without close ties to the declining economic elite. Unlike their predecessors they would not be able to count on either the deference of their francophone colleagues to anglophone power and privilege or the unquestioning support of their own community. Thus they had to earn both the respect of their colleagues and the political support of an electorate that was unprepared for the changes that were transforming Quebec society and politics. As time went on they would face an increasing level of conflict between the aspirations of the community which they represented and those of the francophone society in which it was imbedded. One of them described their dilemma in an interview after he left politics: "You're torn between your constituents and their view of the world which is radically different from the view of the majority of francophone Quebeckers. They live in a different world. It's not the same culturally or politically – the premises aren't the same, the religious expectations are not the same, the whole value system is different. So if you're going to be a bridge between the two communities you're going to get walked on, and we were walked on."[40]

In Kierans' time this dilemma had not yet become acute. Anglophone attitudes towards the Quiet Revolution were generally favourable, although there were scattered exceptions. Kierans' energetic support for the reform agenda of colleagues like Paul Gérin-Lajoie and René Lévesque was not far out of line with the views of his voters, although few of them were as enthusiastic as he was. His successors would have a more difficult task as worried anglophones perceived a threat to their civil society from an encroaching bureaucratic state propelled by Quebec nationalism.

ANGLOPHONE ATTITUDES AND THE QUIET REVOLUTION

Anglophone responses to the Quiet Revolution, the Lesage government, and the end of Duplessism were initially friendly, and for the most part remained so. Quebec nationalism and constant feuding with the federal government had become so closely identified with Duplessis and the Union Nationale that they were expected to end with the old leader's demise and the defeat of his party. This naive assumption ignored the undercurrents of nationalism in the Liberal Party, as well as the fact that Duplessis' relations with Ottawa had in fact improved after the arrival of the Diefenbaker government. Nonetheless, it was given some credence by the fact that Premier Lesage quickly announced Quebec's acceptance of hospital insurance and the Trans-Canada Highway. (The other major dispute, over university grants, had already been resolved by Premier Sauvé.) In fact the early phase of the Liberal government, up to the election campaign of 1962, was not marked by a great deal of nationalism, relative to what came before or afterwards.

Apart from nationalism, the Duplessis regime had been associated in the minds of anglophones with political corruption, dubious electoral practices, excessive use of patronage, inefficient administration, reactionary views on social questions, and a failure to live up to North American standards, or even Canadian standards, regarding the separation of church and state. English-speaking Quebeckers had been complaining about these aspects of Quebec life since Confederation, and tended to attribute them to any political party that held office in the province for an extended period of time. After 1960, and for the first time, the same criticisms of Quebec society and politics that anglophones had always expressed to one another were being expressed by the Quebec government itself. Moreover, the Lesage government actually took steps to ensure that the criticisms would no longer be valid. It was thus understandable that the government was viewed with great enthusiasm and that Liberal support in the west end of Montreal was so overwhelming in the elections of 1962 and 1966. Even *The Montreal Star* and *The Gazette* endorsed the Liberals in those two elections, despite some misgivings about the nationalization of the electric companies.

The issue of electricity raised some concerns in the English-speaking community, but the existence of those concerns is perhaps less interesting and significant than the fact that they were neither particularly widespread nor particularly deep and thus had little political impact. It has already been noted that George Marler, then still the most prominent and important political anglophone spokesman, was an opponent of nationalizing the companies. On the other hand, publicly he appeared to accept the policy once the cabinet had arrived at a collective decision, did not say anything in public to indicate his dissent, and did not resign from the government. (His resignation three years later, long after the takeover of the companies was a *fait accompli,* attracted little attention and was apparently not related to the issue of electricity.) By acting in this way, he prevented the issue from dividing Quebeckers along ethnic or linguistic lines, as it might very easily have done had he acted in a less responsible manner.

The anti-nationalization sentiment which existed among some of the anglophone population could not be exploited by the Union Nationale for two reasons. In the first place, the party's position on the issue was extremely ambiguous, obviously reflecting a compromise between different factions. Secondly, the party was so discredited in English-speaking Montreal, and its leader so widely distrusted, that its opposition to any policy would probably have made that policy more popular with west end voters.

In a few west end ridings, where the Union Nationale label would be the kiss of death, independent candidates ran on a platform of opposition to the takeover of the power companies. The principal target of the anti-hydro campaigns was Lévesque, the minister of natural resources, who was portrayed as a socialist and extreme nationalist. One leaflet depicted him as a baby about to stick his fingers in an electric wall outlet and bore the caption "Don't let him play with electricity." The publicity also suggested that if electricity was nationalized, other and presumably anglophone-owned sectors of the economy would soon suffer the same fate. The campaigns were assisted and loosely coordinated with one another by a group of federal Progressive Conservatives including Egan Chambers, the MP for St Lawrence-St George between 1958 and 1962, and David Angus, then a law student and later appointed to the Senate by Brian Mulroney.[41]

The most prominent of the anti-hydro candidates, then and later, was Richard Holden, a young lawyer from a prominent family, who ran in Westmount. (He would win the same riding for the Equality Party in 1989, and later still would join the Parti Québécois.) When asked about it in an interview many years later Holden seemed somewhat embarrassed by the memory of his 1962 campaign, and claimed that "halfway through the election I wished that I hadn't got involved because I didn't really have my heart in it." At the time, however, he seemed perfectly serious, even if he got off to a bad start by fainting on the platform at his nomination meeting. He performed well in a pre-election debate against his Liberal opponent Richard Hyde, who was himself rumoured to have misgivings about the government's electric power policy. Holden achieved an accolade of sorts when André Laurendeau compared him to the European settlers in Algeria. He ended up with a second-place showing and 22 per cent of the vote, with most of his vote apparently taken from the Union Nationale rather than from the Liberals.[42] English-speaking Quebeckers had no real enthusiasm for the nationalization of electricity, but most were prepared to accept it, particularly since Montreal and its suburbs had been served by Hydro-Québec since 1944. In any event, it was difficult to regard as radical a measure for which Conservative Ontario had provided the precedent almost half a century earlier.

In the 1966 election there was another attempt to stir up anglophone resentment against the Lesage government's economic policies, this time under the rubric of a "Quebec Conservative Party" which claimed not to be affiliated with any other party having a similar name. On this occasion the *bête noire* of the discontented was not Lévesque but Kierans, who was alleged to be selling out anglophone interests by his support for Quebec nationalism.[43] Luke Dougherty, who had been the anti-hydro candidate in NDG in 1962, ran there against Kierans in 1966 and came a distant second with less than 12 per cent of the votes. John P. Boyle, the party's "acting chairman," managed only a fourth-place showing in Robert-Baldwin; there were only two other candidates. The party treasurer, who did not present himself as a candidate, was Alan Singer, who would become well known after 1977 for his litigation against the Lévesque government's language legislation. The failure of all of these campaigns, in both 1962 and 1966, suggests that most English-speaking Quebeckers trusted the Liberals and did not take the accusations of socialism and extreme nationalism seriously.

Although economic nationalism, with its various implications for the anglophone-dominated economy, was an important theme of the Quiet Revolution, the revolution's greatest immediate impact was in the area of social policy, including education. Although education, health and welfare had long been recognized as responsibilities of the government in other parts of Canada, these fields of provincial jurisdiction had, in Quebec, been virtually delegated to the Roman Catholic Church and to private or quasi-private agencies or institutions that served the Protestant and Jewish minorities. The Quiet Revolution saw the shift fo these responsibilities to the state. Two Royal Commissions appointed by the Lesage government, the Parent Commission on education near the beginning of their six-year term in office and the Castonguay-Nepveu Commission on health and welfare towards the end, foreshadowed the emergence of *l'état-providence* in a modernizing Quebec.

English-speaking Quebeckers were initially favourable to these developments, because they seemed to make Quebec more "normal" and more similar to other provinces. When the Legislative Assembly debated Bill 60, the controversial measure to establish a ministry of education, the bill was praised by Glen Brown of Brome, a former Protestant teacher, and by Harry Blank as the unofficial spokesman for the Jewish community.[44] Even Frank Hanley expressed enthusiasm for the bill, and claimed some credit for persuading the Irish Catholic clergy and laity to accept it.[45] Henry Somerville, the Union Nationale, and Protestant, member for Huntingdon, did not really oppose it in principle, although he expressed some dissatisfaction with the provisions for Protestant representation on the proposed Council of Education.[46] In fact Bill 60 left the autonomy of the Protestant system virtually intact in practice. There was still a Protestant committee, which now reported to an associate deputy minister responsible for the Protestant sector. The Protestant school boards continued as before. Not until 1981, under the Parti Québécois, did a minister of education impose a common curriculum on all the schools of the province.

Another reason for satisfaction was that educational and social institutions, including those that served the English-speaking population, received much more funding under the Lesage government than under Duplessis. Not only was there more flexibility, at least initially, in allowing direct or indirect access to federal funds, but the Quebec government itself was more generous than it had been, and not nearly so capricious and unpredictable in its allocation of funds.

Yet, in the longer term at least, these developments had more disturbing implications for an English-speaking community whose relations with the provincial level of government had always been minimal in scope and mediated through a consociational process of elite accommodation. Apart from claiming their share of the petty patronage distributed in rural areas, anglophones had never had much interest in working for the provincial government. The fact that the public service in Quebec City employed hardly any anglophones had been of no concern to them, given the better opportunities available to them in the private sector or in Ottawa and the very limited involvement of the Quebec public service in their affairs. After 1960 the petty patronage largely disappeared and the public service became much larger, more competent, more effective, and potentially more intrusive into domains previously considered private or at least non-governmental. At the same time it would remain almost entirely French, with little input from the English-speaking community and little understanding of that community's way of life.

Anglophones, particularly non-Catholics, who welcomed the declining role of the Church in education and social affairs were implicitly supporting its inevitable corollary, the expansion of the state. They failed to appreciate that the Catholic Church, paradoxically, had been the best friend and ally of non-Catholics in Quebec. By preventing the growth of a bureaucratic state and by providing services only to its

own adherents, it had allowed, encouraged, and protected the autonomy and separateness of non-Catholic civil society. Even Catholic
anglophones had been allowed a degree of separateness and self-
management within the framework of the Church that a bureaucratic
state would be unlikely to allow them. The extensive and well-devel-
oped (at least in Montreal) anglophone Catholic educational system
was the most visible evidence of this but there were also anglophone
Catholic hospitals and other institutions, as well as English-speaking
parishes whose geographical boundaries overlapped with those of the
French parishes.

The consequences for anglophones of the rise of the bureaucratic
secular state would become more apparent in the 1970s, but there
were some undercurrents of discontent or anxiety even in the 1960s,
particularly in rural areas. Elizabeth Cahill's study of Pontiac County
and Rosalind Zinman's of Lachute (a small town in Argenteuil County
with a substantial anglophone minority) both discuss the adjustments
imposed on English-language education in the 1960s.[47] Cahill found
that many English-speaking Catholics in Pontiac were sending their
children to be educated in Ontario.[48] In 1966 Union Nationale
member Henry Somerville charged that "Since the adoption of Bill
60 there has been a steady erosion of the rights of the Protestant
minority" to manage their own educational system;[49] he had supported
Bill 60 at the time of its adoption. His Liberal successor Ken Fraser,
speaking a year later in opposition to a bill that ordered striking
teachers back to work, observed that "The cause of the uneasiness
among the Protestant sector is a mistrust of too much government
control ... The fear of being swallowed up by the majority is as strong
in the English minority in Quebec as it is in the French minority in
Canada."[50]

English-speaking Catholics in Montreal were also discontented and
anxious over educational issues. One grievance that pre-dated the
Quiet Revolution concerned the inability of Loyola College, located
in NDG, to grant its own degrees. Nothing was done by the Lesage
government, even though Eric Kierans was a graduate of Loyola.[51]
There was discontent with the Montreal Catholic School Commission,
which was accused of not committing enough resources to the expansion of the English-language school system in the west end.[52] Another
and related concern, frequently expressed in letters to the editor of
the *Montreal Star* as early as 1962, was an apparent assumption by
the Catholic school authorities that immigrants of non-official
mother tongues should be educated in French rather than in
English.[53] Finally, the proposals to reorganize school boards, recommended by the Parent Commission and implemented to a limited

extent by the government, met with a mixed response and a number of counter-proposals.[54]

In general, however, the tenth decade after Confederation was a happy time for English-speaking Quebeckers. John Turner, in an interview long afterwards, recalled how it was when he was elected to Parliament in 1962: "There were very few tensions. There were the two solitudes, but the minority felt very comfortable in Quebec. I guess the nationalization of Shawinigan was a little disturbing for them – they wondered how far that was going to go. But the Quiet Revolution didn't bother my constituents. They felt it was good that Quebec was coming out of the clerical era. There was a general feeling that it was a breath of fresh air. There was no anxiety among the English-speaking population in the 1960s. Right through into Expo."[55]

NATIONALISM AND THE THREAT OF SEPARATION

By far the most serious anxieties and concerns of English-speaking Quebeckers, beginning in the latter part of 1962 and increasing for the rest of the decade, were brought about by the resurgence of Quebec nationalism and the possibility that Quebec might eventually secede from the Canadian federation to become a sovereign state. As noted previously, the Lesage government had rather soft-pedalled the nationalist theme during its first mandate. In 1961 Marcel Chaput, and his book arguing the case for an independent Quebec, had some impact on the consciousness of Quebec anglophones,[56] but "separatism" was initially more a subject of jokes than of serious apprehension. This changed with the first episodes of FLQ terrorism in the spring of 1963, the demonstration against the royal visit to Quebec City in the following year, and the apparent flirtation with dreams of sovereignty by leading personages in both major provincial parties. Coincidentally or not, there was at the same time a sharp deterioration in Quebec's relations with the federal government, even though the federal Liberals returned to office in April 1963. A series of disputes over pension plans, conditional grants, taxation, the patriation of the constitution, and Quebec's ventures into international diplomacy continued without interruption until the end of the decade, further fanning the flames of nationalism. By 1966 two independence-minded parties ran candidates in the Quebec election, receiving in total almost 10 per cent of the vote. In 1967 Lévesque finally left the Liberal Party to found the Mouvement Souveraineté-Association, which was replaced a year later by the Parti Québécois.

These developments were observed by an English-speaking community that was itself in a period of transition. Montreal's Class C city councillors, nominated by interest groups, had been abolished in the fall of 1960, following a referendum in which francophones had voted overwhelmingly for abolition while anglophones were evenly divided.[57] Railways, the city's greatest industry, declined rapidly in the 1960s, as did passenger shipping. Out-migration weakened the community since anglophones were 2.5 times as likely as francophones to leave Quebec in the 1960s, more for economic than political reasons.[58] Immigrants increasingly came from Italy, Portugal or Greece, rather than from England, Scotland or the United States. The Protestant school system, a constitutionally entrenched bulwark of anglophone power, was losing its importance. By 1970 almost half of English-language enrollments were in Catholic schools, compared to less than a quarter in 1950.[59] As the business elite lost its grip on power, leadership in the anglophone community, such as it was, passed increasingly to a new group of academics and professionals. Television brought the cultural revolution of the 1960s from New York, Berkeley, and Los Angeles into the living rooms of English-speaking Montreal. Adapting to these changes while coming to terms with Quebec nationalism imposed a double challenge on the community.

There was never any prospect that significant numbers of Quebec anglophones would support the sovereignty movement. As one student of ethnic relations in Quebec, Leslie S. Laczko, has rightly observed: "For most of Quebec's history anglophone Quebecers perceived themselves as part of the anglophone *majority* in Canada, and an important part at that."[60] In addition they might perceive themselves as British subjects or North Americans, Montrealers or Townshippers, Scottish or Irish, Protestants, Catholics or Jews, but Quebec as such was a minimal part, if any, of their self-identity. In these circumstances the idea of a sovereign Quebec could have no attraction for them. Instead it was viewed by the overwhelming majority of English-speaking Quebeckers as destructive and senseless, and an expression of an ethnically defined nationalism that excluded anyone whose ancestry was not French.

Attitudinal studies in the 1960s, like those later, demonstrated the gulf between anglophones and francophones in their perceptions of Quebec nationalism. A survey of Quebec law students in the spring of 1968 found that 77 per cent of the anglophones identified solely with Canada, to the exclusion of any Quebec identity, while 86 per cent of the francophones identified either solely or primarily with Quebec, to the exclusion of Canadian identity.[61] In her study of Pontiac County

based on field work conducted in 1967, Cahill found that francophones had a much more positive orientation towards the province
than anglophones, and that there was no significant difference between
anglophone Catholics and anglophone Protestants in this regard.[62]

As the independence movement in Quebec became a serious prop-
osition, English-speaking Quebeckers were forced to define their own
identity. The "British" identity which many had cherished as recently
as 1960 was rapidly discarded. According to Kenneth Price's dissertation on the identity of English-speaking Quebeckers, a content analysis
of the letters to the editor in *The Montreal Star* showed a very sudden
and permanent decline in the use of British themes and symbols by
1964.[63] Significantly, although Price does not say so, this was the year
of the disastrous royal visit to Quebec, which ended in a violent police
attack on nationalist demonstrators, and the ludicrous parliamentary
debate on the adoption of a Canadian flag. The British connection
now appeared to be not only anachronistic, but counterproductive
from the standpoint of those who wished to maintain a united Canada.
On the day that the new Canadian flag became official – 15 February
1965 – there was not a Union Jack to be seen on Montreal Island.
Price's explanation for this sudden change, although not proven,
seems intuitively credible: "The earlier theme of British symbolism
ended at virtually the same moment as the English anti-separatist
argument began. While no evidence exists in our data one can spec-
ulate and leave for historians to examine the hypothesis that the
English consciously downgraded the British connection in order to
create the sense of an independent Canada, a pan-Canadianism that
hopefully could be a counter to French nationalism."[64]

To some extent anglophones tried to understand French-Canadian
aspirations and to show their sympathy. French immersion classes for
anglophone children, an idea that would eventually spread across the
country, began in the Montreal suburb of St-Lambert in the mid-
1960s. Although few anglophones went as far as Kierans in his enthusiasm for the Lesage government's quest for greater autonomy, many
seemed to believe that by giving qualified support to the more moderate variety of Quebec nationalism, the threat of separatism could be
lessened. Coleman Romalis' study of the Jewish community found that
this view was particularly characteristic of the affluent and the well-
educated, perhaps because they were more inclined than the less
affluent or less educated to take the threat of separatism seriously.[65]
While J.R. Mallory was perhaps too optimistic when he suggested a few
years later that "This liberal and generous spirit is the most likely
bulwark against the ultimate separation of Quebec,"[66] the good intentions were genuine. *The Montreal Star* began to publish a regular

column by the editor-in-chief of its French-language counterpart, Gérard Pelletier of *La Presse*. McGill students dedicated their yearbook to Premier Lesage. F.R. Scott and Michael Oliver, both Quebec-born McGill professors, edited a book of translated political essays by prominent French Canadians entitled *Quebec States Her Case*. In large type the front cover proclaimed its message: "What does Quebec want? Its grievances are desperate enough to produce violence, urgent enough to threaten Confederation. English Canada, jolted from a state of comfortable indifference, is now forced to see and understand the plight of the Québécois."[67] Glen Brown, the Liberal opposition member for Brome, struck a similar note in the Legislative Assembly in 1967 when he urged his fellow anglophones to learn French and to become better-informed about their francophone compatriots: "... the greatest contribution we could make to Canada and to Quebec is to explain and clarify to the rest of Canada our friends here in the province of Quebec ... We are living in a tolerant province with a great future ... We should organize ourselves to take part ... in the forward march of raising the Quebec economy to a parity with any place in the North American continent."[68]

This mood of *bonne entente* and liberal optimism culminated in the centennial celebrations later that year, when Montreal seemed briefly to be the centre of the world. The city opened its long-discussed rapid transit system, the Metro, just in time for the festivities. Montrealers of both language communities celebrated the spectacular, and somewhat unexpected, success of Expo 67. Even the brief and carefully guarded visit of the Queen was not marred by any incidents, in contrast to the disaster of 1964. But the much more memorable visit of President Charles de Gaulle, later in the summer, was a reminder that all was not well in the state of Quebec.[69] There would be further reminders in the decade that followed.

A minuscule minority of English-speaking Quebeckers went beyond the cautious liberal support for the moderate nationalism of the Quiet Revolution and became supporters, at least for a time, of the Quebec independence movement. Most were students and other young people caught up in 1960s radicalism. Some of them were married to francophones. Some inherited the Jewish-radical tradition that had elected Fred Rose as Canada's only Communist member of parliament in 1943. Some were Irish Catholics who saw a parallel between the two white Catholic nations that had endured a British conquest. Some were Catholics of various other ethnic origins. Hardly any were of British-Protestant background, a background that made it almost impossible to reject the status quo in Quebec, however radical one might be in relation to other issues. The anglophone pro-separatists viewed Quebec as a young, radical-chic nation struggling against capitalism and colonialism, like Algeria, Cuba, or Vietnam. They surfaced at, or around, McGill University in the mid-1960s. Many of them, perhaps most, eventually became disillusioned with Quebec nationalism.

Marxist pro-separatists were a tiny and almost insignificant minority within an English-speaking population that for the most part regarded the rise of the independence movement with a mixture of horror and incredulity. By 1968 most of this population had as yet suffered no real inconvenience as a result of Quebec nationalism, but at the same time they were beginning to feel nervous, unhappy and frustrated. They believed that they had treated their French-Canadian compatriots with sympathy and understanding, only to be repaid with ingratitude and incomprehension. There seemed to be no end to the threats, demands, demonstrations, manifestos, and general unpleasantness. Anglophones were always accused of having too much power, but from their perspective the election of 1966, the subsequent behaviour of the Union Nationale government, the disintegration of the Liberal opposition, and the emergence of the Mouvement Souveraineté-Association all seemed to suggest that they were powerless. Yet Québécois nationalists in 1968 were equally frustrated and unhappy, for francophone control over the economy had not really been accomplished, nor had Quebec achieved either of the alternatives defined by Daniel Johnson: equality with the rest of Canada, or independence. With both sides in an unhappy mood, the stage was set for a confrontation.

Consociational democracy, which had served Quebec well for a century, was thus approaching the end of the road in 1968. Its end would come over the next few years and would impose on Quebec anglophones a painful task of adaptation. This would be all the more difficult, as J.R. Mallory predicted in 1971, because when it was protected by elite accommodation "the English minority allowed its direct political role to atrophy, and after a century of disuse it could only be revived effectively in conditions of political calm."[70] By trial and error, and without much support from Canadians outside Quebec, a beleaguered community would have to discover new ways to protect its interests in a changing Quebec. While conscious of its diminishing influence, it would still be regarded as a threat by many francophones who feared the overwhelming predominance of the English language in North America.

Given the changes within Quebec, and in Quebec's relations with the outside world, the end of consociational democracy was inevitable. Its survival for a century was a considerable achievement and its peaceful end, at least relative to those of its counterparts in Lebanon or Cyprus, was a tribute to the civility of both the anglophone and francophone communities in Quebec.

FEDERAL POLITICS IN
THE DIEFENBAKER-PEARSON ERA

English-speaking Quebeckers, identifying themselves primarily as Canadians, were predisposed to regard the federal level of government with more enthusiasm than the provincial. In rural areas like Pontiac, as Cahill found in her study of that county, this preference coexisted with a realization that the provincial government and its policies on agriculture, forests, roads and local government had more direct influence on the lives of rural residents than the federal.[71] In Montreal and its suburbs, where most English-speaking Quebeckers lived by the 1960s, this was not the case. Federal policies concerning transportation, trade, banking, defence production and other matters had more influence on the city's economy than those of the provincial government. The provincial government's influence over civil society, while potentially great, was moderated by the virtual delegation of much of its authority to private and religious agencies. Although this began to change during the Quiet Revolution, and although the rise of a new and more threatening variety of Quebec nationalism caused more attention to be directed to that level of government than had previously been the case, there was still a general tendency to agree with Margaret Westley's informant, quoted in the preceding chapter, that "Ottawa was the real government."

Federal and provincial politics were more closely linked in Quebec at this time than they would be later. The federal and provincial wings of the Liberal Party did not separate until 1964, and even the Union Nationale was loosely associated with the federal Progressive Conservatives. Politicians and party organizations at one level could have a decisive impact on nomination contests or elections at the other, and voting behaviour at the two levels was at least tenuously related. Even the issues were similar, since the polarization of provincial politics around the issue of independence versus federalism had not yet taken place.

The Diefenbaker government after the election of March 1958 had a comfortable majority of the Quebec seats in the House of Commons and had made substantial inroads even into the Liberal fortress of Montreal. Fifty Conservatives were elected in Quebec, including nine anglophones, numbers that had not been attained since the days of Sir John A. Macdonald. Most of them, however, lacked experience and stature, and Diefenbaker was not particularly successful in finding a strong contingent of Quebec representatives for his cabinet.

Bill Hamilton, the only Quebec anglophone and the only Montrealer in the cabinet, served as postmaster-general until he lost his seat in the election of 1962. Diefenbaker did not like Hamilton, for perhaps more than one reason.[72] In any event, he never promoted Hamilton to a more senior position which his administrative ability probably would have merited. The post office portfolio was traditionally given to a minister from Quebec, where its considerable resources of petty patronage were deemed to be appreciated. Hamilton did not endear himself to his francophone colleagues, most of whom had learned their politics in the school of Duplessis, by announcing soon after he took office that patronage would be eliminated.[73] To make matters worse, he actually carried out his promise. This brave initiative caused Peter C. Newman, a journalist not known for excessive charity towards the Diefenbaker government, to call Hamilton the best postmaster-general in Canadian history,[74] but it earned the minister few laurels in his own province.

The patronage issue may have been the beginning of Hamilton's unpopularity in the Quebec caucus, but it was probably not the only reason for it. Hamilton spoke no French and, according to his friend and fellow member Heward Grafftey, had no rapport with French Canadians. (He did not need any to win election in NDG in the 1950s, although by 1962 there was a somewhat larger francophone minority in the riding.) Soon after the 1958 election he proposed that the Quebec anglophones should have their own caucus. Grafftey, who represented a rural and predominantly French-speaking riding, refused to support the idea and it apparently was not implemented.[75] Nonetheless the nine anglophones, of whom five were from the west end of Montreal, remained a rather isolated group in what was really a Union Nationale caucus.

Pierre Sévigny, who served with Hamilton in the cabinet, later wrote of him that "rightly or wrongly, he was soon to acquire a reputation for being anti-French, and this eventually contributed to his defeat in June of 1962."[76] Although Sévigny wrote that the accusation was undeserved, he also noted that Hamilton was unpopular with his colleagues and was rarely consulted on Quebec's problems. Hamilton's policy regarding patronage and his dislike of the Union Nationale, a party which was almost universally despised in his riding, may have explained this in large part, but he could also be insensitive to French-Canadian sentiments. Very early in his ministerial career an international postal conference was held in Ottawa, and facilities for simultaneous translation were installed in the Parliament Buildings for the occasion. A

Liberal francophone member from Quebec asked the postmaster-general whether the facilities could be retained and used for parliamentary debates. Hamilton replied that this would not be feasible since the translators would have difficulty if two or more members were speaking simultaneously, the equipment could only be accommodated by reducing the size of the press gallery, and the "feeling" of one language could not be effectively translated into the other.[77] This was too much even for John Pratt, the Conservative member for Jacques-Cartier and former mayor of Dorval, who had been born in England but publicly stated that he was "100 per cent in favour" of simultaneous translation.[78] Simultaneous translation was finally introduced two years later.

The deaths of Duplessis and Sauvé and the defeat of the Union Nationale left the Diefenbaker government without a power base in Quebec, and this fact was reflected in the outcome of the 1962 election. Montreal returned to the Liberals while Social Credit erupted unexpectedly in the hinterlands. Only fourteen Progressive Conservative members survived, of whom Grafftey in Brome-Missisquoi was the sole anglophone. Hamilton lost his seat to Liberal candidate Eddie Asselin, who was Irish on his mother's side and the son of J.O. Asselin, a prominent municipal politician from the Houde era. The younger Asselin had consolidated his control over the sometimes fractious NDG Liberal organization and did particularly well in the partly francophone east end of the riding. His victory left the government without a minister from Montreal for the brief remainder of its term in office.

On the Liberal side of the house, Alan McNaughton was re-elected in Mount Royal and Leon Crestohl in Cartier. C.M. "Bud" Drury, a Westmount patrician and former protégé of the recently deceased Brooke Claxton, won St-Antoine-Westmount. John Turner, the Rhodes scholar once befriended by Duplessis, won a narrow victory in St Lawrence-St George over Egan Chambers. Chambers, a popular member who was not expected to lose his seat, received some help from the Frank Hanley machine, but to no avail. Turner's campaign was managed by Brooke Claxton's son, John Claxton.[79] Bryce Mackasey and Raymond Rock, two local business proprietors with experience in municipal politics, won the contiguous ridings of Verdun and Jacques-Cartier-Lasalle. All of these members would be re-elected in 1963 apart from Crestohl, who died before the 1963 election and was replaced by another Liberal lawyer, Milton Klein. They were joined in that election by Ian Watson from Chateauguay-Huntingdon-Laprairie, whose riding included a substantial anglophone population as well as the Mohawk reservation at Kahnawake.

English-speaking Montrealers gave comfortable majorities to the federal Liberals throughout the 1960s, and beyond, but it was not until 1968 that rural and small-town Quebec anglophones finally deserted the Conservatives. Another interesting, although temporary, development was the rise of the New Democratic Party, which by 1965 had replaced the Conservatives as the second-ranking federal party in the English-speaking neighbourhoods of Montreal. Some of its support came from former Conservatives who found Diefenbaker's nostalgia for the old British Canada increasingly anachronistic and embarrassing in a rapidly changing Quebec. Some came from former Liberals who disliked Lester Pearson's abrupt change of policy regarding nuclear weapons in 1963 as well as the many scandals and fiascos of his accident-prone government. More speculatively, it may be suggested that the heavy NDP vote among Montreal anglophones, particularly the less affluent, was perhaps an early expression of anglophone misgivings about the resurgence of Quebec nationalism, a sentiment for which none of the parties competing at the provincial level provided a vehicle. The NDP could not be stigmatized as reactionary or anti-French, because its leading spokesmen, particularly McGill professors Michael Oliver and Charles Taylor, were obviously sympathetic to the Québécois. At the same time it was unique among parties competing in Quebec in the almost total absence of francophones from its ranks, apart from Robert Cliche who was named leader of the party's Quebec wing and ran unsuccessfully in a rural riding in 1965. This absence was both a symptom and a cause of the party's irrelevance in Quebec, but it may also have been secretly viewed as an advantage by many non-francophones who voted for NDP candidates.

On the other hand, Montreal anglophones in the 1960s did not yet feel the need for the federal government to protect them against Quebec nationalism. Their members of parliament often praised Quebec in their speeches, paid tribute to the good relations between English and French that allegedly existed there, and attempted to explain Quebec developments to the rest of the country, but they hardly ever discussed issues or concerns specific to the English-speaking community. Gérard Pelletier recalled in his memoirs that as late as 1968, when he became the minister responsible for official language minorities in the federal government, Montreal anglophones hardly thought of themselves as a minority. When his department contacted the educational, social service, and media elites of the community, they complacently informed him that they were flourishing and in no need of help. He discovered, however, that there was less complacency among the scattered English-speaking minorities outside of metropolitan Montreal.[80] Unfortunately these minorities had minimal representation in Parliament.

Following the Liberal victory in the 1963 election, Alan McNaughton became speaker of the House of Commons. C.M. Drury entered the cabinet, initially as minister of defence production and within three months as minister of the newly formed Department of Industry. He proved to be one of the government's more effective ministers and was the acknowledged representative of the Montreal business community and of English-speaking Quebec more generally. John Turner joined the cabinet soon after the 1965 election, initially without portfolio but later as registrar general and finally in another newly-formed portfolio, consumer and corporate affairs. Bryce Mackasey also served as minister without portfolio in the last few weeks before Prime Minister Pearson's retirement. Both Turner and Mackasey would play more prominent roles in the Trudeau government from 1968 onwards.

When Parliament was dissolved in 1965 Alan McNaughton was appointed to the Senate. Eddie Asselin did not run again because of an alleged conflict of interest of which he was later found innocent. Both Mount Royal and NDG were traditionally "English" ridings, and there was some sentiment to the effect that, as McNaughton put it later, "There were only five English seats and if you give up one of those it's lost for ever."[81] The Jewish community also felt that Mount Royal should have a Jewish candidate, since Cartier no longer had a predominantly Jewish electorate and would probably be eliminated in the next redistribution. On the other hand the Liberals were seeking a safe seat for their new recruit, Pierre Trudeau, whose well-advertised contempt for Quebec nationalism made him too controversial to run in most of the French ridings. Both the Mount Royal and the NDG riding associations were approached and both indicated that Trudeau was welcome to seek their nominations but would have to compete against local candidates. Trudeau finally opted for Mount Royal but faced two strong Jewish opponents for the nomination, Victor Goldbloom and Stuart Smith. Smith, a psychiatrist who later moved to Ontario and led the provincial Liberal Party there, withdrew at the last moment, but Goldbloom stayed in the race until the end.[82] His strong showing perhaps helped him to become the provincial member for D'Arcy-McGee, which included part of the federal Mount Royal constituency, a year later.

Another, although less publicized, nomination contest occurred in NDG, which was now considered as much a safe Liberal riding as Mount Royal. Richard Lord, a prominent Liberal of Caribbean ancestry, announced his candidacy despite the handicap of living in St-Antoine-Westmount. Warren Allmand, a young college teacher who had worked in Asselin's campaigns, emphasized his closer attachment to the riding. This argument may have been decisive given the strong local pride and community spirit in NDG. The support of Asselin may also have helped, although Asselin's popularity had declined and his support was therefore a questionable asset.[83] Allmand won and became one of Canada's most durable members of parliament, serving in the House of Commons until 1997.

In the campaign to succeed Lester Pearson as prime minister and leader of the Liberal Party there were three candidates from the west end of Montreal: Trudeau, Turner, and Kierans. Turner had the support of his own riding and ended up with a respectable showing, although he was by far the youngest of the candidates. Kierans was handicapped by his lack of federal experience and the fact that the federal and provincial organizations of the party had now separated. NDG, which he had represented provincially, followed Warren All-mand's lead and gave its support to Trudeau.[84] Kierans withdrew from the race after the first ballot at the convention, which gave him less than 5 per cent of the vote, and Trudeau finally won on the fourth ballot, with Turner staying in until the end.

The election campaign that followed was fought on the basis of new constituency boundaries. (The old ones, based on the 1951 census, had been used in six general elections, an all-time Canadian record.) Turner's riding of St Lawrence-St George disappeared, along with Cartier and Ste-Anne. Since his feisty leadership campaign had not endeared him to the hierarchy in the Quebec wing of the party, Turner had little prospect of being nominated in another Quebec riding, and he withdrew to the Ontario riding of Ottawa-Carleton.[85] Kierans ran in the francophone suburban riding of Duvernay partly because he did not wish to be typecast (again) as the spokesman for Quebec anglophones and partly because the Liberals in another riding which he considered apparently expected him to finance the campaign out of his own pocket. He was warned by Jean Marchand that Duvernay would be a difficult riding since the NDP candidate, Robert Cliche, had been cultivating it for some time.[86] In retaliation for Kierans' role in the rejection of sovereignty-association by the provincial Liberals, Cliche received strong support from the Mouvement Souveraineté-Association and the Rassemblement pour l'indépendance nationale. Kierans won a narrow victory nonetheless.

In the predominantly anglophone ridings of the west end, and even in the anglophone enclaves along the American border and in the Ottawa Valley, the Liberals won overwhelming majorities, while the

Progressive Conservative and New Democratic Party vote fell dramatically. The rate of participation in the anglophone ridings was also noticeably higher than in other parts of Quebec, a phenomenon that had not occurred in previous elections.[87] English-speaking Quebeckers were not pleased by what they viewed as the flirtation of the Conservative and New Democratic parties with Quebec nationalism. They respected and admired Trudeau as a French Canadian who represented the liberal and individualistic aspect of the Quiet Revolution while being resolutely hostile to nationalism: the best of all possible French Canadians from their point of view. They hoped that somehow he would bring harmony to Canada, and to Quebec, by reconciling French-speaking Quebeckers to the federal system. Although they loyally supported Trudeau until the end of his political career, this hope was to be largely disappointed in the years to come.

4 Consociationalism Destroyed: The Politicization of Language, 1968–76

1968 was a year of turbulence and upheaval in a large part of the world. In France what began as a student rebellion at the University of Paris came close to overturning the Fifth Republic. In Czechoslovakia a nation-wide experiment in humane socialism was cut short by the invading armies of the country's "allies" in the Warsaw Pact. In Northern Ireland the Catholic civil rights march of 24 August and the decision by the authorities to ban a second march on 5 October (which took place nonetheless) launched a generation of civil conflict. In Vietnam the Tet offensive weakened the resolve of the United States to resist the unification of north and south and led to the early retirement of President Johnson. In the United States itself Martin Luther King Jr and Robert Kennedy were assassinated, inner-city ghettos were sacked and burned by their inhabitants, and the Democratic Party's convention was disrupted by anti-war demonstrators. Richard Nixon's election as president, largely a consequence of the shift of Democratic voters to the racist and populist George Wallace, indicated the end of the New Deal coalition that had governed the country for most of the preceding thirty-five years.

In Quebec the year was also something of a watershed. The choice of Pierre Elliott Trudeau as leader of the federal Liberals in April and his subsequent endorsement by the Canadian electorate in June placed a determined opponent of Quebec nationalism in command of the central government. In September the death of Premier Daniel Johnson began the unravelling of the Union Nationale. Less than a month later the formation of the Parti Québécois, uniting René

Lévesque's Mouvement Souveraineté-Association with Gilles Gré-
goire's Ralliement National, precipitated the realignment of Quebec's
party system around a polarization between sovereignty and federalism. In effect this marked the end of the Quiet Revolution, placing
the citélibrists and the neo-nationalists in opposing camps where each
found allies among some of those who had once supported the
Duplessis regime. Both Trudeau and Lévesque could claim with some
legitimacy to be the heirs of the Quiet Revolution, and the emergence
of the forces that each represented indicated that its immediate goals
had been achieved and that Quebec had moved on to a new and more
difficult agenda.

The fall of 1968 was also marked by the beginning of a series of
bomb-planting incidents, some of them successful, which continued
for well over a year and marked the re-emergence of the terrorist FLQ,
which had been dormant since the summer of 1966.[1] A demonstration
against the federally regulated taxi monopoly at Dorval Airport by a
group calling itself the Mouvement de libération du taxi ended in
violence and the destruction of property.[2] Quebec's network of CEGEPs
(junior colleges), which had been in operation for only a year, was
disrupted and then occupied by disgruntled students. Most significantly, perhaps, the culmination of a series of events in the Montreal
suburb of St-Léonard precipitated the emergence of language policy
as a major issue in Quebec politics.

All of these developments indicated that a considerable segment of
the population – although it was difficult to say just how many – were
dissatisfied with the outcome of the Quiet Revolution. Middle-class
revolutions tend to disappoint those who are without property or
prospects, as well as those who crave the ideological certainties of a
closed society, and there were many Québécois in 1968 who fell into
one or both of these categories. The developments of the preceding
eight years had drastically reduced the power of the Church, secular-
ized the politics and the culture of Quebec, promoted the rise of a
new middle class employed in the public sector and state-owned enterprises, and contributed to the *de facto* decentralization of Canadian
federalism. Probably no part of Canada has ever changed as significantly in so short a time as Quebec between 1959 and 1968, except
for the prairie west in the decade that followed the construction of
the Canadian Pacific Railway.

Nonetheless, for some Québécois the changes wrought by the Quiet
Revolution were not enough. Their discontent and frustration focused
on three targets which they viewed as interdependent and related: the
capitalist economy, the federal state, and the existence of an English-
speaking minority in the province. It was probably not clear, even to

them, which they most resented, so it was understandable that they would attack the weakest of the three. In the end events would prove that there was no alternative to capitalism, in Quebec or elsewhere on the planet. The faltering federal state regained some of its vitality under Trudeau's direction and would last for at least another generation. Only the English-speaking minority in Quebec, with no real allies outside its own ranks and no real place in the changing Canadian economy, would find itself in the eye of the storm.

ST-LÉONARD AND THE POLITICS OF LANGUAGE

The politicization of language began in St-Léonard in the same sense that Germany's bid for the mastery of Europe began with an assassination in Sarajevo. The larger events were the product of larger causes and would have happened in any case, but their timing was precipitated by an immediate cause in a particular location.

One of the major consequences of the Quiet Revolution was a sudden decline in the birth rate of the French-speaking population in Quebec, a birth rate which had previously been among the highest in the Western world. Declining deference to the teachings of the Church, the changing role of women in society, and the necessary trade-off between acquiring more consumer goods and bearing more children all reinforced the impact of the birth control pill, which coincidentally became available in North America while the Lesage government was in office.

The decline in the birth rate, like most other developments in Quebec, had political implications. Traditionally the high birth rate had been part of an equation that maintained a rough but fairly stable balance between the English-speaking and French-speaking populations in Canada and in Quebec. The higher birth rate of the francophones was a counterweight to the ability of the anglophones, in Canada and in metropolitan Montreal, to reinforce their numbers through immigration. Anglophone losses in rural Quebec through out-migration roughly balanced francophone losses in other parts of Canada through assimilation. The percentage of francophones in Canada (about 30 per cent), on Montreal Island (about 60 per cent) and in Quebec (about 80 per cent) hardly changed in the first six decades of the twentieth century. No one felt threatened.

The sudden decline of the francophone birth rate caused many Quebec nationalists to fear that Quebec's population would decline as a percentage of the total Canadian population and also that Quebec itself would become less French. Significantly, it was in 1968 that

Quebec established a Department of Immigration. Unfortunately immigration, while the obvious solution to the first problem, risked exacerbating the second problem. France was not a significant source of immigrants. The children of immigrants in Quebec tended to become anglophones, partly because English was viewed as the language of both geographic and social mobility, partly because non-Catholic children were required to attend the Protestant schools, and partly because even Catholic immigrant children were often encouraged by school administrators to enrol in the non-French (originally Irish) sector of the Catholic school system. None of this had seemed to matter as long as the French birth rate remained high. But now it no longer was.

One ethnic group, the Quebeckers of Italian descent, found itself at the centre of controversy when concern about these issues became politically significant in 1968. In the 1951 census only 34,165 residents of Quebec had claimed Italian ancestry but the number increased to 108,552 in 1961, and 169,655 in 1971.[3] Between 1950 and 1966 there were only two years – 1953 and 1957 – in which Italy was not the largest source of immigrants to Quebec.[4] By 1961 Italians were the largest non-British and non-French ethnic group in Quebec, a position previously occupied by Jews. Like most of Quebec's other ethnic minorities, they were overwhelmingly concentrated on Montreal Island.

Until the 1960s the Italian community enjoyed relatively good relations with the francophone majority, to whom they seemed much closer, in religion, culture, and socio-economic status, than they were to the anglophones. They were one of the few ethnic groups, apart from the French, that were almost entirely Catholic, and the only non-aboriginal ethnic group, according to the 1961 data of the Royal Commission on Bilingualism and Biculturalism, that ranked lower than the French in average income. They shared with the French a deeply rooted cultural conservatism that was quite compatible with voting Liberal in federal elections. In provincial elections the Italians, unlike other ethnic minorities, gave significant support to the Union Nationale. Many worked in the construction industry, which benefitted from Union Nationale patronage during the long reign of Duplessis.

A study of Montreal Italians conducted in 1964 and 1965 discovered that a larger proportion could speak French than could speak English. They were more likely to have francophone than anglophone friends and more likely to marry francophones than to marry anglophones. They did not wish to be forced to take sides between the French and the English, although they were overwhelmingly opposed to the separation of Quebec from Canada. However, they preferred, for essentially pragmatic reasons, to send their children to English schools.[5] In this regard they differed from the smaller Italian community that had existed before the immigration of the 1950s, for in those days Italian children in Quebec had usually attended French schools.

Why did relations between French and Italian Quebeckers deteriorate in the 1960s? Anxiety over the declining birth rate, encouraged by demographers who published pessimistic forecasts about the future of the French language in Montreal, is certainly part of the explanation. One student of the subject, Paul Cappon, suggests that French Quebeckers more or less expected most other immigrant groups to gravitate towards the anglophone community but felt betrayed and hurt when the Italians, a group so similar to themselves, did so.[6] Parallels can also be drawn with French-Canadian attitudes towards the Irish in the nineteenth century and towards the Jews in the first half of the twentieth. In each case an immigrant group that was growing rapidly and apparently competing with French Canadians for jobs became a target of resentment. In each case the resentment reached its peak at a time when the immigration had already begun to decline.

St-Léonard, like many other Montreal suburbs, was originally a rural French parish. In 1955 it had only 800 residents, but in that year it was chosen as the locale for an experiment in building low-cost private houses, and its population began to grow rapidly, although it remained predominantly French.[7] By the time the experiment ended in 1963 a second wave of migration to St-Léonard had begun, with Italian contractors building houses and selling them to other Italians. By 1968 the population was about 35,000, with 53.1 per cent being French and 27.6 per cent Italian.[8]

Until 1962 the Catholic school board of St-Léonard provided education only in French, but in that year an English program was introduced to serve the immigrant population. In 1963 the English program was replaced by a bilingual program in which some subjects were taught in English and some in French. Most Italians chose to place their children in this program rather than in the all-French program. In 1967 some francophone residents of St-Léonard began to campaign for the abolition of the bilingual program, arguing that it encouraged immigrant children to adopt English as their working language. Early in the following year supporters of the bilingual program, mainly Italians, responded by forming the Association of Parents of St-Léonard (APSL), headed by school principal Frank Vatrano. Their opponents almost immediately formed le Mouvement pour l'intégration scolaire (MIS), headed by Raymond Lemieux, who had been active in the Société St-Jean-Baptiste and was also a member of Lévesque's Mouvement Souveraineté-Association (MSA).[9]

The two groups squared off for the school board election which took place in June and was accompanied by a referendum on the issue of whether bilingual education should continue. Slightly more than half of those eligible to vote did so as compared to a usual participation rate of from 10 to 15 per cent.[10] The MIS won both the election and the referendum, and immediately announced plans to become a province-wide organization. It also illegally occupied a local high school in which some students were being taught in English, preventing the school from opening on schedule for the fall term. When Lévesque condemned this action, Lemieux publicly tore up his MSA membership card.[11] Meanwhile Vatrano resigned as president of APSL and was succeeded by a more militant leader, Robert Beale. APSL conducted demonstrations and protests, including a visit to Ottawa where it met with Prime Minister Trudeau, after the new school board announced plans to terminate bilingual education.[12] The English-speaking community of Montreal and its media argued that bilingual education must be allowed to continue. APSL conducted private bilingual classes and encouraged Italian parents to enrol their children in these classes rather than in the unilingual schools.

Both senior levels of government refused to intervene, but while the agitation was still in progress Premier Daniel Johnson died of a heart attack. Johnson had juggled the more nationalist and more federalist wings of his party with remarkable skill, never fully committing himself to either. His successor, Jean-Jacques Bertrand, was identified with the federalist wing and was not strong enough to control the nationalists in the party, who included his minister of education, Jean-Guy Cardinal. At the same time he needed to reassure the business and financial communities, whose confidence in Quebec and in the government had declined precipitously following the events of the recent months.

By-elections were needed to fill Johnson's seat and also to replace Eric Kierans, who had gone to the House of Commons. Cardinal, who had been appointed to the Legislative Council when he entered the cabinet in 1967 because no seat had been available in the elected house, decided to run in Johnson's former riding of Bagot. Bertrand wanted a credible anglophone lieutenant in his government and the by-election in Kierans' former riding of NDG seemed to provide at least a faint possibility of achieving this objective. Through the intermediary of Brian Mulroney he recruited John Lynch-Staunton, a popular municipal politician who had considered running as the Liberal candidate in the same by-election if Liberal leader Jean Lesage would endorse his candidacy for the nomination. Lesage refused to take sides in the nomination contest, but Bertrand was more accommodating and also indicated to Lynch-Staunton that his government would do something to support the Italians in St-Léonard. He kept this promise sooner than expected by promising to introduce Bill 85, which would guarantee parents the right to choose between English and French education for their children, while the by-election campaign was still in progress. To appease the nationalists he also promised a full-scale inquiry into the status of the French language in Quebec, subsequently known as the Gendron Commission after its chairman, Jean-Denis Gendron. It was formally appointed on 9 December 1968, and its five commissioners included one anglophone, Professor Edward McWhinney of McGill University's Faculty of Law, who eventually moved to British Columbia and became a Liberal MP from that province.

The timing of Bill 85 was obviously a rather crude attempt to influence the NDG by-election, and the measure itself was anathema to nationalists, both inside and outside the Union Nationale. From their perspective, Bill 85 would open the door for Montreal to become a predominantly English-speaking city, since all immigrants, and even some francophones, would presumably send their children to English schools. On the other hand "freedom of choice" appealed to conservative Catholics – like Bertrand himself – because it gave the family priority over the state. For the same reason Duplessis, and many of the clergy, had opposed making school attendance compulsory when the Liberal government legislated to do so in 1943.

With an improvised organization, a riding that had never supported the Union Nationale, and an anglophone electorate that now looked back on the Lesage years as a golden age of harmony and progress, Lynch-Staunton was predictably and badly defeated by Liberal candidate William Tetley. First reading of Bill 85 was delayed until the week after the by-election because of widespread resistance to it within the governing party. The government then moved to send it to a committee although anglophone Liberal members urged that it be adopted without delay. Soon afterwards Bertrand suffered a mild heart attack and Jean-Guy Cardinal became acting premier.[13] On the same day Liberal member Glen Brown, in the course of a speech supporting Bill 85, told the Legislative Assembly that he had overheard organizers of a demonstration against the bill boasting that certain members of the cabinet were on their side and would prevent the bill from being adopted. Brown said that he had conveyed this information privately to Premier Bertrand, who represented the county adjoining his own, and to the provincial police.[14] Brown's revelations were soon given credence, for the government under Cardinal's leadership allowed the bill to die in committee.

The situation in St-Léonard remained unresolved. Italians boycotted the now-unilingual schools and their unofficial bilingual classes, which the government insisted were illegal, continued through the 1968–69 academic year. Liberal MLA Victor Goldbloom tried to mediate a compromise. Cardinal eventually offered to recognize the bilingual classes as a private school, entitling them to a subsidy of 80 per cent of their operating costs, but both sides rejected this solution.[15] Tensions were exacerbated in March 1969 by a massive nationalist demonstration at McGill University, demanding that it be turned into a French-language institution, and in September a violent confrontation between Italians and Quebec nationalists in St-Léonard led to the reading of the Riot Act.[16]

In June 1969 the Union Nationale held a convention at which Bertrand, who had never formally become leader of the party, was forced to contest a leadership ballot against Cardinal. Anglophone delegates, who almost unanimously supported the premier, were warned not to do so too publicly lest they provoke a nationalist backlash in favour of Cardinal.[17] In the end Bertrand won by a vote of 1325 to 938, but since about 250 delegates were anglophones his majority among the francophones was exceedingly small.[18] Armed with this rather dubious mandate, he decided to make another effort to legislate freedom of choice, camouflaged this time with some concessions to the nationalists. Bill 63, introduced in October, combined freedom of choice with a requirement that all high school students must have a working knowledge of French in order to graduate and a provision that immigrants should be encouraged, although not required, to educate their children in French. The measure was somewhat optimistically entitled "An Act to Promote the French Language in Quebec"[19] but the nationalists were not impressed.[20] Raymond Lemieux predicted that Bill 63 would cause French to disappear from Quebec.[21] Massive demonstrations against the bill took place in both Montreal and Quebec City. Two Union Nationale members voted against Bill 63 and subsequently left the party. However the Liberals supported the bill and it passed by a large majority.

Bill 63 was presented as part of a package that originally included Bill 62 as a *quid pro quo* for the nationalists. The latter measure would have reduced the number of school boards on Montreal Island, eliminated the distinction between Protestant and Catholic boards, and provided that all members of school boards would be elected by the taxpayers. (The Liberals in 1965 had provided for appointed Jewish representatives on the Protestant School Board of Greater Montreal, to avoid confronting the delicate constitutional problem of allowing Jews to vote as Protestant taxpayers.)[22] Bill 62, whose main purpose was to redistribute tax revenues from the more prosperous Protestant system to the Catholic system, was abandoned by the Bertrand government after it encountered strong opposition from the Protestant and Jewish communities and from the Board of Trade.[23] The principal of McGill University even claimed that it would lead to the disappearance of the English language from Quebec.[24] In his thesis on the controversy over school board reorganization Pierre Fournier has argued that the Protestants were really defending economic privileges but that they succeeded in portraying the issue as one of minority rights and cultural survival, thus winning more sympathy than, in his judgment, they deserved.[25] English-speaking Catholics generally supported Bill 62, which would have provided more resources for their schools while somewhat diluting the preponderance of francophones on the school boards which served their community.[26] Quebec nationalists contrasted the fates of bills 63 and 62 and concluded that the Bertrand government was more concerned with appeasing anglophones than with improving educational opportunities for francophones.[27]

Although the Union Nationale thus alienated the nationalists, it won no gratitude from English-speaking Quebeckers for Bill 63. The party was still widely distrusted by anglophones, at least in Montreal, and there was a suspicion that some hidden nationalist agenda lurked behind the seemingly harmless facade of Bill 63, particularly with Cardinal as minister of education. The Protestant School Board of Greater Montreal opposed even the requirement that English-speaking students become competent in the French language, arguing that this was an inappropriate interference with the autonomy of school boards.[28] William Tetley recalls reminiscing at the legislative committee hearings on the bill that in his childhood French had been taught in the Protestant schools as a foreign language. The chairman of the school board, who was present, amused the largely francophone audience by blurting out: "But it is a foreign language!"[29]

Regardless of the government's policies, the seemingly endless series of demonstrations, riots and terrorist incidents, as well as a strike by Montreal police officers in October 1969 that led Bertrand to request the intervention of the Canadian armed forces, convinced English-speaking Montrealers – and many francophones as well – that the Union Nationale government could not maintain law and order in Quebec.

Anglophones were further alienated by two other initiatives of the Bertrand government. The first was the re-naming of the Legislative Assembly as the National Assembly, simultaneously with the abolition of the Legislative Council. Not many mourned the upper house, but the change of name attracted more attention and more criticism, even though Frank Hanley bravely spoke in its favour.[30] The second initiative was the creation of the Montreal Urban Community (MUC), a regional government for the entire island of Montreal.[31] Residents of the mainly English-speaking suburbs predictably resented this measure, since the MUC would have a francophone majority. Several Liberals voted against it, although the Liberal Party as a whole did not.[32]

St-Léonard and Bill 63 probably sealed the fate of the Union Nationale, although the death of Johnson and the formation of the Parti Québécois had made the party's future rather problematical in any event. More importantly, the damage inflicted on the social fabric of Montreal and its environs by these events was irreversible, and is still visible after almost thirty years. Quebec nationalists and non-francophones henceforth confronted one another warily, each group convinced that the other group posed a threat to the survival of its language and way of life. Nationalists feared (or professed to fear) that the combination of immigration, freedom of choice and a low French-Canadian birth rate would again make Montreal a predominantly English-speaking city, as it had been for a few decades following the Irish migration of the nineteenth century. Non-francophones dismissed such fears as failing to take into account the continuing exodus of anglophones from the province. (The non-francophones were correct, as one of the demographers responsible for raising the alarm, Jacques Henripin, admitted years later.)[33] From their perspective, St-Léonard indicated that the nationalists were determined to eradicate the English language from Quebec. For the first time they sensed that the continuation of their inherited rights and privileges could not be taken for granted. John Parisella, who would later play a significant role in Quebec politics, described the new situation in his MA thesis on St-Léonard: "The politicization of the English-speaking community was also a significant event, for it had never organized itself against any nationalist threat. This proved that any nationalist movement must now be careful not to infringe on English-speaking minority rights, or else organized opposition will follow."[34]

THE RETURN OF THE LIBERALS

The election of April 1970 confirmed the fundamental realignment of Quebec politics, and ended the dichotomy of *rouge* and *bleu* that had lasted for more than twelve decades. The Union Nationale, always an unstable mixture of nationalism, populism and conservatism, disintegrated into its component parts. Nationalists abandoned it for the Parti Québécois, populists for Social Credit (which had belatedly entered the provincial arena) and most conservatives for the Liberals, who were henceforth the party of big business, the religiously observant, and the ethnic minorities – similar to the *bleu* party of Cartier and Chauveau a century earlier. The Liberals won practically all of the non-francophone vote, about one-third of the francophone vote, and two-thirds of the seats. The Union Nationale salvaged enough rural seats to be the official opposition. The Parti Québécois won almost half the francophone vote in metropolitan Montreal and more votes overall than the Union Nationale, but only seven seats, fewer than Social Credit. Their leader lost the riding of Laurier which he had won three times as a Liberal, a riding in which 28 per cent of the voters were non-francophones.[35] The New Democratic Party, entering the provincial arena for the first time, ran a dozen candidates in ridings with large non-francophone populations, but none received more than a few hundred votes.

In their successful election campaign under their new leader, Robert Bourassa, the Liberals promised a return of order and prosperity. They also exploited the fears of the non-francophones by campaigning against "separatism," although there was never the slightest possibility that the newly-founded Parti Québécois would win the election. The highlight of the campaign was a masterpiece of political theatre, subsequently known as *l'affaire Brinks*. A convoy of armoured trucks from the well-known security transfer firm paraded through the financial district and then departed in the direction of Ontario, persuading the credulous that capital was fleeing from the threat of separatism but would return once order had been restored by the Liberals. Frank Hanley, whose twenty-two years in provincial politics finally ended, attributed his defeat to the impact of this event on English-speaking voters.[36] The anglophone response to the victory of the Liberals was euphoric. Richard Holden's eight-year-old son captured the mood of Westmount in his response to the news: "Good, now we don't have to speak French anymore."[37]

Bourassa formed a strong cabinet that included three anglophones. William Tetley, the victor in the NDG by-election of 1968 and a prominent lawyer, initially received the traditional anglophone portfolio of revenue, two of whose four previous incumbents had also been from NDG. After a few months Tetley was given the new Department of Financial Institutions, Companies, and Co-operatives, which included a variety of regulatory responsibilities. In this capacity he introduced in 1971 the first legislation for the protection of consumers in Quebec, a subject in which he took a great interest.[38]

Dr Victor Goldbloom, the member for D'Arcy-McGee since 1966, seemed a natural choice for minister of health but that portfolio was earmarked for Claude Castonguay, a new member who had previously headed the Lesage government's royal commission on social services. Goldbloom entered the cabinet initially as a minister without portfolio attached to the Department of Education, where his presence reassured anglophones who recalled his support for bilingualism in St-Léonard. After seven months, however, he was made minister of state for the environment. While a minister without portfolio he had urged Bourassa to make the environment a priority and he was pleasantly surprised to be given this newly created position.[39] In 1973 Goldbloom also became minister of municipal affairs, while retaining his environmental responsibilities. Later in that year a full Department of the Environment was created and Goldbloom held both portfolios until the defeat of the government in 1976.

The third anglophone minister, Kevin Drummond, had been born into the Westmount elite but decided to immerse himself in a French environment and spent two years in the Quebec public service, an unusual accomplishment for an anglophone. Subsequently he was executive assistant to Westmount's federal representative, President of the Treasury Board C.M. Drury. He was asked to run in 1970 by Bourassa, since Richard Hyde was retiring from politics, on the implicit understanding that he would receive a cabinet position.[40] He became minister of lands and forests, where he served for five years before being shifted to the Department of Agriculture. Despite his background Drummond was one of the more left-wing ministers, a fact not always appreciated by the paper companies with whom he dealt in his first portfolio. His plans to increase government control over the forests were opposed by some cabinet colleagues and had to be largely abandoned under pressure from the industry.

Harry Blank from St-Louis became deputy speaker of the National Assembly (as it now was) and held that position until the government left office in 1976. On the backbenches Glen Brown from Brome and Ken Fraser from Huntingdon were joined by George Springate, who had defeated Frank Hanley in Ste-Anne. Springate was a former policeman whose other occupation, which he continued to pursue while a member of the National Assembly, was kicking field goals for the Montreal Alouettes.

The major events of the government's first term were the October Crisis in 1970 and the general strike of the three labour federations in 1972. The government's handling of both episodes probably strengthened the alliance of nationalists and leftists in the Parti Québécois, but cost the government little if any support among non-francophones. That support remained firm, as the election of 1973 was to show, but along the way there were some relatively minor irritations.

The first of these was the abolition of the protected ridings, which had been constitutionally entrenched in 1867 to ensure adequate representation for the English-speaking minority. The ridings had been incrementally modified over the years with the consent of their representatives, and the English-speaking populations in most of them had long since dwindled to insignificant levels, making them quite irrelevant to their original purpose.[41] Their populations were also considerably smaller, on the average, than those of other ridings in the province. In 1970 the majority of them finally elected Liberals, which they had failed to do in the 1960s, and this fact permitted the Bourassa government to bring about a complete overhaul of the electoral map, something which had not been possible for Lesage and not wanted by Johnson or Bertrand. Abolition of the protected ridings was promised in the first throne speech, implemented a few months later, and followed by the establishment of an independent commission to revise electoral boundaries, which had previously been set by the government.

This issue was of no real interest in Montreal, which could expect to benefit if the electoral map was reformed. The two remaining English-speaking representatives of protected ridings were Glen Brown of Brome and Ken Fraser of Huntingdon. Fraser appeared to accept the inevitability of change, perhaps because in return for his support he had managed to extract from the government a promise to build a hospital in his county, something for which he had campaigned since 1966.[42] Brown was much less accommodating, accusing his party of neglecting rural voters and predicting that no rural anglophones would be elected if the protected ridings were abolished. He also expressed some bitterness about his own exclusion from the cabinet when three Montreal anglophones with much less legislative experience were included.[43]

The issue returned at the third session when the actual changes recommended by the new independent commission were debated in the National Assembly. This time Fraser was more vigorous in his opposition than Brown, since the commission proposed to include the industrial and francophone city of Valleyfield in his riding.[44] He was successful in having it excluded.

Besides creating two new anglophone ridings, Pointe-Claire and Mount Royal, the redistribution on Montreal Island featured a complicated manœuvre in which most of the ethnic voters in St-Louis were redistributed into the ridings of Premier Bourassa and Justice Minister

Jérome Choquette, both of whom feared losing their ridings to the Parti Québécois at the next election. St-Louis retained its name but was shifted further west, to include what remained of the old Square Mile. Harry Blank made a deal with Claude Charron, the Parti Québécois member for neighbouring St-Jacques, whereby the boundary between their ridings was adjusted to make St-Jacques almost totally francophone while the new St-Louis had even fewer francophones than the old riding of the same name.[45]

Meanwhile, *The Gazette* had published a report in February 1971 that the Bourassa and Trudeau governments had agreed to amend Section 133 of the Canadian constitution so that English would no longer be an official language of the National Assembly or the courts. This was immediately denied by both leaders, and soon afterwards Francois Cloutier, Bourassa's minister of cultural affairs, condemned unilingualism in an effort to reassure English-speaking Quebeckers.[46]

Another issue was the amendment in December 1971 of the law establishing the Montreal Urban Community, which had been adopted by the Bertrand government two years earlier. The amendment, which was part of the original plan but had been postponed because of its controversial nature, merged all the police forces of Montreal Island into one. This was greatly resented in anglophone suburbs which had had their own, English-speaking, police forces.[47] In Westmount a mass meeting of some six hundred people filled the community hall and booed their provincial representative, Kevin Drummond. The city's mayor urged the provincial government to recognize that "Westmount is to Quebec as Quebec is to Canada."[48] Drummond was eventually able to prevent the closing of the local police station in Westmount, but the disappearance of Westmount's independent local police force was a *fait accompli.*[49]

The third and most complex issue was the reorganization of school boards on Montreal Island, a problem which the previous government had tried and failed to solve with Bill 62. The Liberal successor to this bill, known as Bill 28, was introduced in 1971 after a year of consultations. Minister of Education Guy St-Pierre, who was sympathetic to the anglo-Protestant establishment, and his minister of state, Victor Goldbloom, tried hard to avoid the opposition that had led to the abandonment of the earlier bill. While retaining the eleven unified boards proposed in Bill 62, Bill 28 would have added Protestant and Catholic confessional committees to each board. It also provided for the appointment of two members of the linguistic minority to any board if no minority representative was elected.[50] K.D. Sheldrick, a prominent member of the Protestant School Board of Greater Montreal who had helped to draft the Board of Trade's brief in opposition to Bill 62, was shown a copy of Bill 28 before it was presented to the National Assembly, a courtesy apparently not extended to any representative of the Catholic boards.[51] Goldbloom's eloquent plea in the National Assembly for anglophones to understand the need for reform was apparently quite successful, and no anglophone members spoke against the bill.[52] However, it was delayed and eventually withdrawn when the Parti Québécois, not very astutely, tried to amend it in a way that would effectively repeal Bill 63. In its place the government introduced, and the National Assembly adopted, Bill 71, which merely reduced the number of boards on the island while retaining the distinction between Catholic and Protestant boards.[53] As later events were to show, this was about all that could be done without amending the Canadian constitution, but it seemed a very limited result after several years of discussion.

A much more significant measure than any of the above – although its significance does not seem to have been appreciated by many anglophones at the time – was Bill 65, which the National Assembly adopted in December 1971.[54] This measure really completed the work of the Quiet Revolution by bringing health and social service agencies under the direct control of the government, eliminating what remained of the influence of religious orders and middle-class volunteers. To coordinate and manage the various agencies twelve regional social service centres were established, later to be supplemented by a large number of local centres (known as CLSCs) which reported to the regional centres. Most of the regional centres had exclusive responsibility for a geographical area, but there were some exceptions. On Montreal Island three separate agencies were established. The Montreal Metropolitan Social Services Centre looked after the needs of francophones, the Jewish Family Services Social Services Centre served the Jewish community, and the Ville Marie Social Services Centre was for everyone else. (Originally the intent had been to place the Jewish agencies under the jurisdiction of Ville Marie, but they refused to accept this and were given their own centre in 1974.)[55] In the extreme eastern part of the province there was also a departure from the territorial principle, with one centre for anglophones and one for francophones. Thus Quebec's traditional consociational pattern of cultural segmentation was partly incorporated into the welfare state, for a time at least. This would prove to be a precarious compromise.

George Springate emerged during the government's first term as the most forceful and uninhibited defender of the anglophone minority in Quebec politics, despite the fact that his riding of Ste-Anne contained a majority of francophone voters. Springate combined Frank Hanley's populism with a rather truculent attitude towards francophones, something which Hanley had always avoided. Not having and probably not expecting a seat at the cabinet table, Springate could say whatever he liked on the floor of the National Assembly, and what he said was not always welcomed by the government. In the fall of 1971 *The Gazette* published a sensational story that William Tetley was blackmailing Springate with a secret file of information about him in an effort to make him less outspoken. The Union Nationale naturally made the most of the story, but Tetley denied it. Springate, while not exactly denying it, told the National Assembly that as a football player and former policeman he could look after himself and that he had no intention of leaving the Liberal Party.[56] He remained as outspoken as ever.

In the election of October 1973 the Liberals won an overwhelming majority of 102 out of 110 seats, a landslide eclipsing even Duplessis' triumph in 1948. Both the Union Nationale and Social Credit collapsed completely, throwing practically all of the federalist vote to the Liberals. Despite the preponderance of francophones in their enlarged ridings, both Glen Brown and Ken Fraser were re-elected easily. Harry Blank also survived despite the relocation of his riding of St-Louis. Art Seguin ran and won as the official Liberal candidate in the new riding of Pointe-Claire, which was separated from Robert-Baldwin. The new riding of Mount Royal, largely carved out of the old Outremont constituency, elected John Ciaccia as its Liberal member. Ciaccia was a Montreal lawyer who had spent two years in the federal Department of Indian Affairs and Northern Development, helping to draft the James Bay agreement with the Cree which enabled Premier Bourassa to proceed with his dream of tapping the hydro-electric potential of the rivers flowing into the bay. Bourassa then persuaded Ciaccia to become a candidate, explaining that the Liberals needed someone from a non-British ethnic minority.[57] Ciaccia had emigrated from Italy to Montreal when he was four years old and received his education in English. He was the first person born in Italy, and only the second of Italian ancestry, to be elected to the National Assembly. He proved to be one of its most durable and successful members and was the senior member of the house in years of service after 1994, before retiring in 1998.

Although the size of the government's majority might have suggested that it had nothing to fear from its opponents for the foreseeable future, this was a superficial view. The Parti Québécois had increased its share of the popular vote to about 30 per cent and was clearly now the only possible alternative to the Liberals. Prudence therefore demanded that the Liberals make some gestures to the portion of the electorate that the Parti Québécois represented.

Although still a pro-business and pro-federalist party, they made some efforts to soften those aspects of their image over the next three years. Their most important initiative in this regard would be in the field of language policy, a time bomb that had certainly not been defused by the fiasco of Bill 63.

BILL 22 AND THE END OF AN ILLUSION

It will be recalled that in 1968, simultaneously with the introduction of Bill 85, the Bertrand government appointed a commission of inquiry into the state of the French language in Quebec which was known as the Gendron Commission. Although the federal government's Royal Commission on Bilingualism and Biculturalism was still in existence and had published several volumes of reports, it would probably have been unthinkable for a Quebec government to rely on the findings of a federal inquiry to shape its policy on so sensitive an issue. In any event, the provincial commission was a necessary gesture to nationalists concerned over the future of the language and disturbed by what they saw as the assimilationist potential of Bill 85. Finally, the inquiry, like many others in Canadian history, could serve the useful purpose of delaying a controversial issue and reducing the pressure on the government to act immediately.

The Liberals inherited the linguistic dossier when they won the 1970 election, but they succeeded in postponing the necessity of dealing with the issue until the 1973 election had taken place. When first established the Gendron Commission had been required to complete its work within twelve months, but in the end it received three extensions by order in council and was not required to submit its report until the end of 1972. Although its public hearings were completed by May 1970, less than two weeks after the Liberals took office, the report was not completed until the last possible day, 31 December 1972, and not made public until February 1973. The latter event followed two weeks after the unauthorized publication of most of its findings in *Le Devoir*; it is not clear whether the Bourassa government would have published the report then, or at all, if this had not happened.[58]

The findings and recommendations of the Gendron Commission were presented in three volumes.[59] The first dealt with the language of work, which the commission regarded as the most important aspect of the status of the French language. The second was a collection of legal and historical studies, some of them rather tenuously related to the matter at hand. The third contained findings and recommendations concerning the integration of immigrants into Quebec, including the highly sensitive subject of the language of education. There were ninety-two specific recommendations in the first volume and eighty-one in the third.

The Gendron Commission's findings, if carefully read and fairly interpreted, suggested the same comment about the French language that Mark Twain once made about himself: rumours of its death were greatly exaggerated. Indeed, there had perhaps been some progress since the Quiet Revolution began, although since the data were not directly comparable with the earlier data assembled by the federal Royal Commission it was not easy to verify this possibility. According to the Gendron Commission's findings the majority of francophone workers in Quebec, 1,165,000 out of 1,820,000 or about 64 per cent, worked exclusively in French. The percentage of anglophones who worked exclusively in English was almost identical: 216,000 out of 344,000 or about 63 per cent. Admittedly the situation was very different if Montreal was considered in isolation. In Montreal only 45 per cent of francophones, and 67 per cent of anglophones, enjoyed the luxury of working in their own language exclusively. Outside of the city their situations were reversed, with 77 per cent of francophones and 49 per cent of anglophones not needing to use the other language.[60]

It was the findings about Montreal that attracted almost all the attention, and that seemed to inspire many of the commission's recommendations. The report's first volume proposed as its first recommendation that the Quebec government set itself the goal of making French the common language of Quebeckers, in the sense that everyone would know French and French would be used in communications between francophones and non-francophones. The second recommendation was the passage of a law proclaiming French the official language of Quebec while retaining the status of English insofar as required by Section 133 of the 1867 Constitution Act. The third recommendation was that steps be taken to make French the language of internal communication in workplaces in Quebec. Recommendations 4 and 5 provided that this goal would be achieved in stages. In the first stage the goal would be to ensure that French would be the working language of francophones, although anglophones would continue to use their own language. In the second stage French should be made the language of oral communication, and in the third stage the language of written communication, between francophones and anglophones.

Several other recommendations may be noted. Number 22 was that a working knowledge of French should henceforth be a condition for admission to the practice of any trade or profession. The right of consumers to be served in French should be guaranteed, according to recommendation 49. Number 72 was that municipalities and school boards should be guaranteed the right to publish their official documents in French only, unless their clientele included an anglophone minority of at least 10 per cent. Recommendation 57 was that organizations created under Quebec law, including business corporations, should be required to have and to use French names, although they might have English names also. Even the names of places in Quebec should be reviewed, according to recommendation 65, and those which did not have a French name should be given one "wherever justified."[61]

These recommendations were, however, somewhat balanced by the commission's moderate approach to the English-speaking minority; several recommendations emphasized the need to negotiate changes with those who would be affected by them. In addition, the imposition of French as the official language in recommendation 2 was qualified by the stipulations that both English and French should be recognized as "national" languages of Quebec and that English should still be the language of instruction in English schools, both Catholic and Protestant.

The recommendations in the third volume were even more moderate.[62] The commission noted that most children from homes where neither English nor French was spoken attended English schools, mainly in the Catholic system. In fact in the English sector of the Montreal Catholic school system, such children greatly outnumbered those whose language spoken at home was actually English. However, the commission attributed this to the perceived greater usefulness of English in the economy, the fact that English as a second language was taught poorly and inadequately in French schools, and the fact that francophone Quebec had not always made immigrants feel welcome. It argued that "generally speaking, the school situation does not involve the degree of urgency or primacy which is sometimes attributed to it."[63] For this reason it did not recommend any coercive measures to make immigrant children, or any children, attend French schools. Instead it suggested that measures to improve the position of French in the economy would create a natural incentive for immigrants to choose to educate their children in French, provided that English was taught adequately as a second language.

The government's legislative program in 1973 included only one item of a linguistic nature. An amendment to the Companies Act, introduced by William Tetley, provided that henceforth companies would only be incorporated if they had a French name. Some sixty thousand existing firms with solely English names were requested to adopt bilingual names on a voluntary basis, but very few complied, even after the five hundred leading companies received a personal letter from the minister.[64] Tetley later recalled that even former premier Jean Lesage, a director of Great Lakes Paper, was indignant at the suggestion that the company should be asked to change its name.[65]

The Quebec Liberal Party's program in the 1973 election devoted more attention to economic and social policies than to cultural policy. It did contain references to French as the language of work and to "cultural sovereignty," which it defined as the extent of freedom of action (for Quebec) necessary for the protection and development of the French language.[66] Victor Goldbloom later recalled that "the 1973 election campaign had been conducted without any indication whatsoever of Mr Bourassa's intention to introduce language legislation."[67] Goldbloom considered in retrospect that the resentment expressed by non-francophones when legislation was introduced was understandable in the circumstances. John Ciaccia, a freshman member of the National Assembly at the time, had a similar recollection: "There was no inkling that this legislation was part of the program of the Liberal Party at the time. It sort of came as a surprise to the communities, the English-speaking community and the minorities."[68]

The inaugural speech – after 1969 it was no longer called the speech from the throne – that launched the legislative session of 1974 hinted that freedom of choice in education would soon be abandoned. With the Union Nationale no longer represented in the National Assembly defence of freedom of choice, such as it was, was left to non-francophone backbenchers on the government side of the house. In their contributions to the debate that followed the inaugural speech, both George Springate and John Ciaccia indicated their strong opposition to any attack on freedom of choice. Ciaccia pointedly reminded the house that he had defended that principle when campaigning for votes as a Liberal in the recent election.[69]

A few months later the government introduced its Official Language Act, Bill 22, which proclaimed French to be the official language of Quebec.[70] The bill followed some of the recommendations of the Gendron Commission, but its provisions for promoting French in business and the economy – the subject which the commission had considered to be of primordial importance – were much weaker. Only firms that did business with the government, or that wished to receive "premiums, subsidies, concessions or benefits from the public administration" would be required to comply with the provisions relating to the use of French within the firm. Provisions relating to firm names, contracts, product labelling, advertising and signs were compulsory for all. The requirements relating to public administration, the professions, municipalities and school boards were similar to the Gendron recommendations. Most provisions of the bill would not take effect until 1975, or 1976, or an indefinite date to be fixed by order in council.

The provisions relating to the language of instruction were quite contrary to the Gendron Commission's advice. Instead of avoiding coercive measures in this area and relying on progress in the work world to give immigrants an incentive to have their children educated in French, Bill 22 opted for a more forceful approach. School boards would continue to provide education in English and could not terminate it or reduce it without the approval of the minister of education. However, access to English-language education would not be open to all but only to pupils who already had a sufficient knowledge of English. To determine whether this criterion was met, the minister of education was given authority to set tests of English proficiency at different levels and to require school boards to reassign pupils on the basis of the results of those tests.

More than one-third of the text of Bill 22 was devoted to machinery for supervision and enforcement. It established a nine-member regulatory agency, the Régie de la langue française, which would combine a number of functions: advising the minister or the government on various matters, cooperating with business firms in elaborating and implementing programs for the greater use of French in their operations, conducting inquiries to determine whether the law was being observed, awarding certificates of "francization" to business firms that succeeded in upgrading the use of French, and improving the quality of the French language itself by various means, including measures to standardize the vocabulary used in Quebec and to accept or reject new expressions.

Reminiscing to an academic audience many years later, Premier Bourassa claimed that expediency had not entered into the decision to introduce Bill 22 since there was no great public demand for it at the time and the government lost rather than gained support because of it.[71] William Tetley remembered, rather more accurately, that the Liberals had to adopt a language bill if they were to be seen as a government that looked after the interests of the majority.[72] According to Kevin Drummond: "I didn't like Bill 22 particularly, but it was something that had to be done."[73] Tetley, Drummond and Goldbloom all agree in remembering that Bill 22 was extensively discussed in cabinet before it was made public, that there were some disagreements within the cabinet about specific provisions, and that each of the anglophone ministers had the opportunity to provide some input into its content. According to Goldbloom, by no means all of these disagreements had been worked out when the bill was presented to the National Assembly.[74]

The original plan was to present two bills, one relating to the language of instruction and the other conforming more closely to the Gendron recommendations. At the last moment Premier Bourassa decided that this would merely double the time required for the legislative process so the two bills were combined into one.[75] François Cloutier, the minister of education, was given the responsibility of steering the combined bill through the National Assembly, a decision which naturally reinforced the public perception that the provision restricting access to English schooling was the most important part of the bill. Kevin Drummond stated subsequently that his first preference would have been to maintain freedom of choice in the language of instruction, as the Gendron Commission had recommended.[76] Relations between both Drummond and Tetley on the one hand, and Cloutier on the other, apparently deteriorated. Goldbloom, who happened to be friendly with Cloutier, remained on good terms with all three and tried to conciliate their differences, but without great success. All three English-speaking ministers realized that the restriction of freedom of choice would cause serious political difficulties with non-francophone voters.

The most controversial aspect of Bill 22 was the provision for testing the English language competence of children entering school and refusing them access to English schools if they failed the test. This idea had been first proposed by the Montreal Catholic School Commission in their brief to the Gendron Commission, but apparently they later had second thoughts.[77] Not only would the tests be traumatic for the children and possibly unreliable for that reason, but in addition the procedure seemed to draw an invidious distinction based on ethnicity and language, since anglophone children were not subject to it. Even Bourassa admitted in retrospect that, although he was proud of Bill 22 as a whole, the provision for testing was a mistake.[78] At the time, however, he seemed to have no misgivings about it.

Despite their unhappiness over certain aspects of Bill 22, and the certainty that the measure as a whole would be widely resented in the constituencies which they represented, none of the English-speaking ministers seems to have seriously considered resigning over the issue. As Victor Goldbloom later explained: "The three of us felt that to withdraw all English representation from the cabinet would have been a grave disservice to the English community."[79] By remaining in the government they could make the views of anglophones known to their colleagues and also try to ensure that the legislation would be implemented in ways that minimized the adverse impact on English-speaking Quebeckers. This was particularly significant since the real impact of Bill 22 would be largely determined by the many regulations which it empowered the government or a minister to make.

Tetley and his department were involved in drawing up regulations concerning the language of work and the language of business. Goldbloom's responsibility for municipalities, his knowledge of the Department of Education where he had previously served as minister of state, and his friendship with Cloutier also gave him some influence over the process of implementation. Drummond's portfolio of lands and forests had little to do with the controversies over language and gave him less opportunity for input.

Public hearings on Bill 22 took place in June and July. A large number of English-speaking groups and organizations appeared and their comments were almost uniformly hostile.[80] The restriction on freedom of choice in education was by far the aspect most frequently criticized, but by no means the only one. The Montreal Board of Trade and the Canadian Jewish Congress both opposed the idea of requiring businesses to apply for certificates of francization, even though the requirement would apply only to firms doing business with the government or receiving favours from it. The English, Irish, Scottish and Welsh benevolent societies, in a joint brief, opposed the requirement that professionals demonstrate competence in the French language. The benevolent societies, the Provincial Association of Protestant Teachers and the Provincial Association of Catholic Teachers all complained that the bill gave too much discretionary power to government officials. The benevolent societies, the United Church of Canada, the Canadian Jewish Congress, the Protestant Teachers, the Association of English-Speaking Catholic Teachers and even the Liberal Party association in the riding of Pointe-Claire all argued that English should be recognized as an official language of Quebec. The Presbyterian Church claimed that the bill "would make Quebec a ghetto, policed by a flying squad of bureaucrats hunting down the use of English, tearing down English billboards, cancelling licenses, and handing out largesse as a normal service function."[81] The Anglican Church, in contrast, was considerably more restrained and advocated only some fairly minor amendments.

Unrestricted freedom to choose the language of instruction was demanded by all of the groups and organizations mentioned in the preceding paragraph, apart from the Anglican Church, the United Church, and the Pointe-Claire riding association. The Board of Trade and the Quebec Association of School Adminstrators (a Protestant group) both expressed concern that Bill 22 would make it more difficult for francophones to learn English as a second language. Other demands for freedom of choice came from an assortment of anglophone educational bodies including the Protestant School Board of Greater Montreal, the Lakeshore School Board, the Quebec Association of Protestant School Boards, the Quebec Federation of Home and School Associations and the Committee for the Co-ordination of Anglophone Catholic Education, and from the Lakeshore chapter of the University Women's Club.

In the debate on second reading the English-speaking ministers did their best to defend the bill, while the English-speaking backbenchers opposed it. Goldbloom said that Bill 22 would both ensure the survival of French and protect the rights of minorities.[82] Drummond argued that the survival of the anglophone minority was not threatened and defended the testing of school children as "an acceptable compromise," which was not his private view.[83] Both Goldbloom and Tetley referred to a promised amendment, which never in fact materialized, to guarantee the existence of an English-language school system. Tetley, the only one of the three to give his speech in English, attributed some significance to the fact that most of the opponents of the bill were over the age of thirty.[84]

Comments more representative of the actual sentiments of English-speaking voters were made by some of the backbench members, although Glen Brown's speech seemed to avoid taking any clear position.[85] Harry Blank claimed to support Bill 22 in principle but argued for freedom of choice and against the broad powers that would be given to the Régie de la langue française. He also questioned why government documents pertaining to anglophones and contracts between anglophones needed to be in French, and he referred to Cloutier's professed objective of "making Quebec as French as Ontario is English" as a false analogy.[86] George Springate insisted on freedom of choice and said that Bill 22 was hostile to bilingualism. He promised to vote "the way my conscience dictates."[87] John Ciaccia alleged that provisions of the bill stating that the French texts of statutes and government documents would be more authentic and authoritative than the English texts violated the constitution of Canada. He also said that Bill 22 gave too much power to bureaucrats, particularly in view of the virtual absence of non-francophones from the public service.[88] Ken Fraser scoffed at the notion that the French language was in peril and predicted that Bill 22 would drive away both immigrants and investors. He noted that his opposition to the bill was well-known but that his decision on how to vote would be "political," given the fact that his riding was two-thirds francophone.[89]

Outside the Assembly, and particularly in Montreal, the reaction of English-speaking Quebeckers was more vociferously hostile than to any measure of public policy since the Rebellion Losses Bill of 1849. An editorial in *The Montreal Star* described Bill 22 as "dangerously flawed … arbitrary, unfair, intrusive and unworkable."[90] A petition was organized and signed by several hundred thousand persons, who each paid fifty cents towards the cost of collecting the signatures. The leading English radio stations, CFCF and CJAD, did their best to keep the pot boiling. Professor Frank Scott denounced the bill as unconstitutional in interviews with both *The Gazette* and *The Montreal Star*.[91] Drummond, Goldbloom, and Tetley all faced angry and hostile reactions in their ridings. A gigantic protest meeting at Loyola College, in Tetley's riding of NDG, lasted for three hours and featured denunciations of the Bourassa government by most of those present, including George Springate and the federal MP for the riding, Warren Allmand. Tetley appeared and was shouted down and verbally abused when he tried to speak, although he eventually succeeded in doing so.[92]

In the end closure was imposed to force Bill 22 through the National Assembly in July 1974. Ciaccia and Springate voted against it on both the second and third readings. Ken Fraser voted for second reading, despite his personal opposition to the bill, but took a vacation in Ireland as an excuse not to be present for the vote on third reading.[93] Blank, who had also criticized the bill, voted for it on both readings.[94] The Parti Québécois opposed it on the grounds that it did not do enough to protect the French language.

Bill 22 left deep and lasting scars on the Quebec Liberal Party and the Bourassa government. Most francophone members of the party considered the bill relatively reasonable and moderate, and in the light of what followed it can be seen that they were right. Even at the time Bill 22 was denounced by Quebec nationalists for its many compromises with the interests and sentiments of the English-speaking community. Yet Bill 22 was a tremendous shock to non-francophones, who had been an important part of the Quebec Liberal Party's constituency for decades and had saved it from extinction during the Duplessis years. The passion and rhetoric of the opponents within the caucus reached levels that made harmonious personal relations almost impossible. Fraser referred to Bill 22 as "Nazi legislation," an analogy that Goldbloom found highly offensive.[95] Springate called Bourassa, with perhaps more accuracy than tact, "the most hated man in Quebec."

Springate could not run again in his largely francophone riding and had to retreat to Westmount, which became available when Kevin Drummond decided to retire from politics in 1976. William Tetley also retired, and later reminisced that by 1976 he was "exhausted." At the same time that he was fighting within cabinet for regulations and interpretations favourable to anglophone interests, his constituents in NDG were denouncing him as a sell-out to Quebec nationalism. As he later remembered: "I was fighting in cabinet for interpretations that favoured the English. The way to do it is inside. The other guys were outside, waving their arms."[96] It is not likely that either Drummond or Tetley could have won the Liberal nominations in their ridings if they had decided to run again. Fraser later recalled that politics was no longer enjoyable after Bill 22. He was criticized by francophones for his public opposition to the bill and by anglophones for failing to vote against it. As he subsequently expressed it: "Two-thirds of the people were French. One-third were English and wanted me to go out and fight for the English. I was between a rock and a hard place."[97]

Fraser's experience in Huntingdon was a microcosm of the breakdown of intercommunity relations in Quebec. The Quebec Liberal Party, the only party which had continuously elected both francophones and anglophones to the Quebec legislature in every election since Confederation, the party which had been the first to elect a Jewish member and the first to elect an Italian member, the party of the Quiet Revolution, had fallen between two stools in an increasingly polarized Quebec. Its language legislation was denounced by nationalists as too little and by non-francophones as too much. When the voters are polarized, the task of those who seek a compromise is likely to be a thankless one.

Those whose mother tongue was neither English nor French – a mere 6 per cent of Quebec's population – were arguably the only group to suffer real inconvenience from Bill 22. The provisions for testing their children's competence in English added insult to injury by effectively denying them a freedom of choice that was still, in spite of all the rhetoric, maintained for those whose mother tongue was actually English. In the following year the Bourassa government caused the National Assembly to adopt a Charter of Human Rights and Freedoms[98] whose Article 10 prohibited discrimination or the nullifying of rights or freedoms on grounds of language, ethnicity or national origin, and it is certainly arguable that the provision making success in an English language test a requirement for non-anglophones to enter English schools was contrary to this provision. For that matter, it also discriminated against the relatively few francophones who wanted their children to enter English schools.

Bill 22, as the sequel to the St-Léonard affair of only six years before, thus contributed to the politicization of Quebec's immigrant or "allophone" minorities, particularly the Italians. Within a few months of the adoption of Bill 22 William Cusano and a number of other Italian Quebeckers established the Consiglio Educativo Italo-Canadese, which held English classes in church basements to prepare children for the English-language test. It also lobbied for flexible interpretations of Bill 22 and campaigned against Liberal candidates in the 1976 election.[99]

Soon afterwards it dissolved, but Cusano himself was elected to the National Assembly as a Liberal in 1981.

For Quebeckers whose mother tongue was English – a much more numerous group than the allophones at that time – Bill 22 was a fundamental attack on their collective and individual identities and on the symbolic order in which they had lived throughout their lives. As Raymond Breton has argued, a major change in the symbolic order can disrupt individual as well as collective identities.[100] For more than a century English-speaking Quebeckers had taken it for granted that Quebec was a bilingual province in which the English and French languages enjoyed equal status. They had taken it for granted also that they could live, be educated, and in most cases work in English, in Quebec, without any necessity of learning Canada's other official language. The status of the English language in Quebec, as far as they were concerned, was a right inherent in their status as Canadians, a fundamental part of their understanding of Confederation as a historical event and of Canadian federalism as an ongoing reality. They had never thought of it as a privilege conferred on them by the French-speaking majority of Quebec's population, and the notion that it could be viewed in this way was simply incomprehensible to them. How could it be so, when there had been an English-speaking population in Lower Canada before "Quebec" as a political entity even existed? Besides, Montreal was the largest city in a country where English was the main language, on a continent where English was the main language. The fact that people in Montreal lived in English, and the fact that immigrants to Montreal wanted to live in English, were viewed as part of the natural order of the universe.

English-speaking Quebeckers had lived for more than a decade with the threat of "separatism," and for several decades with the rhetorical nationalism of the Union Nationale. They had never imagined, however, that the Liberal Party, which they had supported in good times and bad for more than a generation, would turn on them and attempt to take away their collective and individual rights and identities. The fact that it bore the same name as the governing federal party, the party of Trudeau, made this even harder to understand, for the distinction between the two Liberal parties since 1964 was not really understood by voters with an average level of involvement in politics.

Even more significantly, anglophones had never imagined that this betrayal could happen when three English-speaking ministers, whose contiguous ridings together comprised the very heartland of English Montreal, sat in the government, supposedly to defend the interests of the English-speaking community. Three anglophone ministers from Montreal, all in charge of important departments, was an unusually large number, which made the betrayal even more inexplicable than it would have been otherwise. It was understandable, in the circumstances, that the anger and resentment should be focused on Drummond, Goldbloom and Tetley, whose efforts to defend anglophone interests were hidden from view by the conventions of cabinet secrecy. For voters who saw only the end product of public policy, and not the process, the proof of the pudding was in the eating: Drummond, Goldbloom and Tetley must have failed to do their jobs, either through incompetence or lack of commitment to the cause. Anglophone rights had been better protected under the Union Nationale, with only one token English-speaking minister from a rural county!

Turning against the three ministers was the initial and almost instinctive response, like shooting the messenger who brings bad news from the battlefront. But if Drummond, Goldbloom and Tetley were not to blame, a logical conclusion to be drawn from Bill 22 was that the whole political strategy followed by Quebec anglophones since Confederation needed to be re-examined. The conditions for consociational democracy no longer existed. As a consequence, elite accommodation within the governing party had not worked, or at least it had not worked well enough. Perhaps it was time to try something else. The anglophone community seemed bereft of leadership, with its political spokesmen discredited and the business elite, with its increasing number of upwardly mobile francophones, no longer as disposed to go to bat on behalf of anglophone interests as in the past. The anglophone media and the school boards and teachers' organizations attempted to fill the vacuum, although they had little experience of community leadership and lacked credibility among francophones. It was far from clear what alternatives, if any, existed for English-speaking Quebeckers, but Bill 22 at least created a situation in which the need for alternatives could be perceived and the search for them could begin.

AN EVOLVING ANGLOPHONE COMMUNITY

While politics, and particularly language legislation, occupied the centre of the stage, economic and social changes continued to alter the nature and circumstances of the English-speaking population in Quebec between 1968 and 1976. Francophones were slowly and belatedly gaining entrance to the economic elite, and what remained of the anglophone business elite seemed less and less willing or able to play the role of community leadership that it had played in the past. The entry of the United Kingdom into the European Community in 1972, its consequent replacement by Japan as Canada's second ranking trading partner, and the energy crisis that began with the Yom Kippur War in October 1973 further undermined Montreal's position as an economic centre, and the role of anglophones within it. Vancouver and Calgary, rather than Montreal, were becoming the serious counterweights to Toronto as rising energy prices and the new interest in the Pacific Rim caused capital and population to move west. The census of June 1976 revealed that the Toronto metropolitan area, as defined by Statistics Canada, had finally overtaken that of Montreal in the size of its population.

Closer to home, immigrants were still coming to Montreal. Anglophones hoped, and francophones feared, that they would provide reinforcements to the anglophone community and clients for its institutions, as the Irish and the Jews had done in earlier times, but Bill 22 demonstrated that this possibility was subject to political manipulation. Meanwhile, the population in the older English-speaking neighbourhoods and suburbs was aging, and in some cases declining, as younger anglophones moved to more distant suburbs or even to other provinces. Francophones in Montreal were also migrating from the city to the suburbs, a fact that helps to explain why the two language groups could simultaneously feel threatened by one another. The total population of Montreal Island, including all language groups, reached its peak of just under two million at the 1971 census. Five years later, but still before the election of the Parti Québécois, it had declined by 90,000.

In his content analysis of the letters to the editor of *The Montreal Star*, Kenneth Price discovered that pessimism and resignation increased between 1970 and 1974, and that "separatism, the economy and the future of the English ... melded into a single issue."[101] The exodus of anglophones from the province, already apparent in the early 1970s, was a particular concern. After 1974, of course, letters also showed a revival of interest in the issue of the language of instruction as it pertained to immigrants, an issue that had been dormant since 1968.[102]

The increasing strength and apparent radicalism of Quebec nationalism after 1968 was disturbing to most anglophones, and ended the naive hopes of the early 1960s that the two solitudes could come together once the legacy of Duplessism had been overcome. Nonetheless, some anglophones continued their efforts to understand what was happening in Quebec. Leslie Laczko's study of anglophone attitudes towards Quebec nationalism, based on field research conducted in 1971, found that some Quebec anglophones were at least moderately sympathetic to the aspirations of their French-speaking compatriots. Anglophones ranking high in education and status seemed most sympathetic. Those with a low level of contact with francophones at work lacked understanding of francophone aspirations, while those with a high level of contact were usually those whose jobs were potentially at risk. The lower middle class (clerical and sales) were most threatened by francophone competition for jobs and therefore were less sympathetic. Blue-collar anglophones perceived francophones as already equal to them in status, so tended to interpret nationalism as an unjustified demand for special privileges rather than a legitimate quest for equality. Young anglophones who had come of age after 1960 were more sympathetic than their elders. Social contact with francophones, as opposed to contact at work, had a clear and positive correlation with sympathetic attitudes.[103]

Sheila Arnopoulos studied a small sample of anglophones who, unlike most others in their community, participated fully in the institutional and social life of French-speaking Quebec. In the conventional manner of sociological studies she disguises her subjects with pseudonyms, but three of them, referred to in the thesis as "Charles," "John," and "Irving," are easily recognizable as David Payne, subsequently a Parti Québécois member of the National Assembly, John Gardiner, a Montreal city councillor at the time, and Herbert Marx, who later succeeded Victor Goldbloom as the Liberal member for D'Arcy-McGee.[104] She concluded that the integration of such persons into the francophone community was a response to the shift of social power towards the francophones but that most Quebec anglophones could not make the transition away from their traditional majority-group psychology in less than one generation. The few who could do so, in her view, were marginal to the English-speaking group.[105] Either they had left-wing sympathies, working class, Irish-Catholic or immigrant backgrounds, or else they were mavericks with no strong attachment to any cultural group.

Some anglophones moved closer to the francophone milieu because of social activism. The trendy Marxism of a small minority in the late 1960s began to subside among Quebec anglophones soon after the October Crisis, although among francophones it lasted a few years longer. However, a number of young anglophones in the early 1970s were involved in struggles over tenants' rights and other issues that brought them into contact with francophones of similar inclinations, as well as the less-advantaged members of their own community. Unlike more privileged anglophones, those who benefitted from such activities tended to live in neighbourhoods where there were also many francophones and allophones, such as Verdun, parts of Ville Lasalle and Lachine, Park Extension, or the southern fringe of NDG along the railway tracks. Yet the barriers did not entirely come down even here.

Two large anti-poverty organizations emerged in Montreal in the early 1970s: a francophone body called L'association pour la défense des droits des assistés sociaux (ADDS) and its anglophone counterpart, the Greater Montreal Anti-Poverty Co-ordinating Committee (GMAPCC). Vaughan Dowie, who was active in the GMAPCC, later recalled that there was a difference in mentality between the activists of the two organizations. The francophones tended to be more ideological, in the style of European Marxism, while the anglophones inclined more to an American-style populism with little in the way of coherent ideology.[106] Nonetheless, there was some scope for collaboration between them.

Another area of potential collaboration was municipal politics, where the divisive issues of language and federalism were less significant than at the provincial or federal levels. In 1970 an effort by francophone radicals to overturn the elitist right-wing regime of Mayor Jean Drapeau was frustrated and largely discredited by the eruption of the October Crisis during the municipal election campaign. Drapeau's forces won every seat on city council. In May 1974, six months before the next municipal election, a new left-wing opposition emerged, which this time included a substantial number of anglophones. It was known as the Montreal Citizens' Movement (MCM). The chances of unseating Drapeau were slim at best, but the party hoped at least to provide some serious opposition to Drapeau's followers on City Council.

Robert Keaton, a CEGEP teacher and part-time graduate student at McGill who played a large role in organizing the MCM, had spent much of his life in the United States. His wife, a francophone, had run for the Parti Québécois against Harry Blank in 1970. Keaton himself was active in the NDP and had run for that party in the federal election of 1972. He later attributed the emergence of MCM to a decision by the NDP throughout Canada to become more involved in municipal politics: "... I was delegated to get things rolling in Montreal to get some democracy against Jean Drapeau. So I helped put together the Montreal Citizens' Movement and ended up by default being a candidate, which I really did not want to do because I was behind on my thesis that I was working on under Charles Taylor. But I ended up getting elected and really I had mixed emotions about that. Eventually I ended up abandoning my thesis and getting all involved in politics."[107]

The most prominent English-speaking member of the MCM was Nick auf der Maur. Born in Montreal of Swiss immigrant parents, he had joined the Mouvement Souveraineté-Association in 1967 but eventually became disillusioned with Quebec nationalism. Subsequently he founded an entertaining populist magazine, *The Last Post*, which lasted for several years. He had also been arrested during the October Crisis, apparently in retaliation for a practical joke directed against *The Gazette* which the police did not find amusing.[108]

As their candidate for mayor the MCM recruited Jacques Couture, a worker-priest who was later minister of labour in René Lévesque's government. On 10 November 1974, election day, Couture won more than 40 per cent of the vote. Somewhat ironically, his best results were in middle-class neighbourhoods with significant numbers of anglophones. The MCM won seventeen seats on city council, almost one-third of the total. They took all three seats in NDG and all three in Côte-des-Neiges, where auf der Maur defeated the mayor's anglophone lieutenant, former Union Nationale candidate and future senator John Lynch-Staunton. Five of the victorious MCM candidates were anglophones: Keaton, auf der Maur, Arnold Bennett, Michael Fainstat, and John Gardiner.[109]

The MCM however proved to be an unstable coalition between moderate reformers and left-wing radicals. Both Keaton and auf der Maur were in the former category but most of the party's elected representatives were in the latter. Auf der Maur seemed to get along better on a personal level with Mayor Drapeau than he did with most members of his own party.[110] As might be expected the reformers in the MCM tended to be federalists and the radicals to support an independent Quebec. In 1976 Keaton and auf der Maur were expelled from the MCM and formed their own party, the Municipal Action Group. At the next election the two anti-Drapeau parties elected only one candidate each: Nick auf der Maur in Côte-des-Neiges and Michael Fainstat in NDG.[111]

Despite the failure of the MCM, municipal politics remained a field where anglophones and francophones could cooperate more easily than at higher levels of government. This was so because the polarization at the municipal level was more based on economic and class issues than on attitudes towards language policy and federalism. There were some English-speaking radicals, like Fainstat, and there were many French-speaking conservatives, as the continuing popularity of Drapeau clearly demonstrated.

At the provincial level, however, the issues of language and, to a lesser extent, sovereignty, brought about a polarization that was largely along ethnic lines. Practically all francophones, left, right and centre, were convinced of the need for legislation to restrict the use of English and promote the use of French, even though many believed that Bill 22 did not go far enough in this regard. After the release of the Gendron report in 1973 this consensus on language, and the willingness of the right-of-centre Bourassa government to cater to it, contributed to a noticeable lessening of the class conflicts among francophones that had been so apparent in the preceding five years. Labour militancy decreased noticeably, although more in the private than in the public sector, the terrorist FLQ ceased to exist, and there were very few mass meetings, marches or public demonstrations of dissent from 1973 onwards. The Parti Québécois, which had been dominated by its left wing in the early 1970s, moved noticeably to the right even before it took office in 1976. Linguistic solidarity took precedence over class or ideology, just as it had in the heyday of Duplessis.

For anglophones and allophones also, linguistic solidarity took precedence over class or ideology, beginning even earlier with the crisis in St-Léonard. Anxieties over language and over the possibility of secession from Canada reinforced one another. This was shown by the collapse of the provincial NDP in 1968 when it appeared more sympathetic to Quebec nationalism than the Liberals, and by the total futility of the party's efforts in the election of 1970. It was also shown by the continuing refusal of all but a handful of non-francophones to consider voting for the Parti Québécois, although many would privately confess that they admired its leader and some of its policies. In effect the politicization of language strengthened conservative political forces on both sides of the language barrier.

FROM THE FRYING PAN INTO THE FIRE: THE ELECTION OF 1976

The aftermath of Bill 22 left anglophones and allophones in Quebec angry, fearful, and uncertain of what political strategy would best serve their interests. Their traditional support for the Quebec Liberal Party had ended, at least temporarily. Yet Quebec's other major party, the Parti Québécois, promised language legislation even more damaging to their identity and their interests than Bill 22 had been, as well as a commitment to promote the cause of an independent Quebec. A vote for that party, while it might punish the Liberals for Bill 22 by removing them from office, thus involved risks that very few non-francophones were willing to accept.

An alternative emerged in the unexpected shape of the Union Nationale, which had apparently been eliminated as a serious force in Quebec politics after the election of 1973. In May 1976 the party elected as its leader a young businessman from the county of Lotbinière, Rodrigue Biron, who had joined the Union Nationale only two months previously. Although his previous experience in politics was confined to the municipal level, Biron proved adept at exploiting a mixture of moderate conservatism, nationalism, and rural discontent with the Liberals, much as Daniel Johnson had done a decade earlier.

Among the three other candidates in the leadership race was an English-speaking dentist, Dr William Shaw, who for a time had headed the Progressive Conservative riding association in the federal constituency of Vaudreuil. He had also been the Union Nationale candidate in Robert-Baldwin in 1970, when he received less than 4 per cent of the vote. Like many other English-speaking conservatives in Quebec, Shaw both understood and regretted the stranglehold which the provincial Liberals held over the votes of the anglophone electorate in Montreal. Bill 22 seemed to anglophones to demonstrate the danger of entrusting their fortunes entirely to the Liberals, and at the same time to create the possibility that anglophones might finally be persuaded to vote for an alternative. A number of persons in the Montreal area persuaded him to run for the leadership of the Union Nationale not so much in the hope of winning as to establish some anglophone presence in the party and give it some credibility with anglophone voters.[112]

Shaw and his friends persuaded a number of anglophones to join the Union Nationale, with the result that Shaw had the support of more than a hundred delegates at the leadership convention. More importantly, the party seemed open to such ideas as a return to freedom of choice, along the lines of Bill 63, and official bilingualism for Quebec. Although Biron was probably the least sympathetic of the four leadership candidates to these ideas, efforts to incorporate them in the party's campaign for the forthcoming election continued after he assumed the leadership. Shaw was placed in charge of the campaign to win anglophone votes in the Montreal area, a campaign which made Bill 22 the major issue and emphasized that the Union Nationale was the party of "freedom of choice." The party's campaign in francophone Quebec, run by Biron, conveyed a completely different message with a strong dose of Quebec nationalism.

Shaw was nominated in Pointe-Claire riding where the popular Liberal incumbent, Art Seguin, had announced his decision not to run again soon after the adoption of Bill 22. In contrast to previous slates of Union Nationale candidates, that of 1976 was almost a rainbow coalition, with a Jewish candidate in D'Arcy-McGee, a Greek in Laurier, Italians in Anjou, Dorion, Mercier and Marguerite-Bourgeoys, and persons of British origin in most of the ridings farther west. Shaw tried to recruit Robert Beale, the former president of the Association of Parents of St-Léonard, in Robert-Baldwin, but was overruled by Biron, who imposed another candidate.[113]

A second vehicle for protest against Bill 22 emerged around Robert Keaton and Nick auf der Maur, who were then still affiliated with the Montreal Citizens' Movement. In 1975 a meeting was held at Charles Taylor's home to discuss political alternatives for progressive anglophones who could not accept the sovereignty proposal of the Parti Québécois and who feared the re-emergence of the right-wing Union Nationale as a vehicle of anglophone protest. Keaton recalls being invited by Michael Stein, a colleague of Taylor in the political science department at McGill who later moved to Ontario. Some of those present, including Taylor, favoured reviving the Quebec NDP, but others argued that the party had been taken over by Trotskyites and therefore would not be of much help to the cause.[114] Eventually Keaton and auf der Maur formed a new party called the Democratic Alliance which would seek the votes of moderately progressive federalists who disliked the Liberal government. It was this initiative that led to their expulsion from the MCM, whose constitution prohibited its municipal representatives from running in provincial elections.

The Democratic Alliance was soon approached by the Parti Québécois. Auf der Maur was friendly with Gérald Godin, who would later defeat Premier Bourassa in the latter's riding of Mercier, and Keaton knew Lévesque through his wife's involvement in the Parti Québécois. Godin and Lévesque hoped that the new party would take votes from the Liberals and enable the Parti Québécois to win a number of normally Liberal ridings in Montreal. According to auf der Maur's recollection, Godin even offered a financial contribution from the Parti Québécois to the Democratic Alliance if the new party would assist the Parti Québécois campaign in this way.[115] Neither auf der Maur nor Keaton wished to be responsible for electing a Parti Québécois government, despite their dislike for the Liberals. They eventually decided to run candidates only in ridings where the non-francophone vote was so large that the Parti Québécois would have no chance of winning. Those were also the ridings where resentment against Bill 22 was most significant and where the Union Nationale was hoping to make gains. Keaton decided to run in NDG and auf der Maur in Westmount, both ridings represented by ministers who were particularly unpopular because of Bill 22. Christos Sirros, a former teacher with the Lakeshore School Board who had just gone to work for a social service agency in Montreal, ran for the Alliance in Laurier, the riding which Lévesque had represented as a Liberal in the 1960s. Graham Weeks, another teacher, ran in Jacques-Cartier. In all there were thirteen candidates, ten of them in ridings that were less than 50 per cent francophone.[116]

The Liberals hesitated about when to call an election. Victor Goldbloom later recalled that the anger over Bill 22 in his riding seemed to subside during 1975, but the party was also losing support among francophones.[117] As early as April 1976 a poll showed it well behind the Parti Québécois in popular support, and the election of Biron as leader of the Union Nationale a month later promised to create additional difficulties.[118] Eventually the election was scheduled for 15 November 1976, apparently on the theory that the opposition parties would be even stronger if the Liberals waited until 1977.

Seeking a new anglophone lieutenant, and obviously not relishing the prospect of George Springate in that role, Premier Bourassa persuaded Bryce Mackasey, who had just resigned as postmaster-general, to give up his federal seat and run provincially in William Tetley's former riding of NDG. Victor Goldbloom decided to run again, although the anger and resentment against Bill 22 revived after the election was called, to the point where some of his advisers thought that the Union Nationale had a chance of winning the riding. In Robert-Baldwin and Pointe-Claire, where the incumbents were not running again, the Liberals found new English-speaking candidates in John O'Gallagher and Roy Amaron, despite the continuing opprobrium over Bill 22. O'Gallagher, who personally supported Bill 22 and did not think that it removed any rights from anglophones, later recalled that the election "certainly had every indication of being lost … I figured I'd be in the opposition."[119]

The defeat was worse than most people expected, for the Liberals won only 33.8 per cent of the vote, their worst showing since Confederation, and twenty-six seats. The Parti Québécois won 41.4 per cent of the vote and seventy-one seats; the Union Nationale won 18.2 per cent of the vote and eleven seats. Two minor parties, Social Credit and the Parti National Populaire, elected one member each.

Non-francophones predictably rejected the victorious Parti Québécois, which had managed to recruit only two English-speaking candidates, but the swing away from the Liberals among this sector of the electorate was even greater than among francophones. It was less noticeable only because the non-francophone vote for the Liberals had been so nearly unanimous in 1973 that even a massive swing left them with a plurality in 1976. For the first time in history the Union Nationale won a larger percentage of the vote in the western part of Montreal and the western suburbs than in the province as a whole. Their strongest support of all was in the three west island suburban ridings of Jacques-Cartier, Pointe-Claire and Robert-Baldwin, where they won a total of 35,274 votes or only 1771 fewer than the Liberals. William Shaw was elected in Pointe-Claire, the first member of his party to win a predominantly anglophone riding on Montreal Island in forty years. The Union Nationale lost by almost 4000 votes in Robert-Baldwin, which it could probably have won with Robert Beale as its candidate, but lost by only 1265 in Jacques-Cartier. It also did well in NDG, where its candidate won more than half as many votes as Bryce Mackasey. Surprisingly, the Union Nationale appeared to have stronger support among voters whose mother tongue was English than among those whose mother tongues were neither English nor French, despite the fact that it was the latter who were most seriously inconvenienced by Bill 22. Off the island Union Nationale candidates defeated Glen Brown in Brome-Missisquoi and Ken Fraser in Huntingdon.

The Democratic Alliance did not determine the outcome in any riding, having rejected the temptation to split the federalist vote for the benefit of the Parti Québécois. Its best showing was in Westmount, where auf der Maur came third with 4534 votes, almost one-sixth of the votes cast. Keaton won 3497 votes in NDG but was narrowly nudged into fourth place by the Parti Québécois candidate.

Unlike the Alliance, the Union Nationale probably threw a large number of ridings to the Parti Québécois. This may not have been displeasing to Rodrigue Biron, who eventually joined that party and became a minister in Lévesque's government. As a result of the split in the federalist vote, the Parti Québécois won even suburban ridings like Vaudreuil-Soulanges and Chateauguay and city ridings like Bourassa, Dorion, Jeanne-Mance, Ste-Anne and St-Henri, which had large non-francophone minorities. The Union Nationale vote in each of these ridings, apart from Dorion, exceeded the difference between the Parti Québécois vote and that of the second-place Liberal. The Liberals held Outremont only because neither the Union Nationale nor the Democratic Alliance ran a candidate there.

Bill 22 was only one of several reasons for the defeat of the Quebec Liberal Party in 1976, but it clearly ended the romance between that party and the non-francophone voters of Montreal which had lasted since the beginning of the Second World War, and it did so at a time when the party was weak and vulnerable for other reasons. Voters punished the Liberals for Bill 22 by shifting a large portion of their votes to the Union Nationale and a smaller portion to the Democratic Alliance. However, they had no reason to rejoice at the outcome. The election realized their worst fears by electing a government that was committed not only to introducing harsher language legislation than Bill 22 but to working for the sovereignty of Quebec; abandoning their traditional Liberal allegiance had helped to fling the non-francophones from the frying pan into the fire. Their search for an effective political strategy would have to continue in even less promising circumstances.

5 Post-consociational Politics: The Search for a New Strategy, 1976–85

The election of the Parti Québécois with a majority of seats in the National Assembly on 15 November 1976 was more significant than most changes of government. A sovereign Quebec, albeit one economically associated with the rest of Canada, was the objective and *raison d'être* of the Parti Québécois. Although the Parti Québécois campaign in 1976 had emphasized the need for better government more than the promise of sovereignty, their victory clearly placed sovereignty on the agenda.

For the English-speaking minority in the province, the outcome of the election was unprecedented in another way. For the first time in Quebec's history, there was no possibility of an anglophone representative being included in the cabinet. Not one of the successful Parti Québécois candidates had a mother tongue other than French, although a few – Robert Burns, Pierre-Marc Johnson, and Louis O'Neill – had surnames indicative of their mixed ancestry. No predominantly English-speaking riding had elected a Parti Québécois candidate. There was no longer a Legislative Council from which non-elected persons could be recruited as ministers. Moreover, the new government gave no indication that it regretted its absence of anglophone representation or was seriously inconvenienced by it, which suggested what the events of the next few years would confirm: Quebec could be governed effectively without any anglophone participation whatsoever. The English-speaking minority was no longer significant enough, demographically or even economically, to necessitate accommodating its interests within the government. In effect, 15 November

1976 marked the end of consociational democracy in Quebec and the beginning of majoritarian democracy. This was a situation for which the English-speaking minority was completely unprepared, and in these unpromising circumstances they would have to deal with at least two major challenges in the new government's first term: new and more restrictive language legislation to replace Bill 22, and the promised referendum on sovereignty-association.

Admittedly, Bill 22 had demonstrated that representation in the government was not necessarily an effective shield against policies detrimental to the interests of English-speaking Quebeckers. Both the disillusionment with the Quebec Liberal Party that followed Bill 22 and the devastating defeat suffered by that party encouraged the search for alternative means of political expression. Even if the Liberal Party became more sympathetic to anglophone interests or eventually revived, it seemed unlikely that it would do either in time to be of any help to English-speaking Quebeckers in the crisis that confronted them. The Democratic Alliance, although it lingered on for a few months, had failed to make a significant impact. The Union Nationale, although it had received an impressive number of anglophone votes, had elected only one anglophone member to the National Assembly. Thus political parties did not offer a particularly promising vehicle for the expression of anglophone interests; other ways would have to be found outside the party system.

MOBILIZING THE COMMUNITY

A number of organizations, two of which proved to be of particular significance, soon emerged to articulate the interests and concerns of English-speaking Quebeckers. While this may seem inevitable in retrospect, it was not so viewed at the time – and with good reason. Although Bill 22 had been a learning experience, English-speaking people in Quebec were not accustomed in 1976 to thinking of themselves as a minority, or as a collectivity of any kind. Second, they had little experience with democratic mobilization and participation at the provincial level, although their experience at the federal and municipal levels could be put to some use.

At least until 1968, probably until 1974, and possibly until 1976, most people in Quebec whose mother tongue or adopted language was English took the language for granted, like the air they breathed. As long as this was so, the language could not serve as a focus of collective identification for them in the way that the French language did for francophones. No sense of a collectivity called English-speaking Quebec really existed. Collective identities were either broader (e.g.

"Canadian") or narrower, being demarcated by religion, ethnicity, or place of residence. The importance of religion (Protestant, Catholic or Jewish) in the provision of education and social services was an enduring aspect of Quebec life that had largely survived the Quiet Revolution. Ethnic identities, even among long-established communities like the Irish, were probably more significant in Quebec, or at least in Montreal, than elsewhere in Canada.

Geography was also an important source of division. The contrast between anglophone Montrealers, who could still live their lives in English even after Bill 22, and the rural minorities, living in regions where French had been the dominant language for generations, resembled the contrast between francophones in Quebec and francophone minorities in the other provinces. Although many English-speaking Montrealers had come from outlying parts of the province, and some had relatives there, most had little contact with, and less understanding of, the scattered English-speaking minorities in the Eastern Townships, the Ottawa Valley, and more remote regions. The non-metropolitan minorities, although their circumstances and problems were similar, had even less contact with one another and tended to view themselves as distinct regional enclaves. In fact they interacted less with English-speaking Quebeckers in other regions than with neighbours outside the province whose media, schools, hospitals, shopping centres and other institutions they sometimes patronized. Anglophones in the Eastern Townships looked to Vermont, those in the Ottawa Valley to Ontario, those in the Gaspésie to New Brunswick, and those on the North Shore to Newfoundland, more than they looked to Montreal, let alone to one another.

In addition to the lack of cohesion, there was the lack of democratic experience, at the provincial level at least. Anglophone political spokesmen had traditionally emerged from the elites of business and the professions, or had been recruited by the francophone leaders of political parties. They rarely, if ever, owed their prominence to a mobilization of the grassroots even in their own ridings, let alone in the English-speaking community as a whole. In the early 1960s, no one considered it anomalous that George Marler, the most influential anglophone in the government, was a member of the appointed Legislative Council rather than the Legislative Assembly. Even elected ministers were often parachuted into ridings with which they had little or no previous connection, nominated without a contest, and elected with only token opposition from the other parties. Yet for as long as these spokesmen seemed to be effective in delivering benefits and protecting English-speaking Quebeckers against the possible dangers of Quebec nationalism, there was a tendency to leave matters in their hands and not to question their authority or legitimacy. As was explained in chapter 1, theorists of consociational elite accommodation argue that it works best when elites enjoy unquestioned authority and when democratic participation at the grassroots is minimized. In Quebec it seemed to work well for most of the time until 1974, so there was no incentive to alter these conditions. Indeed, grassroots participation in any other than the handful of homogeneous ridings would have required a proficiency in French that most anglophones simply did not have.

As 1976 drew to a close, English-speaking Quebeckers could no longer pretend that the old ways would still work. As Peter Leslie argued in an essay published soon afterwards: "The mercantile-industrial elite which has been the pinnacle of this community is in eclipse. It is caught between the self-assertion of the Québécois and the pre-eminence of Toronto."[1] The business community neither could nor would offer effective leadership, the anglophone political elite had been discredited by their failure to prevent the adoption of Bill 22, and the very concept of consociational elite accommodation had been rendered irrelevant by the election of an almost exclusively francophone party as Quebec's new government.

The first response to these new circumstances came from a small group of young professionals, mainly Jewish, who met to discuss the situation on the evening of 17 November 1976, only two days after the election. The meeting was hosted by a young lawyer, Michael Prupas, and those in attendance included two other young lawyers: Eric Maldoff, who had been formally admitted to the Quebec bar the previous day, and Michael Goldbloom, the son of Victor Goldbloom. Some of those present had voted for the Liberal Party in the recent election, while others had supported the Democratic Alliance. All were bilingual, federalist, and committed to spending their lives in Quebec. Viewed from their perspective, recent events had demonstrated that English-speaking Quebeckers were dangerously isolated from the French-speaking majority and from the social, economic and political trends that were reshaping the province. Both the politicization of language and the rise of the sovereignty movement were regarded by most English-speaking Quebeckers as incomprehensible and bizarre. The election of the Parti Québécois had taken most anglophones by surprise, although polls published in the French-language media months before had given ample evidence of its rising popularity. At the same time francophones retained a stereotyped image of the English-speaking minority as isolated, arrogant, privileged and unilingual – impressions that had some basis in fact but were not universally applicable.

Those at the meeting decided that their group, which they named Participation Québec, would promote dialogue between anglophones and francophones, including francophones sympathetic to the Parti Québécois, in an effort to break down stereotypes on both sides. It would seek to demonstrate that the preservation of a viable English-speaking community in Quebec required neither isolation from the francophone majority nor the reversal of the changes in Quebec society and politics that had taken place since 1960. It would be a rallying point for anglophones who were proud to live in Quebec, sympathetic to the aspirations of the francophones, but determined to maintain an environment in which the minority and its institutions could flourish. As its name suggested, it would encourage anglophones to participate fully in Quebec society while maintaining their own institutions and language. It would also seek to persuade the Parti Québécois government that its interests and those of the anglophone minority were not totally incompatible. In particular, it wished to remind the government, and francophones generally, that the old stereotype of anglophones as a privileged caste living in their Westmount castles no longer bore any resemblance to reality. As Eric Maldoff recollected: "We were all more or less bilingual and all young and we weren't carrying the baggage of ten generations of colonial oppressors. We came from a variety of backgrounds. We thought we represented the new English-speaking Quebec generation. We thought there was an opportunity for us to open up lines of communication that didn't exist for the established leadership."[2]

Participation Québec never became, or sought to become, a mass organization which recruited large numbers of members. In fact it never had more than fifty to a hundred members, and, despite the manifesto outlined above, it was never clear exactly who, or what, it represented. Nonetheless, it was the real precursor of Alliance Quebec, which was not formed until five years later and which eventually became the principal organization representing English-speaking Quebeckers. The prominence of Participation in the early days reflected the talents of its few members, a point of view that was subtle enough, or ambiguous enough, to be recognized as legitimate by both the federal and provincial governments, and the eclipse of the anglophone community's traditional leadership.

Not long after the formation of Participation Québec another anglophone group emerged in Montreal with somewhat similar objectives. Like Participation, the second group grew out of an informal meeting of anglophones to discuss the implications of the Parti Québécois victory. In this case the meeting was a luncheon at the Faculty Club of McGill University and its initiator was a professor in the Department of Philosophy, Storrs McCall.[3] Several of the persons invited to this luncheon, and to a second one in late December, were professors at McGill, including Charles Taylor of the Department of Political Science and Sheila Goldbloom – wife of Victor Goldbloom – of the School of Social Work. Others were alumni of the university but not affiliated with it. They included Alex Paterson, a lawyer who had assisted the Bourassa government in negotiations with the public sector unions, and Reford McDougall, an investment broker with a talent for fundraising.

Not surprisingly, given the location and participants of the first two meetings, the future of McGill was a major topic of discussion. A considerable number of professors were known to be exploring the possibilities of employment outside of Quebec. The anglophone exodus which seemed to be gaining force had broader implications for the English-speaking community as a whole, and not just for the university. If the best and the brightest left, either because they feared the impending language legislation of the Parti Québécois or because they expected the cause of sovereignty to triumph in the referendum, the community would lose much of its vitality and its will to resist unwelcome changes. Also, if enough federalist voters left to tip the balance, the anticipation of federalist defeat in the referendum might become a self-fulfilling prophecy. Persuading anglophones and other federalists to stay in Quebec thus became a major preoccupation of the new group, and perhaps the most conspicuous of its activities. A second major objective, which assumed greater importance after the first year or so, was to prepare for the referendum with the aim of maximizing the federalist vote. To a large extent, of course, the two objectives were interdependent.

The minutes of the second meeting record the observation (not attributed to any specific person) that "the academic community could provide the intellectual framework" to "articulate the aspirations of anglophones in Quebec." While no one seems to have disagreed, some participants emphasized that organization, mobilization, and fundraising were at least equally important. Alex Paterson suggested that the leaders of the anglophone community be identified and contacted to enlist their support. This was done with considerable success: by 30 April 1977 the group was able to publish a full-page newspaper advertisement signed by 115 prominent members of Montreal's anglophone community. Probably more readers scanned the list of signatories to look for familiar names than read the entire advertisement, which was a detailed critique of the Lévesque government's White Paper on language policy.

The young organization was initially known as "the group" or even "the McCall group" but after a few months a sub-committee was appointed to devise a more appropriate name. The name chosen was Positive Action, which had the merit of being similar in French. However, it came to be more widely known as the Positive Action Committee, or PAC. At about the same time as it chose its name, the organization selected Storrs McCall and Alex Paterson as co-chairmen.[4] As Paterson later described their respective roles, he was the communications and public relations person, while McCall was the major source of ideas.[5] By the fall of 1977, Positive Action had a full-time executive director and an office on Park Avenue, a few blocks east of the McGill campus. It was funded by voluntary donations from its members. The organization continued to publish newspaper advertisements, most devoted to the theme that English-speaking Quebeckers should stay in Quebec and work for the survival of their community, rather than taking the easy option of moving to another province.

An initial effort to include federalist francophones in Positive Action was quickly abandoned since very few were willing to be publicly associated with what was perceived as an organization fighting to preserve the anglophone community. In the pre-referendum period francophone federalists found other outlets for their energies, including the various federal and provincial political parties, the Association Québec-Canada, founded by Liberal MNA Michel Gratton, and the well-funded Council of Canadian Unity, which eventually spread to all ten provinces.

Positive Action however did not lack support, and the list of persons who signed its newspaper advertisement published on 30 April 1977 comprised some of the most influential English-speaking people in Quebec at that time. They included the principals of all three English-language universities, Bishop's, Concordia and McGill, the heads of both the Protestant and anglophone Catholic teachers' unions, assorted chairs and past chairs of school boards and federations of school boards, past and present municipal politicians John Lynch-Staunton and Robert Keaton, the mayor of Westmount D.C. McCallum, former member of parliament Egan Chambers and his wife Gretta (a future chancellor of McGill), political philosopher Charles Taylor, who was Gretta Chambers' brother, and an impressive number of lawyers, business executives, and investment brokers. Also on the list were two future members of the National Assembly, Joan Dougherty and Maximilien Polak, who would be elected as Liberals in 1981. Both had lengthy service as members of school boards. Peter Blaikie, a lawyer active in the Progressive Conservative Party, was another signatory who would subsequently play a prominent role in the politics of anglophone Quebec. However, he soon dropped out of Positive Action, considering that its approach lacked political realism.[6]

Participation Québec and Positive Action were not fundamentally different in their objectives or beliefs, but there were differences in emphasis and style that seemed to make them complementary rather than competitive. Participation's members were much younger and less prominent than those who launched Positive Action, and had fewer ties to the community's institutions. They also did not attempt to recruit a mass membership, while Positive Action claimed in June 1977 to have a membership list of thirty thousand persons.[7] Positive Action was much more overtly federalist and became increasingly preoccupied with the referendum; Participation concentrated more on internal issues than on Quebec's relations with Canada, largely because some of its members feared that an overtly federalist stance would be viewed as partisan and would prevent any dialogue with the Parti Québécois government. Participation had a relatively larger Jewish component while Positive Action, if the names of the signatories to its advertisement is any indication, had a remarkable preponderance of English, Scottish and Irish members. Neither organization had much support among first-generation immigrants or among the rural and small-town population outside of metropolitan Montreal.

Other organizations also appeared, although some were of brief duration. A social worker named Carol Zimmerman launched a group known as Quebec For All, but it was quickly branded as too extreme in its views and failed to make much of an impact. Probably it failed because its portion of the political spectrum was more effectively occupied by the Freedom of Choice movement, which included some anglophone Union Nationale supporters like William Shaw as well as the remnants of the short-lived Conservative Party which had challenged the provincial Liberals in the election of 1966. Unlike Participation Québec and Positive Action, these groups favoured a more confrontational style and were openly hostile to Quebec nationalism. They insisted that anglophones should not be expected to adapt to the recent changes in Quebec and that any effort to make them do so would be disastrous for the economy.

At the other extreme were a small number of anglophones who felt some affinity for the Parti Québécois, either because of its social democratic program or because they believed that anglophones had enjoyed too many privileges in the past. Some also believed that the Parti Québécois goal of "sovereignty-association" could be the starting point for a reorganization of Canada into a bi-national state. They formed a group known as the Anglophone Committee for a United

Quebec soon after the 1976 election. Gary Caldwell, a sociologist at Bishop's University, and Henry Milner, a political scientist at Vanier College, were among the more prominent members. The group claimed to have 110 declared members in June 1977, as well as a number of secret sympathizers who were not prepared to reveal their support.[8]

Somewhat later on, regional anglophone organizations began to emerge in the rural hinterlands. The earliest and largest of these was the Townshippers' Association, founded in 1979. Although based in Sherbrooke, it recruited members throughout the region by holding meetings in a variety of locations. Perhaps because townshippers had long since been resigned to their minority status, it tended to be less insistent on anglophone "rights" and more conciliatory towards the Quebec government than most of its counterparts. Other regional organizations appeared over the next two years in the Ottawa Valley, the Chateauguay Valley, Quebec City, the Gaspésie, and the North Shore. Most were similar to Participation Québec and Positive Action in their generally non-confrontational approach, but the Chateauguay Valley English-Speaking People's Association, based in Huntingdon County, was marked from the outset by a more abrasive and somewhat francophobic style reminiscent of Robert Sellar and his *Huntingdon Gleaner* almost a century earlier.

An important stimulus to this organizational activity was the announcement by Secretary of State John Roberts, who visited Montreal in the fall of 1977, that funding would be made available to Quebec anglophone groups under his department's program for the support of official language minorities. Francophone organizations in the other provinces had already been in receipt of such funding for several years. It will be recalled that a previous secretary of state, Gérard Pelletier, had been informed by Quebec anglophones in 1968 that they neither needed nor wanted any help from the federal government. By 1977 their views in this regard had changed rather drastically, and the offer was much more warmly received. Participation Québec received some federal funds, as did a variety of regional and ethnic organizations which already existed or were formed over the next few years. Storrs McCall, however, was opposed to federal funding since he believed this would reduce Positive Action's independence.[9]

The offer from the secretary of state contributed to the formation of an umbrella organization, the Council of Quebec Minorities, in November 1978. There was some concern that both Positive Action and Participation Québec were failing to attract immigrants and allophones, whose support would obviously be needed and whose numbers were increasing while the number of Quebec-born anglophones still living in the province was declining. The Council was intended to be more inclusive, incorporating the already existing organizations of various ethnic groups, and to accept federal funds, which Positive Action would not because of McCall's objections. The Council also provided an outlet for the energies of Eric Maldoff, who disagreed with Participation Québec's refusal to become involved in the forth-coming referendum campaign. Maldoff had been in charge of exter-nal relations at Participation Québec and had thus made contact with the ethnic organizations of which the Council would be largely com-prised. He became chairman of the Council of Quebec Minorities.

The Council used part of its federal funding to hire an executive director and a research assistant, but according to Maldoff's recollec-tion it was "incredibly weak" and leading it was "a horrible and frus-trating experience."[10] It had little influence and no control over the many organizations of which it was comprised. The ethnic organiza-tions that had their own sources of funds guarded their independence against any direction from the Council. So did Participation Québec and Positive Action, which also adhered to the Council, and so did the regional organizations which joined the Council from 1979 onwards. Freedom of Choice regarded the Council's approach as excessively moderate and conciliatory and refused to join. The Council itself had no individual members, being merely a loose federation of organizations and groups or, as Prime Minister Joe Clark might have put it, a community of communities. It was not able to participate effectively in the political debates over language policy, the referen-dum, and other matters. Its main achievement was to compile a data base about the anglophone community in Quebec, its institutions and resources.[11]

ANGLOPHONES AND THE CHARTER OF
THE FRENCH LANGUAGE

The organizational development described in the preceding pages was still in a very early stage when English-speaking Quebeckers were confronted with the necessity of reacting to the new government's initiatives in the field of language policy. The Parti Québécois, which had opposed Bill 22 on the grounds that it did not adequately protect the French language, had promised a new language law as its first priority, and it wasted no time in carrying out its promise. A White Paper on language policy was presented to the National Assembly on 1 April 1977. Less than four weeks later, and before there was much time for public discussion of the White Paper, the government intro-duced Bill 1, the Charter of the French Language. Neither Participation

Québec nor Positive Action, nor the anglophone community as a whole, was yet in a position to rally opposition to the bill or even to provide an informed critique of its provisions. The Quebec Liberal Party was still recovering from its crushing defeat in the recent election. For the second time in four years the National Assembly sat through much of the summer to consider a language bill. By 26 August the legislative battle was over and the government had a Charter of the French Language that differed only slightly from their original proposals.[12] For better or for worse, it would be their most lasting and important achievement, despite subsequent challenges to some of its provisions in the courts. The episode revealed that the anglophone community was no better organized or better prepared to defend its interests than it had been at the time when Bill 22 was introduced in 1974.

Bill 1 and its slightly modified successor, Bill 101, reproduced several provisions of Bill 22 but differed from the Liberal government's language legislation in a number of ways. Section 9 of the Charter provided that only the French text of statutes would be considered official. Section 13 made a similar provision regarding the judgments of the courts. Section 11 provided that litigation involving "moral persons" such as corporations, rather than natural persons, must be in French unless all parties agreed to conduct it in English. Sections 43 and 44 stated that collective agreements and arbitration awards in labour disputes must be in French. Section 45 provided that no employee could be dismissed, suspended or demoted for inability to speak a language other than French. Section 53 stated that business firms must publish their catalogues, brochures and flyers in French. Section 55 provided that business contracts "could," rather than "must" as in Bill 22, be in English if the customer so requested. Section 58 required that commercial signs must be in French only, although other sections allowed for exceptions in certain circumstances. Section 136 required that all firms with fifty or more employees, and not just those doing business with the government, must acquire a certificate of francization.

The rules regarding access to English-language education were far more restrictive than those in Bill 22, although the controversial provision for the testing of allophone children was eliminated. In fact there was no need for it since all immigrants, including those from English-speaking countries, were denied the right to educate their children in English. Migrants from other provinces of Canada were also denied this right – a victory for the hardliners in the cabinet which Premier Lévesque personally opposed. The only concession to the premier's more liberal point of view was Section 86, which would allow the restrictions to be relaxed for migrants from provinces that guaranteed French-language education to the children of francophones from Quebec. Section 73 allowed only four categories of children to receive an English education: those whose father or mother had attended an English school in Quebec, those whose father or mother had attended an English school in another province and were already living in Quebec when the bill was adopted by the National Assembly, those who were legally enrolled in an English school in Quebec before the bill was adopted, and the younger siblings of those who qualified under the third criterion.

The Régie de la langue française established by Bill 22 was replaced by a variety of new bodies. Section 100 established an Office de la langue française, primarily to make regulations. Section 122 established a Commission de toponymie to invent French replacements for English place names. Section 158 provided for a Commission de surveillance to investigate possible infractions of the law. Section 186 provided for a Conseil de la langue française to advise the minister and the government.

Bill 1 had differed from the final version of the Charter of the French Language in only two significant respects: its preamble implied that only those of French mother tongue were true Quebeckers and it contained a notwithstanding clause allowing the application of the language law to override Quebec's Charter of Human Rights and Freedoms. Bill 101, which lacked these two features but was otherwise virtually identical with its predecessor, was substituted for the original document on 12 July. The minister principally responsible for both versions, Dr Camille Laurin, justified the need for stringent legislation by an assertion which he borrowed, without attribution, from a nineteenth-century French historian and reactionary politician, the comte de Montalembert: "Between the strong and the weak it is liberty that oppresses and intervention that liberates."[13] Ironically, Montalembert was an Englishman who abandoned his original language and nationality to become a spokesman for ultramontane Catholicism in France.

A large number of anglophone groups and organizations appeared before the legislative committee that examined Bill 1 in June and July of 1977. Apart from the Anglophone Committee for a Unified Quebec, all were critical of the proposed legislation. On the other hand most of the significant groups, including Positive Action, Participation Québec, the Canadian Jewish Congress, and the Protestant School Board of Greater Montreal, claimed to support the bill's objective of promoting the French language, at least in theory.

The Protestant School Board of Greater Montreal was predictably critical of the restrictive rules for access to English education, and claimed that 56 per cent of its existing students would be "illegal" under the terms of the proposed law. This was somewhat misleading since the bill allowed those children legally enrolled in English schools at the time of its adoption to remain there. The Protestant board also complained of the provisions requiring predominantly anglophone school boards to write their internal and external communications in French.[14]

The brief by Positive Action was one of the longest, most detailed, and most critical. It argued that in principle parents, rather than the state, should select the language of instruction for their children but admitted that some departure from this principle might be justified if the French language was in danger. However, it recommended that all English-speaking immigrants, and all allophones who were already resident in Quebec as of 1977, should be allowed to send their children to English schools. Positive Action also criticized the prohibition of English on commercial signs and the excessive powers which the legislation would give to appointed officials. In addition, it argued that the provisions for "francization" of enterprises should be relaxed for the head offices of Canada-wide enterprises to avoid the danger that these offices would relocate to other provinces.[15]

The brief by Participation Québec appeared slightly more sympathetic to the bill. On the issue of access to English education it differed slightly from Positive Action by arguing that all immigrants who arrived after the bill came into effect, including anglophones as well as allophones, should be required to send their children to French schools. However, migrants from other provinces would still be allowed to send their children to English schools – a proposal that came to be known as the "Canada clause" and that was eventually incorporated in the Canadian Charter of Rights and Freedoms. Participation Québec used one of Dr Laurin's favourite words to denounce the provision prohibiting commercial signs in English, arguing that no "normal" society imposed such a restriction. It also called for measures to increase the number of non-francophones in the Quebec public service.[16]

The brief by the Canadian Jewish Congress, one of the last to be presented, repeated many of the same criticisms regarding access to schools, prohibition of English on commercial signs, and the requirement that anglophone school boards and municipalities communicate in French. It also opposed the abolition of official bilingualism in legislation and the judicial system. The Congress was particularly critical of the exclusive way in which the preamble defined the term "Québécois" and of the provision allowing the government to override Quebec's Charter of Human Rights and Freedoms.[17] Both of these provisions were eliminated soon afterwards, when Bill 101 was substituted for Bill 1.

In the plenary debate opposition members repeated many of the same criticisms. The Liberals presented amendments that would have allowed all anglophones, and all allophones who were already residents of Quebec in 1977, to send their children to English schools. Another amendment suggested that the bill be delayed for three months. William Shaw suggested a law that would guarantee anglophones the right to receive health care and social services in English.[18] Bryce Mackasey and Harry Blank accused the government of wanting to drive anglophones out of the province, and predicted that the bill would have that effect.[19] John Ciaccia said that while he understood the resentment of francophones at their lack of economic power, it was not true that the French language was in danger; the rights of non-francophone minorities were in danger.[20] Victor Goldbloom suggested that it was illogical to claim that the situation of the French language made it necessary to deny migrants from other provinces access to English schools, and then to allow the granting of access through interprovincial agreements.[21] John O'Gallagher, the new member for the suburban riding of Robert-Baldwin, noted that the English-speaking population of Montreal was already declining and called the bill hypocritical, separatist, unconstitutional and unrealistic. He accused the government of promoting "a Quiet Revolution in reverse" and "a backward journey to the time of Duplessis," which would make Quebec "a closed, isolated society controlled by a privileged elite."[22] Needless to say, none of these arguments had any effect on the government's resolve to have the bill passed with as little delay as possible. On 26 August 1977, towards the end of what O'Gallagher remembered as "a long hot summer," it was adopted by the National Assembly.[23]

Looking back almost two decades later, Eric Maldoff considered that the experience of Bill 101 indicated the lack of unity and cohesion in the English-speaking community and their political ineffectiveness:

So this community of roughly a million people reacts and it was really quite a sight ... When the Bill 1 hearings were going on it was a joke, because all of these organizations, institutional leadership and whatever showed up for the hearings, each purporting to speak for the community. There was absolutely no coherence between the submissions, there was no common view, and furthermore there wasn't even a data base ... There was nothing! Nobody knew anything about the community. This community was run out of the hip pocket of a very small group of people. So the community looked ridiculous. It looked preposterous and it was totally ineffective in its presentations.[24]

The only hope for at least a symbolic victory over Bill 101 was to challenge the legislation in the courts, with the aid of a Canadian constitution that did not yet include the Charter of Rights and Freedoms. The Protestant School Board of Greater Montreal had contested the restrictions on access to English schools under Bill 22, alleging that they violated the constitutional guarantee of denominational education, but the Quebec Superior Court had rejected their arguments.[25] Their appeal from that decision was still pending when Bill 101 was adopted and was later dismissed on the grounds that the relevant legislation had been repealed. They saw no reason to repeat the exercise. Section 133 of the 1867 Constitution Act, which entrenched bilingualism in the National Assembly and the courts, offered better prospects of success. The Bourassa government had been careful to avoid violating this section in Bill 22 but the Lévesque government, whether by accident or design, had included provisions in Bill 101 that were directly contrary to the constitutional guarantee of official bilingualism. Peter Blaikie, whose name would be forever linked to the successful challenge of these provisions, thought that they were intended as a deliberate provocation: "It was obvious to me that Lévesque had put them in simply to provoke. Lévesque thought that somebody would take the bait, which was inevitable, he knew they would win, and he thought there would be a political benefit for him. Absolutely! And it was so blatantly obvious …"[26]

Someone convened a meeting at which twenty or thirty members of the bar in Montreal discussed how and whether the provisions should be challenged in court. Some of those present argued that a challenge was inadvisable, at least prior to the referendum, since Lévesque would be able to cite his government's defeat in court as evidence that federalism was contrary to Quebec's interests. This view did not prevail, but to the disappointment of those who favoured challenging the legislation on constitutional grounds, most of the large Montreal law firms did not wish to be publicly associated with their initiative.

In the end it was decided that three lawyers, Peter Blaikie, Roland Durand, and Yoine Goldstein, would be the litigants while three others, Andre Brossard, Robert Litvak, and Donald Johnston, would act as their counsel. (The case would be labelled as *Blaikie* because Peter Blaikie's name was the first in alphabetical order.) The participants were deliberately selected to provide a balanced slate of Protestants, Jews and francophones.[27] Although the Quebec government argued that the National Assembly had merely exercised its constitutional right to amend the constitution of the province, this argument was rejected by the Superior Court, the Court of Appeal, and finally, on

13 December 1979, the Supreme Court of Canada.[28] The Supreme Court ruled that Section 133 was an entrenched provision that could not be altered by either level of government. It took the opportunity to demonstrate its impartiality between provinces by handing down a judgment requiring official bilingualism in Manitoba on the same day.[29]

What effect did the Charter of the French Language really have on the lives of English-speaking people in Quebec? In Montreal, with its heterogeneous and constantly changing population, the most immediate and direct impact was probably that of the new rules governing access to English-language education. Enrollment in English language schools declined from 16.4 per cent of total school enrollment in 1976 to 13.2 per cent in 1981, and 10.5 per cent in 1986.[30] In order to preserve some of their allophone clientele under the new rules the Protestant boards, which had traditionally offered practically all of their instruction in English, converted some of their schools into French-language institutions.[31] This practice served the interests of the boards but weakened their ties with the English-speaking community. Many English schools, both Protestant and Catholic, simply closed because of rapidly declining enrollments.

In rural areas where anglophones lived, particularly the Eastern Townships where anglophones had been the first white settlers, the first shock came from the changes in geographical names that were imposed by the Commission de toponymie. The new names promptly appeared on directional signs along the roads and highways, where they provoked some anger, some ridicule, and a great deal of confusion.[32] For middle-class anglophones, and for some francophones as well, the onerous French-language tests required to continue in the practice of certain professions were a major grievance, even though Bill 22 had provided for the eventual imposition of the same requirement. There were cases of francophones, including a former minister in the Bourassa government, Oswald Parent, failing the test because their spelling or grammar was deemed inadequate. An even more celebrated case was the saga of Joanne Curran, a nurse who failed the French test three times and then gave a fluent interview on French radio to demonstrate her command of the language. In another bizarre episode, the Commission de surveillance investigated St Mary's Hospital, one of the largest hospitals in Montreal, after allegations that a francophone patient had not been given the opportunity to "die in French."[33]

Most difficult to measure is the effect of "francization" requirements on capital investment and employment in the province. While it seems incontestable that Quebec's economy suffered in those years, and

while jobs requiring the use of English were probably disproportionately affected by the slowdown of investment and the flight of capital,
it is difficult to separate the effects of the language legislation from
those of changes in taxation, anxiety about the referendum, economic
policies perceived by the business community as excessively left of
centre, such as the revised Labour Code, and the general tendency of
capital to flow to the West in those years of high resource and energy
prices. Even Ontario was losing employment and investment to the
western provinces in the 1970s. Probably the most that can be said
with certainty about the Charter of the French Language is that it
made English-speaking Quebeckers feel uncomfortable and unwelcome, and that these feelings included those anglophones who owned
capital as well as those who had nothing to sell but their labour.
Whether they were justified in feeling uncomfortable and unwelcome,
or whether they over-reacted to the situation, are certainly questions
that can be debated. Nonetheless, the feelings were genuine and many
anglophones reacted, as Lenin said of the soldiers who deserted from
the Imperial Russian Army in 1917, by voting with their feet.

THE ANGLOPHONE EXODUS

As discussed above, a major objective of Positive Action, and a major
theme of their advertising campaign, was to discourage English-speaking Quebeckers from leaving the province in response to the election
of the Parti Québécois, or in anticipation of an unfavourable outcome
to the promised referendum. It is impossible to estimate how many,
if any, remained in Quebec as a result of this campaign who would
otherwise have left. It is indisputable, however, that a great many did
leave. Between the census conducted in June 1976 and the one
conducted five years later, the number of persons in Quebec identifying English as their mother tongue declined by more than 94,000,
reducing the absolute number to about what it had been in the early
1960s. This was apparently the first time in history that the number
of anglophones in Quebec had decreased from one census to another.
During the same five-year interval the number of Quebec residents
whose mother tongue was neither English nor French declined by
about 20,000, while those of French mother tongue increased by
about 318,000.[34]

The exodus of anglophones was not a new phenomenon in Quebec.
For more than a century they had been moving out – to Ontario, the
western provinces, or the United States – in search of opportunities.
For much of this period there was also a substantial exodus of francophones, particularly to the New England states and to Ontario. Prior

to 1931, according to a study based on census data, almost 60 per
cent of those who emigrated from Quebec were French Canadians.
Even then, however, the smaller English-speaking population had a
greater propensity to leave Quebec (calculated by the ratio of emigration to the total population of the group), and the disparity widened
with time. Between 1956 and 1961 francophones accounted for
slightly more than a third of those who left Quebec. After 1966
francophones always comprised less than 30 per cent of the emigrants,
indicating that anglophones had a far greater propensity to leave.[35]
The effect of this phenomenon was lessened by the fact that departing
anglophones were generally replaced by new ones attracted to the
economic opportunities of Montreal, or by the assimilated children of
allophone immigrants. Thus the English-speaking population of
Quebec continued to grow in absolute terms, although declining in
relative terms, until the Parti Québécois took office in 1976.

After 1976 the accelerating exodus of anglophones, and the dearth
of new arrivals to compensate for it, became conspicuous even to a
casual observer. Real estate signs sprouted like mushrooms in the
anglophone neighbourhoods and suburbs of Montreal. School enrollments declined. Everyone seemed to know someone who was leaving.
Fears that the community was actually disintegrating were reinforced
by the demise of the *Montreal Star* in September 1979, even though
that event was apparently part of a general shakedown in the Canadian
newspaper industry, and the newspaper itself had been weakened by
a strike from June 1978 until February 1979. Nonetheless, its death
was a severe blow to an already beleaguered community, particularly
since its coverage of Quebec politics had, since the end of the
Duplessis era, been significantly better than that of its rival *The Gazette*.

Associated with the departure of individual anglophones, and contributing significantly to it through the relocation of jobs, was the
transfer of corporate head offices from Montreal to other Canadian
cities. The most conspicuous and symbolically important departure
was that of the Sun Life Insurance Company, which had long been
one of Montreal's largest sources of white-collar employment –
although notorious for its reluctance to hire francophones in more
than token numbers. The Sun Life Building on Dominion Square
(officially known as Place du Canada after 1960) was the largest and
most prominent office building in the city and until the 1960s was
often alleged to be the largest in the British Commonwealth. On
6 January 1978 the company announced that it was moving its head
office to Toronto. It claimed to be motivated by fears that Quebec
would become an independent state, although some observers
believed that its unwillingness to comply with the "francization"

requirements of Bill 101 was the true reason. Richard Holden, who held a policy with Sun Life, threatened the company with an injunction and succeeded in delaying its departure by three months. Despite his efforts and those of Positive Action, which also tried to discourage the move, Sun Life soon departed.[36] According to a study released in November 1978 by Reed Scowen, a newly elected Liberal member of the National Assembly, at least forty-two major companies moved all or a major part of their head office operations out of Quebec in the two years after the election of the Parti Québécois.[37]

A number of sociological and demographic studies of the anglophone exodus were conducted in the years immediately following the election of 1976. One by Robert Maheu, already cited, suggests that Bill 101 had a significant, although temporary, impact on the volume of anglophone out-migration. Between 1976 and 1981 the propensity of Quebec anglophones to migrate was 17.5 times that of Quebec francophones. This was an increase in the traditional disparity, which had been 14.9 times in 1971–76 and 12.9 times in 1966–71. Between 1981 and 1983, however, anglophones were "only" about ten times as likely to leave Quebec as francophones, a ratio similar to that of 1956–61. It seems reasonable to assume that those who were particularly offended by Bill 101 left as soon as possible, and that those anglophones who were still living in Quebec in 1981 were more willing to adapt to the new realities of Quebec. Maheu's study however fails to take into account another reason for out-migration after 1976: anxiety concerning the outcome of the promised referendum. By 1981 the federalist cause had won at the polls, and it was widely assumed that the threat of a separation between Quebec and the rest of Canada had disappeared for at least a generation.

Gary Caldwell studied a sample of students who had graduated from, or dropped out of, Quebec's English-language high schools in 1971. He contacted them in 1976, again in 1979, and finally in 1982–83. He found that 31 per cent had already left Quebec by 1976, just before the Parti Québécois took office, that 38 per cent had done so by 1979, and that 45 per cent had done so by 1982–83. The sample included a number of allophones and francophones who had been educated in English, since this was allowed at the time when they were in school. Of those students whose mother tongue was actually English 33 per cent had left by 1976, 41 per cent by 1979, and 50 per cent by 1982–83. By the latter date only 19 per cent of the francophones in the sample had left (compared to 15 per cent in 1976) and only 23 per cent of the allophones (compared to 19 per cent in 1976). Caldwell concludes that anglophones continued to leave in large numbers after the Parti Québécois took office while other graduates of English high schools did not.[38] However the rate of departure for all three groups, even before 1976, seems quite high. Those who lacked fluency in French and those whose parents had come to Quebec from another province were the most likely to leave.

Melanie Jane Lange wrote a master's thesis in sociology based on interviews with a sample of 332 Montreal anglophones interviewed in the summer of 1978.[39] (The sample of course excludes the considerable number who had already left the province in the nearly two years since the victory of the Parti Québécois.) She hypothesized that out-migration was a response to stress brought on by social distance between anglophones and francophones and that younger and more educated anglophones would be less socially distant and therefore less likely to leave than those who were older or less educated. These hypotheses were disproved but another hypothesis, that Jewish anglophones would experience more social distance and thus be more likely to leave than those of British origins, was confirmed. Jewish respondents were much more likely than others to perceive prejudice and discrimination against anglophones in Quebec. More than one-third of the total sample said that they would probably or certainly leave the province. The most important reasons cited for wanting to leave were the individual's economic situation, the general political situation in Quebec, and the impact of language legislation. Lange found that intention to leave Quebec was not significantly associated with education, occupation or income and had a relatively weak association with the degree of fluency in French and the extent of social contacts with francophones. Even attitudes towards francophones and towards Quebec had a relatively weak impact on the probability of leaving the province. Marriage to a francophone, however, did significantly lessen the desire to leave Quebec.[40]

Lange distinguished between what she called "innovative migrants," who move in order to better their situation, and "conservative migrants," who move to escape a perceived threat.[41] Contrary to her expectation, more than two-thirds of the potential migrants fell into the innovative category. She concluded therefore that much of the anglophone exodus was probably part of a normal ongoing process of population movement not directly related to the Parti Québécois, Bill 101 or the referendum. On the other hand, there were anglophones who felt threatened and for whom "voicing one's intention to leave Quebec may simply be a response to feelings of impotence and disapproval of the situation."[42] She suggested that the phenomenon of out-migration would be better understood if the two types were distinguished.

A longitudinal study of anglophone out-migration and of attitudes towards the Parti Québécois was conducted by Uli Locher for the Conseil de la langue française.[43] It was based on interviews with 332 persons in 1978 and re-interviews with as many of them as could be contacted in 1983. One-fifth of those who could still be located in 1983 had left the province. Of those who had left and were re-interviewed, 29 per cent cited language laws or political conditions as the primary reason for their departure, while 24 per cent cited as the primary reason the fact that they, or a family member, had been transferred out of Quebec by their employers.[44]

Locher found that the level of satisfaction with the Quebec government among his interviewees was very low in 1978 and even lower in 1983.[45] Opposition to the Charter of the French Language was almost unanimous on both occasions.[46] About three out of every four respondents considered that they would leave Quebec if it became independent.[47] Like Maheu, Locher noted that the decline in the anglophone population was only partly explained by out-migration. A large part of it resulted from the fact that fewer anglophones were moving to Quebec from other provinces. (This fact could also be attributed in large measure to the election of the Parti Québécois.)[48]

Albert O. Hirschman, in a work often cited by political scientists, suggests that what he calls "exit" and "voice" are alternative responses to declining satisfaction with both economic and political institutions.[49] One can choose "exit" by no longer shopping in a store, belonging to an organization, or living in a country. Alternatively, one can choose "voice" by staying and trying to improve matters. Exit is usually, although not always, easier, and "The presence of the exit alternative can therefore tend to atrophy the development of the art of voice."[50]

Many Quebec anglophones, particularly young, educated persons and a good portion of the economic elite, chose "exit" after the politicization of language began in the late 1960s, and particularly in the period between the 1976 election and the 1980 referendum. The availability of this option may explain in part, as Hirschman's theory would suggest, the anglophone community's lack of effectiveness in defending its interests in the political arena during that period. The tendency to exit declined after the referendum and there seemed to be at least a modest increase in political activity and political effectiveness. At first political activity took the form of a revived enthusiasm for the Liberal Party, but after the party's unexpected failure to return to office in 1981 attention shifted to interest group politics, building on the foundations laid by Positive Action and Participation Québec.

These developments will be discussed in the remaining portions of this chapter, along with the efforts by the Parti Québécois to build some bridges to the anglophone community.

CLAUDE RYAN AND
THE LIBERAL REVIVAL

The Quebec Liberal Party reached the nadir of its fortunes in the election of 1976. There was even some doubt, given the apparent revival of the Union Nationale, whether the party would survive as a major force in Quebec politics. As we have seen, among anglophone voters in particular, disillusionment with the Quebec Liberals ran very deep in the aftermath of Bill 22. Nonetheless, it seemed after the election that there were no real alternatives to the Liberals. The Parti Québécois was not a possible option for most anglophones. The Democratic Alliance soon faded out of existence. Robert Keaton, who remained active in municipal politics and to some extent in Positive Action, concluded, in retrospect, that the formation of the Democratic Alliance had been a mistake.[51] The Union Nationale abandoned its half-hearted commitment to "freedom of choice" within a few months of the election.

The Union Nationale's change of policy disillusioned William Shaw, who continued to support freedom of choice in the language of instruction. Shaw finally resigned from the party in February 1978 and devoted his energies to the Freedom of Choice organization, which transformed itself into a political party in time to run a candidate in the NDG by-election that summer. Shaw continued to be an articulate defender of anglophone interests in the National Assembly: he was one of the first politicians to raise the issue of the scarcity of non-francophones in the public service, and he also criticized the government for imposing geographical boundaries on the three social service centres in Montreal, which the Liberals had allowed to serve their respective ethnic clienteles regardless of location.[52] Some of his initiatives were perhaps less well-considered, such as his parliamentary question in December 1979 regarding an unsubstantiated rumour that the Office de la langue française had prohibited the use of the name Santa Claus.[53] He remained credible, however, until just before the 1980 referendum, when he ill-advisedly co-authored a book on the possible partition of Quebec.[54] This topic was then considered beyond the pale of respectable discourse, and the effect on Shaw's political career was disastrous.

Meanwhile the Liberals had begun to revive under their new leader Claude Ryan, the former publisher of the intellectual and nationalist daily newspaper *Le Devoir.* Ryan's ascent to the Liberal leadership was unexpected, since he had advised his readers to vote for the Parti Québécois in 1976. However, his integrity and intellect were widely and deservedly respected and he had never ceased to be a federalist. Efforts to recruit him for the Liberals began in the summer of 1977, after Robert Bourassa had resigned his leadership and left for a lengthy sabbatical in Europe and the United States. At first Ryan said that he was not interested but in January 1978 he announced that he was, and by the time the leadership convention opened in April his victory was considered a foregone conclusion. He defeated his only adversary, Raymond Garneau, by a margin of better than two to one.

Ryan was initially not particularly well known to anglophones, very few of whom read *Le Devoir.* He made a favourable impression, however, in the course of his leadership campaign, when he released a statement of his views on language policy. He proposed to eliminate the ban on bilingual commercial signs, to allow all anglophone children access to English schools, to guarantee the availability of health and social services in English, and to allow municipalities to conduct their business in both languages. He also promised that a Ryan government would communicate with anglophone Quebeckers in their own language and would dismantle much of the bureaucratic machinery created by the Charter of the French Language.[55]

Not all anglophone Liberals, however, were Ryan supporters. Bryce Mackasey, who had never appeared to enjoy the National Assembly as much as the House of Commons, resigned his seat a few days after the leadership convention. He returned to the House of Commons, representing an Ontario riding, two years later. Victor Goldbloom had supported Garneau's unsuccessful bid for the leadership and found himself on rather cool terms with his new leader as a result. In 1979 he resigned from the National Assembly to accept a position as executive director of the Canadian Council of Christians and Jews, after Ryan had made no effort to dissuade him from doing so.[56]

The departure of Mackasey precipitated the first of eleven by-elections, all of them won by the Liberals, that took place in the years 1978 through 1980. Ryan decided to wait until a predominantly francophone riding became available, rather than running in NDG. He was elected in the Argenteuil by-election the following year. The Liberal candidate in NDG was Reed Scowen, who won the nomination with Ryan's blessing. His opponents included Richard Lord, who had unsuccessfully sought the federal nomination in 1965. Scowen was from the Eastern Townships, where he had run a family-owned manufacturing business for several years before becoming a public servant, first at the provincial level and then at the federal. Bourassa had tried to recruit him as a replacement for Kevin Drummond in Westmount in 1976, but Scowen had declined to run at that time.[57] In 1978 Scowen was executive director of the Pépin-Robarts Task Force on Canadian Unity, a position to which he had been appointed after working with Jean-Luc Pépin on the Anti-Inflation Board. The NDG by-election was an easy victory for the Liberal candidate; the only serious opposition came from the Freedom of Choice candidate, David de Jong, who won 25 per cent of the vote, 4 per cent less than the Union Nationale had won in 1976.

The by-election in D'Arcy-McGee to replace Victor Goldbloom took place in November 1979. The Liberal candidate, Herbert Marx, was a professor in the Faculty of Law at the University of Montreal and a specialist in human rights. He was also one of the few anglophones who had known Ryan reasonably well before Ryan became leader of the party, since Marx had written a number of articles for Le Devoir when Ryan was publisher.[58] Like Ryan himself, Marx had no previous connection with the Liberal Party. Ryan encouraged his candidacy in a subtle way, as he had encouraged Scowen's, but was in principle opposed to candidates being imposed on ridings by the leader and insisted on a genuine contest for the nomination. He thus did not discourage another possible candidate, Maximilien Polak, who expressed interest in running. Polak, who had emigrated to Montreal from the Netherlands at the age of twenty-one, was a trilingual lawyer, a member of the Protestant School Board of Greater Montreal, and a part-time municipal judge in Côte St-Luc until he resigned from that position to seek the nomination. He was not actually Jewish, although his father had been, and this fact may have hindered his campaign for the nomination. In any event, Marx won easily.[59] Some of Polak's supporters felt that Ryan had treated their candidate unfairly, but Polak later received the Liberal nomination in another riding and was elected to the National Assembly in 1981.

The by-election in D'Arcy-McGee was little more than a formality, with Marx receiving 96.7 per cent of the votes; neither the Union Nationale nor Freedom of Choice bothered to contest the by-election. The Parti Québécois managed to find a credible young Jewish candidate, David Levine, whose campaign emphasized his roots in the suburban riding. (Marx, who was sixteen years older, had grown up in downtown Montreal.) The almost unanimously federalist voters were not impressed and Levine received only 791 votes. With the additions of Scowen, Ryan and Marx, and the capture of two seats from the Parti Québécois and one from a minor opposition party in additional by-elections, the Liberals now formed a strong opposition to argue for federalism and bilingualism in the National Assembly.

By the time Marx was elected, the referendum on sovereignty-association was only six months away and increasingly it took over the political agenda. The ground rules for the referendum required that a single committee be in charge of the campaign on either side, and since the committee on the federalist side was dominated by the Quebec Liberal Party many federalists were naturally drawn into a closer association with the party. The decisive federalist victory in the referendum on 20 May 1980, and the winning of four additional by-elections by the Liberals later that year – three of them in ridings which the Union Nationale had won in 1976 – also persuaded most Quebec anglophones that the next general election would restore the Liberals to power. This perception, the referendum victory itself, and Ryan's vision of a pluralistic Quebec where minority rights would be respected as in the past, had a noticeable effect on the morale of English-speaking Quebeckers and on their interest in the Quebec Liberal Party. Although the Council of Quebec Minorities and its various components continued to exist, they attracted little attention or enthusiasm. With an election expected in the fall of 1980, or at the latest in 1981, electoral politics returned to the centre of the stage and interest group activity – a somewhat uncongenial pastime which Quebec anglophones had embraced only out of desperation – no longer seemed such a high priority.

On the day after the Supreme Court of Canada handed down its decision in the *Blaikie* case, Reed Scowen described the decision as "an opportunity and an invitation for the English-speaking people of the province to take a fuller and more complete role in the government of Quebec."[60] Some were already in the process of doing so. John Trent, a University of Ottawa professor who lived in western Quebec and a tireless political activist, had not supported the party in 1976 but joined it in time to play a part in Ryan's leadership campaign. Ryan appointed him to the party's constitutional committee, which produced a pre-referendum blueprint for renewed federalism, popularly known as the Beige Paper.[61] John Parisella, a teacher for the Montreal Catholic School Commission and the author of a master's thesis on the St-Léonard crisis, joined the party in 1978 and hoped to run in the NDG by-election. He later described himself as "a product of the Claude Ryan renewal phase of the party."[62] As a volunteer Parisella helped to stimulate support for federalism in the anticipated referendum, organizing coffee parties in the homes of Liberal members. At the end of 1979 he took a leave of absence to work for the party, organizing the referendum campaign in the fourteen ridings in the west end of Montreal. After the referendum he continued as a pre-election organizer responsible for a total of eighteen ridings, with one of his tasks being to encourage suitable persons to present themselves as candidates.

The party and its leader wanted a credible slate of minority candidates for the forthcoming election and in the circumstances there was little difficulty in finding them. On the West Island the redistribution conducted by the Parti Québécois government had divided William Shaw's riding of Pointe-Claire between Jacques-Cartier, which became more anglophone as a result, and a new riding of Nelligan, which also acquired part of Robert-Baldwin. Since Shaw was considered unlikely to win wherever he chose to run, this created three safe anglophone seats for the Liberals. Ryan decided that Noel St Germain, the veteran member for Jacques-Cartier, should be replaced by an anglophone. Joan Dougherty, the chair of the Protestant School Board of Greater Montreal and an admirer of Ryan, had been active in the referendum campaign in Mount Royal, where she lived, and decided that she would like to be a candidate. She took the initiative of contacting the party, met Parisella, and had a meeting with Ryan. Eventually it was decided that she would challenge St Germain for the nomination in Jacques-Cartier, which she did successfully.[63] An unexpected entry into the nomination contest was Shaw, who later alleged that Claude Ryan "set me up" by expressing interest in his candidacy.[64] Because he had sought the Liberal nomination, Shaw had to leave the Freedom of Choice party and run in the election as an independent.

In Robert-Baldwin the sitting member, John O'Gallagher, had been effective in his first term and was renominated without a contest. In Nelligan, the farthest west and the most affluent of the three ridings, there were nine candidates for the nomination. The one who most impressed Parisella was Clifford Lincoln, who had been born in Mauritius and lived in British Columbia for several years before moving to Quebec in 1964.[65] Lincoln was a long-time federal Liberal, having belonged to that party even when he lived in British Columbia, but his interest in provincial politics had not really been stimulated until Ryan became leader. As Lincoln later reminisced, "It was a very uplifting time when he took over the party in 1977–78. He really brought about this notion of Quebec for all and tremendous involvement of the grassroots ... Just a tremendous time for small-l liberals and people who believed in a broader and more inclusive society."[66] Lincoln began to recruit party members and by the date of the convention six of the nine original candidates had dropped out. He was successful on the first ballot.

In the Ottawa Valley, the redistribution restored Pontiac, which had been combined with Temiscamingue in the 1973 and 1976 elections, as a riding about evenly divided between anglophones and francophones. Aylmer, an Ottawa suburb just outside the county boundary, was added to Pontiac to bring the riding's total population closer to the provincial average. Michel Gratton, the member for Gatineau and a militant federalist, was expected to run in Pontiac as a result of this change, since he lived in Aylmer. John Trent would then have run in Gatineau, a more francophone but equally federalist riding, with a near-certainty of being elected.[67] Instead Gratton decided to stay in Gatineau and encouraged his friend Robert Middlemiss, a civil engineer and member of the Aylmer town council, to run in Pontiac. Middlemiss, the child of a mixed marriage, had the advantage, as he later put it, that the anglophones thought he was an anglophone and the francophones thought he was a francophone.[68] Trent decided not to challenge Gratton for the nomination in Gatineau.

George Springate's decision in 1980 not to run again made Westmount available to another anglophone representative. The most logical candidate, and a certainty for cabinet office if the Liberals won as anticipated, would have been Alex Paterson. Paterson was approached but was not interested in running.[69] (There was also some interest in recruiting Storrs McCall, possibly for a West Island riding, but he too refused.) In the end the contest in Westmount was between Robert de Fougeyrol, a prominent businessman without political experience, and Richard French, a young McGill professor who had worked in the Privy Council Office in Ottawa. The party's head office preferred French, who had been an active fundraiser in the riding, and he succeeded in winning the nomination.

In the ethnically mixed ridings of central Montreal a number of non-francophones were nominated. Ste-Anne did not have a nominating convention, since the Parti Québécois was believed to have infiltrated the Liberal riding association.[70] Instead Maximilien Polak was parachuted in. Christos Sirros, who had run for the Democratic Alliance in 1976, defeated four other candidates to become the Liberal nominee in Laurier, the stronghold of the city's Greek community. He subsequently claimed to have signed up more than two thousand new members.[71] Cosmo Maciocia, an insurance agent, and William Cusano, a school administrator, both natives of the same Italian region as John Ciaccia, were nominated in Viger and Viau respectively. Cusano had been a leading opponent of Bill 22 and had helped to organize the classes which prepared immigrant children to pass the English test required by that statute.

The Liberals thus entered the 1981 election with an impressive slate of non-francophone candidates, although they had lost one promising prospect in John Trent and had failed to recruit either Alex Paterson or Storrs McCall. The candidates represented both the established anglophone community and the newer immigrant groups, and included persons who had opposed Bill 22 as well as some who had supported it. According to Joan Dougherty's recollection, however, Ryan's encouragement of diversity only went so far. When she suggested finding a black person to run for the Liberals, Ryan's reply was that it was a little too early to consider such a radical step.[72] Jean Alfred, an immigrant from Haiti, had already been elected to the National Assembly as a Parti Québécois member in 1976. Richard Lord, a long-time Liberal of Caribbean origin, would run for the Equality Party in 1989. At the time of writing, the Quebec Liberal Party has still not nominated any visible minority candidates.

ANGLOPHONES AND THE PARTI QUÉBÉCOIS

In its first few years in office the Parti Québécois realistically recognized that it had no hope of attracting significant support from anglophones. It also had no need for their support, since Bill 22 and the election of 1976 had clearly demonstrated their political impotence. Whether or not it was motivated by vindictiveness and a desire for vengeance against anglophones, as some Liberal politicians charged, Bill 101 was certainly not the action of a government that was seriously interested in courting anglophone support. The preamble to the original version of the bill, which seemed to exclude non-francophones from Quebec society, sent a particularly unfortunate signal to the community, although admittedly they would not have liked the bill in any event. On the other hand the language legislation seemed to unite the different factions of a party that had suffered conspicuously from internal feuding during its years in opposition, and to be popular in most sectors of francophone Quebec, apart from the higher echelons of the business community.

As the referendum approached, and as the initial shock and outrage of the anglophone community towards Bill 101 subsided, the government began, rather ineptly at first, to build bridges to the English-speaking community. This effort was originally the responsibility of Dr Camille Laurin, the minister responsible for language policy and as such a natural focus for anglophone resentment. When he moved to the education portfolio in the fall of 1980 the bridge-building role was assumed by the newly appointed minister of immigration, Gérald Godin. In May 1981 the phrase "cultural communities" was added to the name of Godin's portfolio. During the committee discussion of his department's estimates a few weeks later, Godin was asked by Maximilien Polak whether he considered anglophones a cultural community. The minister replied that if anglophones considered themselves a cultural community he would welcome them as such. He also asserted that the government rejected the concept of a melting pot and believed in "the friendly and fraternal coexistence of communities which would totally keep their identities" while sharing a common language (sic) and a common territory.[73] This appeared to be little different from the concept of multiculturalism espoused by the federal government and most of the English-speaking provinces.

The government's efforts to open a dialogue with anglophones were paralleled by those of the Parti Québécois itself. In 1976 the party already had a few English-speaking members including David Levine, the public health administrator who would later run in the D'Arcy-McGee by-election, and David Payne, a British-born community college teacher and former Catholic priest. Both were promptly hired as advisers to ministers. Levine worked in the office of Economic Development Minister Bernard Landry and Payne in that of Camille Laurin, whom he had met while working at the Vatican in 1967.[74] There were also some sympathizers, mainly on the left, some of whom had been active in the Montreal Citizens' Movement or in interest groups where they encountered Parti Québécois members. The disintegration of the NDP in Quebec and the failure of the Democratic Alliance suggested that a left-wing federalist party in Quebec might be an oxymoron, and those whose left-wing sentiments were stronger than their allegiance to federalism thus drifted towards the Parti Québécois, even though they recognized that, particularly outside of Montreal, it was a coalition of left, right and centre rather than a truly left-wing party. The Committee of Anglophones for a United Quebec, formed soon after the 1976 election, was an early manifestation of this tendency.

Just as the referendum campaign tended to draw individuals and groups on the federalist side into the orbit of the Liberal Party, it tended to draw those on the other side closer to the Parti Québécois. The Committee of Anglophones for a United Quebec was succeeded early in 1979 by the Committee of Anglophones for Sovereignty-Association, headed by Henry Milner, which was somewhat more closely associated with the party. As Milner later recalled, "I was very much involved in the yes organization even though I wasn't formally involved in the PQ, but in reality there wasn't much distinction between the PQ and the yes organization. So in the process I worked with people right at the top. It meant that those links were strengthened."[75]

The committee published an advertisement with the names of fifty-five anglophones who supported sovereignty-association. Most were young academics or students although the list, which specified occupations as well as names, also included a truck driver, a nurse, a librarian, a housewife, the Quebec director of the United Auto Workers, Robert Dean, and the eminent Marxist historian Stanley Ryerson. Another advertisement, published in the *McGill Daily*, listed ninety-nine McGill students (less than 1 per cent of the total number) who supported sovereignty-association, but more than half of the students on the list were francophones.[76]

During the referendum campaign Premier Lévesque found time to attend a few meetings with groups of sympathetic, or perhaps merely curious, anglophones. On 23 March 1980 he delivered a major speech, in English, which he addressed "to the English community," although those actually in attendance were mainly sympathizers with his party.[77] The speech was part of a one-day workshop on sovereignty-association conducted in English and organized by the party. The event was somewhat marred by anonymous telephone calls making bomb threats but nothing actually happened. In the speech Lévesque emphasized that his definition of "Québécois" was inclusive of different languages, religions and ethnic backgrounds, and defended his party against charges of ethnocentrism. He also praised the courage of those anglophones who supported sovereignty-association, although he admitted somewhat ruefully that they were very few in number. While stating that he respected the right of anglophones to choose federalism, he added that he could not be expected to applaud the fact that they did so in such overwhelming numbers.

In the course of the referendum campaign the Committee of Anglophones for Sovereignty-Association had identified about two hundred anglophones who were sympathetic to the cause.[78] The only prominent anglophone who became a convert during the referendum campaign was Kevin Drummond, the former representative of Westmount who had held two cabinet posts under Premier Bourassa. Although he never joined the party, Drummond announced that he intended to vote for sovereignty-association, and campaigned with Premier Lévesque in the last days before the referendum. As he later explained: "I've always wanted the most independent Quebec possible, no matter what the structure is, be it federalist or sovereignty-association, to get there with the least trauma. So that had always been my approach. Especially when you're in the Quebec government you just find that there's not a lot of empathy between the various provinces, except for strategic alliances in various circumstances. You always seem to be at war with the federal government, one way or another, and surely there's a better way of operating, that's all. A better way of living together."[79]

After the referendum the Parti Québécois set up a National Anglophone Committee, with Henry Milner as chairman, in the hope that more anglophone supporters, members and candidates could be recruited before the next election. Since Lévesque had promised to place the pursuit of sovereignty on the back burner for the remainder of his government's existence, it seemed possible that some anglophones might be attracted by the government's generally good performance, its remarkable absence of corruption, and its moderately progressive policies, some of which had already been implemented. The committee also hoped to sensitize members of the Parti Québécois to the importance of the anglophone minority and the legitimacy of its collective rights. A document to this effect was prepared for discussion at the meeting of the party's National Council in November 1980.[80] It pointed out that anglophones had lived in Quebec for two centuries, that they comprised 13 per cent of the population, and that they could not be considered merely one among several ethnic minorities. It was agreed that the party would devote some funds and a part-time staff person to strengthening its anglophone component.

On 7 February 1981 the party published an advertisement in *The Gazette,* signed by Premier Lévesque and including his photograph. The message, addressed to "English Speaking Quebecers," noted that some anglophones already belonged to the Parti Québécois but "far too few to be representative of the important place of the English-speaking community in Quebec" even though "many anglophones share our priorities and support our programs and policies." It invited English-speaking readers to join the party and promised that the National Anglophone Committee would help them to "integrate into the structures of the party" if they decided to do so.

Few responded to this invitation, but the party did manage to recruit seven English-speaking candidates for the 1981 election, two of whom had not signed the sovereignty-association advertisement a year earlier. Four of the seven ran in predominantly anglophone ridings: Henry Milner in Westmount, Kevin Henley in NDG, Donald Waye in Jacques-Cartier, and Bill Bedwell in Pontiac. (David Levine did not run again in D'Arcy-McGee, where a francophone candidate carried the party's banner.) In addition Judith Anne Scott ran in Chomedey, a portion of suburban Laval with a substantial number of anglophones. Robert Dean of the United Auto Workers was the candidate in Prevost, which included the General Motors plant at Ste-Thérèse, and David Payne ran in Vachon on the south shore of the St Lawrence near Montreal. Both Dean and Payne were elected in their almost entirely francophone ridings. (Dean eventually was appointed to the cabinet as minister of revenue, the traditional anglophone portfolio, in March 1984.) In ridings with substantial numbers of English-speaking voters the party's performance at the polls was as discouraging as ever.

Although there were two anglophones on the government side of the house after the 1981 election there was no prospect of restoring the old consociational arrangements, even if the government had wished to do so. Neither Dean nor Payne represented a riding with significant numbers of anglophones and neither had any rapport with the English-speaking community. Dean was not interested in playing the role of an anglophone spokesman and took little interest in linguistic issues. Payne was more interested, but the English-speaking community did not take him seriously, partly because they suspected that his own party, with the exception of Camille Laurin, did not take him seriously either. Payne seemed a man of contradictions: he was associated with Laurin, the nationalist most hated by English-speaking Quebeckers, yet he flaunted his English origins with odd gestures, like seeking unanimous consent so that the National Assembly might congratulate the Prince and Princess of Wales on the birth of their son. (Predictably, unanimous consent was not given.)[81] Anglophones concluded that Payne was simply irrelevant.

THE FORMATION OF ALLIANCE QUEBEC

The election of April 1981 was a severe shock for the Quebec Liberal Party, which had almost taken it for granted that it would win a majority of seats and replace the Parti Québécois in office. Although the Liberal share of the vote increased to 46 per cent (from 34 per cent in 1976), the share of the Parti Québécois also increased, from 41 to 49 per cent, and the government retained nearly two-thirds of the seats in the National Assembly. The Liberals even lost several of the seats that they had won in by-elections since 1976. The result demonstrated that a federalist vote in the referendum did not automatically translate into a Liberal vote in the election, even though the electorate was polarized between the two main parties. The Liberal popular vote in April 1981 fell short of the federalist vote less than a year earlier by more than half a million; the vote for the Parti Québécois exceeded the "yes" vote in the referendum by almost 300,000.

The share of the vote going to minor parties and independent candidates was the lowest since 1962. The Union Nationale collapsed, with most of its anglophone voters apparently returning to the Liberals while many erstwhile francophone supporters followed their former leader, Rodrigue Biron, to the Parti Québécois. Freedom of Choice ran a dozen candidates but made little impact; its best showing was in Pontiac where its candidate won about 8 per cent of the vote. William Shaw, running as an independent in Jacques-Cartier (where there was no Freedom of Choice candidate), received less than 4 per cent of the vote in that riding.

Claude Ryan, whom the party had welcomed with such enthusiasm when it needed him, rapidly became the scapegoat for the Liberal defeat. He was alleged to be too austere, too religious, too rigid in his views, and – the most fatal accusation of all – too sympathetic to the anglophones. The latter accusation seems to have convinced even Ryan himself, at least in part.[82] His English-speaking colleagues in the National Assembly were saddened by his defeat and refused to blame him for it, although most eventually recognized that he would have to resign the leadership. By the time he finally resigned on 10 August 1982 he had only six supporters in the caucus, including Herbert Marx, Reed Scowen, and Christos Sirros. Daniel Johnson, the newly-elected Liberal son of the late Union Nationale premier, also continued to support Ryan. When a successor to Ryan was chosen the following year, most of the anglophones and allophones supported Johnson's candidacy.

English-speaking voters were almost as shocked by the Liberal defeat as the party itself. They had voted Liberal almost unanimously, resisting the blandishments of both Freedom of Choice and the Parti Québécois. Relying almost entirely on the English-language media for their knowledge of Quebec politics, they had naively assumed that the rest of the province would follow their example and reject the Parti Québécois. Some had even believed that the referendum result signalled the end of Quebec nationalism.[83] Certainly since the referendum most of them had viewed the Parti Québécois government as a temporary interruption in the normal pattern of Liberal rule. Now they were faced with the prospect that the Parti Québécois would remain in office indefinitely. While the government had promised not to hold another referendum during its second mandate, this assurance cut both ways, since it might mean that the government would feel less need to pursue conciliatory and consensus-building policies so as to maximize the support for its constitutional option. Furthermore, since anglophones had almost unanimously rejected the Parti Québécois in both the referendum and the election, the party might understandably feel that any further efforts to appease them would be a waste of time. The second half of 1981 gave some credence to this interpretation, as the government began to implement the prohibition of bilingual signs, challenged Prime Minister Trudeau's efforts to amend the Canadian constitution, and prepared for a major educational reform that would abolish denominational school boards.

The effect of all these anxieties, and above all of disappointment with the election, was a revival of preoccupation with interest group politics, which had taken a back seat to electoral politics during the years when the Liberal Party was reviving under Ryan's leadership.

Participation Québec, Positive Action, and the Council of Quebec Minorities had been somewhat dormant since before the referendum. In the fall of 1981 the Council established a task force on organization and structure that included Geoffrey Chambers, John Claxton, and Michael Goldbloom – all sons of prominent politicians – as well as Eric Maldoff. It recommended forming yet another organization which would provisionally be called the Coalition of English-Speaking Quebeckers. There was a general feeling that Participation Québec and Positive Action had similar objectives and that the distinction between them made little sense. At the same time, the Council had not worked well because of the constant need to defer to the different organizations which comprised it. An inclusive organization which would have individual members – although it might also have some affiliated organizations – was perceived to be essential.

There was also a belief that a single comprehensive organization with a mass membership would have a more credible claim to speak for the community as a whole than a collection of smaller organizations and would thus be more likely to attract significant funding from the federal government. Federal funding for the various English-language groups in Quebec had increased from about $86,000 in 1978 to about $400,000 in 1981, but the latter figure was considerably less than the amount made available to official language minorities in the other provinces.[84] Casper Bloom, a lawyer who had been active in Positive Action and who became the chairman of the Coalition of English-Speaking Quebeckers, recalls that the secretary of state's department put "pressure" on the anglophone groups to combine into one group if they wanted a significant increase in their funding.[85]

A declaration of principles was drawn up in the name of the Coalition of English-Speaking Quebeckers and published as an advertisement in several newspapers on 3 December 1981 with instructions that readers could fill in a coupon to indicate their support. It provoked a surprising response, given the traditional resistance of Quebec anglophones to participatory democracy. Several thousand persons returned the coupons – a revealing indication of the dismay that followed the election of 1981. The lists of names were used to organize a series of regional meetings which also met with an enthusiastic response. As Maldoff recalled: "The turnouts were unbelievable. A thousand people in Westmount. A thousand in NDG. Around the province we were getting – a small crowd was two hundred. Frequently in the eight hundred range or more."[86]

The public meetings were used to sign up members for the new organization and in some cases to launch regional chapters. A second round of meetings elected delegates to a province-wide convention which would take place in the spring of 1982. Sheila Finestone, a policy adviser in Claude Ryan's office and later a member of parliament, was contacted to ensure that the Liberal party and caucus would have no objection to a new organization of Quebec anglophones.[87] By March the organization was using the name Alliance Quebec, which was first suggested by Michael Goldbloom.[88] The name had the virtues of being short, almost identical in English and French, and avoiding the awkward term "English-speaking" which seemed to exclude most immigrants. Alliance Quebec formally came into existence at the founding convention, which took place on 29–30 May 1982 at the Loyola campus of Concordia University. The three predecessor organizations – Participation Québec, Positive Action, and the Council – all ceased to exist.

Alliance Quebec's organizational structure has remained much the same since it was founded.[89] A province-wide convention is held each year in May to elect the officers, discuss policy, and hear reports on the organization's activities. Between conventions Alliance Quebec is governed by a board of directors and an executive committee, whose members also sit on the board. The executive committee includes the president, chairman, two vice-presidents of whom one must be from outside the Montreal Urban Community, a treasurer, a secretary, and three members-at-large. The chief executive officer, elected each year but eligible for an unlimited number of terms, is called the president. The first two presidents, Eric Maldoff and Michael Goldbloom, were unremunerated volunteers, but later presidents have received a stipend. The chairman presides over the board of directors and assists the president but otherwise plays a less active and more honorific role. This office was occupied in the first year by Alex Paterson, and then by James Ross, a medical doctor from the Eastern Townships, until 1985. There is also an advisory council which includes, but is not limited to, most of the former presidents and former chairmen. The remunerated staff, headed by a full-time executive director, are organized into branches responsible for such topics as health and social services, education, community development, communications, and research. The first executive director was Geoffrey Chambers, who held the position until 1985.

The individual members of Alliance Quebec belong to regional chapters, whose numbers and boundaries have varied somewhat over the years. There are three on Montreal Island and several others within commuting distance of the metropolis although some are far-ther afield. The chapters were set up at the same time as Alliance Quebec itself, or in some cases later. There are also a number of what are called Autonomous Regional Organizations, which existed before Alliance Quebec and whose members belong to Alliance Quebec indirectly through the affiliated body. They jealously guard their autonomy and distinct character against Alliance Quebec, just as they did against the Council of Quebec Minorities, and tend to have polit-ical perspectives and priorities characteristic of their regions. The most important of these are the Townshippers' Association and the Outa-ouais Alliance, representing the two largest concentrations of English-speaking population outside of Montreal. There are also the Coasters' Association on the North Shore, the Committee for Anglophone Social Action in the Gaspésie, the Voice of English Quebec in the capital city, and the rather more militant Chateauguay Valley English-Speaking Peoples' Association in the southwestern corner of the prov-ince. The existence of these autonomous bodies testifies to an anti-Montreal sentiment among anglophones in the hinterlands of the province. According to Michael Goldbloom, the second president of Alliance Quebec, there were always tensions between the autonomous regional organizations and the Montreal-based headquarters.[90] The appointment of a chairman from the Eastern Townships in 1983 was considered a necessary gesture to reconcile the Townshippers to their status as part of a Montreal-based organization.[91]

The subsidy from the secretary of state amounted to $730,000 in the first year of Alliance Quebec's existence, a significant improvement over the level of funding received by the predecessor organizations in the previous year. In the second year, federal funding increased to about $1 million. In that year the modest sum of $33,000 was also received from the province under Gérald Godin's program of aid to cultural communities.[92] Membership fees and donations provided the remainder of the organization's revenues.

ALLIANCE QUEBEC AND THE PARTI QUÉBÉCOIS: A USEFUL DIALOGUE?

Even before its founding convention, Alliance Quebec took advantage of the government's efforts to open a dialogue with English-speaking Quebeckers. On 20 March 1982, *The Gazette* published an article by Premier Lévesque which professed goodwill towards the English-speaking community but regretted their negative attitude towards his government and, as he saw it, towards the promotion of the French language. The headline was "Lévesque asks for dialogue." Eric Maldoff, who was already acting as president of Alliance Quebec although not yet confirmed as such by the members, wrote a lengthy response taking issue with some of the premier's comments and also called an acquaintance in Lévesque's office to arrange a meeting.[93] Maldoff and Lévesque met on 26 March at the premier's office. Maldoff, who later described the meeting as "pretty cordial," explained to Lévesque that Alliance Quebec was intended to be a province-wide organization of moderate anglophones and that it hoped to enter into a constructive dialogue with the government.

A second meeting took place soon after the founding convention. Maldoff now had a mandate to represent the English-speaking community, having been elected president by the members. In the process he had defeated an opponent, Patrick Curran, who wished Alliance Quebec to move towards a more militant Freedom of Choice position and to demand that the English and French languages have equal status in Quebec. (Curran was the husband of Joanne Curran, the nurse who had been dismissed for failing her French language test.) Lévesque could thus be reminded, however subtly, that if he failed to make concessions to the more moderate leadership of the English-speaking community, he might eventually have to deal with those who were less moderate.

At his second meeting with Lévesque, Maldoff presented polling data to demonstrate that the majority of francophones agreed with Alliance Quebec's six principal objectives, including broader access to English education, guarantees of health and social services in English, greater anglophone representation in the public service, English as the language of communication within anglophone institutions, an end to mandatory French tests for professionals educated in Quebec, and acceptance of bilingual signs. He asked, orally and in writing, whether the government would accept these requests, hoping thereby to provoke a test of strength between the moderate Lévesque and Camille Laurin, who was viewed as the chief spokesman of the party's more anglophobic wing.

There was no immediate response to Alliance Quebec's requests, but in November 1982 Lévesque rejected all six of the organization's suggestions for changes to the Charter of the French Language. Both he and Gérald Godin, the minister responsible for language policy, may have been offended by an episode earlier that month. *The Gazette* published a leaked, and obviously outdated, list of ethnic community leaders, with short biographies of each, which had apparently been prepared in the Department of Immigration about three years previously, and probably as part of the referendum campaign. The newspaper, many of the people on the list, and a number of Liberal politicians used the document as a pretext to lambaste the Parti Québécois for its allegedly invidious attitudes towards minorities.[94] Maldoff, who was described on the list as the vice-president of Participation Québec, reacted moderately and sensibly, but the episode of the "ethnic list" was a setback for relations between the English-speaking community and the government.

Nonetheless, Godin announced in October 1983 that the National Assembly would conduct hearings on possible changes to the Charter of the French Language. Remembering the anglophone community's incoherent response to the original legislation in 1977, Alliance Quebec came well-prepared to the hearings. Vaughan Dowie, who had just gone to work for the organization, subsequently remembered his amazement that the office functioned twenty-four hours a day, seven days a week, and that the staff worked extra hours without complaining.[95] Alliance Quebec's sixty-page brief was accompanied by so many research studies and supporting documents that, as Eric Maldoff remembered several years later, a group of anglophone school children on a class visit to the National Assembly were recruited to carry the mountain of documents into the committee room. Godin seemed dismayed by the professionalism of the presentation, and left the hearings without speaking to the delegation from Alliance Quebec.[96]

The committee consultations nonetheless led the government in November to introduce Bill 57, which was considered a significant victory for Alliance Quebec. The bill amended the charter in a number of ways. Section 1 amended the preamble to state that the National Assembly respected the institutions of the English-speaking community of Quebec. Section 2 exempted municipal, educational and social service institutions which served a predominantly anglophone clientele from the requirement that all employees must be fluent in French, provided the institutions had enough bilingual employees to be capable of serving francophones in French. Section 6 provided that municipal, educational, and social service institutions serving a mainly anglophone clientele could communicate with one another in English, and that written communications within such institutions could be in English only. Section 7 removed the requirement that predominantly anglophone school boards provide a French translation of their pedagogical communications. Section 9 relaxed the requirement for French language testing of professionals by providing that those who had been educated in French, or those who graduated from any Quebec high school in 1986 or later, would be automatically exempted from the test. There were also some minor and essentially cosmetic changes to the provisions regarding commercial advertising and access to English schools.

The National Assembly considered Bill 57 in December 1983. Since the subject had already been discussed in lengthy committee hearings the usual protracted committee stage after first reading was replaced by four days of discussion in committee after second reading. In the National Assembly Reed Scowen congratulated Godin on his flexibility, but the Liberals nonetheless complained that the bill was inadequate since English on commercial signs would still be prohibited and migrants from other provinces would still be denied access to English schools.[97] After a relatively brief debate the bill received royal assent on 22 December 1983.[98]

Meanwhile another major issue had appeared on the political agenda. As mentioned above, the government's plans to reform the educational system and eliminate denominational school boards had become common knowledge in the latter part of 1981, and had contributed to the mobilization of anglophone opinion leading up to the formation of Alliance Quebec. Petitions demanding the maintenance of the denominational system were circulated in English-speaking neighbourhoods of Montreal and a number of them, with lengthy lists of signatures, were presented in the National Assembly by Liberal members. In June 1982, soon after the Alliance Quebec convention, Camille Laurin released the long-rumoured White Paper on educational reform.[99] Although it did call for an end to the denominational system and for reducing the powers of school boards generally, it differed from an earlier draft whose contents had been leaked several months previously in at least one important respect. It proposed that on Montreal Island there would be linguistic school boards, English and French, rather than the unified boards envisaged for the rest of the province. This change was a significant victory for English-speaking Quebeckers, and at least indirectly for Alliance Quebec.

The proposal for linguistic boards nonetheless drew attention to a division in the English-speaking community and created a dilemma, in the short term at least, for Alliance Quebec. Anglophone Catholics tended to favour linguistic boards since they were a minority of taxpayers, students and trustees on all of the French-dominated Catholic boards. Jews, never comfortable with their anomalous status under the denominational system, would also be better served by boards based on language. However many Protestants, or at least the Protestant educational establishment, still insisted that the denominational system must be maintained and that the constitutional guarantee of Protestant schools in Quebec was the only reliable defence of English-language education. The latter argument gave little comfort to anglophone Catholics and by 1982 was questionable for two other reasons. First, the recently adopted Canadian Charter of Rights and Freedoms guaranteed minority language educational rights regardless of religion and second, the Protestant boards themselves were converting many of their schools from English to French so as to retain their immigrant clientele despite the Charter of the French Language.

Alliance Quebec favoured linguistic boards but at first did not emphasize this preference for fear of offending the Protestant school boards. Its initial response to the White Paper was thus extremely critical. When the government announced in October 1982 that the introduction of legislation based on the White Paper would be delayed until the following year, Lévesque was able to interpret the delay as evidence of his reasonableness towards the demands of Alliance Quebec. For its own reasons Alliance Quebec chose to accept this interpretation.

By the following year Alliance Quebec was ready to take a clearer position on the issue. The Townshippers' Association held a friendly meeting with Laurin in April 1983 and seemed to accept the substance of his proposals. The second annual convention of Alliance Quebec endorsed the idea of linguistic boards, with or without a constitutional guarantee. The Protestant school boards appeared to be isolated, although they soon found powerful allies among francophone Catholics who feared any further secularization of the school system. Laurin's educational bill died in committee, largely because of this francophone opposition, and Laurin himself was shifted to another portfolio in March 1984. His successor introduced a modified version of the bill which was adopted in December, but after a judge of the Quebec Superior Court ruled it to be unconstitutional the government lost interest in the issue and did not bother to appeal the decision. The issue was nonetheless still alive, and the delay had allowed the English-speaking community to move much closer to a consensus in favour of linguistic boards. Alliance Quebec could take some credit for providing leadership in this regard.

Several different factors help to explain the vitality and vigour of Alliance Quebec from 1982 through 1985, and its success in establishing a working relationship with the Parti Québécois government. In the first place, Eric Maldoff was a skilful and effective leader who devoted great energy and enthusiasm to the cause. His principal lieutenants Michael Goldbloom (who succeeded him in May 1985) and Geoffrey Chambers were also important assets to the organization. Significantly, all three were veterans of Participation Québec, although Chambers had also been involved in Positive Action. They belonged to a new generation that was functionally bilingual and had grown up in post-Quiet Revolution Quebec, without the inherited intellectual and emotional baggage of another era. While determined to maintain a viable English-speaking community in Quebec, they also knew enough not to make unreasonable or reactionary demands. In a sense they represented the "new middle class" of English-speaking Quebec just as the Parti Québécois represented the new middle class of French-speaking Quebec, so the two sides had much in common.

The situation of the English-speaking community in the early 1980s was also conducive to the success of Alliance Quebec. There were anglophones who found life in a nationalist Quebec intolerable, or who were totally unwilling to adapt to it, but the most vigorous and articulate of those who fell into this category had largely departed during the exodus between 1976 and 1980. Most of those who remained were realistic enough to accept the moderate leadership of Alliance Quebec, but also dissatisfied enough to perceive a real need for the organization. At the same time the failure of the Liberal Party to win the 1981 election encouraged them to invest their energies, at least for the time being, in interest group activity rather than party politics.

Interest group activity, to be successful, requires that the government accept both the legitimacy of the interest that is being represented and the mandate of the organization to represent the interest in question.[100] Both conditions were fulfilled in the years between 1982 and 1985. The Parti Québécois must have realized that it would never win anglophone votes in large numbers, but appeasing anglophones was necessary because their conspicuous dissatisfaction was bad for the economy and bad for Quebec's external image. Thus defence of anglophone interests was considered legitimate.

The other condition was fulfilled because Alliance Quebec seemed the best available organization to represent the anglophone point of view. Premier Lévesque knew that the small anglophone wing of his own party did not represent the community's views, and he also knew that the radical or militant element represented by Freedom of Choice would not engage in a fruitful dialogue with his government. Alliance Quebec with its middle-of-the-road position avoided the disadvantages of both extremes. At the same time Alliance Quebec was avowedly non-partisan and, although presumably federalist in its sympathies, did not emphasize constitutional issues or its opposition to a sovereign Quebec. In this regard it followed in the tradition of Participation Québec by concentrating on relations between communities within the province.

Alliance Quebec did have its weaknesses, and these became more apparent at a later date. In the first place it essentially represented middle-class persons of English mother tongue and British, Irish, or Jewish origins. It had little appeal to the working class, who were not interested in such issues as allowing merchants to display bilingual signs or exempting professionals from language tests. It also had little rapport with allophones, who still preferred to rely on their own ethnic associations or on the Liberal Party for support.

In the second place, community support for Alliance Quebec depended on the perception that it was continuing to win meaningful concessions from the government. Bill 57 was a significant victory that maintained the organization's momentum for some time, but if additional victories did not follow from time to time the community would become disillusioned and lose interest. If this happened anglophones might lapse into apathy, resume their outward migration from the province, or follow more militant and radical leaders rather than the moderate leadership of Alliance Quebec.

6 False Hopes Betrayed:
Bill 178 and
the Anglophone Reaction,
1985–94

In *The Caine Mutiny*, Herman Wouk's novel of the Pacific War, the ill-fated minesweeper is commanded initially by a gruff, but capable, officer named Captain de Vries. Willie Keith, the naive young ensign from whose perspective the story is told, at first welcomes the replacement of de Vries by the superficially pleasant but emotionally unstable Philip Queeg. Like the rest of the crew, he later changes his mind when the morale and efficiency of the ship deteriorate under Queeg's leadership. In the book de Vries does not reappear, but Hollywood could not resist giving the story a more dramatic ending. The movie ends, after the mutiny, the court martial, and the ruin of Queeg's career, with de Vries returning to the ship. As the last reel unwinds, he is seen striding down the pier to assume command, while an incredulous Willie Keith looks on and martial music plays in the background.

From the perspective of English-speaking Quebeckers, Robert Bourassa was the Captain de Vries of Quebec politics. They had never felt much affection for him during his first government, and had tended to underestimate him even while they voted for him. After Bill 22 they had willed his departure and in 1976 they had received their wish, only to discover that they had jumped from the frying pan into the fire. No one then had foreseen that he would ever return, but life sometimes imitates art, as Oscar Wilde observed. In December 1985, after a decade that had seen the English-speaking community of Quebec literally decimated, Robert Bourassa was premier of Quebec once more. However, the de Vries analogy is faulty in one important respect. Bourassa's second term of office would be much more traumatic for English-speaking Quebeckers than his first, and perhaps even more so than the interregnum under the Parti Québécois.

Claude Ryan's resignation as leader of the Quebec Liberal Party in August 1982 was followed by a period of interim leadership under Gérard D. Lévesque, who had represented Bonaventure riding since the days of Duplessis. "Gerry D.," as he was known to his colleagues, had no wish to lead the party through an election campaign, and the would-be successors were soon jockeying for position. Robert Bourassa's leadership campaign did not officially begin until August 1983, three months before the convention, but in fact he had been preparing for a comeback since 1979, and had participated in both the referendum campaign of 1980 and the election campaign of 1981. In the race to succeed Ryan he was "the most left-leaning and the most nationalist of the candidates,"[1] appealing to those Liberals who thought that the party had lost in 1981 because it was too conservative and too sympathetic to the anglophones. Bourassa won the leadership with an overwhelming vote on the first ballot, his percentage of the delegates exceeding even that attained by Jean Lesage in 1958.[2]

Bourassa's return to the leadership owed nothing to the party's nonfrancophone element. Most of the anglophone and allophone Liberal members of the National Assembly supported Daniel Johnson, who came third in the race. Joan Dougherty and Maximilien Polak were the only exceptions, and they supported Pierre Paradis, a young member from the Eastern Townships, who surprised some observers by coming second. Richard French and Herbert Marx were the least hostile to Bourassa of the English-speaking members, but both were deterred from supporting him by the overwhelming opposition to him in their constituency associations. For French the choice of Johnson was easy since Johnson was a personal friend as well as the choice of the party members in Westmount. French also thought that he would be considered an opportunist if he voted in those circumstances for Bourassa, who was certain to win.[3] Marx, who liked and admired Bourassa, did not feel he could justifiably defy the strong anti-Bourassa sentiment in his riding; he was warned by Bourassa's chief organizer, Marc-Yvan Cote, that his failure to support the new leader would be remembered.[4]

Bourassa led the party for some time without a seat in the National Assembly. During this period he asked Harry Blank to resign and open a seat for Bourassa to contest in a by-election, as the member for

Argenteuil had done when Claude Ryan needed a seat in 1978.[5] Blank refused on the grounds that he had first been elected in 1960 and wanted the distinction of serving for a quarter of a century. In fact Blank had no intention of retiring at all, and he was renominated early in 1985 as the Liberal candidate in St-Louis.

By this time Bourassa had won a by-election in Bertrand, a solidly francophone suburban riding on the south shore of the St Lawrence that had been won by the Parti Québécois in 1981. He would run there again in the general election. However he needed a seat for a star candidate from the business community, Pierre MacDonald, who was a francophone in spite of his surname. Blank celebrated his twenty-fifth anniversary by telling the National Assembly, in what proved to be his last parliamentary speech, that he hoped to serve for a few more years.[6] When the election was called in October, Blank was again approached and asked to resign with an implied promise of patronage but again refused. This time the party overturned Blank's nomination in St-Louis only to discover that MacDonald, a business executive without political experience, had no desire to run in a downtown riding where there was a chance of being defeated by the Parti Québécois. Bourassa then asked John O'Gallagher, the member for Robert-Baldwin, to step down. O'Gallagher had been planning to run again but was persuaded to retire when the election was called and not seek renomination. MacDonald was nominated in Robert-Baldwin, where the Liberal candidate scarcely needed to campaign.

The effect of these machinations was that the Liberal caucus lost two of its English-speaking members. O'Gallagher left quietly but Blank decided to run as an independent against Jacques Chagnon, the president of the Quebec Federation of Catholic School Commissions and the last-minute choice of the Liberals in St-Louis. Blank won just over 4000 votes, fewer than the Parti Québécois candidate and less than half as many as Chagnon. This episode cost him any hope of patronage but gained him considerable sympathy. In what Gérald Godin saw as poetic justice, Bourassa lost his riding to the Parti Québécois.[7] As a result the premier was forced to run in a by-election in St-Laurent, a riding with a large English-speaking minority.

The only new English-speaking candidate in 1985 was John Parisella, who had left his job in party headquarters after the 1981 election to work for the Council of Quebec Minorities, then for Alliance Quebec, and finally for the federal Commissioner of Official Languages. He ran against Godin in Mercier, the riding which Bourassa had lost to Godin in 1976. Godin managed to defeat Parisella in a close race, but the Parti Québécois elected only five members on Montreal Island, the lowest number in the party's history. Robert Dean and David Payne both lost their seats, as did more than thirty other incumbent members of the Parti Québécois, including several ministers. Overall the Liberals won ninety-nine seats and the Parti Québécois only twenty-three.

Although none had supported him in his leadership campaign, Bourassa named four anglophones to his cabinet. John Ciaccia became minister of energy and resources, Richard French minister of communications, Clifford Lincoln minister of the environment, and Herbert Marx minister of justice. The justice portfolio, one of the most important in the government, had not been held by an anglophone for more than a hundred years, but Marx's expertise in constitutional law and civil liberties made him the most obvious choice, with the possible exception of Gil Rémillard who was appointed to intergovernmental relations. Constitutional discussions with the federal government were expected to loom large on the new government's agenda.

The major surprise of the new cabinet was the fact that Reed Scowen was not included. NDG had been represented at the cabinet table in every Liberal government since 1939, and the bestowing of a portfolio on its representative had almost attained the status of a constitutional convention. Scowen had more experience in the National Assembly than French, Lincoln or Marx, and he could indirectly represent the English-speaking communities outside of Montreal, since he had spent most of his life in the Eastern Townships. However, he had been one of the most vocal opponents of Bourassa's return to power and it was said that some of the new premier's advisers thought he needed to be taught a lesson. As a consolation prize he was made both legislative assistant and economic adviser to the premier, and was later placed in charge of a task force on deregulation. He also acted as a channel of communication for many anglophone individuals and groups seeking access to the premier. Disappointed by his exclusion from the cabinet, he later concluded that "there were a lot of forces arrayed against me."[8]

Whether they were appointed to the cabinet or not, most of the anglophone members were at first pleasantly surprised with Bourassa. He did not appear to bear grudges against those who had failed to support his campaign for the leadership, and was generally pleasant to work with. He also seemed open and sympathetic to the concerns of the English-speaking community, although he had not previously had that reputation. Even Reed Scowen thought in retrospect that Bourassa had personally accepted the idea of a bilingual Quebec and that he was less of a French-Canadian nationalist than Ryan, despite appearances to the contrary.[9]

On the other hand, the composition of the Liberal caucus in the National Assembly had changed in a way that did not bode well for the concerns of anglophones and other minorities. The Liberal members who had survived the 1976 election, and the somewhat larger number elected in 1981, had mainly represented constituencies with significant non-francophone populations. Almost half of those elected in 1981 were from Montreal Island, and more than half of the Montreal Island members themselves had a mother tongue other than French. The 1985 election brought to the National Assembly a large number of francophone Liberals whose constituencies were almost entirely francophone and sympathetic towards Quebec nationalism. Most of these new members were young and tended to be nationalists out of conviction, even if opportunism had not inclined them in that direction. Clifford Lincoln recalled that these younger Liberals, many of whom were not bilingual, had "a very different mindset." They were "nice, articulate, smart, but petrified of French losing its force in Quebec and being threatened."[10]

The caucus also lost an important spokesman for the English-speaking community in June 1987, when Reed Scowen resigned his seat to become Quebec's delegate-general in London. His departure necessitated a by-election in NDG, the fourth experienced by that riding in twenty-five years. There was some feeling at party headquarters that this might be the time and the place for a visible minority candidate, but John Parisella had already approached Harold Thuringer, a social worker from Saskatchewan who had lived in NDG since coming to Quebec in 1970. The by-election, like the three previous in that riding, was little more than a formality and Thuringer took his seat in the National Assembly in the fall of 1987.

ANGLOPHONES AND
THE LIBERAL AGENDA

One major issue of concern to English-speaking Quebeckers had already been settled before Bourassa returned to office, and in a way compatible with Quebec Liberal Party policy. The Canadian Charter of Rights and Freedoms had come into effect on 15 April 1982, despite the objections of the Lévesque government. Section 23:1(b) of the Charter gave Canadian citizens resident in Quebec who had received an English education anywhere in Canada the right to have their children educated in English. This provision, which came to be known in Quebec as the "Canada clause," coincided with the policy of the Quebec Liberals. Section 59 of the Charter, a last-minute concession to Quebec, exempted Quebec from Section 23:1(a), a somewhat broader definition of minority language educational rights imposed on the other provinces. Section 59 also provided that the exemption could be ended by a resolution of the National Assembly accepting Section 23:1(a), but no one seriously expected that to happen.

Since Section 23 was obviously incompatible with the very restricted access to English schools imposed by Sections 72 and 73 of the Charter of the French Language, the Association of Quebec Protestant School Boards wasted little time in taking the issue to court. Its demand that Sections 72 and 73 be struck down was upheld by the Superior Court, the Court of Appeal, and finally, on 26 July 1984, the Supreme Court of Canada. In its unanimous decision the Supreme Court ruled that, since Section 23 "was in large part a response" to Sections 72 and 73 of the Charter of the French Language, the provision in Section 1 of the Charter of Rights and Freedoms subordinating rights to "such reasonable limits prescribed by law as can be demonstrably justified in a free and democratic society" could not be used to uphold those sections.[11] While the Court's decision fell far short of requiring freedom of choice, it was an important, although entirely predictable, victory for the English-speaking community. It also removed from the Quebec Liberal Party the responsibility of legislating their own policy into effect when they took office. Legislation imposing the Canada clause in the absence of a court ruling would certainly have caused a lengthy and bitter debate within (and also outside of) the National Assembly.

The new Liberal government sent the right signals to the English-speaking community in a number of ways. The previous government's practice of routinely invoking the notwithstanding clause in the Canadian Charter of Rights and Freedoms so as to shield all legislation from possible challenges in the courts was discontinued almost immediately. Claude Ryan, who had been appointed minister of education, introduced Bill 58, the so-called amnesty bill, which was adopted early in the session.[12] Bill 58 recognized the fact that many school boards had continued to defy the terms of the Charter of the French Language after 1977 by enrolling children in English schools who were not strictly speaking eligible. It allowed such children to remain in English schools and removed from them the stigma of being "illegal."

A much more significant measure in terms of the number of people affected concerned the question of access to health care and social services in the English language. Six months before the election, the General Council of the Liberal Party had adopted an important resolution on policies towards the English-speaking community.[13] The preamble noted that the English-speaking community was the largest and the most deeply rooted of the minority groups in Quebec and that it represented in Quebec "one of the two founding peoples of our country." The resolution itself made four specific promises:

- A Liberal government would recognize the right of the community to direct and administer its own educational, cultural, health and social service institutions.
- A Liberal government would ensure that public and parapublic services were available to anglophones in their own language.
- A Liberal government would make efforts to increase the representation of anglophones in the public and parapublic sectors to a level commensurate with their numbers.
- A Liberal government would respect the right to display signs in languages other than French, bearing in mind the obligation to respect the rights of the francophone majority.

The adoption of this resolution by the party, and particularly of the first two points, was in part the consequence of a systematic pressure campaign by Alliance Quebec. After the adoption of Bill 57 by the previous government, English-language health care and social services became Alliance Quebec's first priority. This was partly because of dissatisfaction with the Lévesque government's insistence that the three social service centres on Montreal Island have geographic boundaries rather than serving an ethnically defined clientele regardless of location. It also reflected the priorities of a population with an increasing proportion of older people following the exodus of young people after 1976. In addition, there was a realistic chance of progress on this issue because it did not seem to have the same symbolic importance for Quebec nationalists as the issues of commercial signs and access to English-language education.

Although the Quebec Liberal Party was now on record as supporting the demand for a guarantee of English-language health and social services, lobbying efforts continued after they took office in order to ensure that the party would not forget its promise. Michael Goldbloom, who had become president of Alliance Quebec before the election, was assisted in this effort by Eric Maldoff as past president and by Vaughan Dowie, who had succeeded Geoffrey Chambers as executive director in 1984. As mentioned in chapter 4, Dowie was a community activist with an interest in social issues. Also working on the file was Russell Williams, the director of the social affairs department of Alliance Quebec, who would later be elected to the National Assembly as a Liberal.

The result of their efforts was that the government introduced Bill 142 in 1986. This relatively brief measure added a new section to the Health Services and Social Services Act which provided that "Every English-speaking person is entitled to receive health services and social services in the English language, taking into account the organization and resources of the establishments providing such services." It amended Section 3 of the same act to provide that health and social services in each region of Quebec must be adapted to "the physical, geographic, linguistic and sociocultural characteristics of the region." It also gave the government the power to designate by regulation which health and social service institutions would be required to make services available in English.[14]

Christos Sirros, as parliamentary secretary to the minister of social affairs, was given the task of piloting the bill through the National Assembly. While doing so he worked closely with Russell Williams of Alliance Quebec – an indication of the reputation and influence which the organization enjoyed at that time.[15] The Parti Québécois, recognizing an issue that might help to restore the party's fortunes, argued that the bill would encourage immigrants to assimilate into the English-speaking community. Sirros denied this and argued that the bill was a humanitarian measure that merely gave immigrants a choice between services in French or in English, recognizing the fact that some of them had more knowledge of English than of French.[16] Reed Scowen noted that Bill 142 would also help anglophones in remote regions not served by anglophone institutions.[17] Robert Middlemiss pointed out that it would give anglophones in Pontiac less incentive to go to Ontario for health care and social services.[18] The bill was adopted on a roll call vote on 18 December 1986, with the Parti Québécois voting against it.

During the second session of the National Assembly, the Liberals undertook to resolve the seemingly intractable problem of school board reorganization, which had resisted the efforts of previous governments for twenty years. Claude Ryan introduced Bill 107, a measure to amend the Education Act. This provided for linguistic school boards, English or French, throughout the province, except that within the city boundaries of Quebec City and Montreal Catholic and Protestant boards would be retained for the time being in accordance with the constitution of Canada.[19] Mindful of the previous government's experience, Ryan also stated that Bill 107 would not be implemented until the Supreme Court of Canada had ruled it to be constitutional. The Supreme Court so ruled in 1993,[20] but the statute had still not been brought into effect when the Liberals left office more than a year later.

As mentioned in the previous chapter, Alliance Quebec had gradually built a consensus within the English-speaking community in favour
of linguistic boards, while its own position had evolved towards one
of enthusiastic support for the idea. Among anglophone politicians,
only Joan Dougherty, the former head of the Protestant School Board
of Greater Montreal, continued to espouse the traditional view that
denominational Protestant boards must be preserved.[21] The fact that
such boards were formally "Protestant" rather than English allowed
them to retain control of their French-language schools, which were
the only growing part of the "Protestant" system. Their opposition to
Bill 107 was thus an obvious expression of institutional self-interest.
Dougherty later argued, no doubt sincerely, that she opposed it
because "I didn't like the idea of anglos being ghettoized. The so-
called confessional boards allowed for more contact."[22]

Alliance Quebec, however, saw linguistic boards as the only realistic
way to maintain a viable system of education controlled by anglophones and guaranteeing access to English-language education
throughout the province. Protestant boards were increasingly bilingual
institutions and if their growing French-language sectors became predominant they would no longer be anglophone institutions under
anglophone control. Royal Orr, who succeeded Michael Goldbloom
as president of Alliance Quebec in 1987, was a Protestant teacher from
the Eastern Townships, where the decline and the aging of the
English-speaking population had had a particularly severe impact on
school enrollments. He knew that the English-speaking community
could no longer afford to remain divided along religious lines. As he
explained in 1988 to the legislative committee considering Bill 107,
enrollment in English-language schools throughout Quebec had
declined by 53 per cent between 1975 and 1986. In the same period
the proportion of "Protestant" school children who received their
education in French had increased from 2 to 20 per cent. The remaining English-language enrollment was almost evenly divided between
the Protestant and Catholic systems. Orr expressed the hope that
denominational boards in the two major cities would be eliminated as
soon as possible, for the same reason that he supported their elimination elsewhere. He urged the government to request that the Canadian constitution be amended so as to guarantee the preservation of
English-language boards, rather than of Protestant boards.[23]

By the time the Liberals celebrated their third anniversary in office
there had been some progress in achieving the objectives which Alliance Quebec had defined at the time of its foundation, but in two
significant areas there had been none. The first was the representation
of anglophones in the public service, which continued to be as minimal

as ever. The second and far more contentious issue was the question of bilingual signs. By the end of 1988 this issue could no longer be contained and it finally erupted in dramatic fashion, with a lasting impact on Quebec politics. To understand why and how this happened it is necessary to retrace our steps and examine the evolution of the issue over the years since the Charter of the French Language came into effect.

SIGNS AND SYMBOLS

In the early days after the adoption of the Charter the issue of commercial signs was somewhat overshadowed by other matters, and particularly by the restrictions on access to English education. The administrative machinery necessary to implement the legislation pertaining to signs was not put in place immediately, and the regulation specifying the detailed requirement for signs did not assume its final form until June 1979. Some time elapsed before anyone was prosecuted for violation of the law which provided that commercial signs must be only in French.

In one sense the issue had little practical importance. Even if displaying commercial signs in English is a "right," it is one of which relatively few people wish to take advantage. It directly concerns only those engaged in certain kinds of business, particularly retail trade. Those who read signs are obviously much more numerous than those who display them, but most English-speaking Quebeckers by 1977 had the minimal degree of bilingualism necessary to recognize the few French words most likely to appear on commercial signs. If they did not at the time, they presumably soon acquired it. Proper names, trademarks and pictorial symbols were of course affected very little, if at all.

Yet in another sense the issue was very important to both sides. In chapter 4 Raymond Breton was quoted regarding the disruptive effect on individuals and groups of changes in the symbolic order of society. In a society where commercial enterprise plays as large or larger a role in everyday life as government or religion, advertising is an important part of the symbolic order. For years many francophones had resented the "English visage" of western Montreal and the western suburbs, where English language advertising was as conspicuous and obtrusive as in other North American cities of comparable size. It seemed to symbolize the affluence and economic power of the English-speaking minority and the traditional subordination of the French to the dictates of North American capitalism. Although the economic gap between the two language groups had greatly diminished by 1977, the resentment remained and the temptation to seek revenge through the ballot box and the statute book was irresistible. A related and somewhat more practical consideration was the fear that immigrants, seeing English signs, would conclude that English was still the dominant language in Quebec and that there was no need to learn French.

The issue was also symbolically important for English-speaking Quebeckers. Sheltered from the French-speaking society that surrounded them before the Quiet Revolution, they had witnessed its gradual encroachment on their way of life since the rise of the bureaucratic state after 1960. Bill 22 had begun to restrict, however slightly, the privileges which the minority regarded as "rights," but it did so in a way that continued to give the English-speaking community some recognition. The prohibition of English or bilingual signs seemed like an effort to deny that the minority language and the community that used it even existed. Section 58 of the Charter of the French Language seemed to say, in effect, that the existence of an anglophone minority was a shameful fact that must be concealed from public view.

The first legal challenge to the sign law was launched in 1978 by Allan Singer, the owner of a store in NDG that sold office supplies and stationery. Singer, who had been one of the founders of the short-lived Quebec Conservative Party in 1966 and would later be a candidate for the Freedom of Choice Party in 1981, refused to remove a unilingual English sign from his store. When prosecuted he challenged the validity of several sections of the Charter of the French Language, claiming that they intruded on federal jurisdiction and were contrary to Quebec's Charter of Human Rights and Freedoms. The Superior Court ruled against him in 1982, less than a month before the Canadian Charter of Rights and Freedoms came into effect. Singer appealed the decision.

In November 1983 the president of the Quebec Human Rights Commission, Francine Fournier, advised the legislative committee considering possible changes to the language law that the prohibition of the English language on signs violated freedom of expression, a right guaranteed by both the Canadian Charter of Rights and Freedoms and Quebec's Charter of Human Rights and Freedoms.[24] Three months later a new court challenge was launched by Valerie Ford, who operated a wool store in Pointe-Claire, and by four locally owned business enterprises incorporated under Quebec law. All five plaintiffs had been charged with displaying bilingual signs at various locations on Montreal Island. Unlike Singer, they did not claim the right to display signs in English only, but only to include English as well as French. Ford's store, for example, had a French name and only one English word ("wool") had appeared on the offending sign. The

Superior Court ruled in their favour on 28 December 1984 and the Quebec government appealed. The appeal was still pending when the Liberals returned to office.

As noted above, the Quebec Liberal Party was on record since June 1985 as supporting the right to display signs in languages other than French. Pressure from Alliance Quebec, the enthusiastic support of Reed Scowen, and the declining popularity of the Lévesque government in its last months had contributed to the adoption of this policy. Some Liberals, including some anglophones, had misgivings about making such a categorical commitment and creating an issue which the Parti Québécois might use to the party's disadvantage. Nonetheless, Robert Bourassa repeated the promise to allow bilingual signs during the election campaign, notably during a debate on the leading English-language radio station CJAD.[25]

Probably the best time to implement a controversial policy is immediately after a successful election campaign, when the government's popularity is at its peak and the opposition is in disarray. For whatever reason, Premier Bourassa passed up this opportunity, using the pretext that it would be more appropriate to wait for the decision of the Court of Appeal on the case launched by Valerie Ford and her co-plaintiffs. Meanwhile, as Justice Minister Herbert Marx explained to the National Assembly in April 1986, the government was not prosecuting businesses that displayed bilingual signs but would prosecute those whose signs were in English only.[26] When opposition leader Pierre-Marc Johnson accused the government of tolerating illegal behaviour, Marx pointed out that the previous government had pursued the same policy while its appeal in the *Ford* case was pending.[27]

Quebec nationalists were beginning to rally their forces to defend the Charter of the French Language, and in June 1986 the General Council of the Quebec Liberal Party adopted a new resolution relating to signs which differed somewhat in emphasis from that adopted a year earlier.[28] The General Council resolved that the government should take all the measures necessary to preserve "*l'image française du Québec,*" that it should allow the use of a language other than French on signs, but that in such cases French must be more prominent than the other language. The Parti Québécois continued to accuse the government of failing to enforce the sign law, and in October introduced a motion of censure which referred to the issue. In response, Marx repeated that businesses displaying bilingual signs would not be prosecuted until the Court of Appeal handed down its decision.[29] On 19 December 1986, however, he asserted that the government had waited long enough for the decision and would begin to prosecute bilingual signs after all.[30]

Three days after Marx's announcement the Court of Appeal ruled in favour of Valerie Ford and the four other business enterprises which had displayed bilingual signs. At the same time it ruled against Allan Singer, on the grounds that requiring a sign to include French as well as English did not violate freedom of expression. Over the next few days, unidentified persons vandalized several stores owned by anglophones, including that of McKenna Inc., a prominent florist and one of the five businesses involved in the *Ford* case. Although the Court of Appeal had in effect endorsed the Liberal Party's policy of allowing bilingual signs but prohibiting those in English only, Premier Bourassa continued to hesitate rather than carrying out his promise to amend the law. In March the government announced that it would appeal the decision to the Supreme Court of Canada for "technical reasons," giving itself another pretext to delay. At the same time the Quebec Department of Justice quietly agreed to pay the legal costs of the government's ostensible opponents. Herbert Marx would later say that this was done without his knowledge, but the furore that ensued when it became known made it politically inadvisable for Bourassa to retain Marx as justice minister.[31] Bourassa, who remained on friendly terms with Marx, offered him a choice between a judicial appointment and another portfolio. Marx chose the latter option and became solicitor-general on 23 June 1988, with the understanding that the portfolio would be given more responsibilities than in the past. A few weeks later his title was changed to minister of public security.

Meanwhile, in March 1988 the federal commissioner of official languages, d'Iberville Fortier, had described the continuing prohibition of bilingual signs as "disturbing" in his annual report. He also expressed the view that "the salvation of French ... must surely lie in positively asserting its own demographic weight, cultural vigour and innate attractiveness, and not in humbling the competition."[32] The Parti Québécois introduced a motion denouncing the commissioner's comments and claiming that Quebec was in danger of being anglicized. Premier Bourassa told the National Assembly that he considered Fortier's comments neither realistic nor responsible. He also stated that Quebec's French majority was too vulnerable to run the risk of accepting "unconditional and unlimited bilingualism."[33] Bourassa introduced an amendment to the opposition motion which toned it down slightly and to which the opposition agreed. The motion was then adopted unanimously.

Several of the English-speaking members later regretted their participation in this vote and their failure to defend the commissioner for expressing sentiments that were shared by most of the voters in their ridings. Joan Dougherty was particularly reluctant to support the resolution and was persuaded to do so only at the last moment. Harold Thuringer also had serious misgivings. Their silence on this issue, as well as later events, would cost both Dougherty and Thuringer their seats in the 1989 election. At the time most of the anglophones rationalized their vote by the argument that a motion which had no legal force was not a serious enough matter to justify a public breach of party solidarity. The English-speaking ministers, if not perhaps the backbenchers, were also aware that a more serious conflict between party discipline and anglophone interests would probably arise in the near future, when the Supreme Court of Canada handed down its decision on the question of bilingual signs.

That moment came in December 1988, when the Supreme Court of Canada released its decision on the government's appeal in the *Ford* case.[34] The decision on Allan Singer's appeal was handed down simultaneously. As most informed observers had expected, the Supreme Court's rulings were not much different in substance from those of the Court of Appeal. The Court found freedom of expression to include the right to advertise in the language of one's choice. While constitutional rights were subject to "reasonable limits" under Section 1 of the Canadian Charter of Rights and Freedoms and under Section 9.1 of Quebec's Charter of Human Rights and Freedoms, a prohibition of English was not a reasonable restriction, although a requirement that the message be repeated in French or even that the French inscription be more prominent could be considered reasonable. The requirement that signs be in French only had been shielded against the Canadian Charter of Rights and Freedoms by the Lévesque government's use of the notwithstanding clause in Bill 57, but this protection was to expire on 1 February 1989, the fifth anniversary of when Bill 57 (which had re-enacted the original prohibition in slightly modified form) came into effect.

Nationalists responded with predictable denunciations of the Supreme Court of Canada. The rhetorical nadir of the language debate was perhaps reached when Paul Rose, who had been paroled after serving eleven years of a life sentence for his part in the kidnapping and murder of Labour Minister Pierre Laporte during the October Crisis, described the Court's decision as "very extremist."[35] At the request of the Parti Québécois opposition, the National Assembly held a debate on the "emergency" brought about by the Supreme Court's decision. By this time, as his behaviour over the past three years and his remarks in the d'Iberville Fortier debate had suggested, Premier Bourassa had concluded that his electoral promise to allow bilingual signs was not politically viable. Within a few days of the decision the government introduced Bill 178, which would continue to require that most commercial signs be in French only.[36] However, signs located inside a business establishment, and thus presumably directed at those who had already decided to do business there, might be partially in "another language," provided that the French inscription was predominant. The bill would also give the government extensive powers to make regulations specifying the precise requirements. Because this measure would admittedly violate the right to freedom of expression as defined by the Supreme Court, the notwithstanding clauses in both the Canadian Charter of Rights and Freedoms and Quebec's Charter of Human Rights and Freedoms would be used to bring it into effect.

This measure came as a tremendous shock to English-speaking Quebeckers, and particularly to anglophone members of the Quebec Liberal Party. Joan Dougherty later described it as "the end of everything we had fought for."[37] It created a painful dilemma for the English-speaking ministers, Ciaccia, French, Lincoln and Marx, who knew that they must either acquiesce in a measure that offended most of the voters in their ridings or resign from the government. Bourassa, who had survived a similar crisis over Bill 22 without losing any of his ministers, seems to have expected that his anglophone colleagues would also accept Bill 178. He later told William Cosgrove, a Liberal candidate in the 1989 election, that he had expected the anger in the anglophone community to die down after two or three months.[38]

But anglophones did not forget or forgive. They might have expected something like Bill 178 from the Parti Québécois, but they felt betrayed by a party that had received the overwhelming share of their support in 1985. Unlike Bill 22, Bill 178 broke an explicit promise to the English-speaking community and it was also admittedly contrary to the Canadian Charter of Rights and Freedoms, a document which had become an important symbol for English-speaking Canadians, not least those who lived in Quebec. Moderate anglophones in the Liberal Party recognized that the French language needed some protection in North America, and some felt guilty about the economic power that Quebec anglophones had enjoyed in the past. Privately at least they accepted the legitimacy of Bill 22 and even, to some extent, of Bill 101. But Bill 178, introduced after the Supreme Court of Canada had offered the government another option and at a time when the anglophone community had already been weakened economically and numerically, seemed unnecessarily vindictive. It appeared to deny that the English-speaking community had any right to exist. Joan Dougherty was "devastated" when Claude Ryan, whom she greatly admired, brusquely told her that the anglophone voters in her riding were "living on another planet" and she was wasting her time by trying to represent their views.[39]

Clifford Lincoln, who of the four ministers was the most offended by Bill 178, met with the premier and urged him to reconsider and to make some compromise with the views of the anglophone community.[40] Bourassa, as he later explained to an academic audience and in his book, believed that Bill 178 was itself a compromise which would be criticized by Quebec nationalists, and that it would have been politically most expedient to re-enact the original terms of Bill 101.[41] He refused to compromise any further. Perhaps, as Lincoln later believed, Bourassa had hoped until the last moment that the Supreme Court would hand down a decision that gave him more freedom to manoeuvre.[42]

Lincoln's riding of Nelligan had a large and growing francophone population and he could probably have been re-elected if he had gone along with the government's decision. He loved his work as minister of the environment and was deeply committed to it. Nonetheless, he decided that his conscience would not allow him to remain in the government. As he told the National Assembly in a celebrated speech explaining his decision: "Rights are rights are rights. There is no such thing as inside rights and outside rights ... There are no partial rights. Rights are fundamental rights. Rights are links in a chain of fundamental values that binds all individuals in a society that wants to be equitable, and just, and fair."[43]

Neither French nor Marx felt as deeply about the issue as did Lincoln, but both represented ridings that had larger percentages of anglophones than Lincoln's riding, including many business proprietors who would be directly affected by Bill 178. Both realized that they could not accept Bill 178 and retain any political credibility in their ridings, or with the broader English-speaking community which in a sense they represented. Both therefore decided to resign. In contrast to Lincoln, both realized that Bourassa was not likely to change his mind and they made little effort to dissuade him. On the other hand, both recognized the depth of francophone concern about the future of the French language and sympathized with Bourassa in his dilemma.[44] Both used their resignation speeches to plead for mutual understanding between anglophones and francophones.

John Ciaccia, the only one of the four who had been in the National Assembly at the time of Bill 22, had voted against that measure as a backbencher. Now that he was a minister, a decision to break party solidarity would have much more serious consequences. He was being urged by the Italian community to remain in the government, and he regretted the fact that allophones seemed often to be caught in the crossfire of disputes between French and English.[45] He decided not to resign, although many of his constituents in Mount Royal were not happy with his decision. He told the National Assembly that he was "disappointed" in Bill 178 but that the English-speaking community must try to understand the concerns of francophones about their language. He also said that "by staying I can do more than by leaving."[46]

In addition to the three ministers who resigned, Joan Dougherty and Harold Thuringer, whose ridings had large anglophone majorities, refused to support the bill. Robert Middlemiss, with a riding almost evenly divided between anglophones and francophones, shared Bourassa's view that the Liberals would risk losing the next election if they allowed bilingual signs throughout the province. Middlemiss told the National Assembly that he was ambivalent about the bill but would vote for it, in part because he had been assured that bilingual signs might be allowed in municipalities that were predominantly English-speaking.[47] This compromise, which never actually materialized, would have satisfied most of the anglophone voters in Pontiac, where the two language groups tend to live in different municipalities. Members representing ethnically mixed ridings with large immigrant populations had no difficulty supporting Bill 178, because their voters generally did not share the anger of Quebec-born anglophones.

Usually in a parliamentary system the simultaneous resignation on an issue of principle of three respected ministers, all holding important portfolios, is a major crisis that may even precipitate the fall of the government. In Canadian federal politics the collapse of the Diefenbaker government in 1963, and of the Bowell government in 1896, may be cited as examples. During the Second World War the Mackenzie King government survived a similar crisis over conscription, but its survival seemed by no means inevitable at the time. The resignation of three ministers over Bill 178, however, did not seriously threaten the stability or the survival of the Bourassa government. The Liberals were easily re-elected in September 1989 and it is even possible that Bill 178 contributed to their success in that election. John Ciaccia remained the sole representative of the English-speaking and minority communities in the cabinet until October 1989, almost a year after the resignations of French, Lincoln and Marx.

Bill 178 thus demonstrated, even more clearly than Bill 22 in 1974 or Bill 101 in 1977, the political impotence of the English-speaking community in Quebec. After 1974 it had been possible to argue that a credible threat to resign by the anglophone ministers might have prevented the adoption of Bill 22. After 1977 it had been possible to consider the outcome an aberration caused by the election of a nationalist party without significant anglophone support. But after 1988 there could be only one conclusion. Anglophones had been well represented in a cabinet and caucus formed by the party which they traditionally supported, their representatives had carried their protest to the point of resignation, and it had made no difference. The point was not lost on English-speaking voters, whose fury and frustration knew no bounds. The Quebec Liberal Party, as they saw it, had betrayed them again by breaking its promise and adopting legislation which from their perspective seemed unnecessary, petty and vindictive. Alliance Quebec, for reasons that will be explained, had proved ineffective if not irrelevant. The moderate anglophone leadership of both organizations, which had argued that anglophones could count on the goodwill and moderation of the francophone majority, was discredited. New – and some not so new – voices emerged in the English-speaking community to argue for a different approach.

ANGLOPHONE ANGER AND THE ELECTION OF 1989

Premier Bourassa's expectation that the resentment over Bill 178 would subside proved to be erroneous. As they had done in 1976, but to an even greater extent, English-speaking voters turned against the Liberals in 1989. Two new political parties emerged as vehicles of anglophone protest, one in rural Quebec and one in Montreal.

The rural movement, known as the Unity Party, was in effect an offshoot of the Chateauguay Valley English-Speaking People's Association (CVESPA). On 5 January 1989 CVESPA's board of directors held a special meeting to plan a campaign against Bill 178. Maurice King, the founder and president, proposed a plan of action that included a petition to the United Nations, declaring that Bill 178 was in violation of the International Covenant on Civil and Political Rights, a treaty that Canada had signed. The plan was adopted and volunteers, including King himself, began to travel through southwestern Quebec and the Eastern Townships to collect signatures for the petition. In doing so, as King later explained, they encountered significant sentiment in favour of creating a new party as an alternative to the Liberals.[48] King decided to follow this advice and was given a leave of absence by the CVESPA board of directors to devote his energies to organizing the party, of which he became the first leader.

King was a retired railwayman born in Montreal and a former mayor of Greenfield Park, a suburban municipality across the river from Montreal which at that time had a predominantly English-speaking population. He had bought a farm in the Chateauguay Valley in 1965 and eventually retired there, although his retirement proved to be more active than most. After founding CVESPA in 1983 he had devoted most of his time to it and, after 1987, to a monthly publication called

Dialogue which circulated across Canada. In three months of organizing the Unity Party he claimed to have formed associations in fifteen rural ridings and to have signed up five thousand members. Before the election was called he handed over the leadership of the party to James Atkinson, a resident of Huntingdon. (King continued his efforts to have Bill 178 condemned by the United Nations, organizing a petition on behalf of three English-speaking business proprietors in southern Quebec.) The party ran sixteen candidates in the election of 1989, including Atkinson but not King. None of the candidates was widely known outside of his or her local community.

The Montreal-based Equality Party, which would prove to be the more long-lived and successful of the two protest parties, began a little later than its rural counterpart but its origins went back to before the introduction of Bill 178. In March 1988, just after the National Assembly voted to censure the commissioner of official languages, a young architect named Robert Libman met with a few friends to discuss the implications of the vote for English-speaking Quebeckers.[49] Libman, who was only twenty-seven years old, had no previous political experience but he had become concerned about the future of anglophones in Quebec when he noticed how many members of his McGill graduating class were leaving the province. He had become disillusioned with the Liberals after voting for them in 1985 and the unanimous vote to censure d'Iberville Fortier was, as he later put it, "the last straw."[50] He decided that neither the Liberals nor Alliance Quebec could be relied upon and that Quebec anglophones needed either a new party or a new pressure group to defend their interests.

The project did not immediately come to fruition, but further meetings took place. In June Libman attended a public meeting organized by Carol Zimmerman, the social worker who had founded Quebec for All in the aftermath of the 1976 election. She had just founded another group called the Coalition of Canadian Quebeckers, from which she would be expelled less than two months later for being "too radical."[51] Libman attended several meetings of this group where he discussed his idea of a new party and was advised to get in touch with Maurice King. This advice was not immediately taken, but he and his friends began to canvass for the still non-existent political party in Dollard-des-Ormeaux, a largely Jewish suburb that was part of Robert-Baldwin riding. Meanwhile some new supporters had been attracted including Lionel Albert, who had co-authored with William Shaw the book on partition that had proved so disastrous to Shaw's career.[52] Albert subsequently recruited Neil Cameron, a history professor at John Abbott College, the anglophone CEGEP on the West Island.

The movement finally went into high gear after Bill 178 was adopted. In January 1989 a bookseller named Stephen Nowell, who refused to comply with the sign law, organized a public protest meeting at Victoria Hall in Westmount which attracted a thousand people. Neil Cameron, who knew Nowell, was one of the speakers on the platform. Robert Libman was not impressed by Nowell's idea of a civil disobedience campaign but saw the Victoria Hall meeting as evidence that his proposed party would be viable. He decided at last to contact Maurice King, who gave him some useful advice about political organization. The Equality Party really began with a public meeting in NDG on 13 March 1989, which attracted more than three hundred people, many of whom joined the party. Over the next few weeks similar meetings were held in a number of other ridings. In April the Equality Party was given the status of an official political party in Quebec, entitling it to issue tax receipts for donations and to be named on the ballot.

As the anticipated election approached Libman began to look for candidates. He approached some prominent persons including Peter Blaikie, Joan Dougherty, and George Springate. Blaikie was sympathetic but would not commit himself. Dougherty preferred to run again for the Liberals. Springate had apparently abandoned hope that anything could be done to save the anglophone community in Quebec. Libman's overtures were also rejected by Graeme Decarie, a history professor who was chairman of Alliance Quebec, by Bernard Lang, the mayor of Côte St-Luc, and by Joel Hartt, the chairman of the Lakeshore School Board.[53]

One potential candidate who volunteered without being asked was William Shaw, the former Union Nationale member for Pointe-Claire. Shaw's overtures created what Libman described as a "dilemma" for the party.[54] Libman's ideological mentor was Pierre Elliott Trudeau, and he genuinely believed in a bilingual Quebec that was part of a united, bilingual, and liberal Canada. He hoped to attract other persons of like mind, including francophones if possible, and he was greatly concerned lest the party be labelled extremist or reactionary. Somewhat hypocritically, Shaw's co-authorship of the book on partition had left him too controversial to be a candidate, even though the other author, Lionel Albert, was a prominent member of the Equality Party. Libman therefore refused to sign his nomination papers, even though Shaw had already won the party's nomination in Jacques-Cartier by an overwhelming vote. This may have been a mistake, for Shaw was an experienced bilingual parliamentarian and much more moderate in fact than his public image suggested.

The most prominent federal politician who publicly supported the Equality Party was David Berger, who had been a member of parliament for almost ten years at the time of the party's formation. Berger had represented the mainly francophone riding of Laurier until it ceased to exist in 1988, and then moved to St-Henri-Westmount, which had a much larger anglophone population. He had known Gordon Atkinson, one of the four Equality members elected in 1989, for many years and was angry with the Quebec Liberal government over Bill 178. In the summer of 1989 Berger attended an Equality Party fundraising reception with his father Sam Berger, the former owner of the Montreal Alouettes football team and a prominent member of the Jewish community. He later attended another Equality Party meeting, but never became deeply involved. Superficial though it was, his interest in the party offended the provincial Liberal organization in St-Henri, which was part of his federal riding and had helped him in the 1988 campaign. Berger later recalled that it took some effort on his part to restore good relations.[55]

Despite Libman's sincere efforts to include francophones in the Equality Party, it was soon apparent that it would attract very few and that these would be viewed with disfavour by others of their community, much like those anglophones who were brave enough to join the Parti Québécois. Realistically this meant that the party could only hope to win in six or seven ridings: D'Arcy-McGee, NDG, Westmount, Jacques-Cartier, Robert-Baldwin, Mount Royal, and perhaps Nelligan. It would show the flag in as many ridings as possible, although avoiding those where the Unity Party planned to run, but these seven were the highest priorities.

Libman considered being the candidate in Robert-Baldwin but eventually decided to run in D'Arcy-McGee, where a Jewish candidate was essential and where efforts to find a prominent member of the Jewish community who was willing to run were unsuccessful. A professor named Adrian Waller, who was also a columnist for *The Gazette*, then volunteered to run in Robert-Baldwin. Jean-Pierre Isore, one of the party's few francophone members, was nominated in Nelligan. Gordon Atkinson, a popular broadcaster on CJAD who had once been a media adviser to Prime Minister Louis St Laurent, was persuaded by Libman to run in NDG, although he was at first reluctant; he defeated five other candidates, including Neil Cameron, for the nomination. Cameron was then persuaded to run in Jacques-Cartier, where Libman had refused to accept the candidacy of William Shaw, and was nominated in that riding. In Mount Royal, where John Ciaccia's vote for Bill 178 might have made him vulnerable, efforts to find a candidate were so unsuccessful that a self-described "sacrificial lamb" from out-side the riding, Nat Bernstein, volunteered on the last day before the deadline.[56] Richard Lord was nominated in Ste-Anne, where the per-centage of anglophone voters was too small to give him any realistic hope of success. Although generally confined to Montreal and the suburbs, the Equality Party also nominated Peter Vernham to run against Claude Ryan in Argenteuil. In all the party fielded nineteen candidates.

Richard Holden, some of whose previous adventures have already been noted, was by this time rather sympathetic to Quebec national-ism, but his libertarian instincts had been offended by Bill 178 and he tried to persuade two of his friends, Peter Blaikie and Egan Cham-bers, to run for Libman's party.[57] Libman heard about these efforts and decided to recruit Holden himself, although Neil Cameron warned him that Holden might be unpredictable and a dubious asset to the party.[58] Holden at first resisted but eventually agreed on several conditions, including the right to support the Meech Lake Accord (which the party opposed) and a stipulation that he do no campaign-ing before noon on any day. Nick auf der Maur, although not really a supporter of the Equality Party, agreed to be Holden's campaign manager.

The unpopularity of Bill 178 and the rise of the Equality Party was soon apparent to Liberals in the predominantly anglophone ridings. Russell Copeman, a Liberal organizer in 1989 and a successful candi-date in 1994, recalled the situation in the earlier election: "Traditional donors shut the tap off, the money dried up, volunteers dried up ... by the time we got into the campaign, for the first time we were having difficulty filling the paid positions the party had – enumeration for example. When you can't find people who are willing to sign on with you to do a paid job, you know you are in trouble."[59]

Both Joan Dougherty and John Ciaccia considered retiring but decided to run again, feeling the need to vindicate their (contrasting) positions on Bill 178. Premier Bourassa hoped that all three of the ministers who had resigned would run again but Clifford Lincoln refused without hesitation. Richard French's mind was made up by a chance encounter with Trudeau, who advised him that it would be inappropriate to run again after resigning on an issue of principle,[60] while Herbert Marx decided against running in the spring, largely because of the strong sentiment in his riding. Maximilien Polak was nominated again in Ste-Anne but decided to retire anyway when he realized that Bourassa had no intention of naming him to the cabi-net.[61] Pierre MacDonald, who had antagonized anglophone voters with an ill-considered remark about "fat English ladies at Eaton's," wisely chose not to run again in Robert-Baldwin, where he would probably have been defeated by the Equality Party candidate. Both Marx and Polak were appointed as provincial judges before the election.

The Liberals managed to find four new anglophone candidates, although none was willing to endorse Bill 178 either publicly or privately. Russell Williams, who had worked on Bill 142 as an employee of Alliance Quebec, replaced Clifford Lincoln in Nelligan. Gary Waxman, a labour lawyer, replaced Herbert Marx in D'Arcy-McGee. Premier Bourassa personally recruited Sam Elkas, the mayor of Kirkland and a Progressive Conservative supporter in federal politics, to run in Robert-Baldwin.[62] Elkas proved an excellent choice and joined the cabinet right after the election, but another candidate recruited by the premier was less fortunate. William Cosgrove, an engineer and a long-time Liberal activist, had been the party's anglophone vice-president during Bourassa's first term as premier, but he had been living in Washington for sixteen years as an employee of the World Bank and was somewhat out of touch with Quebec politics. Bourassa nonetheless persuaded him to return to Quebec and run in Westmount, telling Cosgrove that he needed an English-speaking lieutenant who understood the mentality of anglophone voters.[63] Cosgrove's campaign started disastrously when he was asked at a press conference to comment on Bill 142 and was unable to identify it. Ironically the question came from a friendly reporter who was trying to give Cosgrove an opportunity to discuss what the Liberals had done for the anglophone minority. This episode persuaded Richard Holden, for the first time, that he actually had a chance of winning Westmount for the Equality Party.[64]

On election day the Liberals were easily returned, although the Parti Québécois won six more seats than in 1985. The Unity Party won no seats although their candidate in Pontiac, Mark Alexander, made a strong second-place showing, with 31 per cent of the vote, against Robert Middlemiss. The Equality Party took four seats. Robert Libman won an overwhelming victory in D'Arcy-McGee with 58 per cent of the vote. Gordon Atkinson in NDG, Neil Cameron in Jacques-Cartier, and Richard Holden in Westmount were also successful, although with less impressive pluralities. Adrian Waller lost by only 1384 votes in Robert-Baldwin; his share of the popular vote, at 41 per cent, was actually the same as Holden's in Westmount. Peter Vernham won 15 per cent of the vote in a riding with only 18 per cent of non-francophones, suggesting that Claude Ryan had lost practically all of his anglophone supporters. In the suburban riding of Laporte, where neither new party had a candidate, Steve Olynyk won about 25 per cent of the vote as an independent opposed to Bill 178. Olynyk was Maurice King's successor as the mayor of Greenfield Park.

An analysis of the voting results by Pierre Drouilly, published in *Le Devoir*, revealed that about 70 per cent of English-speaking Quebeckers who voted in ridings where the Equality Party ran a candidate had voted for that party, a higher percentage than pre-election polls had anticipated.[65] According to Drouilly, the Equality Party did particularly well among Jewish voters, exceeding the Union Nationale percentage of 1976 in seven ridings with substantial Jewish populations. Voters whose mother tongue was neither English nor French generally stayed with the Liberals, giving only about 15 per cent of their votes to the Equality Party. The Unity Party received between 40 and 75 per cent of the anglophone vote in ridings where it ran a candidate. Although the results for the new parties were not particularly impressive in terms of seats, this reflected the fact that neither party had significant support among francophones, and there were only a few ridings where a candidate could win without francophone support. Even Mount Royal, Nelligan and Pontiac had more francophone than anglophone voters by 1989, although persons of other mother tongues, many of whom spoke English at home, held the balance of power in Mount Royal and Nelligan. The Equality Party won four of the five ridings where English was the mother tongue of more voters than was French, and it lost the fifth, Robert-Baldwin, by a narrow margin. The Unity Party received as large a share of the anglophone vote in ridings where it ran a candidate as its urban counterpart did in Montreal, but anglophones were too few in rural Quebec to give it a realistic chance of winning any seats. Soon after the election the two parties merged, although some Unity Party members, including Maurice King, did so with great reluctance. King believed that the Equality Party was too sympathetic to the Liberals and also that it lacked the experience and administrative structure to be effective in the rural areas.[66]

In a post-election editorial *The Gazette* congratulated the Equality Party on the election of four members to the National Assembly, but warned that a single-issue party appealing only to anglophones had little potential for growth and would probably not last long. On the other hand, if the party could develop a more comprehensive platform it might appeal to those francophones who supported minority rights and unconditional federalism, enabling it to make a more lasting impact on Quebec politics.[67] These were not far from Robert Libman's own sentiments, despite his generally low opinion of *The Gazette*, but the difficulties of following this advice proved to be insuperable.

ALLIANCE QUEBEC AND
THE LIBERAL GOVERNMENT

It is necessary at this point to go back to the 1985 election to trace the fortunes of Alliance Quebec under the Liberal government. Although officially non-partisan and on relatively good terms with the Parti Québécois government after the adoption of Bill 57, Alliance Quebec was a federalist organization. Its leading activists naturally welcomed the return of the Liberal Party to office in 1985, even though they realized that there would inevitably be disagreements between Alliance Quebec and the new government. However, the change of government did not prove to be an unmixed blessing for Alliance Quebec.

During the reign of the Parti Québécois, Alliance Quebec had been virtually the only channel of communication between the anglophone community and the government, which largely explained its influence and importance. English-speaking Quebeckers, viewing the government as distant and hostile, perceived the need for a strong organization to protect their interests. At the same time the Parti Québécois government itself appreciated the convenience of having Alliance Quebec as a means of liaison with a community that was almost unanimously hostile to, and by its own choice excluded from, the party.

All of this changed in December 1985. The new Liberal government had strong anglophone representatives in cabinet and caucus, and these had many ties with the leading institutions and personalities of the anglophone community. Alliance Quebec was thus, in a sense, superfluous. At the same time English-speaking Quebeckers felt a great sense of relief at the return to office of a federalist party that had promised various concessions to anglophone interests, including the removal of the prohibition on English-language signs. Many English-speaking Quebeckers concluded that Quebec nationalism was in decline, that the anglophone community's problems were over, and that the organization was no longer required. Many ceased to renew their memberships or to make financial contributions to Alliance Quebec, which in turn weakened the organization, increased its dependence on subsidies from the federal government, and undermined its credibility as a representative of the anglophone community.

As noted above, some early Liberal initiatives, such as Bill 142, were welcome to Alliance Quebec and to those whom it represented. Looming over everything else, however, was the issue of bilingual signs. Alliance Quebec had supported the court challenges to the sign law which had begun before the change of government. It continued to do so, but at the same time it tended to assume that Premier Bourassa would carry out his promise to allow bilingual signs. As Michael Goldbloom later recalled, "we weren't overly aggressive" as a result of this faith in the government, and this was probably a mistake.[68] Faith in the government and the continuing pursuit of the court challenges were not considered contradictory, since it was assumed that a victory for English rights and freedom of expression in the courts would make it politically easier for the government to do what it presumably wanted to do anyway.

While both sides were still waiting for the Supreme Court of Canada to hand down its decision, Goldbloom stepped down from the presidency of Alliance Quebec after two years in office. His succession in May 1987 by Royal Orr marked a major change in the organization. While the first two presidents had been Montreal lawyers and veterans of Participation Québec, the third president of Alliance Quebec was a music teacher from the Eastern Townships who had been an undergraduate at Bishop's University in 1976. Orr had grown up in a region where French had been the dominant language for generations. He was not a rights-oriented Trudeauvian liberal like Goldbloom or Eric Maldoff but an old-fashioned Canadian conservative who admired the philosopher George Grant and had little use for the Charter of Rights and Freedoms. He did not really favour Alliance Quebec's policy of challenging the sign law in court, although he recognized that his position had little support on the board of directors. He was also a supporter of the Meech Lake Accord, which was announced two days after he became president and which many Quebec anglophones and most of Alliance Quebec's board of directors opposed, particularly after it was publicly denounced by former prime minister Trudeau.

The combination of Orr's leadership and the misguided faith in the goodwill of the Quebec Liberals meant that Alliance Quebec became less and less aggressive in its dealings with the government. Instead it consciously channeled more of its energies and resources into preserving the cultural heritage of English-speaking communities, particularly outside of Montreal. This made the organization appear less politically relevant and probably contributed to the decline in its membership.

Orr's influence was counterbalanced to some extent by that of Peter Blaikie, who replaced Dr James Ross as chairman of the board at the same time as Orr became president. It would obviously have been inappropriate for both the chairman and the president to be from the Eastern Townships, but an even more important reason for the choice of Blaikie was the desire to improve Alliance Quebec's relations with the business community,[69] which had rejoiced at the defeat of the Parti Québécois and had seen its access to government improve under the

Liberals. Its continuing interest in Alliance Quebec could not be taken for granted.

Alliance Quebec was seriously discredited by the Bourassa government's decision to introduce Bill 178 rather than complying with the Supreme Court's decision on the sign law. The organization's faith in the Quebec Liberals had obviously been unjustified, its leadership had been too passive and moderate, and its reliance on the courts had been rendered irrelevant by the government's willingness and ability to override a judicial decision with the aid of the notwithstanding clause. The Unity Party and the Equality Party soon arose to represent those English-speaking Quebeckers who demanded an alternative to the Alliance Quebec approach. Both of the new parties argued that "Compliance Quebec" had betrayed the interests of its community, that it was merely a front for the Liberal Party designed to lull anglophones into a false sense of security, and that its failure to prevent Bill 178 from being adopted demonstrated the folly and futility of attempting to appease Quebec nationalism. Alliance Quebec's habit of taking positions that were a compromise between anglophone and francophone interests, according to this view, was counterproductive. By demanding less Alliance Quebec ensured that it would receive less, since a Liberal government could not afford to adopt a position identical with Alliance Quebec's demands.

To make matters worse a mysterious fire largely destroyed Alliance Quebec's headquarters in downtown Montreal within a few days of the adoption of Bill 178. Arson was determined, but the perpetrators of the crime were never discovered. Anglophones assumed that the fire had been started by Quebec nationalists. On the other hand, anonymous sources in the police force alleged that Royal Orr had started the fire himself. While ludicrous to anyone who knew Orr even slightly, these rumours appeared to convince some francophones. They were published in *Le Journal de Montréal*, a daily newspaper sympathetic to the Parti Québécois, and broadcast on the TVA television network. Orr and Alliance Quebec sued the media for libel, retaining Peter Blaikie as their lawyer against *Le Journal de Montréal* and Richard Holden against TVA. (Blaikie had been asked to take both cases, but TVA was a client of his firm, which would have created a conflict of interest.) The cases dragged on for several years and were eventually settled out of court.[70]

Orr had understandably had enough and resigned in March 1989 to become a broadcaster at CJAD, leaving Alliance Quebec without an office, without a president, and with most of its records destroyed. Peter Blaikie agreed to serve as acting president until a new president could be found, while simultaneously retaining the position of chairman. Most members of the board still believed that anglophones should support the Quebec Liberal Party, but Blaikie insisted that Alliance Quebec could not do so after Bill 178 if it wished to retain any credibility. He made it clear that he would have to resign if the board insisted on endorsing the Liberals in the forthcoming election, and since the organization obviously needed him the board eventually came round to his point of view.[71] Eleven days before the election Blaikie published a lengthy statement which carefully avoided mentioning the Equality Party or the Unity Party but which stated that "Those who believe the proper course is to fight the Liberal policy from within are living in a dream world. Bill 178 was not an aberration. It represents the consistent approach of the Liberal government toward the anglophone minority." For good measure Blaikie added that anglophones who voted Liberal would "make a mockery of the democratic process."[72] This statement may have decided the outcome in Westmount, where Blaikie's friend Richard Holden defeated the Liberal candidate by just 513 votes. In any event it did not improve relations between Alliance Quebec and the Liberal government.

The election result indicated that few anglophones still supported the moderate and conciliatory approach towards the Liberal government which Alliance Quebec had pursued before the arrival of Blaikie. The board nonetheless sought a president who would return to that approach and in October, not many days after the election, they succeeded in recruiting Robert Keaton, who was then teaching at Dawson College. Keaton had served three years as a citizenship court judge, appointed by the Trudeau government, and had unsuccessfully attempted a comeback in municipal politics in 1986. He was at first reluctant to become president of Alliance Quebec but eventually agreed and served for more than four years. Another academic, Graeme Decarie of Concordia University, replaced Blaikie as chairman of the board. He in turn was replaced by John O'Brien, also a Concordia professor, in 1990.

Keaton's presidency coincided with a period of intense activity directed towards the reform of the Canadian constitution, which is discussed in chapter 8. Perhaps because he was a political scientist, Keaton took an intense interest in these matters. He supported both the Meech Lake Accord and its successor the Charlottetown Accord, although many members of Alliance Quebec and its affiliated organizations did not. Opposition to the two accords was associated with the Equality Party, which was at the peak of its popularity when Keaton assumed the presidency of Alliance Quebec. Inevitably Alliance Quebec and the Equality Party came to be viewed as rivals, although, since one was an interest group and the other a party, there was theoretically no reason for them to be in conflict. Keaton's efforts to improve relations with the government contributed to the animosity between the two organizations, and revived the old accusations that Alliance Quebec was too closely linked to the Liberals. Ironically the Liberals were also disillusioned with Alliance Quebec because of Blaikie's advice not to vote for them in 1989, which they viewed as an endorsement of the Equality Party.

While Keaton was rebuilding the relationship with the Liberals and building a new one with the Equality Party, he also sought to open a dialogue with the Parti Québécois. In particular he hoped to lessen the antipathy of the Parti Québécois to bilingual signs so that the Liberals would not be afraid to replace Bill 178 with a more reasonable sign law. He therefore devoted considerable effort to this endeavour. Keaton believed that a successful interest group must be non-partisan and maintain communications with all parties. He was also by temperament a conciliator and a compromiser who believed, as he put it, that "it takes a lot more courage to take a moderate position than to take an extreme position."[73]

One major concern of the English-speaking community at this time was to ensure that the government's massive reorganization of health and social services, known as Bill 120, did not remove or undermine any of the guarantees given to anglophones by Bill 142. Bill 120 was introduced near the end of 1990 and adopted about eight months later. Alliance Quebec worked closely with Russell Williams, a former employee of the organization, on this bill and was generally satisfied with the final form of the legislation. Even Robert Libman, not normally an admirer of Alliance Quebec, praised their contribution in his speech on third reading, although for a number of specific reasons his party eventually voted against the bill.[74] When it was finally implemented in 1993, Bill 120 virtually dismantled the regional social service centres, including Centre Ville Marie and the Jewish Family Services Centre, transferring most of their functions to the CLSC's. (As an exception, youth protection services on Montreal Island were assigned to two new agencies, one English and one French.) Anglophones accepted this change because Bill 142 had guaranteed their right to be served in their own language, more or less regardless of location.

While Alliance Quebec was caught in the crossfire between the Quebec Liberal Party and the Equality Party it faced a new challenge to its traditional orientation from Reed Scowen, whose term as delegate-general in London had ended in 1990. Early in the following year Scowen published a book which warned that Quebec anglophones could expect little satisfaction from the Quebec Liberal Party, and not much from political activity in general.[75] As a small minority they would simply be ignored, or worse, by francophone politicians, as the experience of Bill 178 had demonstrated. At the same time Scowen criticized the leaders of the anglophone community for their apparently resigned acceptance of the community's dwindling numbers. He argued that it was a fallacy to think that Quebec nationalists would tolerate the anglophone community once it was too small to be a threat, because francophone elites would still refuse to admit that the French could be secure in North America without protection. The small anglophone minority would continue to be attacked, no matter how weak it became, because it was "the symbol of a larger problem."[76] Scowen urged the anglophone community to adopt the goal of replacing the 120,000 anglophones who had left Quebec since 1976.[77]

Scowen's advice was to rely less on politics and more on individual effort and the efforts of the private sector, to insist on the right to use the English language as much as possible, and to encourage as many Quebeckers as possible, including immigrants and francophones, to use English. He deplored the tendency of many anglophones since 1977 to use French in public so as to blend into Quebec society. The English language with its dominant role in the global and North American economy should be regarded as the community's major asset. The community should be defined to include anyone who spoke English as his or her principal language in Quebec, rather than only those who had British, Irish or Jewish roots and who retained the cultural attributes associated with those origins.[78]

Scowen made a number of speeches promoting these ideas and also sought the chairmanship of Alliance Quebec so as to redirect the organization towards the goals and strategies defined in his book.[79] He became chairman in June 1991 and promptly held a press conference in English only to support his view that English must be re-established as a public language in Quebec.

Scowen's views were anathema to most Quebec nationalists, perhaps because they offered a realistic and credible plan for strengthening the position of the English language in Quebec and also because they relied on what all nationalists fear the most: the power of the market. At the same time his views faced considerable opposition within the anglophone community, and particularly within Alliance Quebec.[80] Scowen dismissed Alliance Quebec's traditional emphasis on lobbying as irrelevant and doomed to failure. Anglophones outside of Montreal feared that his market-oriented strategy would abandon them to their fate while reinforcing the English language in the metropolis, where it was already relatively strong. Scowen's insistence that the English-language community must become an inclusive melting pot in order to survive also offended those who viewed Alliance Quebec's mission as one of preserving existing communities of British, Irish or Jewish heritage and their "way of life."

Scowen persuaded Alliance Quebec to establish a task force on job opportunities for young anglophones, largely made up of representatives from the business community.[81] He also caused the organization to issue stickers bearing the letters F/E to businesses willing to serve the public in both languages, the idea being that anglophones, whether residents or visitors to Quebec, could use their own language without embarrassment in establishments where the sticker was displayed. However, Scowen's efforts to change the direction of Alliance Quebec were not successful. At the convention in June 1991 he proposed to amend the constitution of Alliance Quebec so that its basic goal would be to expand the use of English in Quebec rather than to "preserve" the existing English-speaking community. This proposal was considered over the next year and finally rejected by the convention in June 1992. The opposition to Scowen was led by Graeme Decarie, who mobilized the rural members, the elderly, and those of British or Irish heritage in favour of the traditional approach. Scowen resigned as chairman and his immediate predecessor, John O'Brien, resumed the position. Shortly afterwards Scowen was appointed as Quebec's delegate-general in New York.

Meanwhile Robert Keaton continued his efforts to rebuild the strength and credibility of Alliance Quebec, with mixed results. He faced a vicious circle in that evidence of success in winning concessions from the Quebec government was needed to recruit members while evidence of strength at the grassroots was needed to impress the government. During his first three years in the presidency the government made a few token gestures to the anglophone community, such as establishing a task force on English education headed by Gretta Chambers and appointing Charles Taylor to the Conseil de la langue française. Alliance Quebec's membership may have grown somewhat, although it never disclosed the numbers, but was certainly much lower than in the early days of the organization. (Maurice King later alleged that there were only about 1200 members when he ran for the presidency of Alliance Quebec in 1993, apart from those who belonged indirectly through the autonomous regional organizations.)[82] The geographical and partisan differences among the members were further complicated by differing views on the new direction proposed by Reed Scowen and on the various proposals to amend the Canadian constitution.

Keaton's leadership was twice challenged by dissident candidates for the presidency: Irwin Rapaport in 1991 and Maurice King in 1993. Both argued that Alliance Quebec should be more militant in defending anglophone interests and less conciliatory towards the Liberal government. Keaton actually wished to step down in the spring of 1993 so that he could prepare to run for the Liberals in the next provincial election. However, he sought another term as president partly to prevent Maurice King from taking over the organization and partly because the legislation to replace Bill 178 had not yet been adopted.[83] By the end of the year the new legislation was in place and a more moderate successor as president had been found in the person of Michael Hamelin. Keaton resigned in December 1993, a few weeks before the retirement of Premier Bourassa. He could take some credit for having begun the recovery of Alliance Quebec from the low state in which he found it.

THE EQUALITY PARTY IN
THE NATIONAL ASSEMBLY

English-speaking Quebeckers had some reason to be satisfied with their defiance of the Quebec Liberal Party in the election of 1989. They had established their own party and within a few months it had elected four members to the National Assembly – the largest number elected by any new party since the first appearance of the Parti Québécois almost twenty years previously. It was hoped and expected that at the very least the new party would force the Liberals to listen to anglophone concerns. Some even hoped that the party would take root and provide a permanent political home for anti-nationalist Quebeckers of all ethnic and linguistic backgrounds. These hopes were realized only in part. The Liberals knew that their most serious opposition was still the Parti Québécois, and they acted accordingly. The Equality Party itself suffered from tensions among its four elected members, and between the elected members and the party militants, that eventually led to its disintegration.

The four members elected were a rather disparate group, and the group dynamics that developed were not favourable to success.[84] None of the four had really known any of the others until a few months before the election, and they differed in age, in temperament, and in political background. Four is perhaps an unlucky number for a parliamentary caucus in any event, since it can easily polarize into two groups of two. The party's history might have been different if it had won Robert-Baldwin riding, as it would have done with a high-profile candidate like Peter Blaikie or Joel Hartt.

The four quickly established public personae that seemed like characters in a political novel: Libman the earnest and energetic but rather dour young leader, Holden the cynical man-about-town, Cameron the absent-minded professor who never seemed to be awake in time for question period, and Atkinson the grandfatherly war veteran. (In a curious inversion of the usual tendency of politicians, Atkinson encouraged the rumour that he was seventy-five years old, although he was only sixty-seven.)[85] Their differences even extended to their travel arrangements. Libman, who never liked to sit still longer than necessary, always flew the short distance from Montreal to Quebec City. Atkinson, the traditionalist, travelled by train. Cameron, who claimed that train schedules were too complicated to remember, took the bus. Holden, not one to sacrifice his personal comfort, hired a limousine with a chauffeur. Holden's limousine became the target of accusations that he was wasting the taxpayer's money, but in fact he received the same mileage allowance as every other member. Atkinson and Cameron, who pocketed the surplus cash that resulted from their preference for economical transportation, escaped criticism.

The political backgrounds of the four were as various as their personalities. Libman, insofar as he had any political allegiance before 1989, was a Trudeauvian Liberal. Atkinson, who was originally from Winnipeg, was a Liberal of older vintage, at home in the party of Louis St Laurent and C.D. Howe. Cameron, also a westerner by birth, was a one-time 1960s radical who turned deeply conservative after the October Crisis. Holden was a maverick from the Westmount Tory establishment who disliked most Liberals and had an odd affinity for Quebec nationalists, perhaps because they shared his views about Liberals.

Libman, who was only twenty-nine years old, had some difficulty establishing his authority over the others, all of whom were over fifty. Holden, the most politically experienced member of the caucus and the most at home in a francophone milieu, proved to be the greatest source of difficulty in this regard. He made it clear from the outset that he would not be bound by party discipline and soon began to treat his leader with open contempt. Atkinson had a somewhat higher opinion of Libman than did Holden, but he was almost equally independent. These two dissidents soon became friends and formed an alliance. Libman and Cameron, although they also had their differences, formed a counter-alliance in an effort to hold the party together. As it turned out, Cameron was the only one of the four who would stick with the party to the end.

Differences among themselves were rivalled by differences between the elected members and the party grassroots, and these became increasingly serious over time. The Equality Party was a populist movement which the generally moderate elites of the anglophone community tended to view with some disfavour. Like any protest movement, it had attracted its share of ideologues and fanatics, and these persons remained as the hard core of the party membership after members with a less emotional commitment drifted away. (Libman later estimated that party membership fell from 16,000 or more in late 1989 to 4000 three years later.)[86] Some of them seemed to operate on the principle that whatever the francophone majority wanted must be wrong by definition. They accused their elected representatives of being too moderate and too accommodating – accusations that were ironically similar to those which the Equality Party directed against anglophone Liberals and against Alliance Quebec. Richard Holden, who despised the grassroots ideologues and did not hesitate to say so, was the main target of their wrath until Libman expelled him from the party in September 1991. After that the anger of the dissidents increasingly focused on Libman himself, although neither of his two remaining colleagues escaped it entirely.

Nonetheless, the Equality Party for a time was a visible and reasonably effective opposition in the National Assembly. It expressed anglophone concerns openly and vigorously, something that English-speaking Liberals tended to do better when their party was in opposition than when it formed the government. Libman, who proved to be an effective debater in both languages, worked hard to avoid the label of a single-issue party by intervening in almost every debate, but he was also the party's most effective spokesman on linguistic issues. He was generally respected by the Liberals, although he offended them (and delighted the Parti Québécois) in March 1991 by releasing the secret details of some Hydro-Québec contracts. Cameron, whose French was rusty at first but soon improved, had a dry wit and impressive erudition and also spoke on a wide range of issues. Atkinson, who spoke almost no French, concentrated on health, social services, and the problems of senior citizens, all of which he discussed in a constructive manner. He was particularly effective in the discussion of Bill 120. Holden devoted much of his energy to the revision of the civil code and to constitutional matters. In his memoirs Libman accuses both Holden and Atkinson of being lazy and neglectful of their duties.[87] They were probably no worse in this regard than many members of the major parties, but a party with only four elected members required an unusual degree of industriousness by all four if it was to be successful.

Constitutional issues connected with the Meech Lake and Charlottetown accords were the real cause of the party's undoing. Richard Holden was a friend of Prime Minister Brian Mulroney. His insistence on supporting the Meech Lake Accord, even though he had been clear about this from the outset, antagonized the party membership and divided the caucus. Keith Henderson, a professor of English at Vanier College and a member of the Westmount riding association, became active in the party so as to protest against Holden's views.[88] Robert Libman placed Henderson in charge of a committee on constitutional affairs, in which position Henderson became the effective leader of the party's militant extra-parliamentary wing. Holden, who disliked both Henderson and Libman, provoked his own expulsion in September 1991 by releasing to the press a highly critical analysis of the party.[89] He sat as an independent member for almost a year, during which, according to both Robert Libman and William Cosgrove, he made overtures to the Liberals.[90] If so, he was unsuccessful, but the Parti Québécois, with some of whose members Holden had become friendly while serving on the Belanger-Campeau Commission, was more receptive. In August 1992, to the astonishment of most people outside the National Assembly, Holden announced that he had joined the Parti Québécois. It was a strange destination for a man who, two years earlier, had proclaimed in the National Assembly that he was speaking "as a Canadian first and as a Quebecker second."[91]

The departure of Holden from the Equality Party did not greatly improve its internal cohesion. Henderson and his cohorts were as hostile to the Charlottetown Accord as they had been to Meech Lake. Gordon Atkinson supported the Charlottetown Accord and so, after some initial hesitation, did Libman. After Libman campaigned actively for the "yes" side in the referendum of October 1992, Henderson attempted to remove Libman from the leadership. Libman was already considering defecting to the Liberals and decided to resign in January 1993. He retained his seat in the National Assembly but Henderson became leader of the party. A year later Libman withdrew from the party to sit as an independent and Atkinson soon afterwards did the same. Only Neil Cameron chose to go down with the ship.

The collapse of the Equality Party cannot be attributed to any single cause. Its lack of appeal to francophones meant that it had no potential for growth in any case, but it disintegrated more rapidly than many had anticipated. Apart from the personalities involved, it fell victim to a conflict between two roles, that of a militant single-issue pressure group and that of a parliamentary party. In addition, the Liberals were able to win back the anglophone voters by exploiting the fear of "separatism" and by devising a somewhat more acceptable replacement for Bill 178. For all of these reasons the substance of the Equality Party had disappeared by the time of the 1994 election, and only the shadow remained.

BILL 86: THE LIBERALS MAKE AMENDS

As they approached the mid-term of their second mandate the Liberals began, after a fashion, the slow process of rebuilding bridges to the English-speaking community. The process was slow because the party's more nationalist elements, including the youth wing, were reluctant to make any significant moves in the direction of bilingualism. Also there were few anglophone Liberals left, after the rise of the Equality Party, to present the contrary arguments. In the National Assembly, for example, Russell Williams, the new member for Nelligan, was the only Liberal whose parents were both anglophones. On the party executive William Cosgrove, the candidate defeated by Richard Holden in Westmount, represented the anglophone point of view, as did the party's director-general, John Parisella. The party formed an ad hoc committee on the English-speaking community that included some members of the National Assembly and some from the extra-parliamentary wing of the party, in an effort to repair the damage done by Bill 178. Its membership overlapped with that of two other committees, a caucus committee on anglophones which included most of the members who had significant anglophone minorities in their ridings, and an extra-parliamentary committee on language policy.[92] In the course of 1991 Williams prepared an "action plan" on anglophone issues for the attention of Premier Bourassa, and in April 1992 he revealed the existence of this document in the National Assembly (although the document itself was not tabled then or later) and predicted that the government would introduce measures to meet anglophone concerns regarding education and employment.[93]

The English-speaking community remained concerned about the future of their educational system, given the dramatic decline in English-language school enrollments since 1977 and the consequent closing of many schools, particularly in rural areas. The system seemed also to be losing its "English" character, partly because of the increasing tendency of the Protestant boards to give instruction in French and partly because of the rigid curriculum guidelines imposed by the Ministry of Education. The Protestant School Board of Greater Montreal had earlier challenged the constitutionality of these guidelines in court, but the Supreme Court of Canada ruled in 1989 that Section 93 did not preclude the ministry from imposing a curriculum except in regard to religious and moral instruction.[94]

The task force on English education headed by McGill University Chancellor Gretta Chambers was established by the government in September 1991 to respond to these concerns. After consultations throughout the province it reported five months later with twenty-nine specific recommendations.[95] The first, and most controversial, of these was "that access to education in English be widened to include any child who was being educated in English or who has a parent from an English-speaking part of the world." This meant in effect that Quebec should opt in to Section 23:1(a) of the Canadian Charter of Rights and Freedoms, and thus give its official language minority the same rights as were guaranteed to francophone minorities in the other provinces. The task force also recommended the appointment of an assistant deputy minister for English education, a constitutional amendment to protect English-language school boards (which did not yet exist although they had been promised by Bill 107), and the establishment of an English curriculum council to advise the assistant deputy minister.

Both Alliance Quebec and the Equality Party repeatedly urged implementation of the first recommendation. Robert Libman introduced a private member's bill on the subject in May 1992.[96] However, the government stonewalled for more than a year until it was obvious that they had no intention of implementing the suggestion. One problem for the Liberals was that their supporters in the allophone communities disliked the idea of giving anglophone immigrants a right that was not available to other immigrants. Mindful of their experience with Bill 22, the Liberals had no wish to offend this part of their constituency, which had remained faithful to them in 1989, in order to please the anglophones, who had not.

Libman then took up the cause of the proposed constitutional amendment to guarantee linguistic school boards, which was also supported by Alliance Quebec, but the government did nothing about that either. The linguistic boards did not yet exist, so it seemed odd to entrench them, and there were enough controversies about the Canadian constitution without creating another. About all that came out of the Chambers report in the end was the appointment of an assistant deputy minister for English education.

The one linguistic issue that the Liberals could not avoid was that of signs. Bill 178 would have to be replaced by the end of 1993, since legislation whose validity depends on the use of the notwithstanding clause in the Canadian Charter of Rights and Freedoms ceases to have effect five years after it comes into force. The issue had become an embarrassment when Mordecai Richler, the internationally known Quebec writer, wrote a critical article on the sign law in *The New Yorker* and later expanded his comments into a book.[97] The party and the government were deeply divided. Some members were inclined to favour, in effect, re-enacting Bill 178 but the anglophones involved in the debate, principally Cosgrove, Parisella and Williams, argued vigorously, and in the end successfully, against this course of action. Others thought that outdoor bilingual signs might be allowed in municipalities that were predominantly English-speaking, as Robert Middlemiss had hoped in 1988. This idea would do nothing for Montreal, and Alliance Quebec vigorously opposed it. Some anglophone Liberals thought that the opportunity might be taken to allow English-speaking immigrant children into English schools, as recommended by the Chambers report, under the pretext that the new bill would be a general overhaul of the Charter of the French Language. As explained above, there was little support for this option. Claude Ryan, who since 1989 had been the minister responsible for language policy, was particularly adamant against it.

The process of working out an acceptable position within the party and the government began late in 1992, about a year before the deadline. In March 1993 the Equality Party began to put pressure on the government by circulating petitions in favour of outdoor bilingual signs and presenting them in the National Assembly with long lists of signatures.[98] Alliance Quebec was meanwhile quietly lobbying the government to the same effect, citing polls which suggested that most francophones did not object to bilingual signs. On the last day of March the Human Rights Committee of the United Nations finally rewarded Maurice King's efforts by declaring that the sign law did violate the International Covenant on Civil and Political Rights by limiting freedom of expression.[99] Coincidentally the Conseil de la langue française recommended on the same day that English be allowed on commercial signs belonging to small and medium-sized enterprises, provided that the French language occupied at least two-thirds of the space.[100] In April the executive of the Quebec Liberal Party voted in favour of allowing bilingual outdoor signs.

The government introduced its bill in May but decided to delay matters further by holding public hearings on the issue, a decision opposed by both opposition parties. Bill 86 would allow most outdoor bilingual signs provided the French words were more prominent than the English but continued to prohibit English on billboards or on signs carried on public transit vehicles. Other provisions of the bill significantly moderated the impact of the Charter of the French Language. The criteria for access to English schools were revised to bring them into harmony with Section 23:1 (b) of the Canadian Charter of Rights and Freedoms, and also to allow access for children with learning disabilities, whether or not they met the criteria. Other provisions allowed the government to communicate with corporations and other entities in English, allowed English on traffic signs in certain circumstances, and provided that municipal, educational, health and social service institutions presently recognized as bilingual could not be deprived of that status except at their own request. (The latter provision resolved the problem of Rosemere, a Montreal suburb which had been threatened with the loss of its bilingual status after the census of 1986 revealed that it no longer had an anglophone majority.) Bill 86 would also abolish the Commission de protection de la langue française, whose functions would be absorbed by the Office de la langue française.

For almost a month the usual procession of interest groups and institutions presented their briefs, with Robert Keaton appearing for Alliance Quebec and Keith Henderson for the Equality Party. Mayor Jean Doré of Montreal argued in favour of allowing outdoor bilingual signs while his counterpart in Quebec City, Jean-Paul L'Allier, argued in favour of continuing to prohibit them.[101] Ironically, Doré had been a member of the Parti Québécois while L'Allier had been a minister in the Liberal government of the early 1970s. Most of the anglophone individuals and groups who appeared thought that the bill was inadequate. Alliance Quebec was generally satisfied and had agreed to the exceptions made for billboards and public transit vehicles.[102] At the report stage the Parti Québécois moved to delay the bill for six months, which would have brought it close to the deadline, but the government, supported by the Equality Party, easily defeated this request. Bill 86 was finally approved by the National Assembly on 17 June 1993.[103] Both opposition parties voted against it, one on the grounds that it went too far in allowing the use of English and the other on the grounds that it did not go far enough. Gordon Atkinson, who was privately satisfied with the bill, did not participate in the vote.[104]

Thus ended, at least for the time being, the dispute over the language of signs that had divided and disrupted Quebec for nearly two decades, brought about the resignation of three ministers and the establishment of two political parties, and caused Quebec to be condemned by the United Nations for the one and only time in its history. Many in Quebec were dissatisfied with the outcome. Many more contemplated the whole episode with the sentiments of the children in Robert Southey's poem about the battle of Blenheim: "But what good came of it at last?" Alliance Quebec chose to regard Bill 86 as a victory, although a partial one. Gordon Atkinson thought, perhaps rightly, that the Equality Party should also have claimed it as a victory and could thus have argued that the establishment of the party had not been in vain.[105] Both Alliance Quebec and the Equality Party deserved some of the credit for Bill 86, along with William Cosgrove, Maurice King, John Parisella, Mordecai Richler, Russell Williams, and others besides.

Although the Parti Québécois opposed Bill 86 at the time, they essentially kept it in place when they returned to office, suggesting that it was a compromise that represented the balance of linguistic and political forces in Quebec fairly accurately.

Perhaps another Quebecker who deserved some of the credit was Robert Bourassa, whose impressive political talents were never put to a greater test than in this instance. It was to be his last major political achievement, for the cancer that had first been diagnosed in 1990 had recurred, and he retired in January 1994 for reasons of health, although he lived until October 1996. He had never become a favourite with the English-speaking voters of Quebec, but unlike many of his contemporaries he had no hostility or bitterness towards the anglophone minority. Those anglophones who knew him best agreed with what *The Economist* wrote at his death: "Robert Bourassa was everyone's idea of a decent Canadian, warm-hearted and conciliatory. He was a federalist in his aims, if not his methods. For many Canadians, that was the problem."[106]

7 Anglophones in Disarray, 1994-97

The adoption of Bill 86 contributed to a partial reconciliation between English-speaking Quebeckers and the Quebec Liberal Party. However, the reconciliation was not as complete as the overwhelming anglophone support for the Liberals in the election a year later appeared to suggest. Bill 178 was not forgotten, and anglophones supported the Quebec Liberals in 1994 with more resignation than enthusiasm. The party, for its part, seemed to view anglophone voters as a dubious asset since they were difficult to satisfy, of decisive importance in only a few ridings, and at times a source of embarrassment in the party's efforts to broaden its appeal to moderately nationalist francophones. Efforts to recruit prominent anglophone candidates and potential ministers were apparently a much lower priority for the Liberals in 1994 than they had been in most earlier campaigns.

The anglophone community itself, meanwhile, was fragmented and confused, and without recognized leaders and spokespersons. The traditional business and professional elite had long since dwindled away, the provincial Liberals had betrayed the community in 1988, federal parties and politicians, as described in the next chapter, had failed to provide effective support, and neither Alliance Quebec nor the Equality Party had entirely lived up to expectations. The discordant voices of would-be leaders further divided a community already fractured by increasing cultural diversity and weakened by the continuing exodus of its young people from the province. Francophone politicians, accustomed to dealing with reasonably cohesive and organized groups in Quebec's corporatist society, could be forgiven if they found the anglophone community difficult to understand and deal with.

THE ELECTION OF 1994

In September 1993, Robert Bourassa announced his retirement, although he agreed to remain in office until a successor could be chosen. No potential successors appeared other than Daniel Johnson, who was duly acclaimed leader at a party convention on 14 December 1993 and sworn in as premier four weeks later. The lack of competition for the leadership suggested a lack of confidence in the party's electoral prospects vis-à-vis a resurgent Parti Québécois. Although Johnson was a convinced federalist, he offered nothing of substance to anglophones, particularly on the question of broadening access to English schools. Robert Libman was correct when he alleged in March 1994 that the Liberals were again taking anglophone voters for granted.[1]

Johnson's apparent lack of sympathy for Quebec nationalism prompted the former head of the Quebec Liberal Party's constitutional committee, Jean Allaire, to form a new nationalist party known as Action Démocratique. It was headed initially by Allaire, who viewed himself as an interim leader, and then by Mario Dumont, the former head of the Liberal Party's youth wing. Dumont attempted to position the party as a moderately nationalist alternative to the two major parties, much like the Union Nationale in the last days of its existence.

Whatever their prospects in Quebec as a whole, the Liberals were universally expected to win back the four ridings which the Equality Party had taken in 1989. The Equality Party had been shattered by controversies over the Canadian constitution and the adoption of Bill 86 seemed to deprive it of its *raison d'être*. The growing possibility of a Parti Québécois victory made anglophone voters reluctant to split the federalist vote by supporting a third party. The party's new leader, Keith Henderson, professed to see little difference between the two major parties, but few anglophone voters agreed with him.

Soon after his resignation from the Equality Party in early December of 1993, Robert Libman began a serious effort to win the Liberal nomination in D'Arcy-McGee, the riding which he represented in the National Assembly. He began quietly selling memberships and his supporters rented an office and printed a banner reading "Liberals for Libman." However, he had waited too long. Despite Libman's impressive credentials and his popularity in the riding, Daniel Johnson was not well-disposed towards his candidacy. On the day after Johnson became leader, Libman was informed that the party would not accept him as a candidate in the forthcoming election. He therefore withdrew from the nomination contest, in which he was probably the front-runner, and decided to contest the riding as an independent instead.[2]

Libman's withdrawal left four candidates in the race for the nomination. The two most prominent were Joe Rabinovitch, director-general of the Association of Jewish Day Schools, and Jack Jedwab, director of community relations for the Quebec region of the Canadian Jewish Congress.[3] However first Rabinovitch and then Jedwab dropped out of the race. The dark horse candidate was Lawrence Bergman, a notary and the president of a large synagogue in the riding. Bergman won the Liberal nomination by acclamation in March 1994.

In NDG, Gordon Atkinson was also rumoured to be interested in running as a Liberal but did not make a serious effort to win the local nomination. Russell Copeman, an employee of the Liberal Party since 1988 and of Alliance Quebec prior to that, decided to seek the Liberal nomination in early 1993, after receiving an assurance from William Cosgrove that the latter was not interested.[4] Copeman had worked in Premier Bourassa's constituency office and also as a pre-election organizer with responsibility, at one time, for thirty ridings. His campaign for the NDG nomination began early and he was apparently the choice of the party establishment, both locally and at the provincial level. A more prominent candidate was Robert Keaton, still the president of Alliance Quebec, who approached the Liberals about running in NDG soon after the passage of Bill 86. It will be recalled that Keaton had contested the same riding as the Democratic Alliance candidate in 1976. However Keaton, like Libman, waited too long. He wished to remain at Alliance Quebec until near the end of 1993, and this prevented him from waging a serious campaign in NDG. By the time he was available the riding association had scheduled a convention for February 1994, leaving him little time to sell memberships.[5] Copeman, although much less well-known than Keaton, won on the first ballot. Atkinson, after contemplating retirement, decided without much enthusiasm to run as an independent. Keith Henderson, who had a low opinion of Atkinson, was nominated as the Equality Party candidate in NDG.

The redistribution of boundaries that would take effect with the 1994 election combined Westmount with St-Louis, producing a riding that no longer had an anglophone majority. Jacques Chagnon, the member for St-Louis, became the Liberal candidate in the combined riding. William Cosgrove had hoped to run in Westmount but refused to run anywhere else, while the party refused to move Chagnon to a different riding.[6] Thus another prominent anglophone was denied the chance to sit as a Liberal member of the National Assembly. Chagnon became minister of education when the Johnson government was formed in January 1994.

In Jacques-Cartier, the fourth Equality Party riding, the Liberals nominated Geoffrey Kelley, who had been a student of the incumbent member, Neil Cameron, at John Abbott College. Kelley, who had lived practically all of his life in the riding, had subsequently worked for Alliance Quebec and later in Claude Ryan's office. In Robert-Baldwin the Liberal incumbent, Sam Elkas, was excluded from the cabinet by Premier Johnson and decided not to run again. He was succeeded as the Liberal candidate in his riding by a francophone, Pierre Marsan. (To the surprise of some observers, Russell Williams was not appointed to the cabinet as an anglophone replacement for Elkas.) Also excluded from the new government was Deputy Premier Lise Bacon, whose riding of Chomedey, a part of the city of Laval, had a substantial anglophone minority. She resigned her seat and was later appointed to the Senate by Prime Minister Jean Chrétien. To replace her in Chomedy, the Liberals nominated Thomas Mulcair, a former employee of Alliance Quebec. Of mixed Irish and French descent, Mulcair claimed to be descended on his mother's side from Honoré Mercier.[7] The presence of Mulcair, Copeman, Kelley and Russell Williams in the Liberal lineup led Don MacPherson, a columnist with *The Gazette*, to call Alliance Quebec the farm team of the Liberal Party, an observation not appreciated by either organization.

Another former employee of Alliance Quebec, John Parisella, directed the Liberal election campaign, which took place in August and September of 1994. Alliance Quebec, now headed by Michael Hamelin, rather grudgingly endorsed the Liberals as the lesser of two evils. A poll published early in the campaign indicated that 67 per cent of anglophones supported the Liberals, 6 per cent the Parti Québécois, and only 2 per cent the Equality Party.[8] The Equality Party fielded only twelve candidates, including its sole incumbent member, Neil Cameron, in Jacques-Cartier and the formerly notorious William Shaw in Nelligan. It did not run a candidate in D'Arcy-McGee, where its former leader was running as an independent.

The election result on 12 September was closer than most observers had anticipated, with the two major parties winning virtually equal shares of the popular vote. Anglophones and allophones voted overwhelmingly for the Liberals, who won most of the ridings on Montreal Island but only 47 out of 125 in Quebec as a whole. The Equality Party did poorly, as anticipated, with none of its candidates managing better than a third-place showing. Neil Cameron and Keith Henderson were the only Equality candidates to win more than a thousand votes, with Cameron winning 2375. Henderson, with 1406 votes, came fourth in NDG, slightly behind Gordon Atkinson.[9] Robert Libman, running as an independent, won almost a third of the votes cast in D'Arcy-McGee. Although much better known than his Liberal opponent, he was defeated by the voters' conviction that they would help the Parti

Québécois if they failed to elect a Liberal. The last of the former Equality Party foursome, Richard Holden, ran for the Parti Québécois in Verdun. He received 36 per cent of the vote, a record for the Parti Québécois in a riding that had been Liberal since the days of Duplessis.

FROM ELECTION TO REFERENDUM

In 1991, three years before it returned to office, the Parti Québécois had established a task force on the status of the English-speaking community in a sovereign Quebec. Henry Milner and David Payne, two of the party's most prominent anglophone members, were among the seven persons appointed. The task force heard representations from a large number of English-speaking individuals and groups, although not from Alliance Quebec which refused to participate in its deliberations. Its report, published early in 1993, was reasonably moderate in tone, although it insisted that French must be the only official language and explicitly rejected the possibility of broadening access to English schools as recommended by the Chambers report.[10] The published version of the report made no recommendation on the language of signs, citing as an excuse the fact that the task force was still awaiting legal advice on the matter.

Nonetheless, there was some comfort for anglophones. The report recommended that the constitution of a sovereign Quebec should guarantee anglophones the right to use their language in the National Assembly and the courts, as well as the right to manage their own educational institutions. Linguistic school boards should be established to replace the denominational boards required by the Canadian constitution. Access to health and social services in English, and the bilingual status of certain health and social service institutions, should be maintained, as well as English-language radio and television, both public and commercial. There should be an affirmative action program to increase anglophone representation in the public service. The task force also recommended maintaining freedom of choice of the language of instruction at the CEGEP level. This recommendation was contrary to party policy, which favoured restricting access to English CEGEPs in the same way that the Charter of the French Language restricted access to English schools. Although the party policy was not changed, party vice-president Bernard Landry promised in June 1994 that it would not be implemented by a Parti Québécois government.[11]

Soon after the report of the task force the Parti Québécois approved and published its new program, entitled *Quebec in a New World*. At two places in the program it praised the contributions of anglophones to Quebec. It promised to maintain "a solid network of educational, social and cultural institutions" for the anglophone community and also to guarantee the rights of the anglophone minority in the constitution of a sovereign Quebec.[12]

However well-intentioned these promises may have been, they had no visible effect on the outcome of the election. The Parti Québécois nominated only two anglophone candidates, Richard Holden and David Payne, and neither was in a predominantly anglophone riding. Anglophones voted against the party as overwhelmingly as usual. David Payne was elected to the National Asembly as the member for Vachon, returning after an absence of nine years. However, he was again excluded from the cabinet as was his mentor, Dr Camille Laurin.

The new premier, Jacques Parizeau, was known as an unconditional sovereignist who did not favour political ties or common institutions between Canada and Quebec after independence.[13] He had resigned from the government in 1984 after the Parti Québécois had temporarily abandoned the goal of sovereignty. As premier he made the forthcoming referendum his first order of business, rather than waiting until near the end of his mandate as René Lévesque had done.

Anglophones were largely spectators in the elaborate process leading up to the referendum campaign. Both the Liberal opposition and Alliance Quebec refused to participate in the pre-referendum consultations that were supposed to draft the constitution of a potentially sovereign Quebec. Seventeen commissions (fifteen regional commissions, plus additional ones for youth and senior citizens) were set up to collect the popular input, which they did in February and March 1995. Two of the commissions had anglophone vice-presidents. David Levine, a hospital administrator and long-time member of the Parti Québécois who had been the party's candidate in the D'Arcy-McGee by-election of 1977, was named vice-president of the commission for Montreal Island. Gary Caldwell, the Ontario-born sociologist who had been a member of the Anglophone Committee for a United Quebec and was considered sympathetic to the party, although he was not actually a member of it, was named vice-president of the commission for the Eastern Townships. Caldwell later publicly rebuked the government for not taking the input gathered by the commission seriously, and urged people to spoil their ballots in the referendum.[14] Despite his disillusionment, he soon afterwards accepted another appointment from the government, as a member of its Estates General on Education.

Some discord was also to be found in the federalist camp once the actual campaign began. The referendum law, adopted prior to the 1980 referendum and used again in 1992 and 1995, required all participants in the campaign to affiliate with one of the two committees representing the two options provided on the ballot. A group called the Special Committee for Canadian Unity, which included many members of the Equality Party, had been formed in January 1995 to promote the view that the referendum process was illegal and unconstitutional. The Liberal-dominated No Committee, not wishing to be associated with a group which it considered to be extremist, refused the Special Committee permission to affiliate. The Special Committee took its grievance to the Referendum Council, which ruled that the No Committee's decision had been unjust. The No Committee then relented and allowed the Special Committee to affiliate. However, this decision was taken only eleven days before the vote and an absurdly low limit was imposed on the Special Committee's expenditures.[15] Several months after the referendum the Special Committee filed a motion in the Superior Court which charged Daniel Johnson and the No Committee with violating its constitutional rights.[16] Brent Tyler, who had been the Equality Party candidate in Westmount-St-Louis in 1994, acted as the Special Committee's lawyer.

The referendum itself took place on Monday, 30 October 1995. In contrast to 1980, practically all of the constituencies that had voted for the Parti Québécois in the previous election voted for sovereignty. Huge federalist majorities in the more ethnically diverse ridings, and in the Ottawa Valley, gave the federalists a narrow victory. The margin was so slim that if only two of the most federalist ridings had been excluded from the final tally the cause of sovereignty would have triumphed. Some federalists, and Alliance Quebec, later alleged that a disproportionate share of federalist ballots had been rejected by the deputy returning officers. In two ridings with substantial anglophone minorities, Chomedey and Marguerite-Bourgeoys, the number of rejected ballots was certainly large enough to inspire justifiable suspicion.

Premier Parizeau's comment as the returns came in that the will of the majority of Québécois had been frustrated by "money and the ethnic vote" belied his party's formal commitment to a pluralistic society and embarrassed many of his supporters. Anglophones, most of whom had never taken the party's expressions of goodwill towards them seriously, were only slightly mollified by his subsequent resignation. Three months after the referendum Parizeau was succeeded by Lucien Bouchard, who had previously headed the pro-sovereignty Bloc Québécois in the House of Commons.

ANGLOPHONE RESPONSE TO
THE REFERENDUM

Anglophone voters should have felt satisfied with, and even empowered by, the result of the referendum. Federalism had triumphed, as they had almost unanimously wished. Furthermore, and for the first time in living memory, their votes had had a decisive influence on the outcome of a popular consultation in Quebec. In provincial elections their votes, concentrated in a few ridings, had no real influence on the choice of a government, a fact that had been convincingly demonstrated in both 1989 and 1994. Even in federal elections, although the nationwide result more frequently corresponded with their preferences, their influence was minimal. In referenda, where votes are counted equally regardless of location, their influence was potentially much greater, but in 1992 their strong vote for the Charlottetown Accord had been unable to determine the outcome, since most francophones in Quebec, and most anglophones outside of it, disagreed with them. Even in 1980 they had not been decisive, since a narrow federalist victory would have been achieved even without them. Only in 1995 had they clearly and decisively tipped the balance in the direction that they preferred.

This fact was well known to sovereignists as well as to federalists. Premier Parizeau's bitter but accurate comment about "money and the ethnic vote" expressed a truth that anyone could infer from the results. Anglophones should thus have had another reason for satisfaction. Twenty or thirty years earlier, if the will of a clear majority of francophones had been visibly frustrated by anglophone voters in the western suburbs of Montreal, there might well have been violence in the streets. In 1995 there was none. Virtually everyone accepted the legitimacy of the outcome. Francophones, including many nationalists, appeared more dismayed by Parizeau's tactless remark than by the outcome of the referendum itself. Clearly Quebec was a more mature, stable and liberal society in 1995 than it had been a generation before. This gave reason to hope that even if sovereignty did occur, there might be a place in Quebec for an English-speaking minority.

Most Quebec anglophones, however, did not appear to notice these facts, and their response to the referendum was far from happy. Instead of congratulating themselves on the result and on their decisive part in bringing it about, they were dismayed and frightened by the narrow margin of victory. Many also blamed the federal government of Prime Minister Chrétien for its inept and rather inconspicuous contribution to the federalist campaign, which contrasted sharply with the performance of Pierre Trudeau in the 1980 referendum. There was renewed talk of an anglophone exodus from the province, even though a massive exodus, if it occurred, would almost certainly bring about a federalist defeat the next time the Quebec government decided to have a referendum. In March 1996 the most famous of all Montreal-based enterprises, the Canadian Pacific Railway, announced the transfer of its headquarters to Calgary. In contrast to the Sun Life episode almost two decades earlier, there was little public reaction, and no one seriously tried to dissuade the railway's management from leaving the city where they had held sway for more than a century.

A more dramatic and unexpected sequel to the close call in the referendum was a sudden resurgence of support for the idea of partitioning Quebec in the event that another referendum gave a majority to the supporters of sovereignty. The resurgent support for partition, which was evident within weeks of the referendum, was clearly a response to the closeness of the result. The fact that the ridings which rejected sovereignty formed a relatively compact bloc along the southern border of the province, including most of Montreal Island, added to the plausibility of the notion.

Partition was not an entirely new idea. An anti-partition book which made a timely appearance in the spring of 1996 has traced its history back to the 1830s.[17] More recently it had surfaced following the victory of the Parti Québécois in 1976. At that time William Shaw and Lionel Albert were its principal promoters, and their efforts culminated in the appearance of their book *Partition: The Price of Quebec's Independence,* just prior to the referendum of 1980. The decisive federalist victory in that referendum caused the idea of partition to lie dormant for a decade, but it resurfaced in the early 1990s, possibly in response to the resurgent support for sovereignty following the collapse of the Meech Lake Accord. The rise of the Equality Party and a confrontation between the Bourassa government and the Mohawk people at Oka in the summer of 1990 also added fuel to the flames. Interest in the partition of Quebec began to be expressed both outside and within the province.

Two books published outside of Quebec in the early 1990s gave explicit support to the partition of Quebec in the event that the province chose to become sovereign. In 1991 David J. Bercuson and Barry Cooper, respectively a historian and a political philosopher at the University of Calgary, published *Deconfederation: Canada without Quebec.*[18] Although both authors had lived in Alberta for many years, Bercuson was an expatriate Quebec anglophone who had grown up in NDG. Their book was rather inappropriately dedicated to the memory of René Lévesque, who had died in 1987. Bercuson and Cooper argued that an independent Quebec was inevitable and appeared to welcome the idea on the grounds that a Canada without Quebec would be more coherent and viable. While Lévesque had used this argument on occasion when addressing audiences outside of Quebec, he would have been greatly distressed by the second part of the book's thesis, which was that Quebec should be deprived, on various grounds, of more than half of its territory. Bercuson and Cooper claimed that a sovereign Quebec would have no right to the northern territories which had been added to the province in 1898 and 1912, comprising more than half of its land mass after that date. Second, they argued that predominantly anglophone areas in southern Quebec should be detached from the province and remain part of Canada. Third, Canada should retain a "corridor" to provide land communication between Ontario and New Brunswick. Indeed the two academics asserted that "Quebec has no prior claim on the south shore of the St Lawrence."[19]

Hard on the heels of this book came a second one by another western Canadian, which presented a much more detailed plan for the partition of Quebec.[20] Scott Reid, the author of *Canada Remapped*, was a Vancouver journalist and later an adviser to Preston Manning, the leader of the Reform Party. Although he lacked the academic credentials of Bercuson and Cooper, his book was in fact more scholarly in substance and less polemical in tone than theirs. It contained detailed and generally accurate information about the political geography of ethnicity in Ireland, Switzerland and the Balkans, as well as Quebec. Its basic recommendation was that if Quebec chose to become sovereign the boundary should be redrawn so as to minimize the number of federalist voters who would be left in the new state, as well as minimizing the number of sovereignty supporters who would find themselves on the Canadian side of the boundary. To achieve this end, which he clearly valued more highly than geographical coherence or administrative convenience, Reid proposed that every polling division which voted against sovereignty in a hypothetical referendum should remain part of Canada. He also proposed that Canada be guaranteed the ownership and use of a road between Montreal Island and the Ontario border, although the territory through which the road passed would remain part of Quebec. Being primarily interested in satisfying as many voters as possible, Reid rejected legal or strategic arguments which might be used to take additional territory from Quebec, regardless of the wishes of the inhabitants.

Closer to home, the partitionist cause was taken up by Stephen A. Scott, a professor in the Faculty of Law at McGill who was already renowned for his hostility to any form of Quebec nationalism. In a speech delivered to a public meeting in Pointe-Claire in February 1992, Scott asserted that "Any argument designed to prove that Quebec is indivisible proves equally that Canada is indivisible. And any argument designed to prove that Canada is divisible proves equally that Quebec, too, is divisible."[21] Although he claimed that federalists in southern Quebec, and the territory where they predominated, should remain in Canada if Quebec were allowed its independence, Scott devoted much more attention to a legal argument that the northern territories given to Quebec in 1898 and 1912 would remain part of Quebec for only so long as Quebec remained a part of Canada. As he put it, "The Quebec north, to me, is Canada's winning card: and it must be made perfectly clear by everyone, including the Government of Canada, that this card will be played."[22] Prior to the referendum on the Charlottetown proposals, this speech was printed and distributed as a pamphlet.

Such ideas found a responsive audience in the Equality Party, some of whose members were becoming disillusioned by what they viewed as the excessively moderate views of the party's representatives in the National Assembly. As early as March 1991 the party's General Assembly had adopted a resolution stating that any declaration of sovereignty by Quebec should be followed by negotiations on partition and the establishment of new boundaries. Later in the year the General Council of the Equality Party resolved that if Canada recognized Quebec's right to self-determination it should also recognize that federalists within Quebec who wished to remain "politically and territorially part of Canada" had the right to do so.[23] Keith Henderson later claimed that disagreement over the issue of partition was a major reason for Robert Libman's departure from the party in 1993.[24] Even while Libman was still leader, the party's constitutional committee was preparing a document entitled *Territorial Rights: The Partition of Quebec*. The document called for federalist parts of Quebec to remain in Canada, either as a new province, a territory, or through annexation by existing provinces, if Quebec became sovereign. It was finally adopted by the General Assembly of the party in June 1993. William Shaw, whose candidacy had been vetoed by Libman in 1989 because of his pro-partition views, had no difficulty in becoming the Equality candidate in Nelligan in 1994 when Henderson was the leader of the party.

Public support for these ideas increased dramatically in the immediate aftermath of the 1995 referendum. The Special Committee for Canadian Unity, which had been refused affiliation with the referendum's No Committee, became the main standard-bearer for the partition movement afterwards. It held a conference on partition at McGill University in January 1996, followed by a second conference at the Radisson Hotel in Montreal a month later. Each conference was attended by more than a thousand people and featured prominent speakers, including Henderson and Scott. A public opinion poll released between the two conferences indicated that a majority of non-francophones in Quebec were favourable to partition.[25] Even the federal government became involved when the new minister of inter-governmental affairs, Stéphane Dion, suggested publicly that if Canada was divisible, Quebec was divisible also. His comment was promptly endorsed by the prime minister.[26]

By the spring of 1996 both the Special Committee for Canadian Unity and the partitionist movement as a whole were showing signs of internal tension. Some members of the Special Committee thought that it should be a non-partisan organization, and resented its close ties to the Equality Party, particularly since the party appeared to have no immediate prospects of success. Dr Roopnarine Singh, a prominent member of the Special Committee and a former Freedom of Choice candidate in the 1981 election, announced plans to form a new federalist party, the Bloc Canadien.[27] Dr Singh was best known as the organizer of Montreal's annual Canada Day parade. Some Equality Party members, on the other hand, viewed the Special Committee and the partition movement as means by which the Equality Party might be revived.

The partitionist cause began to win symbolic victories as municipal councils, particularly on Montreal Island and in the Ottawa Valley, adopted resolutions affirming their determination to remain part of Canada, whether or not the province chose to do so. Anthony House-father, a municipal councillor in Hampstead and a prominent member of Alliance Quebec, was one of the leading promoters of this devel-opment. By October 1997 forty-four municipalities, for the most part predominantly anglophone, had adopted such resolutions and numer-ous others were considering doing so. However three important Mon-treal Island municipalities, Lachine, Lasalle and Verdun, had rejected partitionist resolutions.[28] The percentage of francophones in all three was similar to that for the island as a whole, and their rejection of the partitionist cause was symptomatic of its almost total lack of appeal to francophones.

As is often true of new ideological movements, the partitionist discourse suffered from a certain lack of consistency and coherence. A variety of criteria – legal, geographical, economic, linguistic or political – were suggested as reasons for amputating one or another part of Quebec's territory, with little apparent appreciation of the inconsistency between them. Some partitionists favoured drawing a linguistic boundary, apparently not appreciating that this would be almost impossible in practice and that it left them open to the same accusations of exclusiveness and intolerance that they frequently directed at the Quebec nationalists. Others wished to retain all feder-alist localities, regardless of language, on the Canadian side of the new boundary. Still others dreamed of making Montreal Island an eleventh province, or even a new state, despite the fact that the eastern part of the city had voted for Quebec sovereignty in the referendum. The most determined partitionists, and the ones with the best legal argument to support their cause, were the Cree and Inuit in northern Quebec, but their project did little to reassure the anglophones in the south, except insofar as it acted as a deterrent to any further move towards sovereignty for Quebec. An even more fundamental ambiguity in the partition movement concerned the question of whether partition was really seriously intended, or whether it was merely being suggested as a theoretical possibility to deter francophones from voting for sovereignty. The partitionists themselves were divided on this question; the federal government, which occasionally seemed to support their cause, was almost certainly taking the latter position.

The partitionist movement was not the only manifestation of anglophone discontent in the aftermath of the 1995 referendum. Two weeks before the vote actually took place, Howard Galganov, the owner of an advertising agency based in Vaudreuil County, west of Montreal, decided that the federal government's lacklustre effort to mobilize the federalist vote failed to meet his professional standards. "As an advertising man," he later observed, "I have never seen a worse campaign for anything."[29] Rather than offering his services as a consultant, he decided to form a new federalist group which he called the Quebec Political Action Committee, anticipating that the need to mobilize and encourage supporters of Canadian federalism would not end on the day of the referendum.

Galganov had sent his Liberal Party membership card back to Premier Bourassa in 1988 as a protest against Bill 178. In the following year he ran rather half-heartedly as an independent candidate in Jacques-Cartier but eventually decided, too late to remove his name from the ballot, that Joan Dougherty deserved to be re-elected. He was not impressed by the Equality Party: "All they talked about was one issue and they didn't talk about the issue in depth. You've got to talk about more than one thing." Essentially a Liberal in the Trudeau tradition, Galganov believed in a strong federal government, bilingualism, multiculturalism, and the use of the federal spending power to maintain social programs. Like most anglophone businessmen in Quebec, he lamented the impact of Quebec nationalism on the economy, but he was never a supporter of partition.

After forming the Quebec Political Action Committee in 1995, Galganov soon demonstrated a talent for organizing political events and activities that attracted attention. His first target was the business enterprises, many controlled outside of Quebec, that had not bothered to display bilingual signs after the adoption of Bill 86 gave them the legal right to do so. In April 1996 Galganov organized a demonstration at the Fairview Shopping Mall in Pointe-Claire which attracted more than two thousand people. Its purpose was to publicize a boycott of retailers, including large chains like Eaton's, Sears, and the Hudson's Bay Company, that continued to comply with the provisions of the now-defunct Bill 178, rather than those of its more liberal successor. Within a week of the demonstration Eaton's restored its bilingual signs. Galganov later claimed that all of the targeted stores had eventually done likewise. His success provoked a curious threat from Minister of Finance and Deputy Premier Bernard Landry, who was beginning to occupy the same role in anglophone demonology that Camille Laurin had occupied between 1976 and 1984. Landry suggested that if anglophones insisted on compliance with the existing law regarding commercial signs, they would risk a backlash resulting in a more restrictive law, presumably along the lines of that adopted in 1977.[30]

Seemingly undeterred, Galganov subsequently opened a store on Monkland Avenue in NDG which violated the law by displaying signs on which English was as prominent as French, if not more so. The store specialized in woollen goods and was appropriately called "Presque Pure Laine," a sarcastic reference to the metaphorical Québécois use of the expression "*pure laine*" to refer to a person of completely French ancestry. Galganov defied the government to prosecute him for violating the sign law, but they wisely refused to do so, not wishing to draw any further attention to his cause.

Galganov's first venture outside of Quebec was to organize a pro-Canada demonstration on Parliament Hill in Ottawa, which attracted about ten thousand people and gained additional publicity. In August 1996 he announced that he would lead a delegation to New York the following month and subsidize the expenses of those who accompanied him. The purpose of the trip was to publicize his campaign against Quebec nationalism and to meet interested Americans. Hundreds of persons expressed interest in the expedition, but space on the chartered bus and at the various media events was limited to a select few, chosen so as to illustrate the diversity of Quebec's anglophone community.[31] Serge Ménard, who had been designated by Premier Bouchard as the minister with special responsibility for the problems of Montreal, denounced the proposed trip as a deliberate effort to undermine Quebec's economy and urged that it be cancelled. Even among anglophones the New York excursion appeared more controversial than Galganov's previous ventures. Michael Hamelin, the president of Alliance Quebec, criticized it in an interview and argued that Quebec's problems could only be resolved at home.[32]

The visit to New York took place in early September and featured a luncheon and press conference at the Harvard Club on 12 September.

The American media largely ignored the story: in fact the ninety-page index to *The New York Times* for the first half of the month listed no articles about Quebec and only sixteen about Canada, ten of which were about hockey. The report on the event in *The Globe and Mail* bore the headline "Wall Street ignores Galganov's visit."[33] Galganov himself professed to be satisfied with the trip, which he later called "the greatest marketing success we could have hoped for."[34] He was particularly pleased to receive a private interview with Congressman Thomas Campbell of California, who later publicly expressed the view that a sovereign Quebec would not automatically become a member of NAFTA. Less than two weeks after the Galganov visit, Campbell organized public hearings of the House of Representatives Sub-Committee on the Western Hemisphere, which summoned four witnesses to discuss the impact of Quebec sovereignty on the interests of the United States.

By the autumn of 1996 Galganov was one of the most famous persons in Quebec, and a biographical profile of him covered half a page in *The Globe and Mail* on 4 November. He had largely financed his various campaigns out of his own pocket, and at the end of the year he announced that he might have to abandon his political activities for lack of funds. More contributions soon appeared, as he had anticipated, and his retirement proved to be of short duration. However, when he announced in March that he would run for Parliament as an independent in the safe Liberal riding of Mount Royal, a number of promised contributions, estimated by Galganov at about a quarter of a million dollars, were withheld or cancelled.[35]

Whatever the future prospects of Galganov and his Quebec Political Action Committee, both the partitionist movement and the Galganov phenomenon provided evidence of the angry and frustrated mood of Quebec anglophones after the 1995 referendum. Not only were they angry at the Parti Québécois; they were dissatisfied with both the federal and provincial Liberal parties. They were also dissatisfied with the established leadership of their own community, and with Alliance Quebec, whose moderate approach seemed to epitomize the alleged failings of the anglophone establishment. Similar anger and frustration, after the adoption of Bill 22 in 1974 and after the adoption of Bill 178 in 1988, had led to protest voting: for the Union Nationale in 1976 and for the Equality Party in 1989. In 1995 no provincial election was imminent and no obvious vehicle for electoral protest seemed to be available. The parallel was perhaps closer with 1976, when the election of the first Parti Québécois government had caused widespread anxiety and had contributed to a proliferation of protest groups. Yet in 1976 what remained of the anglophone establishment, as represented by the Positive Action Committee, had been strong enough to channel the protest in more conventional directions. By 1995 this was apparently not the case.

Alliance Quebec's period of greatest influence had arguably been from 1982 through 1985, when the Parti Québécois had been in office. It might therefore have been expected that its influence would revive after that party returned to office in 1994. In fact Alliance Quebec continued to experience problems in serving as an effective link between the anglophone community and the Quebec government. Perhaps the government distrusted Alliance Quebec because it was both more closely associated with the Liberal opposition, and more financially dependent on the federal state, than it had been a decade earlier. Alliance Quebec's refusal to participate in the pre-referendum consultations on the future of Quebec annoyed Premier Parizeau, who cancelled a scheduled meeting with Alliance Quebec President Michael Hamelin as a result. The francophone media continued to portray Alliance Quebec as an extremist group that refused to accept the realities of Quebec, a characterization that had been propagated fairly consistently since the adoption of Bill 178.

The ironic situation of Alliance Quebec was that, while regarded as extremist by the leaders of francophone opinion, it was considered excessively moderate by most anglophones. By 1994 Alliance Quebec had become an institutionalized group that no longer inspired widespread enthusiasm or commitment among the community which it supposedly represented. It seemed to represent the comfortable anglophone establishment – not the old business elite, which had long since vanished, but the new middle-class establishment which had replaced them. Its moderate, conciliatory approach was sometimes ridiculed and sometimes resented. The issues which it emphasized, particularly maintaining and improving access to English-language education, health, and social services, were extremely important but tended to produce only small and incremental victories, if any. Its quiet diplomacy did not always produce visible results and certainly lacked the drama and excitement of the mass meetings, boycotts and other activities that kept the newer groups in the headlines. It was not easy to see how Alliance Quebec could overcome these problems. At the same time it seemed likely that the need for an organization like Alliance Quebec would persist for the foreseeable future.

THE BOUCHARD GOVERNMENT AND THE ANGLOPHONE COMMUNITY

With the referendum past, the Quebec government, headed after 29 January 1996 by Lucien Bouchard, could look more to other matters. The government's relationship with the anglophone community was one area of concern that seemed to require some attention. At the same time there were other concerns that could adversely affect this relationship, such as the desire to restrain the growth of spending on health and social services and the preference of many Parti Québécois members for more nationalistic language laws and policies.

Almost immediately after taking office, Premier Bouchard invited a number of prominent anglophones to an "off the record" meeting, organized by David Payne. Those in attendance included Peter Blaikie, Gretta Chambers, Michael Goldbloom, David Levine, and Royal Orr. Michael Hamelin refused to attend on the grounds that as president of Alliance Quebec he should receive a private audience, as his predecessors had done with previous premiers.[36] Those who attended would not reveal what was said but seemed reasonably satisfied, and Payne predicted that the government would soon announce measures to make anglophones feel more comfortable in Quebec.[37] Keith Henderson, who was not invited to the meeting, said that the partitionist movement, which held a major rally the following day, deserved the credit for the government's willingness to listen to anglophone concerns.[38]

Bouchard's effort to open a dialogue with the anglophones was countered almost immediately by a response from the more rigid Quebec nationalists. In September 1995 the minister responsible for language policy, Louise Beaudoin, had established an interdepartmental task force to explore and report on the status of the French language. The report had not yet been completed at the time of Bouchard's meeting with the anglophones, but a week later some of its more pessimistic conclusions were leaked to the media by Josée Legault, the director of research for the task force, a Parti Québécois militant, and the author of a highly critical book, based on her master's thesis, about the anglophone minority in Quebec. Since the publication of her book in 1992 Legault had received considerable exposure in the media, including English-language television, as an alleged expert on relations between the two linguistic communities in Quebec and as an articulate representative of the hard-line nationalists. In a letter that soon became public, she accused the government of trying to censor the task force's report in the interests of better relations with the anglophone minority. The leaked report warned that the French language was threatened by the persistence of *de facto* bilingualism. It alleged that French had still not become the exclusive language of public activities in Quebec, that immigrants were still being absorbed into the anglophone community, and that too many concessions to anglophone interests had been made under the previous

Liberal governments.[39] In an effort at damage control, Beaudoin emphasized that the report was only a preliminary draft and that some sections would be rewritten, after consultation with the relevant ministries, before the final version was published.[40]

On 11 March 1996 Premier Bouchard spoke in English to an audience of about four hundred at the Centaur Theatre, a major cultural institution of the anglophone community. As at the more intimate gathering in February, attendance was by invitation only, but this time a greater effort was made to represent the entire spectrum of anglophone opinion. Two prominent partitionists, Keith Henderson of the Equality Party and Brent Tyler of the Special Committee for Canadian Unity, were added to the list of invitees at the last moment. The speech was carried live on television.

Two days before the Centaur Theatre speech several prominent anglophones, mainly associated with Alliance Quebec and its affiliated organizations, published a signed article indicating what Bouchard would have to promise to win the trust of the anglophone community. Their demands included broader access to English schools, continuation of the right to display bilingual signs in accordance with Bill 86, no amendments to strengthen the Charter of the French Language, and measures to increase anglophone representation in the public service. They also demanded, rather unnecessarily, that the government not question the loyalty of federalists to Quebec or the right of federalists to participate in debates over Quebec's future.[41]

Although Bouchard's speech understandably fell somewhat short of this agenda, it was genuinely conciliatory in tone. The premier praised the cultural diversity of Montreal, commended anglophones for helping to launch the Quiet Revolution in 1960 and for supporting the Meech Lake Accord in 1987, and apologized for having said, just before he became premier, that Canada could be partitioned because it was not a "real country." He described linguistic school boards as "an idea whose time has come" and reiterated his party's commitment to maintain English-language education and health care in Quebec, even after the achievement of sovereignty.[42] Most members of the audience who were interviewed by *The Gazette* seemed to be favourably impressed by the speech. On the other hand, the newspaper's editorial, headed "Hold applause for Bouchard speech," was rather cool. Both the op-ed page columnist, Don MacPherson, and the staff cartoonist, Aislin, ridiculed the premier for mispronouncing the name of another columnist, Josh Freed. Freed himself, who was present at the speech, was more generous, describing Bouchard as "a sovereignist you can talk to."[43]

Later in the month the revised report of the task force on the French language was published – without an English translation.[44] It contained a lengthy and comprehensive account of the status of French in the economy, education, cultural life, and the integration of immigrants, fortified by forty-six pages of tables and graphs. A shorter chapter examined the quality, as opposed to the quantity, of French as spoken and written in Quebec. *The Gazette* commented on the final report in an editorial that bore the same title as its editorial on the leaked version exactly one month before: "Bouchard's tough language choice." The second editorial conceded that the data were accurate and the research generally useful, while the conclusions drawn from the data in the revised report were more reasonable than those in the preliminary version. *The Gazette* also noted that the percentage of anglophones in Quebec, enrollment in English schools, and the circulation of English newspapers had all declined considerably since 1971, and suggested that the position of the French language in Quebec had never been stronger. It urged Bouchard to follow the spirit of his Centaur Theatre speech rather than the recommendations of the "zealots" in his own party.[45]

This advice was easier to offer than to follow, and the path to an accommodation between the government and the anglophone minority continued to be strewn with obstacles. Early in April Louise Beaudoin announced that the government was going on a "concerted offensive" to promote French by enforcing the existing language laws more strictly.[46] The day following this announcement was the first day of Passover. Almost simultaneously the Office de la langue française ordered the removal of assorted kosher foods from the supermarket shelves on the grounds that the labelling was in English. The Office later met with representatives of the Jewish community and said that it was all a misunderstanding.

Health care was another area of concern. Quebec, like other provinces, was attempting to control the costs of the hospital sector by closing, merging, or redefining the functions of, a number of institutions. Anglophones argued that the effects of these measures were being disproportionately felt by institutions that had traditionally served a mainly anglophone clientele, and whose bilingual status had therefore been recognized by the Charter of the French Language. There was some evidence to support their case although one proposed restructuring, a plan to combine the five teaching hospitals associated with McGill University into a single institution called the McGill University Hospital Centre, was apparently first proposed within the anglophone community itself.[47] The Parizeau government had announced, early in its mandate, plans to close seven small to medium-sized hospitals in Montreal, mainly in the west end. It also planned to merge the "English" hospital in Sherbrooke with its larger francophone counterpart and to convert Quebec City's "English" hospital, the Jeffrey

Hale, into a geriatric centre. In September 1995 between ten and twelve thousand people participated in a march to support the Queen Elizabeth Hospital, located in NDG, which was the largest of the seven Montreal institutions slated for closure. The petitions against the closing of the hospital were said to have been signed by 135,000 persons.[48] In April 1996 the Bouchard government announced that the Queen Elizabeth would remain open, after a fashion, as the Centre-West Community Health Centre.

This concession did not appease the government's advisory committee on English language health and social services, headed by Eric Maldoff, which had been established under the Liberals. The committee met with the minister of health on 11 April 1996 and later in the month wrote a lengthy letter to him claiming that the availability of health care in English was being jeopardized by the government's plans. Although the letter was ostensibly an internal document, a large portion of it was soon published in *The Gazette*. The committee urged that institutions designated as bilingual must remain so, that they should not be closed or have their status modified until a clear and detailed plan to provide English-language health care was in place, and that as a general rule bilingual institutions should not be merged with unilingual French institutions. The committee also noted the dependence of anglophones outside of Montreal on a handful of institutions, such as the Jeffrey Hale, that had traditionally provided service in English.[49]

The issue was a complex and emotional one, in part because of pressures on the government to control spending on health care, in part because the relative decline of the anglophone community, especially outside of Montreal, made its institutions a tempting target, and in part because the anglophone community was aging and thus health care was a subject of increasing concern. An added complication was that the right of anglophone patients to service in their own language, recognized in law since the passage of Bill 142, clashed with the right of francophone hospital employees to use only their own language, recognized in law since the adoption of the Charter of the French Language.[50] Furthermore, some francophones still alleged that "English" hospitals designated as bilingual did not provide adequate service in French. In August 1996 a francophone journalist who had been treated for a heart attack at the Jewish General Hospital in Montreal claimed that he had been insulted by a nurse who told him to speak English. This allegation promptly led to a demonstration outside the hospital.[51] Although the journalist recovered from his illness, the incident was eerily reminiscent of the episode fourteen years earlier at St Mary's Hospital, only a few blocks from the Jewish

General, when a patient had allegedly been prevented from "dying in French." Karl Marx's famous observation that great historical events occur twice, the first time as tragedy and the second as farce, seemed curiously appropriate.

Meanwhile, in June 1996, the government introduced a new language bill in the National Assembly. Given the depth of concern about linguistic issues among the militants of the Parti Québécois, Bill 40 was a surprisingly modest measure. Its main purpose was to re-establish the Commission de protection de la langue francaise, which had been abolished by the Liberals' Bill 86. Anglophones had hated the Commission because its personnel had been responsible for finding and reporting bilingual signs, but its revival, while unwelcome to them, was merely a logical corollary of Louise Beaudoin's pledge in April to enforce the Charter of the French Language more rigorously. Bilingual signs would continue to be allowed, as they had been since 1993. The only other major substantive provision of Bill 40 was a requirement that computer software, including computer games, must be available in French unless no French version existed. English software could still be sold, provided that the French version was not inferior in quality and was offered on equally favourable terms, apart from price. Computer software had not of course been a concern in 1977, so this was merely an adaptation of the Charter to new circumstances. The modest scope of Bill 40 suggested that Premier Bouchard's remarks at the Centaur Theatre had been quite sincere.

Bill 40 was sent to the standing committee on culture where it was severely criticized by representatives of the anglophone community. Many of the criticisms seemed to reflect long-standing frustration and resentment over language policy, rather than the contents of the bill itself. Michael Hamelin, appearing on behalf of Alliance Quebec, accused the government of introducing unnecessary legislation to "patch over the cracks in the Parti Québécois."[52] He cited a poll commissioned by Alliance Quebec which showed that overwhelming majorities of voters supported access to health care in English, bilingual signs provided French was predominant, and a bilingual status for Montreal. Keith Henderson spoke at great length about bilingual signs and reminded the government that Canada's constitution made English an official language in Quebec. He also urged that Bill 40 be referred to the courts on the grounds that the provisions about computer software intruded on federal jurisdiction over trade and commerce while the powers given to the "language police" violated the constitutional prohibition of "unreasonable search or seizure."[53] Marjorie Goodfellow of the Townshippers said that reading *Le Français langue commune* made her organization feel "discouraged" and "unwelcome" in Quebec. She asked whether the government intended to prohibit any public use of the English language.[54]

The bill returned to the National Assembly for second reading in December, when the Liberals unsuccessfully tried to give it the six months hoist. Russell Williams described the bill as backward-looking, coercive, and divisive, called the government "morally corrupt," and accused them of "continued harrassment of the English-speaking community." He noted that the implementation of Bill 40 would cost $5 million in the first year, more than the construction costs of a French language CEGEP which had been promised to his riding by the previous Liberal government but cancelled by the Parti Québécois.[55] The bill passed on second reading in March and became law in June 1997.[56]

Meanwhile, the dissatisfaction of some party militants with Premier Bouchard's moderate stance on linguistic issues became evident at the Parti Québécois convention in November 1996. Bouchard warned in his opening speech that any evidence of intolerance towards the anglophone minority would damage the cause of Quebec sovereignty, and he specifically ruled out any return to the prohibition of bilingual signs.[57] The following day only 76.7 per cent of the delegates voted to confirm his leadership. Furthermore, a policy workshop dominated by militants from the Montreal ridings voted by a narrow majority to prohibit bilingual signs, although even Camille Laurin urged them not to do so.[58] On the final day of the convention the delegates in plenary session voted by a show of hands to reject the workshop's recommendation, and some of the militants walked out in protest. It was reported that some delegates had voted for the status quo out of fear that Premier Bouchard might resign if the convention failed to do so.[59]

Seemingly undeterred by the discontent among party militants, the Bouchard government showed further evidence of moderation in January 1997 by announcing that firms with between ten and forty-nine employees would not be required to qualify for certificates of francization. Instead they would merely be encouraged to do so.[60] This was a reversal of party policy, but the good news for anglophones was overshadowed a few days later when the National Council of the Parti Québécois adopted a recommendation from party members in the Eastern Townships that health and social service institutions, other than those whose clientele was predominantly anglophone, should not be required to offer service in English. A second recommendation was that the plans for availability of service in English, which Bill 142 required institutions to prepare, should be reviewed by the Office de la langue française to ensure their compatibility with the Charter of the French Language.[61] Premier Bouchard explained to the anglophone media that no change in existing laws was intended and that the purpose of the proposals was merely to protect the rights of francophone employees, but anglophones saw the recommendations as an attack on Bill 142. Alliance Quebec called a protest meeting at the Centaur Theatre which was attended by about 250 persons.[62]

The perennial problem of denominational school boards, which had defied all efforts to resolve it for thirty years, reappeared in 1996 and unexpectedly complicated relations between anglophones and the Bouchard government. The Liberal government's Bill 107, which had been adopted in 1988, would have retained Protestant and Catholic boards only within the boundaries of the two major cities, where the Canadian constitution prevented their abolition.[63] This compromise seemed to create as many problems as it solved and was never implemented. As explained in preceding chapters, most anglophones had come to the conclusion that linguistic rather than denominational boards would be more conducive to maintaining a viable English-language educational system. The main opposition to reform appeared to come from the conservative faction that controlled the Montreal Catholic School Commission and probably had less influence over the Parti Québécois than it did over the Liberals.

In March 1996 Premier Bouchard's speech opening the second session of the National Assembly promised to replace denominational school boards in Montreal and Quebec City with linguistic boards, a reform which he said was supported by "a consensus among all progressive Quebeckers."[64] Bouchard asserted that linguistic boards would make it easier for francophones to integrate new arrivals into Quebec society and would also make it easier for anglophones to ensure the vitality of their community.

In May the minister of education, Pauline Marois, repeated the same two arguments for linguistic boards in the standing committee on education while adding two more: they would increase the influence of parents and local communities over the schools and would guarantee freedom of religion in a democratic manner. Marois noted that she had met representatives of the anglophone community in the Townships who had told her that linguistic boards would help to maintain the anglophone culture and presence in that region.[65] When pressed to clarify the government's intentions she indicated that they had not yet decided whether an amendment of the Canadian constitution would be necessary, and suggested that if one were, there might be a long delay. She was worried that the federal government seemed in no hurry to deal with a request for a similar amendment from Newfoundland, even though the premier of that province had been a member of the Chrétien government until quite recently.[66]

Three months later Marois announced that the whole question of school board reorganization would be postponed since public consultations had persuaded her that there was no consensus on the subject; the Estates General on Education would be asked to recommend a solution. This announcement was not well received in the anglophone community. "We're very disappointed," was the response of Joan Dougherty, the former MNA for Jacques-Cartier and the chairman of Alliance Quebec's committee on education. Alan Butler, chairman of the Protestant School Board of Greater Montreal, had a similar reaction.[67] Don MacPherson's column in *The Gazette* a few days later was headed "Breaking the promise: Reversal on linguistic school-board plan kills whatever's left of the spirit of the Centaur speech."[68]

One might have expected, given this response, that the anglophone community would be overjoyed the following winter when the Quebec government announced that it would, after all, request the federal government to sponsor a constitutional amendment that would allow the elimination of denominational school boards in Quebec.[69] Instead Alliance Quebec unexpectedly responded that the removal of the denominational guarantee in the constitution would only be acceptable if replaced by a new constitutional guarantee entrenching the proposed linguistic boards.[70] Alliance Quebec had admittedly taken the same position in 1988, when Bill 107 was under consideration in the National Assembly. However, the Supreme Court of Canada had ruled in 1990, in a case involving francophones in Alberta, that Section 23 of the Charter of Rights and Freedoms gave linguistic minorities the right to manage and control their own schools.[71] This judgment seemed to suggest that any further constitutional guarantee would be superfluous. Premier Bouchard pointed this out in a televised interview, but Alliance Quebec was not convinced.[72] Two members of parliament from Montreal Island, Warren Allmand and Clifford Lincoln, also insisted that a constitutional guarantee of linguistic boards would be necessary.[73] Both Prime Minister Chrétien and Minister of Intergovernmental Affairs Stéphane Dion indicated that they would have to be convinced that a sufficient consensus existed in Quebec to justify a constitutional amendment. Dion stated specifically that this consensus would have to include the anglophone community.[74] Daniel Johnson announced that the Liberal opposition in the National Assembly would not support the request for an amendment.[75]

Relations between anglophones and the Bouchard government thus appeared to have reached a low state less than a year after the premier's speech to anglophones at the Centaur Theatre. Interviewed by *Le Devoir* in late February of 1997, Bouchard admitted that his efforts at reconciliation with the anglophones had come to naught and blamed "extremist" and "radical" leaders of the anglophone community, whom he suggested might not represent the views of the English-speaking population.[76] He specifically mentioned in this connection the recently expressed views of Alliance Quebec on the question of linguistic school boards, and indicated that he was uncertain whether there was enough consensus to proceed with the government's plans.

In April the Parti Québécois government and the Liberal opposition agreed to a compromise, suggested by Thomas Mulcair, whereby the right of anglophones to manage their own school boards would be explicitly recognized in the law, although not in a constitutional amendment. The compromise appeared to satisfy all of the Liberals, apart from Lawrence Bergman and John Ciaccia, who were both deliberately absent when the National Assembly unanimously resolved to request a constitutional amendment. Bergman's objection was based on the grounds that schools would not be able to choose a religious orientation other than Catholic or Protestant.[77]

A few days after this vote the government introduced Bill 109, which provided for English and French linguistic school boards throughout the province and the abolition of all the Protestant and Catholic boards. Until 30 June of the year following the adoption of the constitutional amendment, the boards in the two major cities would have Protestant and Catholic confessional councils. Until the same date, Catholics or Protestants elsewhere in the province could establish new dissentient boards, if they constituted a religious minority within the clientele of the board that provided instruction in their own language. The government could amalgamate such dissentient boards with others of the same language and religion, even if their territories were not contiguous.

However, further difficulties ensued. The bill originally provided that only those persons who were eligible to send their children to English schools under the Canada clause would be able to vote in elections for the English-language boards. Alliance Quebec argued that immigrants should be allowed to vote for, and pay taxes to, the school board of their choice.[78] Although the government feared that this concession would re-open the question of broadening access to English education, as recommended by the Chambers report, it eventually agreed to a compromise whereby anyone could choose to vote for the English board in his or her locality, thereby forfeiting the right to vote for the French board. However, choosing to vote for an English board did not make the person or the person's children eligible to receive instruction in English, if they failed to qualify under the provisions of the Charter of the French Language. In this modified form the bill became law in June 1997.[79] The Chrétien government, which had been re-elected earlier in June, decided to amend the constitution. Although Clifford Lincoln and Senator Dalia Wood both opposed the amendment, the House of Commons approved it on 18 November and the Senate on 15 December 1997.[80] After more than thirty years, it seemed that the long struggle to abolish denominational school boards in Quebec had finally ended.

All was not well, however, in the anglophone community of Quebec. Three years after the return to office of the Parti Québécois, the anglophone minority were still divided and confused, distrustful of the government, with little confidence in the Liberal opposition and without effective leadership. Alliance Quebec, which the premier had publicly described as too radical and which much of the anglophone population despised for its allegedly excessive moderation, had not regained the influence which it held in its earliest years. The continuing stagnation of the economy in Montreal, and the demographic weakness of the scattered anglophone minorities elsewhere in the province, did not seem to bode well for the community's prospects.

Nonetheless, anglophones could take some satisfaction from the fact that they had survived three years of government by the Parti Québécois without experiencing any serious efforts to curtail their rights and privileges by amending the laws. At most they could complain of neglect and insensitivity, both of which they had been used to under the Liberals, rather than deliberate malice. Bill 40 was essentially innocuous and no new initiatives in language legislation appeared to be contemplated by the government. It seemed that after a generation of controversy over linguistic issues a precarious equilibrium had been reached between the two communities.

8 Quebec Anglophones and the Federal Government, 1968–97

Chapters 4 through 7 of this book have concentrated on politics at the provincial level and referred only in passing to federalism and the central government of Canada. As those chapters have explained, the years after the end of the Quiet Revolution saw the emergence of language policy as a major issue in Quebec politics, growing support for the independence movement, and the collapse of the consociational arrangements that had enabled the anglophone minority to flourish since Confederation. One might expect that in these circumstances Quebec anglophones would look to the federal level of government for support. To what extent did they do so, and to what extent did the federal government respond to their concerns? How did their peculiar situation affect their outlook on federalism and the constitution? This chapter attempts to answer these questions.

For the century prior to 1968 English-speaking Quebeckers, at least in urban areas, had directed most of their political energy and attention towards Ottawa rather than Quebec City. Not only did their identity as Canadians take precedence over any sense of identification with the province, but they were convinced, not without reason, that the central government was more important to them and had a greater impact on their lives than its provincial counterpart. This continued to be so during the Quiet Revolution despite their interest, on the whole sympathetic although not unmixed with apprehension, in the Lesage government's reforms.

1968, however, is a watershed in this regard. It is only from the 1960s onwards that observers began to describe Canada as the world's

most decentralized federation. Increasingly the federal government
withdrew from direct involvement in shared-cost programs, lost interest in Keynesian macro-economic policy and fiscal centralization,
allowed its military forces to deteriorate, and acquiesced (most of the
time) in the erosion of economic and cultural barriers between
Canada and the United States.[1] The rhetorical resistance of Prime
Minister Trudeau to the growing relative importance of the provincial
governments could not obscure the facts, any more than the rhetoric
of Charles de Gaulle or Harold Macmillan concealed the collapse of
western Europe's colonial empires during their terms in office. As
regards Quebec in particular, the greater importance of provincial
government after the 1960s cannot be seriously disputed.

For English-speaking Quebeckers the contrast between the dynamics of Canadian federalism before and after that point in time was even
more obvious than for other Canadians. The politicization of language
in Quebec from 1968 onwards and the simultaneous emergence of
the Parti Québécois turned the attention of English-speaking Quebeckers towards provincial politics to a greater extent than at any time
in their previous history. Although their affective orientation towards
Canada continued to be stronger than towards Quebec, they increasingly realized that the future of their community was in the hands of
the provincial authorities. The energies spent defending the interests
of that community against the threat of the independence movement,
and against the encroaching bureaucratic provincial state driven by
Quebec nationalism, left less time and attention to be devoted to
federal politics, which more and more seemed removed from their
day-to-day concerns. It may also be suggested, although the validity of
the assertion can rest on no more than intuitive and subjective evidence, that after 1968 there was a tendency for the more talented of
the community's political leaders and spokespersons to gravitate
towards the provincial level of politics, at least as often as to the federal
level if not more so. Even those with extensive working experience in
the federal government, such as Kevin Drummond, John Ciaccia, Reed
Scowen, and Richard French, sought election to the National Assembly, where they made significant contributions to the political life of
the province. One suspects that prior to 1968 persons such as these
four would have been elected to the House of Commons and would
not even have considered seeking provincial office.

Nonetheless, the federal level of government cannot be ignored
entirely, even after 1968. This chapter therefore examines its relationship with the English-speaking community of Quebec during the three
decades that followed the federal general election of 1968. It describes
the representation of English-speaking Quebeckers in federal political

institutions during that time and their voting behaviour in federal elections. It also examines the extent to which the community sought and received assistance from the central government and federal institutions in defending its interests against Quebec nationalism and the bureaucratic modernization of the provincial level. A final section will describe the contribution of Quebec anglophones and their organizations to the debate over Canada's constitution, particularly in the sixteen-year period between the formation of René Lévesque's government and the referendum that rejected the Charlottetown Accord proposals for constitutional change in 1992.

REPRESENTATION IN FEDERAL INSTITUTIONS

Chapter 3 described the redistribution of parliamentary constituencies prior to the federal general election of 1968 and the mixed consequences it had for the representation of English-speaking Quebeckers. Long overdue inasmuch as no fewer than six general elections had been conducted under an electoral map based on the 1951 census, redistribution increased the representation of Montreal Island, where most English-speaking Quebeckers lived, from twenty seats to twenty-two and a half. (The new riding of Vaudreuil was partly on and partly off the island.) This would prove to be an all-time high, as subsequent redistributions reduced the island's representation. On the other hand it eliminated the historic ridings of Cartier, Ste-Anne, and St Lawrence-St George, which had been respectively identified with the Jewish, Irish Catholic, and British Protestant elements in Quebec's population.

More generally, this redistribution was the first to be based on the recommendations of independent boundary commissions, one for each province, rather than on negotiations among the elected members themselves. One consequence of this was to make the decennial redistribution required by the constitution a much slower process, so that boundaries based on the 1971 census were not used until 1979, and so forth. A second consequence was that boundaries were based on purely arithmetical criteria, the intent being to make the ridings equal in size regardless of whether areas within a riding shared any real community of interest. Not only the ethnic and linguistic characteristics of the population but even municipal boundaries seem to have been ignored, which probably worked to the detriment of anglophone representation in Quebec. (It was at least equally unfair to other minorities, such as farmers who found themselves in ridings dominated by suburban voters.)

The census did not record the linguistic composition of federal electoral districts until 1976, but on the basis of data for municipalities it appears that the redistribution that took effect before the 1968 election left Quebec with five predominantly English-speaking ridings: Dollard, Lachine, Mount Royal, NDG and Westmount. The redistribution prior to the 1979 election added St-Henri, a working-class francophone neighbourhood, to Westmount, with the result that persons of English mother tongue became a plurality, rather than a majority, of the riding's voters. Its name was appropriately changed to St-Henri-Westmount. Lachine riding was shifted to the west by adding Beaconsfield (previously part of Vaudreuil) and removing half of the city of Lachine (which was added to NDG). This made NDG somewhat less English than before although anglophones continued to be a majority there according to the census of 1976.

The anglophone exodus from Quebec following the election of the Parti Québécois, most of which occured before these new boundaries were actually used in an election, drastically altered the linguistic composition of the five "English" ridings. By the time of the 1981 census St-Henri-Westmount had more voters of French than of English mother tongue. Dollard and NDG had both lost their English mother tongue majorities, although persons of English mother tongue still outnumbered those of French mother tongue in both ridings. These developments left only two ridings in which English was the mother tongue of a majority of the voters: Lachine and Mount Royal.

The next redistribution, taking effect before the 1988 election, returned the eastern half of the city of Lachine to Lachine riding, with the result that NDG regained its English mother tongue majority while Lachine–Lac St-Louis, as it was now called, had only a plurality of anglophones. Mount Royal's anglophone majority also became a plurality owing to an influx of allophones; the population of French mother tongue increased hardly at all. Dollard, now called Pierrefonds-Dollard, lost territory in the east but gained some in the west, with little net effect on its linguistic composition. NDG was now the only riding with an anglophone majority, but it did not retain that status for long. The redistribution prior to the 1997 election added the entire city of Lachine to that riding, reducing its anglophone majority to a plurality and changing the riding's name to NDG-Lachine. The former riding of Lachine–Lac St-Louis, now known simply as Lac St-Louis, regained its anglophone majority as a result of this change, and was extended to the western tip of the island at the expense of Vaudreuil. Mount Royal and Pierrefonds-Dollard retained their English mother tongue pluralities. St-Henri was detached from Westmount, which added some additional territory in the east to become Westmount-Ville Marie, regaining its anglophone plurality.

The details of these changes are less significant than the fact that after the 1968 election there were only five Quebec ridings, and between 1979 and 1997 only four, in which English was the mother tongue of more voters than French. Four is about half the number of ridings which would correspond with the actual size of the anglophone minority, and the same number allocated to the province of Prince Edward Island, whose total population is about one-sixth as large as the number of anglophones in Quebec.

A predominantly anglophone riding does not necessarily have an anglophone member of parliament, and conversely a predominantly francophone riding is not always represented by a francophone. Mount Royal was represented by Pierre Elliott Trudeau from 1965 until his retirement in 1984, although its percentage of francophones was among the lowest of any riding in Quebec. Dollard (or Pierre-fonds-Dollard) has always been represented by francophone Liberals, except when Gerry Weiner held it for the Progressive Conservatives between 1984 and 1993. On the other hand St-Henri-Westmount continued to have anglophone members of parliament until 1994, long after it had lost its anglophone plurality. C.M. Drury, who retired in 1978, was succeeded by Donald Johnston, a prominent lawyer and friend of the prime minister. Trudeau had wanted Johnston to run in working-class Verdun, which had been vacated by Bryce Mackasey more than a year earlier, but Johnston found Westmount, the citadel of the business elite, more congenial.[2] His hopes to succeed Drury as the acknowledged political spokesman for that elite were realized only in part.[3] When Johnston left politics in 1988 the Liberal nomination was won by David Berger, a member of a prominent Jewish family, whose previous riding of Laurier had been abolished in the latest redistribution. Only after Berger resigned the seat in 1995 to become Canada's ambassador to Israel did Westmount acquire a francophone federal representative in Lucienne Robillard. (It had acquired a francophone provincial representative the year before, when Jacques Chagnon succeeded Richard Holden.) Robillard continued to represent Westmount-Ville Marie, a riding with slightly different boundaries and an anglophone plurality, after 1997.

Mount Royal, which many members of Montreal's Jewish community had expected to elect a Jewish member after the retirement of Alan McNaughton in 1965, finally did so after Trudeau's retirement in 1984. Sheila Finestone won the Liberal nomination in a strenuous contest against a francophone Jewish candidate from the Sephardic community. More than four thousand Liberals turned out for the nominating convention in what was probably the safest Liberal riding in Canada. Finestone had worked in Claude Ryan's office and would have liked to run for the National Assembly, but Robert Bourassa had discouraged her on the grounds that he had too many anglophones already in a party that was trying to capture the "soft nationalist" vote. The federal Liberals, on the other hand, were impressed by her strong credentials in the Jewish community and also wanted more women on their slate of candidates.[4] She easily resisted the trend towards the Progressive Conservatives in 1984 and became an articulate spokesperson in Parliament for Quebec anglophones and other minorities.

NDG, now known as NDG-Lachine, and Lac St-Louis were the only Quebec ridings with an unbroken tradition of anglophone representation in the House of Commons. When Warren Allmand finally retired in 1997 the Liberal nomination in NDG was won by Marlene Jennings. There was some local resentment that Jennings, a visible minority woman who lived outside the riding, had been parachuted in by the federal party's Quebec organizer, Alfonso Gagliano, so as to give the party a more pluralistic image. However, she held the riding for the Liberals in 1997 with the usual overwhelming majority.

Lachine–Lac St-Louis was won by Clifford Lincoln in the federal general election of 1993, almost five years after his resignation from the Bourassa government over Bill 178. He held the successor riding of Lac St-Louis, which included part of his former provincial riding of Nelligan, in the 1997 election. Later that year he was a candidate for the speakership of the House of Commons, but was defeated by incumbent speaker Gilbert Parent.

Other ridings in and around Montreal elected English-speaking representatives without having a plurality, much less a majority, of anglophone voters. Bryce Mackasey continued to represent Verdun in the House of Commons until 1976, and Eric Kierans represented Duvernay from 1968 until 1971. In the 1972 election Hal Herbert was elected as a Liberal in Vaudreuil and John Campbell in Lasalle; both remained in the House of Commons until 1984. David Berger held Laurier from 1979 until 1988, when he moved to St-Henri-Westmount. Paul Martin won back Campbell's former seat for the Liberals in 1988. In the same year Shirley Maheu, an anglophone woman married to a francophone, won St-Laurent, a new and mainly francophone riding carved out of the former Dollard.

Outside of the Montreal metropolitan area a number of English-speaking members were also elected by overwhelmingly francophone ridings. Walter Smith and Ian Watson represented rural ridings south of Montreal as Liberals from 1968 until 1979. Heward Grafftey, defeated in 1968, returned four years later to serve three more terms as the Progressive Conservative member for Brome-Missisquoi. In the eastern part of the province Brian Mulroney and Darryl Gray were elected as Progressive Conservatives in 1984 and re-elected in 1988.

Philip Edmonston, an American-born consumer advocate running for the NDP, won Chambly in a by-election in 1990 and held it until the 34th Parliament was dissolved three years later. David Price won Compton-Stanstead for the Progressive Conservatives in 1997. Thus the number of English-speaking members representing Quebec ridings fluctuated between six and ten until 1995. The resignations of David Berger in that year and of Shirley Maheu in 1996, both receiving patronage appointments to open safe seats for Lucienne Robillard and Stéphane Dion respectively, reduced the number of anglophones to four, increasing to five after the 1997 election.

Quebec anglophones showed a consistently greater tendency than Quebec francophones to support the federal Liberals, as can be seen by examining the electoral outcomes in the five ridings with the largest percentages of English-speaking voters: Dollard, Lachine, Mount Royal, NDG, and Westmount. In the five elections between 1968 and 1980 the Liberal share of the valid votes fluctuated between 67 and 77 per cent in Dollard, between 53 and 64 per cent in Lachine, between 75 and 91 per cent in Mount Royal, between 62 and 73 per cent in NDG, and between 58 and 79 per cent in Westmount. In each case the Liberal percentage was lowest in 1974, but increased by about 10 percentage points or more in the following election. Lachine's Liberal percentage was always the lowest of the five ridings, possibly because the traditionally Liberal Jewish vote was negligible in that riding. The highest percentage was always in Mount Royal, Prime Minister Trudeau's riding, but Trudeau never again exceeded 90 per cent of the vote after doing so in his first election as prime minister.

The Progressive Conservatives tended to run more serious campaigns with stronger candidates in Lachine than in the other four ridings. In 1972 the Liberal member, Raymond Rock, defected to the official opposition and became the Tory candidate after the Liberal Party encouraged Rod Blaker, a popular broadcaster, to challenge him for the nomination. Ironically Blaker had earlier been asked to run as a Progressive Conservative by his distant cousin Brian Mulroney, who was helping to organize the party's campaign in the Montreal area.[5] In 1974 John Pratt, who had represented roughly the same area during the Diefenbaker years, attempted a comeback in Lachine riding. In both 1979 and 1980 the Progressive Conservative colours in Lachine were carried by Peter Blaikie. (Blaikie would probably have won the riding if he had made a third attempt in 1984, but his lack of rapport with the party's new leader, Brian Mulroney, made him decide not to do so.)[6] In 1979 the Progressive Conservative slate also featured Richard Holden in Dollard and David de Jong (the Freedom of Choice candidate in the NDG provincial by-election a year earlier) running against Prime Minister Trudeau in Mount Royal. Both did very poorly.

Trudeau's popularity among English-speaking Quebeckers had deteriorated considerably by the time he retired in 1984, and this fact affected the level of support for the Liberals even after he was succeeded by John Turner.[7] The Progressive Conservative vote increased by enough in 1984 to push the Liberals below 50 per cent in all five ridings. Brian Mulroney's leadership, and the fact that the Progressive Conservatives had realistic prospects in Quebec for the first time in a generation, attracted some unlikely recruits to the cause. Robert Layton, whose father Gilbert had served in Maurice Duplessis' first government, won Lachine for the Progressive Conservatives. The younger Layton had sought the federal Liberal nomination in Vaudreuil, without success, in 1972. Gerry Weiner, the mayor of Dollard-des-Ormeaux and a self-described social democrat, took out a party membership and was nominated in Dollard after an interview with Mulroney persuaded him that the leader shared his commitment to minority rights.[8] He was also successful. Nick auf der Maur, another recruit from the left side of the political spectrum, was recruited to run in NDG by his friend Richard Holden.[9] He came close to defeating Warren Allmand but fell short by about two thousand votes. Sheila Finestone and Donald Johnston won the other two ridings for the Liberals without difficulty.

In 1988 the Liberal share of the vote continued its decline in most parts of Quebec, but it increased by more than 10 percentage points in Lachine, Mount Royal, and NDG. The closest race in any of the five ridings was in Lachine where Victor Drury, the son of C.M. Drury, came within a few hundred votes of defeating Robert Layton. There was little change in Pierrefonds-Dollard, where Gerry Weiner retained a comfortable edge over the Liberal candidate, and a continuing Liberal decline in St-Henri-Westmount, where David Berger replaced Donald Johnston as the Liberal candidate. Berger nonetheless retained the riding for the Liberals.

In 1993 and 1997 the Liberal percentages in all five ridings returned to approximately the levels achieved during the Trudeau era. The pro-sovereignty Bloc Québécois, which won most of Quebec's federal ridings on both occasions, was obviously not a factor in the anglophone ridings. The only serious challenge to Liberal hegemony in any of them came from Howard Galganov, the anglophone rights activist, who ran as an independent in Mount Royal in 1997. Galganov based his campaign on the allegation that Sheila Finestone had not done or said enough on behalf of the anglophone minority in Quebec. He won 21 per cent of the vote and Finestone's percentage fell by exactly the same amount, from 83 to 62. A few members of the

Equality Party ran in the federal elections of both 1993 and 1997, but their party did not field enough candidates to be officially recognized at the federal level and they received only a handful of votes.

The rural anglophone vote in federal elections followed somewhat similar trends, judging by the results in four predominantly English-speaking municipalities in different regions of the province: Grosse-Île, Hatley/North Hatley, Lennoxville and Shawville. Grosse-Île, a part of Les-Îles-de-la-Madeleine in the Gulf of St Lawrence, deviated from the norm only in 1974, when it gave the Progressive Conservative candidate a slight majority. Hatley/North Hatley, in the Eastern Townships, was Liberal in every election except those of 1984, 1988, and 1997. Lennoxville, the largest anglophone community in the Townships, was Liberal throughout the Trudeau era but remained loyal to its Progressive Conservative member, Jean Charest, in 1993 and 1997. Shawville, a Protestant stronghold in Pontiac County, was the most idiosyncratic. It voted Progressive Conservative throughout the Trudeau era, although not by majorities as overwhelming as an earlier years. It finally defected to the Liberal camp in 1993.[10]

The Senate continued to count a reasonable number of anglophones among Quebec's twenty-four representatives. Alan McNaughton served until he reached the age of compulsory retirement in 1978. Lazarus Phillips became the first Jewish senator from Quebec in 1968. When he retired two years later he was succeeded by Carl Goldenberg, who served until 1982. Shortly after Goldenberg's retirement Leo Kolber was appointed from a different senatorial district. Prime Minister Trudeau also appointed Dalia Wood, the president of the Liberal association in his riding of Mount Royal, to the Senate in 1979. She became an articulate spokesperson for the anglophone minority in the province. Charlie Watt, an English-speaking aboriginal who had assisted the federalist cause in the referendum of 1980, was appointed in 1984. Prime Minister Mulroney appointed John Lynch-Staunton, the former municipal politician and Union Nationale candidate, in 1990 and David Angus, a prominent Westmount Progressive Conservative who had worked in Richard Holden's 1962 campaign, three years later. Angus replaced the dean of the Senate, Hartland Molson, who had been appointed by Prime Minister Louis St Laurent in 1955, as the member for the senatorial district of Alma. Shirley Maheu received a Senate seat when she resigned from the House of Commons in 1996. After her appointment there were six anglophone senators from Quebec along with two European-born allophones, Philip Gigantes and Pietro Rizzuto. Senator Rizzuto died in 1997.

Quebec anglophones were also continuously represented, and at times over-represented, in the federal cabinet. The Trudeau cabinet as constituted after the 1968 election included no fewer than three

English-speaking Quebeckers, or more than one-tenth of the entire cabinet. C.M. Drury, the acknowledged senior spokesman for Quebec anglophones, was president of the Treasury Board, Bryce Mackasey was minister of labour, and Eric Kierans held the office of postmaster-general, to which was later added the new portfolio of communications. Kierans was not happy in Ottawa, or in a government led by a prime minister with views about federalism quite different from his own. Although determined to leave by the fall of 1970, he decided to remain for a decent interval after the October Crisis.[11] He finally resigned both his portfolio and his parliamentary seat in April 1971 and was replaced by a francophone. Mackasey was shifted to manpower and immigration in January 1972 but dropped from the cabinet in the shuffle that followed the 1972 election. According to Trudeau's memoirs, he was dropped because he refused to change portfolios for the second time in a year.[12]

At the same time that Mackasey left the government, Warren Allmand from NDG entered it as solicitor-general. Mackasey returned to the cabinet as a minister of state (in effect without portfolio) just before the 1974 election. He was promoted to the office of postmaster-general after the election. Mackasey's return brought the number of Quebec anglophones in the cabinet back to three. As Hal Herbert, the Liberal member for Vaudreuil, recalled in his unpublished memoirs: "Bud Drury represented the upper crust, Warren Allmand the middle class, and Bryce Mackassey (*sic*) the blue collar workers."[13] With the prime minister also representing an anglophone Quebec riding, the community probably had more influence in cabinet than any of the four western provinces.

This was not to last, however, for Drury and Mackasey left the cabinet simultaneously on 13 September 1976. Mackasey resigned his seat to run in the provincial election, as described in chapter 4. Drury remained in the House of Commons for more than a year as a private member before accepting an appointment as chairman of the National Capital Commission. Their departures from the cabinet left Warren Allmand, who was moved to the portfolio of Indian affairs and northern development, as the only representative of anglophone Quebec in the government. In September 1977 Allmand changed portfolios again, becoming minister of consumer and corporate affairs. He remained in the government until the Liberals were defeated in 1979.

After 1976 the normal quota of Quebec anglophones in the cabinet returned to one, which had been the usual number in the much smaller cabinets prior to the Trudeau era. Heward Grafftey of Brome-Missisquoi served as a minister of state, first for social affairs and then for science and technology, in the short-lived government of Joe Clark. Warren Allmand was not reappointed when the Liberals returned to office in 1980, and spent the rest of his parliamentary career on the back benches. Donald Johnston, the lawyer who had represented Westmount since the by-election that followed Drury's retirement, entered the cabinet as president of the Treasury Board. Johnston had been one of the lawyers involved in the *Blaikie* litigation and was also a friend of Trudeau, who would later join the law firm in which Johnston was a partner. Johnston held four different portfolios in less than five years, ending up as minister of justice in the short-lived government of John Turner.

Brian Mulroney became prime minister in September 1984, the first Quebec anglophone to hold that office since John J. Abbott in 1891–92. Robert Layton joined the Mulroney government with the minor portfolio of minister of state for mines. It will be recalled that mines had been the traditional anglophone portfolio at the provincial level in the era of Maurice Duplessis. Perhaps unconsciously, Mulroney emulated Duplessis' political style in a number of ways and this appointment might be an example, although Layton's professional experience as an engineer would have made the portfolio a natural choice in any event.

Layton was dropped from the cabinet in June 1986 and replaced by Gerry Weiner, who played a much more significant role in the Mulroney government. Weiner was at first minister of state for immigration and then minister of state for multiculturalism. In January 1989 he became secretary of state and as such responsible for implementing the Official Languages Act. He held that portfolio until April 1991 when he was shifted to the new ministry of multiculturalism and citizenship. He held the latter portfolio until the Progressive Conservatives left office in 1993.

Upon the return of the Liberals, Paul Martin Jr, representing the riding of LaSalle-Émard, became minister of finance. Although originally from Ontario, like his famous father and namesake, he had lived in Montreal as a businessman for two decades before being elected to the House of Commons in 1988. Martin was joined in the new government by Sheila Finestone, who became secretary of state for multiculturalism and the status of women. She was dropped from the cabinet in January 1996.

Apart from the House of Commons, the Senate, and the cabinet, another important institution should be mentioned in connection with the federal representation of Quebec anglophones. Douglas Abbott, the former minister of finance who had served on the Supreme Court of Canada since 1954, took early retirement in 1973, almost two years before reaching the age of seventy-five. He attempted, without success, to persuade the minister of justice that his successor should also be an anglophone.[14] Since Abbott's retirement there have always been three francophones from Quebec on the Supreme Court, and six justices from the common-law provinces.

When the number of justices on the Supreme Court was increased from seven to nine in 1949, Abbott, then a minister, had urged that one of the new seats be reserved by convention for an English-speaking Quebecker.[15] The idea had been rejected then and had no more success a quarter century later. On both occasions it was certainly proper and understandable that the government should want three of the nine justices to be francophones from Quebec. On the other hand, this convention appears to have the consequence that Quebec anglophones are the only Canadians, outside of the northern territories, with no realistic chance of being appointed. In this connection it may be appropriate to recall that the Supreme Court Act requires "at least three" of the justices to be from Quebec.[16] In other words, the customary number of three is a minimum but not a maximum. Given the large number of anglophone lawyers and legal scholars in Quebec, and the particular significance of the Charter of Rights and Freedoms for official language minorities, it would be reasonable to appoint an anglophone as a fourth justice from Quebec at least occasionally, even if this meant having only five justices from the common-law provinces.

FEDERAL INSTITUTIONS AND COMMUNITY INTERESTS

Quebec nationalists have a tendency to suspect that the federal government systematically acts to reinforce the anglophone minority in Quebec. The reasons, if any, why the federal government would be interested in doing so are not specified, but the suspicion is understandable given the overwhelmingly federalist sentiments of Quebec anglophones and, in the days of the National Policy, the strong ties between Montreal's anglophone business elite and the federal state. Trudeau's not entirely voluntary choice of an anglophone riding when he entered federal politics, his hostility to Quebec nationalism, and his announced intention to restore the influence and legitimacy of the federal level of government, naturally made the suspicion more plausible. In a book published after Trudeau's retirement, Josée Legault alleged that Trudeau, while ostensibly denying the existence of collective rights, had in practice reduced the rights of francophone Quebeckers to the benefit of those of the anglophone minority.[17]

From the perspective of Quebec anglophones themselves, the situation looks rather different. English-speaking members who represent anglophone ridings in the House of Commons, like their counterparts in the National Assembly, have repeatedly been accused by their constituents of not doing or saying enough to protect the minority's interests. Most of these members have felt some sense of obligation to defend those interests, but their power to do so is limited by party discipline, by their small numbers, and by the federal government's reluctance to drive more francophones into the sovereignist camp by pursuing policies that might be viewed as hostile to Quebec. The anglophone representatives have themselves been frustrated by the apparent inability of their constituents to understand these realities. They and the federal government have often been convenient targets for anglophone resentment and frustration, since they appear unable, or perhaps unwilling, to reverse the long decline in the role and status of the English language within Quebec.

A classic instance of the unrealistic expectations of some Quebec anglophones concerns the power of disallowance. Although the federal cabinet can legally disallow any provincial statute within a year of its adoption, this power has not been used against any province since 1943 and not against a Quebec statute since 1911. Its use against Quebec under modern conditions would offend even diehard federalists and would be politically unthinkable. It would probably also be futile since, as John A. Macdonald found out more than a century ago, a determined provincial government can simply re-enact the offending statute every year until the federal government loses interest in contesting it. Nonetheless, there were demands from English-speaking Quebeckers for the disallowance of Bill 22 in 1974, of Bill 101 in 1977, and of Bill 178 in 1988. The first of these measures was introduced by a Quebec Liberal government while a federal election campaign was in progress, and probably hurt the federal Liberals by stirring up latent francophobia throughout the country. Warren Allmand, a minister at the time when Bill 22 was introduced, recalled later that he was angry over the timing of the measure and that "none of the federal members were very happy with Bourassa."[18] Bill 178 probably ensured the collapse of the Meech Lake Accord, whose entrenchment in the constitution was an important priority for the federal government of the day. Prime Minister Mulroney urged Premier Bourassa not to use the notwithstanding clause.[19] In all three cases the federal government clearly disapproved of the legislation but in all three cases it rejected the option of disallowance, preferring to rely on public opinion or on the courts to resolve the problem. This was true even in 1974, when a petition calling for the disallowance of Bill 22 was signed by nearly one-tenth of those living in Quebec at the time. While both Trudeau and Mulroney may have believed in principle that the power of disallowance was an undemocratic anachronism, a calculation of political costs and benefits would undoubtedly have led them to the same conclusion. There are simply too few Quebec anglophones to weigh very heavily in any federal government's calculations, when compared with the perils of antagonizing francophone opinion in the province. The same inexorable arithmetic affects the internal dynamics of the federal political parties and their caucuses in Parliament.

Within the major federal parties, particularly the one that forms the government at any given time, the situation of Quebec anglophones has not always been easy. Typically the governing party has a large and overwhelmingly francophone Quebec caucus within which the handful of anglophones are a weak and rather discordant voice. They are expected to raise large contributions to party funds from their (presumably affluent) ridings but otherwise to be as inconspicuous as possible. Under both Trudeau and Mulroney they discovered that the prime minister, although a Quebecker himself, delegated responsibility for the Quebec caucus and for political affairs within the province to a "Quebec lieutenant" who was not viewed as particularly sympathetic to anglophones. Matters were no better under Chrétien, who had once publicly predicted without visible sorrow that the anglophone minority in Quebec would eventually dwindle to an insignificant number.[20] Warren Allmand was not offered a cabinet portfolio and was later deprived of a committee chairmanship for a breach of party discipline. Sheila Finestone was dropped from the cabinet after a short time in office. Donald Johnston was not invited back. David Berger, who had ruffled some feathers by opposing the Meech Lake Accord and supporting the Equality Party, was sent to Israel, and a francophone candidate was parachuted into Westmount for the first time in the riding's history.

In these circumstances friction seems to be endemic. Two former members interviewed said that their careers suffered because they did not raise as much money for the party in their ridings as the Quebec wing of the party expected. Raymond Rock said he was "blackballed" by the then-Quebec lieutenant, Jean Marchand, for insisting on the right to speak English in caucus, and attributed his defection from the Liberals in large part to this cause.[21] Bryce Mackasey was apparently so unpopular with his francophone colleagues that he had to run in an Ontario riding when he returned to federal politics after his brief stint in the National Assembly.

Members like C.M. Drury, who supported anglophone interests and concerns very discreetly, if at all, seemed to have the most successful careers in federal politics. Those who were less discreet generally did not fare as well. Warren Allmand probably ended any hope of returning to the cabinet by his public dissent over the patriation of the constitution, described in the next section of this chapter. Donald Johnston did not run for re-election in 1988 after disagreeing with party policy regarding the Meech Lake Accord, although he attempted a comeback two years later by seeking the party leadership. Robert Libman alleges in his memoirs that Liberal Party leader John Turner rebuked David Berger for supporting the Equality Party in 1989.[22] Berger was not the only Liberal member of parliament from Quebec who refused to vote for the provincial Liberals in the election that year, but others were more discreet about it. Turner, whose hopes of winning the election in 1988 had probably been doomed by the tacit alliance between Bourassa and Mulroney, was desperately trying to rebuild the relationship between the federal and provincial Liberals and the federal party's support among francophone voters.

None of the foregoing is intended to suggest that the federal level of government has been of no help to the English-speaking community in Quebec, for any such conclusion would be clearly exaggerated. Support for official language minorities, a category that includes the anglophones in Quebec as well as the francophones in each of the other provinces, has been an explicit goal of federal policy under Trudeau from near the beginning of his term in office and under all of his successors. This support has been expressed in a number of ways, including the adoption of two Official Languages Acts, the entrenchment of some minority rights in the Canadian Charter of Rights and Freedoms, funding for second language education and for interest groups representing the official language minorities, assistance with constitutional litigation, and the activities of the commissioner of official languages. In each case Quebec anglophones benefitted, although from their perspective perhaps not enough, from policies whose primary purpose was to demonstrate that the French fact existed throughout Canada and should not be exclusively identified with Quebec, much less with the movement for Quebec sovereignty.

Federal support for official language minorities began in the very early days of the first Trudeau government. It will be recalled from an earlier chapter that Gérard Pelletier, the first minister given the responsibility for this dossier as secretary of state, found little interest on the part of Quebec anglophones, most of whom at the time still felt secure enough not to need much help from the federal government.

The first Official Languages Act, adopted by Parliament in 1969, was mainly concerned with strengthening the francophone communities outside of Quebec and with improving the status of the French language in federal institutions.[23] It declared English and French to be the official languages of Canada, required federal departments and agencies to practice bilingualism, provided for "bilingual districts" (which were never actually established) within which all federal services would have to be available in both languages, and established a commissioner of official languages to oversee and report on the implementation of the act.

The annual reports of the various commissioners over the years provide useful insights into the evolution of official language policy. The first commissioner, Keith Spicer, was a journalist from Ontario who apparently saw his primary role as one of persuading English-speaking Canadians to accept and welcome the French fact in their country. His observations were sometimes thoughtful, sometimes witty, and usually designed to attract attention. Spicer's six annual reports, although detailed and verbose in their coverage of the federal scene, devote little attention to developments at the provincial level and scarcely mention the anglophones of Quebec. Spicer's most noteworthy comment on the latter subject, for which he later apologized, was made at an academic conference in Washington DC in the spring of 1973, when he referred to them as "Westmount Rhodesians."[24] English-speaking Quebeckers had more or less forgiven René Lévesque for describing them so three years earlier, but thought it an odd comment from a federal public servant.

Spicer's successor, Max Yalden, was a former diplomat, a profession for which Spicer would have been ill-suited. He was appointed in 1977, soon after the Lévesque government took office in Quebec, and served for seven years. Yalden's first annual report was the first to devote a section to the situation of the anglophones in Quebec. It excused the absence of such a section in earlier reports on the grounds that "on the whole they have fared well in that province" but noted a perception that this might no longer be the case in future.[25] Nonetheless, it tended to downplay the impact of the Charter of the French Language. In the following year Yalden's report still asserted that "Quebec's anglophones are much better off than their francophone counterparts in other provinces."[26] His third report, covering the year 1979, gently criticized the federal government for neglecting English-speaking Quebeckers.[27] It was not until his fourth report, published after the referendum on sovereignty-association, that he expressed any criticism of the Quebec government, observing that "anglophones in Quebec are now experiencing more difficulties than heretofore in enjoying facilities and receiving services in English." He also noted the under-representation of anglophones in the province's institutions.[28] His fifth annual report was more sharply critical, asserting that "... the language rights they believed themselves to have are being eroded. What began as a legitimate language reform on behalf of French has deteriorated at times into something a good deal less commendable."[29]

Yalden's sixth report noted that Quebec anglophones felt threatened and that, while they might still be better off than other official language minorities, this was no reason for the federal government not to support them. He criticized the low level of federal assistance to Alliance Quebec, noting that the official language minority groups in Ontario and New Brunswick together received about five times as much funding for roughly the same number of people. He also criticized Petro-Canada, then a federal crown corporation, for displaying unilingual French signs at its service stations in Quebec so as to conform to the province's language law.[30] In his final report Yalden was able to report some good news for the anglophone minority in the shape of Bill 57, but noted the continuing exodus and relative decline of Quebec's English-speaking community.[31]

Yalden's successor, d'Iberville Fortier, was another former diplomat and the first francophone to hold the office of commissioner of official languages. He began the practice of including a province-by-province survey of the official language minorities in each report. Although best remembered for the comment in his fourth report about "humbling the competition," to which the National Assembly replied with a unanimous condemnation, Fortier acknowledged the need for some legislative protection of the French language in Quebec. His third report noted that "the French language is threatened even in Quebec and ... needs protecting."[32] Two years later he recognized that "Bill 101 has led to an improved feeling of cultural security that in our view should not be unduly disturbed by changes brought about either by the Supreme Court or even by Quebec's own National Assembly."[33]

The next commissioner, appointed by the Mulroney government in 1991, was none other than Victor Goldbloom. Appointing a prominent and distinguished member of their own community was an important gesture to Quebec anglophones, who had been profoundly shaken by the experience of Bill 178. Commissioner Goldbloom forthrightly condemned Bill 178 in both of his first two annual reports.[34] He also usually reviewed developments in the fields of health and social services, a matter of particular concern to him because of his medical background. In his fifth and sixth reports Goldbloom noted the difficulties of the English educational system in Quebec to which the Chambers task force had drawn attention.[35] Using his contacts in the province to good advantage, Goldbloom met frequently with community groups in Quebec, with Alliance Quebec, and with officials of the provincial government. Although certainly not neglecting francophones in the other provinces, he demonstrated more genuine concern for the anglophones of Quebec than any previous commissioner. Times had clearly changed since the days of Keith Spicer.

One matter to which commissioners' annual reports repeatedly drew attention, beginning with Yalden's report submitted to Parliament in 1983, was the lack of anglophone representation in that portion of the federal public service located in Quebec. This was a matter of particular concern in the Eastern Townships, where there were not many other jobs for anglophones and where federal personnel were particularly conspicuous at the many customs and immigration offices along the international border.[36] Four years after Yalden first raised the issue, d'Iberville Fortier noted that "Anglophone participation rates in the federal Public Service in Quebec have fallen over the years to intolerable levels."[37] In 1976 anglophones had comprised 12.6 per cent of the personnel and in 1987 only 5.5 per cent. The Treasury Board set up a committee with representation from the anglophone community to study the situation. Fortier was able to report a year later that the percentage of anglophones had ceased falling, but it did not improve.[38] Victor Goldbloom noted the lack of improvement in the report which he submitted to Parliament in 1997, fourteen years after Yalden had first drawn attention to the situation.[39]

In addition to the commissioner's office, the parliamentary committees which considered the annual reports helped to draw attention to the situation of official language minorities. A Special Joint Committee on Official Languages was established in 1980, with Hal Herbert as one of the original members. In January 1986, with Herbert no longer in the House of Commons, Warren Allmand was added to the committee and remained on it for as long as it existed. Senator Dalia Wood became co-chair of the committee at the same time. In 1991 the Special Joint Committee ceased to exist and was replaced by a standing committee of the House of Commons, of which Warren Allmand was also a member. After the Liberals returned to office under Chrétien the standing committee was discontinued and the Special Joint Committee was revived. Senator Wood, however, was not included in the new Committee.

Meanwhile, the Mulroney government had introduced Bill C-72, a new Official Languages Act. It was adopted by Parliament in 1988, prior to the September election. The preparation of the new statute had actually begun more than two years earlier, and involved significant input from Alliance Quebec. Like its predecessor, the new act was adopted by a nearly unanimous vote in the House of Commons, with a handful of rustic Tories from English-speaking Canada comprising the only opposition. The 1988 act cited as one of its three purposes to "support the development of English and French linguistic minority communities and generally advance the equality of status and use of the English and French languages within Canadian society."[40] It also provided the secretary of state with authority to "enhance the vitality of the English and French linguistic minority communities in Canada and support and assist their development."[41] Furthermore, the secretary of state could take measures to "encourage and assist provincial governments to support the development of English and French linguistic minority communities generally and, in particular, to offer provincial and municipal services in both English and French and to provide opportunities for members of English or French linguistic minority communities to be educated in their own language."[42]

Soon after this legislation was introduced in Parliament, Quebec's Conseil de la langue française complained that by promoting the English language in Quebec it would violate the Charter of the French Language.[43] The Parti Québécois, then in opposition, took up this refrain, and Jacques Brassard introduced a motion to censure the Bourassa government for not opposing the legislation. Claude Ryan, then the minister responsible for language policy, replied that he was generally satisfied with Bill C-72 and that the government would cooperate in its implementation. He pointed out that "language" was not a single field of jurisdiction but that responsibility for it was divided between the two levels of government.[44]

Federal spending power has been used to support official language minorities, including the anglophones of Quebec, in a number of ways. One of the last major conditional grant programs to be established in Canada, the Official Languages in Education Program, began in 1970 when Gérard Pelletier was secretary of state. It provided federal funds to the provinces to assist the education of official language minorities in their own language. On a more modest scale funding was also provided to teach English as a second language in Quebec and French as a second language in the other provinces. Total expenditure under the program between 1970 and 1983 was almost $1.8 billion.[45] About half of this expenditure went to Quebec, mainly to assist in the cost of educating anglophones in English. The program was extended by bilateral agreements in 1983, 1988, and 1993. In recent years Quebec's share of the funding has declined to about one-third, owing to declining English-language enrollments in Quebec and increasing French-language enrollments in the other provinces.[46]

The secretary of state also offered subsidies, beginning in 1977 when John Roberts held that portfolio, for the support of organizations representing official language minorities. As described in chapter 5, this initiative contributed to the creation of the Council of Quebec Minorities and, indirectly, to that of its successor organization, Alliance Quebec. The secretary of state's grant to Alliance Quebec reached a peak level of $1,591,000 in 1992 but subsequently declined, presumably because of efforts to reduce the federal deficit.[47] For all but the first few years of its existence Alliance Quebec has derived practically all of its revenue from the federal grant, a somewhat unhealthy situation which casts doubt on the willingness of the anglophone community in Quebec to support the organization out of their own resources.[48] A persistent grievance articulated by Alliance Quebec, and occasionally by the commissioner of official languages, is the fact that funding to Alliance Quebec has always been only a fraction of that made available to francophone organizations in the other provinces.[49] This is despite the fact that there are almost as many anglophones in Quebec as there are francophones in the rest of Canada.

Another form of assistance which the federal government provided to official language minorities was financial support for litigation on behalf of their constitutional rights. The Court Challenges Program was established in 1978 to fund the costs incurred by individuals who wished the courts to clarify the extent of their denominational and linguistic rights under Sections 93 and 133 of the Constitution Act 1867. The adoption of the Canadian Charter of Rights and Freedoms in 1982 caused the program's terms of reference to be expanded to include the language rights and minority language educational rights guaranteed by the Charter. Three years later Section 15 of the Charter, guaranteeing equality rights, came into effect and the Court Challenges Program assumed responsibility for funding litigation related to that section also. At the same time the management of the Court Challenges Program was entrusted to the Canadian Council on Social Development so as to ensure its independence from the federal government. Two independent panels were established to study applications for assistance under the program, one dealing with language rights and the other with equality rights. In 1990 management of the program was taken over by the Human Rights Research and Education Centre at the University of Ottawa.

In 1992 the Mulroney government unexpectedly announced the termination of the Court Challenges Program, on the grounds that a sufficient body of case law had already been established and also that the funding of court challenges could be more economically managed by the Department of Justice on an ad hoc basis. There was considerable criticism of this decision and in the election campaign the following year both Prime Minister Kim Campbell and the opposition Liberals pledged to reinstate the program. After consultations between the new government and various interested groups the Court Challenges Program resumed in October 1994. It was placed under the auspices of the Department of Canadian Heritage, the successor to the former Department of the Secretary of State, but with an independent board of directors. Like its predecessor, the revived program had two independent panels, one for language rights and one for equality rights.[50] Language rights litigation receives only 20 per cent of the total budget, or $550,000 per annum, even though the terms of reference of the language rights panel have been expanded to include the Official Languages Act and the new Section 16.1 of the Charter, which entrenches the collective rights of the Acadian community in New Brunswick.[51] Casper Bloom, ex-chairman of the Coalition of English-Speaking Quebeckers, was one of five persons named to the language rights panel in 1994.

A report prepared for the commissioner of official languages after the Mulroney government announced the termination of the Court Challenges Program in 1992 attempted to assess the program's impact on language rights.[52] Without reaching any firm conclusion, the report noted that the program had funded eighteen language-related cases up to 1985 and another seventy-seven between 1985 and 1992. It would appear that only a few of these directly concerned the anglophone minority in Quebec. Quite understandably the smaller and weaker official language minorities in other provinces, particularly those seeking to exercise their minority language education rights under Section 23 of the Charter of Rights and Freedoms in provinces where French-language education had previously been minimal or non-existent, received most of the funds.

The cases in which Quebec anglophones did receive funding for court challenges included the *Blaikie* case, as well as the subsequent rehearing of the same case when the Quebec government requested clarification of whether and how the decision applied to delegated legislation, municipalities and school boards.[53] The program also assisted the challenge to Quebec's language law in *A.G. Quebec v. Association of Quebec Protestant School Boards*.[54] Alex Paterson, who as chairman of Alliance Quebec was involved in the request for funding, later recalled that federal funding was provided rather reluctantly, and that most of the necessary money had to be raised from private donors.[55] The litigation relating to the language of commercial signs was not funded at all because it related to fundamental freedoms rather than to language rights in the narrow sense.

Another case that was funded was *MacDonald v. City of Montreal*, in which an English-speaking resident of Quebec challenged the validity of a speeding summons that was written in French only.[56] Alliance Quebec intervened on behalf of D.C. MacDonald, the recipient of the summons. The attorney-general of Canada, oddly enough, joined the attorney-general of Quebec in intervening against MacDonald and on behalf of the city. The Supreme Court found that Section 133 did not require a summons to be issued in both official languages, but rather that it was intended to give court officials the option of issuing such documents in either language, in the same way that politicians were given the option of speaking either language in the legislature. Only Justice Bertha Wilson, a minority of one, argued that the municipality should be required to issue a summons in the language of the official language minority.

In a later case, *Regina v. Cross*, Justice Greenberg of the Superior Court of Quebec ruled that anglophones who requested and received a trial in English were not entitled to demand that the crown prosecutors conduct all the proceedings in that language or that they be able to do so.[57] The case concerned three aboriginals who were tried in 1991 for their alleged participation in the disturbances at Oka in the previous year. The judge ruled that Section 530.1(e) of the Criminal Code, which appeared to require that the prosecutors speak the same official language as the defendants, did not apply in Quebec by virtue of Section 133 of the Constitution Act 1867. In other words, anglophones on trial in Quebec had fewer rights than francophones on trial in Ontario: Section 133 protected the rights of the francophone prosecutors rather than those of the defendants. Alliance Quebec received funding from the Court Challenges Program to appeal, but at the time of writing the Supreme Court of Canada has not handed down a decision.

On balance it must be concluded that the Court Challenges Program was of limited usefulness to the anglophone minority in Quebec, although some of the cases involving francophones in other provinces may establish precedents that will be useful to them in the long run.

The second Official Languages Act provided the secretary of state (known since 1993 as the minister of Canadian heritage) with an open-ended mandate to encourage bilingualism in areas of provincial jurisdiction, in cooperation with the provincial governments. One of the first results of this mandate was an agreement signed in May 1989 by Secretary of State Gerry Weiner and Quebec's Minister of State for Health and Social Services Louise Robic. It provided that the federal government would contribute half of certain costs involved in providing health and social services in English. Federal funding in the first year of the agreement amounted to $550,000.[58]

Whether the interests of the anglophone community in Quebec were better served by Liberal or by Progressive Conservative federal governments is a question not easily answered. Prime Minister Trudeau articulated a pluralistic and liberal vision of Canada and Quebec that was very congenial to Quebec anglophones. Both Alliance Quebec and the Equality Party largely adopted the Trudeau vision as their own, despite the sometimes different conclusions which they drew from it. The Trudeau government's various policies and programs to support official language minorities, although designed in the first instance to help francophones outside of Quebec, did prove useful to anglophones in Quebec in several ways. So, perhaps, did the Canadian Charter of Rights and Freedoms although, as will be argued below, its benefits should not be overestimated.

Trudeau's official language policies also encouraged a political alliance of convenience between anglophones in Quebec and francophones outside of Quebec. This began in the late 1970s when Positive Action supported the efforts to restore bilingualism in Manitoba, and later made contact with francophone organizations in several provinces. The widespread perception, inside and outside of Quebec, that Quebec anglophones were a privileged group who deserved little sympathy made it politically expedient to identify their cause with that of the francophone minorities. The alliance is not without friction. Quebec anglophones complain of the more generous funding given to other official language minorities by the federal state. Francophones outside of Quebec envy the institutional strength and what they see as the privileges of Quebec anglophones, and some of them are sympathetic to Quebec nationalism. Nonetheless, the alliance continues to exist as a lasting legacy of the Trudeau era.

Mulroney was less successful than Trudeau in articulating a vision, and he never matched Trudeau's popularity among Quebec anglophones. Nonetheless he was one of them, which Trudeau was not, and he was a great improvement, from their point of view, over his two immediate predecessors as leader of the Progressive Conservative Party. Neither Robert Stanfield nor Joe Clark made any real effort to win the votes of English-speaking Quebeckers. Mulroney sought an alliance, as they did, with Quebec nationalists, and he succeeded in forming one where they had failed, but he never forgot where he had come from or who he was. Mulroney had known the experience of belonging to a linguistic minority in a remote town where services for anglophone Catholics were so rudimentary that he had to attend high school in New Brunswick.[59] Bilingualism, in Quebec and elsewhere, was one of the few things in which he strongly believed. At the time of the 1980 referendum he reacted angrily when Louis Laberge of the Quebec Federation of Labour implied that a majority vote among francophones should suffice as a mandate for sovereignty.[60] His dislike of the notwithstanding clause was expressed on more than one occasion.[61] The references to official language minorities in the Official Languages Act of 1988 and the appointments of Gerry Weiner as secretary of state and Victor Goldbloom as commissioner of official languages suggest that his commitment to the preservation of Quebec's anglophone community was as strong as Trudeau's, if not more so.

In the last analysis, however, there was a limit to what any federal government could or would do on behalf of Quebec anglophones. As Trudeau had written before he joined the Liberal Party, the political power of francophone Quebec was based on its ability to break the country.[62] No responsible prime minister could ignore that fact, or the fact that a quarter of the members of the House of Commons were elected by francophone votes. Quebec anglophones could not break the country, even if they had wanted to, and their votes were decisive in only four or five constituencies. Alex Paterson was not far from the truth when he summed up the attitude of the federal Liberals towards Quebec anglophones as follows: "We were a kept group. They knew they had our votes. The only thing we had that they wanted was our money."[63]

QUEBEC ANGLOPHONES AND THE CONSTITUTIONAL DEBATE

Like most other Canadians, most Quebec anglophones gave little thought to the Canadian constitution prior to the election of the first Parti Québécois government in 1976. Insofar as attention was directed towards constitutional matters there was a general tendency to support the federal government in its disputes with Quebec and other provinces over constitutional interpretation, acceptance of occasional constitutional amendments, such as those related to old age pensions and survivors' benefits in 1951 and 1964, and some perplexity at the Quebec government's repeated rejections of the amending formulae proposed by the federal government in 1961, 1965, and 1971. Demands by Quebec nationalists for a completely new constitution, or at least a radical overhaul of the existing one, met with no sympathy whatsoever.

Since the whole subject was not considered highly salient, there was no reason for the English-speaking community of Quebec to formulate a constitutional position. In any event there was no body or institution, apart from the two levels of government which they shared with their French-speaking neighbours, that could have formulated one on their behalf or that had any reason to do so. When the Société St-Jean-Baptiste summoned the Estates General of French Canada to convene for a constitutional debate in 1967, Quebec anglophones were not invited to participate and were not offended by the absence of an invitation. There was no suggestion that they hold an Estates General of their own and the whole event, coming a few months after President de Gaulle's celebrated intrusion into Quebec's affairs, seemed a picturesque and faintly ridiculous aberration.

One English-speaking Quebecker who did have deeply held and clearly formulated convictions on constititutional matters during those years was Frank R. Scott. In later years, when the community began to devote more attention to such matters, his influence would prove to be highly significant. Scott taught constitutional law at McGill University for four decades, from the 1920s to the 1960s, and ended his academic career as the dean of the Faculty of Law. No one who studied law at McGill during that long period can have failed to come into contact with Scott and with his views on the constitution. This is highly significant because most of Quebec's English-speaking lawyers graduated from McGill, and because lawyers, after the decline of the traditional business elite, assumed an increasingly prominent role as the leaders of, and spokespersons for, the anglophone community. Apart from his teaching and writing, Scott's constitutional views were expressed in his court battles against the Duplessis government in the 1950s, his service on the Royal Commission on Bilingualism and Biculturalism in the 1960s, and his comments on public affairs even afterwards. (His opposition to Bill 22 was mentioned in chapter 4 of this book.) In addition to his influence on the anglophone community, Scott was also an intellectual and political mentor, although never actually a teacher in the formal sense, of Trudeau.

About a decade after Scott's death, William Tetley, who was then teaching in the same faculty of which Scott had once been the dean, described Scott as a great man but added that Scott's idea of federalism had been "peculiar."[64] Whatever one may think of the value judgment implicit in that remark, Scott certainly had a different view from that of governments in Quebec City, including the government to which Tetley had earlier belonged. Scott believed in a broad construction of the federal power to make laws "for the Peace, Order, and Good Government of Canada," and a correspondingly narrow construction of the provincial jurisdiction over property and civil rights. He deplored Quebec's traditional preoccupation with provincial autonomy, which he considered detrimental to the real interests of French Canadians as a people, not to mention the interests of Canadians more generally. He favoured the transfer of the amending power from the United Kingdom Parliament to Canada, with a flexible amending formula that would allow the federal government to assume new responsibilities subsequent to the transfer. He also favoured a constitutionally entrenched charter of rights, binding on both levels of government, to prevent the abuses of civil liberties that he had observed under Duplessis.[65]

Scott was too old and ill to take much part in the debate over the patriation of the constitution between 1980 and 1982, but he influenced it profoundly. The constitutional proposals introduced and promoted by Prime Minister Trudeau, although not the last-minute concessions to the premiers of Newfoundland and the western provinces, expressed the Scott vision of Canadian federalism. This was also, for reasons suggested above, the vision of most English-speaking Quebeckers, insofar as they had one, at the time when patriation took place.

The Special Joint Committee on the Constitution of Canada, which Parliament established soon after Trudeau announced his plan to patriate and amend the constitution without provincial consent, provided an opportunity for groups and individuals to express their views on constitutional matters, particularly the proposed Charter of Rights and Freedoms. Among the groups that appeared before the committee were the Council of Quebec Minorities, Positive Action, and the Protestant School Board of Greater Montreal. All expressed general satisfaction with the government's proposals but recommended some improvements.

Speaking for the Council of Quebec Minorities, Eric Maldoff recommended that Section 133, requiring bilingualism in the legislatures and the courts, should be extended to apply to Ontario and New Brunswick.[66] Alex Paterson, on behalf of Positive Action, suggested that the constitution should guarantee official language minorities the right to receive health care and social services in their own language.[67] Both Positive Action and the Protestant School Board criticized Section 23, concerning minority language educational rights, which Joan Dougherty for the Board described as "totally inadequate" and "an expedient compromise."[68] She demanded freedom of choice between English and French education for all children, regardless of background. Storrs McCall of Positive Action argued that all persons of English mother tongue, and not just Canadian citizens, should be allowed to send their children to English schools in Quebec. He also said that the phrase "where numbers warrant" should be deleted.[69] Later, when questioned by Warren Allmand, he admitted that Positive Action really favoured freedom of choice but that they had adopted a compromise position to indicate their sympathy for francophone concerns about the French language.[70]

The Quebec Liberal Party, then led by Claude Ryan, had a somewhat different vision of Canadian federalism than that of the federal Liberals. The provincial party's view was expressed in a document usually known as the Beige Paper, which was published prior to the referendum of 1980.[71] Drawn up by a committee of eleven Liberals, including Claude Ryan ex-officio and John Trent as the sole representative of the English-speaking minority, the Beige Paper expressed a more classic and balanced view of federalism than that of Scott, with significant powers being transferred to the provinces. The party hoped that its blueprint would be acceptable to moderate Quebec nationalists, who might thus be dissuaded from voting for sovereignty-association in the referendum. Nonetheless, the Beige Paper also called for an entrenched charter of rights, it would have retained a federal government with meaningful powers, and it would have guaranteed the anglophones of Quebec control over their own schools and access to health and social services in their own language.

In September 1981, the Supreme Court of Canada indicated that Trudeau's plan to seek the patriation and amendment of the constitution with the support of only two provincial governments was legally permissible but violated constitutional convention. In response the Parti Québécois government called a special session of the National Assembly. They introduced a motion calling on Trudeau to re-open negotiations with the eight provincial governments that opposed his plan and stating that amendments reducing provincial powers without Quebec's consent were not acceptable. Ryan apparently believed that the Quebec Liberals could only retain credibility if they supported the motion.

Like Bill 22 a few years earlier and Bill 178 a few years later, this episode revealed the fragility of the alliance between anglophone and francophone federalists in the Quebec Liberal Party. This is not to say that all anglophones in the party disagreed with Ryan or even that all francophones agreed with him, but the distribution of sentiments in the two communities was clearly different. Most anglophones, reared in the Scott tradition, welcomed the substance of Trudeau's proposals, especially the entrenchment of linguistic, educational and mobility rights, without significant reservations. They had little emotional commitment to the provincial level of government which had recently, as they saw it, been systematically engaged in curtailing the very rights which the Charter would protect. They cared even less for western provincial governments that were using their control over natural resources to undermine Montreal's precarious economy. It seemed ridiculous to most of them that Trudeau should further prolong negotiations with the very people who were obstructing his plans, and thus run the risk that the provinces would demand more powers in return for their acquiescence.

The result, and perhaps the intention, of the Parti Québécois motion was to expose Liberal members who represented largely non-francophone ridings to serious cross-pressures. If they voted with the majority they would offend their constituencies, and perhaps their personal convictions as well. If they represented the views of the people who had elected them less than six months earlier, they would breach party discipline. Ryan and his lieutenant, Gérard D. Lévesque, made strenuous efforts to secure a unanimous vote, but they were not successful.[72] Only two francophones voted against the motion, Lucien Caron of Verdun and Michel Gratton of Gatineau, but the non-francophone Liberals divided evenly. John Ciaccia, William Cusano, Joan Dougherty, Richard French, Clifford Lincoln, Cosmo Maciocia, and John O'Gallagher voted against it. Those who voted for it included Mark Assad, Harry Blank, Herbert Marx, Robert Middlemiss, Maximilien Polak, Reed Scowen, and Christos Sirros.

All of the non-francophone members, whether or not they supported the party line, were uncomfortable about this episode. Ciaccia, who had already broken party ranks over Bill 22, felt particularly cross-pressured since he knew that Cusano and Maciocia would follow his lead if he decided to vote against the motion.[73] Both would be severely criticized by Italian voters if they voted for the motion and Ciaccia did not. In the National Assembly, where he was the only dissident allowed to speak, Ciaccia made a careful statement in French to the effect that he disapproved of unilateral patriation but could not support a motion on the subject introduced by the Parti Québécois.[74] (To demonstrate his middle of the road position, he later refused to attend the ceremony at which the Queen signed the constitution on 15 April 1982.) Dougherty, French and O'Gallagher all thought that they should represent what they knew to be the strong pro-patriation sentiment in their ridings. Dougherty and French later recalled that Ryan was very unhappy about their votes and could not seem to understand the feelings of anglophone voters about the issue.[75]

Herbert Marx, like Ciaccia, represented part of the riding represented by Trudeau in the House of Commons, and his voters supported Trudeau's constitutional initiative almost unanimously. Yet Marx had studied and taught law at the University of Montreal, not McGill, and had spent most of his professional life in a francophone milieu. He disagreed with Trudeau's action and preferred to defy the wishes of his voters. Reed Scowen had been executive director of the Pépin-Robarts Task Force on National Unity whose report was even more decentralizing in tone than the Beige Paper. He also disapproved of Trudeau's actions, as did Christos Sirros. All three, however, were severely criticized by their voters, and were perhaps fortunate that the next election was four years away.[76]

Warren Allmand, whose federal riding corresponded roughly with Scowen's provincial riding, expressed views more typical of NDG residents that same autumn when he defended the right of all anglophones in Quebec to have their children educated in English. On 23 October 1981, Allmand asked Minister of Justice Jean Chrétien about a rumour that the government was planning to weaken Section 23 to make the Charter more compatible with Quebec's language legislation. Chrétien did not directly answer the question but expressed the view that all English-speaking Canadians who moved to Quebec should have access to English schools.[77] Allmand repeated his question on 9 November and received another reassuring reply from Chrétien's parliamentary secretary.[78] A few days afterwards, the government announced that Section 59, which would delay the application of Section 23:1(a) to Quebec until such time as the National Assembly chose to adopt it, had been added to the Charter of Rights and Freedoms. Donald Johnston, the only Quebec anglophone in the cabinet at the time, later said that Section 59 had not been what he wanted, but he deferred to the views of francophone colleagues. Johnston expressed similar sentiments about Section 33, the notwithstanding clause, which was inserted at the behest of certain English-speaking provincial premiers.[79]

On 1 December, the day before the House of Commons would vote to accept the revised constitution, Warren Allmand informed the House that he could not vote for it because of Section 59. He described Section 59 as offensive, discriminatory, and "a betrayal of all that I have ever supported and stood for in this House."[80] He quoted statements by government spokesmen over a fifteen-year period to the effect that minority language education rights should be applied equally across the country. On the following day, Allmand was one of only three members from Quebec to vote against the constitutional motion. He would continue his crusade against Section 59 until he retired from politics in 1997.

The Canadian Charter of Rights and Freedoms, a document which expressed and entrenched the Scott/Trudeau vision of Canada's constitutional order, was welcomed by most English-speaking Quebeckers as at least a step in the right direction. However, its contribution to the welfare of anglophones in Quebec should not be overestimated. Section 23, especially when limited in its application by Section 59, did not undo much of the damage done to English-language education in Quebec by Bill 101. There were few anglophone Canadians moving to Quebec who could benefit from the Canada clause, and the National Assembly will probably never agree to bring Section 23:1(a) into effect. Enrollments in English schools did not increase significantly following the adoption of the Charter and the Supreme Court's decision in *A.G. Quebec v. Association of Protestant School Boards.*

Most other provisions of the Canadian Charter of Rights and Freedoms were subject to the notwithstanding clause, which was unpopular with English-speaking Quebeckers but apparently necessary to secure the assent of the western provinces. The decisive importance of this clause, at least in Quebec where the provincial government had no scruples about invoking it, was to be demonstrated by the controversy over bilingual signs discussed in chapter 6. It is also significant that "language" was not included among the prohibited grounds of discrimination in Section 15 of the Canadian Charter of Rights and Freedoms, even though it is a prohibited grounds of discrimination under Section 10 of Quebec's statutory Charter of Human Rights and Freedoms.[81]

No part of the 1982 Constitution Act, including the Canadian Charter of Rights and Freedoms, gave explicit recognition to the existence of an anglophone minority in Quebec, nor did it impose bilingualism on any province, apart from New Brunswick which requested that its commitment to bilingualism be constitutionally entrenched. Section 27 of the Charter, which directs that it be interpreted in a manner consistent with the preservation and enhancement of the multicultural heritage of Canadians, might conceivably be of some use to anglophones in Quebec, although its potential in this regard has not been realized. Josée Legault, in her critical book on Quebec's anglophone community, has suggested that Quebec's legislation restricting the language of signs might have been challenged more effectively with the aid of Section 27, which is not subject to the notwithstanding clause, than by relying on the guarantee of freedom of expression in Section 2(b).[82]

All in all, the Charter produced very limited benefits for Quebec's anglophone community, especially if the benefit is measured against the disgruntlement of many Quebec francophones over the circumstances in which it was imposed on their province. If it did in fact increase the likelihood of a sovereign Quebec at some time in the future, as many believe, who is to say that Quebec anglophones would not have been better off without it?

In any event, patriation and the Charter did not end Canada's constitutional debates, which resumed five years later with the signing of the Meech Lake Accord. The anglophone community was ambivalent about the accord, and divided in its sentiments. On the one hand, the accord promised an end to constitutional controversy if it would give the Canadian Charter of Rights and Freedoms more legitimacy in Quebec, but on the other hand there was some apprehension that the distinct society clause would weaken minority rights within the province. Alliance Quebec was also divided. Appearing in May 1987 before the National Assembly committee that was studying the accord, Michael Goldbloom expressed cautious support for Meech Lake but criticized the wording of the distinct society clause and the proposed procedures for making appointments to the Supreme Court of Canada and to the Senate. He regretted that Quebec had begun public hearings on the accord before the final text had even been agreed upon by the eleven heads of government. Alliance Quebec also was disappointed that nothing had been done in the accord to strengthen minority language educational rights, even though Minister of Intergovernmental Affairs Gil Rémillard's speech at Mont Gabriel had indicated that Quebec might support the deletion from Section 23 of the qualifying phrase "where numbers warrant" and the clarification of the right of minorities to control their own schools.[83]

Almost simultaneously with the signing of the Meech Lake Accord, Alliance Quebec experienced a change of leadership. Its new president, Royal Orr, supported the final text of Meech Lake while some board members and much of the membership were inclined to oppose it.[84] Alliance Quebec's brief to the Special Joint Committee of Parliament which studied the accord criticized the process by which the accord had been negotiated and the provisions regarding appointments to the Supreme Court and the Senate. It called for an explicit assurance that the distinct society clause would not diminish any rights under the Charter and expressed the wish that the notwithstanding clause be repealed as it was "an embarrassment to all Canadians."[85] In his appearance before the committee Orr suggested that Parliament and the legislatures should be obligated to "promote," rather than "preserve," Canada's linguistic duality.[86] However, he indicated that he approved the accord in principle.

On the following day the Special Joint Committee heard a wholesale attack on the accord by the Freedom of Choice movement, whose spokesman, William A. Sullivan, predicted that acceptance of Meech Lake would mean the beginning of the end of Confederation.[87] Similar sentiments were expressed before a Senate committee in March 1988 by David Savodnick, a spokesman for the Quebec For All movement.[88] Even the Townshippers' Association, one of the most moderate anglophone groups in Quebec, expressed misgivings about the accord, which they had originally supported, on the grounds that it might enhance Quebec's ability to "protect collective objectives at the expense of individual rights."[89] The Quebec Federation of Home and School Associations, representing parents whose children attended Protestant schools, expressed concern that the distinct society clause might undermine denominational education rights. Their president, Helen Koeppe, said that the Meech Lake Accord was unnecessary since Quebec was already subject to the constitution. She also suggested the repeal of Section 59.[90]

In the House of Commons Sheila Finestone initially supported Meech Lake, although she was disappointed that the notwithstanding clause had not been removed from the Charter.[91] By the autumn of 1987 she had had second thoughts, and worried that the accord would undermine the rights of Quebec anglophones.[92] Gerry Weiner, the spokesman for Quebec anglophones in the cabinet, insisted that the distinct society clause would not weaken the Charter and promised that Prime Minister Mulroney would "defend with every ounce of his being the rights of English-speaking Quebecers."[93] Robert Layton assured Quebec anglophones that "I would not be promoting the Meech Lake amendments if I felt that any rights of the community have been taken away."[94] Despite these assurances both David Berger and Sheila Finestone eventually voted against the Meech Lake Accord, as did Donald Johnston, who introduced a whole series of amendments to it. Berger, who specifically objected to reducing the federal role in immigration, lost his position as opposition critic for science and technology because of his position on Meech Lake.[95] Warren Allmand somewhat surprisingly voted in favour, but three of the seven votes against the accord in the House of Commons on 22 June 1988 came from Quebec anglophones.[96] Finestone later recalled in an interview that "I hated Meech Lake ... I haven't changed my mind. It wasn't inclusive of the English-speaking minority, it didn't protect language rights ... it needed to be amended."[97]

The Equality Party, which was not formed until nearly two years after Meech Lake was negotiated, also opposed the accord, mainly on the grounds that the distinct society clause might be used to interfere with minority rights. However, Robert Libman indicated that he did not oppose the five conditions for Quebec's acceptance of the constitution which Rémillard had specified in his Mont Gabriel speech of May 1986. Libman argued that a distinct society clause in the preamble to the constitution would be acceptable, and would meet Rémillard's conditions. The actual distinct society section in the Meech Lake Accord was unacceptable because it was placed in the body of the constitution and phrased as an interpretative clause. Libman supported the efforts by Premier Frank McKenna of New Brunswick to modify the Meech Lake Accord in the spring of 1990.[98]

On the other hand, the Meech Lake Accord had significant support in Quebec's anglophone community. None of the English-speaking Liberals in the National Assembly opposed it. The Friends of Meech Lake, a non-partisan group which lobbied for the ratification of the accord in Manitoba, New Brunswick and Newfoundland, had its origins in Montreal. Among the prominent persons who participated in it were Casper Bloom, William Cosgrove, Richard Holden, Storrs McCall, Alex Paterson, and Charles Taylor. Taylor's nephew, Geoffrey Chambers, subsequently recollected his impression that most English-speaking Quebeckers had really supported Meech Lake.[99]

The failure of Manitoba and Newfoundland to ratify the Meech Lake Accord before the deadline of June 1990 produced a resurgence of nationalism in Quebec, creating great difficulties for Premier Bourassa and the Quebec Liberal Party. The party had staked its future on the accord and its leading members, including the anglophones, were bitterly disillusioned. Bourassa, as is clear in retrospect, remained committed to federalism throughout the crisis that ensued. At the same time he placated, and eventually defeated, the nationalists by a display of calculated ambiguity that even William Lyon Mackenzie King never surpassed.[100] He established a constitutional committee of the Liberal Party, headed by Jean Allaire, to draft new constitutional proposals. At the same time his government caused the National Assembly to establish the Bélanger-Campeau Commission which would consider all possible options, not excluding sovereignty. The latter initiative was supported by both opposition parties.

William Cosgrove represented anglophone Liberals on the Allaire committee, as John Trent had done on the committee that drafted the Beige Paper a decade earlier. Cosgrove's task was far more difficult than Trent's had been, for the mood in the party was highly nationalist and he was frequently a minority of one. He later recalled that "I felt pretty lonely."[101] Most members of the committee believed that a radical report was needed to shock the rest of Canada into entering serious negotiations. Cosgrove was rightly sceptical about the merits of this strategy. The first draft of the report was so radical that he refused to sign it, whereupon a slightly more moderate version was produced. Cosgrove still hesitated, for even the second version left Canada as little more than a common market. Bourassa reportedly feared that his English-speaking ministers would resign in protest against the document.[102] Cosgrove reluctantly agreed to sign it after other anglophone Liberals urged him not to split the party along linguistic lines, but he refused to say anything in its defence.[103]

Cosgrove's misgivings were shared by Claude Ryan, who suffered the indignity of having the microphone deliberately shut off while he was standing in line to speak against the report at the party convention in

March 1991.[104] Both Ryan and Cosgrove left the convention in disgust. Cosgrove returned the following day, at the urging of John Parisella, in time to hear Premier Bourassa deliver a speech that praised the Allaire committee for its work but was decidedly more federalist in tone than the report itself.[105]

Meanwhile the Bélanger-Campeau Commission pursued its deliberations and reported on 27 March 1991, two months after the Allaire committee. The commission was carefully constituted to provide a balance between sovereignists and federalists, and between elected politicians and members of interest groups. Although it was supposed to be broadly representative of Quebec society, its thirty-nine voting members included only four non-francophones: Russell Williams and Cosmo Maciocia representing the Quebec Liberal Party, Richard Holden representing the Equality Party, and Mrs Cheryl Campbell Steer as one of four representatives from the business community. Robert Libman was appointed as a non-voting member.

Predictably such a heterogeneous committee could agree on little of substance, but it did recommend that a referendum on sovereignty be held either in June or October of 1992 and that the National Assembly establish two special committees, one to examine "matters related to Quebec's accession to sovereignty" and one to consider constitutional offers from the federal government, should any be made. Williams, Maciocia and Steer signed the report with addenda clarifying their continuing support for federalism. Holden, after consultation with Libman, refused to sign at all. Instead he appended a statement, actually written by Libman's executive assistant, Tony Kondaks, which expounded the Equality Party's constitutional position, including demands for the repeal of both Section 33 and Section 59 of the Canadian Charter of Rights and Freedoms. Holden later claimed that he had not actually bothered to read the statement.[106]

Bill 150, embodying the recommendations of the Bélanger-Campeau Commission, was adopted by the National Assembly on 20 June 1991, with both opposition parties voting against it. The only Liberal to vote against it was Russell Williams, who had reluctantly signed the Bélanger-Campeau report but could not accept a referendum on sovereignty. Several other Liberals were absent for the vote including four ministers: John Ciaccia, Sam Elkas, Robert Middlemiss and Claude Ryan. Richard Holden and Gordon Atkinson were also absent, although both had made resoundingly federalist speeches a week earlier.[107]

On the day after Bill 150 was approved, Parliament established a Special Joint Committee on a Renewed Canada, beginning yet another round of constitutional consultations. The Mulroney government also produced its own proposals in a document entitled *Shaping Canada's Future Together*, the genesis of what became the Charlottetown Accord. Robert Keaton appeared before the Special Joint Committee on behalf of Alliance Quebec in December 1991. He supported most of the federal proposals but also called for the removal of the notwithstanding clause from the Canadian Charter of Rights and Freedoms.[108] The notwithstanding clause was also attacked by Marjorie Goodfellow, speaking for the Townshippers' Association, and by Max Bernard of the Canadian Jewish Congress, presenting a joint brief on behalf of the Jewish, Greek and Italian communities in Quebec.[109] The Equality Party, which was divided on the question of whether a distinct society clause should be included in the constitution, was represented by Robert Libman, who expressed his ambivalence about the idea.[110] Keith Henderson, the chairman of the party's constitutional committee, presented a brief totally opposed to a distinct society clause. Admitting that his brief had not yet been accepted as party policy, he presented it on behalf of "Canadians for Equality of Rights under the Constitution."[111]

Libman was critical of the Special Joint Committee's proposals when they appeared early in 1992, but he still urged Premier Bourassa to enter constitutional discussions with the other heads of government.[112] Bourassa eventually did so, and negotiated what came to be called the Charlottetown Accord. As was noted in chapter 6, the Charlottetown Accord, and the referendum that followed, virtually destroyed the Equality Party. Most of the party militants, including Keith Henderson and Tony Kondaks, opposed the accord and campaigned against it, but Libman defended it, claiming that the new version of the distinct society clause, which appeared as part of a section listing the characteristics of Canada, would not threaten minority rights. He argued that federalists should vote for the Charlottetown Accord, and that members of his party who campaigned against it were playing into the hands of the Parti Québécois.[113] Both Libman and Gordon Atkinson predicted, correctly, that their ridings would vote heavily in favour.[114] Neil Cameron also supported the Charlottetown package, which he personally disliked, because he knew that his voters in Jacques-Cartier were heavily in favour of it.[115] Richard Holden, by this time a member of the Parti Québécois, adopted that party's position of opposing Charlottetown, even though he had been a strong supporter of Meech Lake.[116]

Although disagreeing on the subject of the Charlottetown Accord, Libman and his party were agreed in their opposition to the provisions of the Referendum Act which required participants in a referendum campaign to join or affiliate with the national committees in support of one or the other option.[117] Libman and the Equality Party jointly brought a motion in the Superior Court for a declaratory judgement declaring portions of the Referendum Act unconstitutional. They lost in the Superior Court and the Equality Party decided not to pursue the matter. Libman appealed the trial judgement, on somewhat narrower grounds than those contained in the original motion, and lost again in the Court of Appeal. He was finally vindicated in 1997, when the Supreme Court of Canada unanimously ruled that certain provisions of the Referendum Act that pertained to "regulated expenses" violated the freedom of expression and freedom of association guaranteed by the Canadian Charter of Rights and Freedoms. The Court noted that its decision would have been the same if it had been based on Quebec's statutory Charter of Human Rights and Freedoms.[118]

Alliance Quebec supported the Charlottetown Accord, and was particularly happy that the so-called Canada clause, listing the characteristics of the country, included as one of its sub-sections a reference to the official language minorities, meaning anglophones in Quebec and francophones elsewhere. The provision allowing Quebec to elect its senators indirectly rather than by direct popular vote was also considered to be desirable, since it would make the choice of an anglophone for at least one of the senatorial seats much more likely.[119]

On 26 October 1992, the voters of Quebec rejected the Charlottetown Accord, with only 42.4 per cent of the vote being cast in favour. This was a slightly lower percentage than in the rest of Canada. However, the results in predominantly anglophone ridings in Quebec were very different. D'Arcy-McGee voted more than 90 per cent in favour, Jacques-Cartier, Robert-Baldwin and Westmount more than 80 per cent, and NDG more than 70 per cent. The results were similar in ridings where anglophones were close to forming a majority: Mount Royal was over 80 per cent in favour, Nelligan and Pontiac more than 70 per cent. All the linguistically mixed ridings in Montreal and southwestern Quebec voted in favour.[120] An academic study of the referendum result concludes that 71 per cent of Quebec anglophones voted "yes" (a lower estimate than that of most other observers) but the same study also discovers a paradox: 57 per cent of Quebec anglophones did not think the Charlottetown Accord was a good thing for their community.[121] Obviously some concern about the impact of the distinct society clause on minority rights continued to exist.

How does one explain the fact that a majority of Quebec anglophones voted for constitutional changes which a majority thought would not benefit their community? It can be explained in terms of the dilemma that shaped Quebec anglophone attitudes towards the constitutional debate over the decade and a half that preceded the

Charlottetown Accord. The two predominant concerns of the community over this period were to protect their linguistic and educational rights as a minority and to reduce the likelihood that Quebec would choose to become a sovereign state. Yet these two goals did not always lead to the same conclusions. Protecting minority rights meant limiting the freedom of action of the Quebec government and the National Assembly, either through a more centralized form of federalism or through an activist judiciary and a strong Canadian Charter of Rights and Freedoms. The dilemma was caused by the fact that most francophones in Quebec preferred the Quebec government and the National Assembly to have more freedom of action, not less. Measures to make minority rights more secure ran the risk of making francophones more discontented, and thus making Quebec sovereignty more likely. Those anglophones who opposed unilateral patriation in 1981, who supported Meech Lake in 1987, and who supported Charlottetown in 1992 were doing so because they feared sovereignty more than they feared curtailment of their minority rights. Those who took the opposite position in each case were more concerned about the threat to rights than about the threat to federalism. Since neither threat could be measured precisely, both sides were acting rationally according to their assessments of the situation. It is hardly surprising that the community was divided and ambivalent more often than not in its views on constitutional issues.

Neither Meech Lake nor Charlottetown was successful in producing a consensus for constitutional change, but the informal and incremental decentralization of authority and influence in the Canadian federation continued under the Liberal government that took office in 1993.[122] By the time of the 1995 referendum the federal government's influence on the economy and civil society, and on the everyday lives of Canadians, was at a much lower level than it had been in 1980. Possibly this made federalism more palatable to francophones in Quebec, but it is at least equally likely that it made the federal level of government seem an irrelevant and unnecessary burden that collected taxes and provided few benefits in return. The very narrow margin of victory for the federalists in the 1995 referendum gives some credence to the latter interpretation.

Whatever the future of Canada and Quebec may hold, it seems certain that the centralized form of federalism envisaged by Macdonald, Cartier, and Galt, the form of federalism in which F.R. Scott believed, is a thing of the past. The conditions, in Quebec, in Canada, and in the world, that might have allowed it to exist have vanished forever. The Chrétien government's strategy for preserving "national unity" appears to involve further decentralization, while

Intergovernmental Affairs Minister Stéphane Dion has advocated "a unilateral devolution of power over language only to the legislature of Quebec."[123]

If the anglophone community in Quebec is to survive, it will have to do so without much help from Ottawa. The final chapter of this book explores the possibilities that are still available to the community, and the prospects for its future.

9 Prospects and Strategies for Survival

Preceding chapters have described the political involvement of English-speaking Quebeckers, their relationship with the provincial and federal governments, and the impact of both those governments on their community over a period of 130 years. The political drama, if it may be called such, has been performed against a background of the community's slow but almost continuous decline: in economic power, in political influence, and in numbers relative to the growing populations of Quebec and Canada. The decline has been brought about by changes in the Canadian, North American, and global economies, by social and ideological changes (sometimes described under the rubric of modernization) in French-speaking Quebec, and by political and constitutional developments. Among these political and constitutional developments Confederation itself, involving the creation of a semi-autonomous and predominantly francophone province of Quebec, was arguably the most detrimental to the long-term welfare of the anglophone community, but its full impact was delayed for a century by the economics of the National Policy and the institutional and ideological power of the Roman Catholic Church. While the anglophone community's territorial base, and its size in relation to Quebec's population, declined in the century that followed Confederation, the community remained remarkably viable until after the Quiet Revolution. Thereafter the rise of a francophone bureaucratic state, as well as the sovereignty movement that was its logical and perhaps inevitable corollary, cast long shadows over the future of a community whose traditional role in the Canadian economy had coincidentally become largely obsolete and superfluous after the Second World War.

The Bourassa government's Official Language Act of 1974, better known as Bill 22, marked the effective end of consociational democracy in Quebec, since a measure of fundamental importance to the anglophone community was adopted despite the community's overwhelming opposition to it. That this was not a temporary aberration was revealed three years later, when the Lévesque government adopted the Charter of the French Language, or Bill 101, without even the pretence of consulting the anglophone community. Furthermore the Lévesque government, admittedly through no fault of its own, lacked even token anglophone representation in the cabinet or the caucus. Consociational democracy was replaced by majoritarian democracy in Quebec.

In the circumstances that have prevailed over the last generation, it is legitimate to raise the question of whether the anglophone community in Quebec has any prospects other than eventual disappearance. As discussed in chapter 2, Robert Sellar raised this question not long after Confederation, and one need not admire the rather paranoid flavour of his writings on the subject to conclude that his pessimism may have been merely ahead of his time. Richard Joy, an expatriate Quebec anglophone, engineer, and amateur demographer, privately published in the centennial year of Confederation a book called *Languages in Conflict.* Joy used census data to suggest that Canada was evolving towards two territorially distinct unilingual societies, French in Quebec and English elsewhere. He predicted that the anglophone exodus from Quebec, which was already significant when he wrote, "may well accelerate as the French language increases in power and prestige" and as more francophones became qualified for jobs traditionally filled by non-francophones in the province.[1] He also predicted the gradual assimilation of francophone minorities outside Quebec. Joy urged governments to inform Canadians that the decline of linguistic minorities was a natural phenomenon. He feared that otherwise the "psychological shock" when the minorities disappeared would be more harmful to national unity than their actual disappearance.[2]

Possibly Jean Chrétien, then Minister of Justice, was following Richard Joy's advice in the spring of 1982 when he publicly predicted that the anglophone minority in Quebec would dwindle to the point of insignificance, in spite of the recently adopted Canadian Charter of Rights and Freedoms.[3] Chrétien's comment provoked an indignant response from Storrs McCall of the Positive Action Committee but made no impression on the rest of Canada.[4] *The Globe and Mail* did not even report the story.

Table 9.1
English Mother Tongue and English Home Language in Quebec, 1971–96

Year	Mother tongue	Home language
1971	789,185	887,875
1976	800,680	No data
1981	706,110	809,145
1986	680,120	791,377
1991	666,923	761,813
1996	621,862	762,455

Source: Calculated from data in Canada, *Census*, 1971–96.
Note: Since 1986, those who give multiple responses have been divided among the categories – thus half of those responding "English and French" are included as English.

Chrétien was speaking in the aftermath of the most precipitous demographic decline in the community's history, which took place between the census of 1976 and that of 1981. The number of persons of English mother tongue in Quebec and the number of Quebec residents who speak English at home have both continued to decline since 1981, as shown in table 9.1. However, the decline has not been rapid enough to suggest that the community is in imminent danger of disappearing. The 1996 census data on home language even suggest a slight reversal of the trend, or at least the end of the decline.

Regardless of the numbers, there is no realistic prospect of the revival of consociational democracy as Quebec anglophones experienced it for more than a century after Confederation. The community is no longer strong enough or influential enough, economically or politically, to claim the status of an equal partner in a bilingual province. More to the point, the arrangements of the past are no longer compatible with the aspirations of the francophone majority. Since the 1970s both major parties in Quebec, and most francophone elites, have asserted that French must be the common public language of Quebec, as English is the common public language of Ontario. In particular, they have asserted that immigrants to Quebec should learn French and accept the public predominance of that language, just as their counterparts in Ontario or the western provinces learn English and take for granted the public predominance of English. Since the 1970s, policies directed towards this objective have achieved some success.

Although it violates tradition, the idea that immigrants should accept French as the common public language of Quebec is not intrinsically unreasonable. Nor, despite the romantic nonsense about anglophone Canada's "multiculturalism," is it substantially different from the universal acceptance of English as a common language west of the Ottawa River. Like other Canadian provinces, Quebec allows, and even assists, its "cultural communities" to retain their own cultural attributes, provided the public predominance of the majority language is accepted. Modern Quebec nationalism has largely abandoned the ethnic and religious exclusivity of old-style French Canadian nationalism, at least officially.

Yet, however benign it may be, the new idea of an assimilating, pluralistic French Quebec is incompatible with a consociational regime, because recognition of an autonomous anglophone segment as a partner in the governance of Quebec is incompatible with the notion of French as the common public language of all Quebeckers. Furthermore, it would convey to immigrants the message that they are free to join either linguistic segment, French or English, and that the government is indifferent to their choice. Given the predominance of English in North America, francophones fear that English might be the more rational choice for most immigrants, just as it was before the Quiet Revolution.

There is, however, relatively little support in today's moderate and liberal-minded Quebec for removing the acquired rights and institutions that Quebec anglophones still enjoy. As a tolerated linguistic minority, anglophones occupy a rather anomalous but reasonably secure position in the symbolic order of post-consociational Quebec. They are too diverse, too deeply rooted, and perhaps too self-sufficient to be recognized as a minority "cultural community" like the Greeks or the Vietnamese, even though anglophone cultural institutions like the Centaur Theatre in fact receive aid from governments of both parties. Their existence is a fact of life which none can deny and which few are seriously inclined to challenge. It is largely up to them to decide what they choose to make of their anomalous position.

OPTIONS AND STRATEGIES
FOR SURVIVAL

Whatever the future may hold for the community in Quebec, its own choices and actions will have a significant and perhaps decisive impact on the outcome. Historically the community has identified itself with larger English-speaking groups of which it considered itself a part: the British Empire, Canada, and North America. The military, political, economic and cultural achievements of these larger entities, to which Quebec anglophones have made contributions at least proportional to their numbers, have provided psychic satisfaction, and will probably continue to do so. The larger entities have also provided demographic reinforcements to the community, economic relationships that contributed to its prosperity and growth, and at times even political support. These benefits, however, cannot be expected to continue. Relatively few anglophones nowadays migrate to Quebec, even from other parts of Canada. Montreal's historic role as a commercial, financial and transportation centre appears to be obsolete in the global and North American economies at the end of the twentieth century. As for political support, there is little evidence to suggest that many people outside of Quebec care deeply about the Quebec anglophone community's future. The United Kingdom, since 1982, can exert no influence over Canada or Quebec, even if it wished to do so. The United States wants political and economic stability on its northern border and the elites of Canada outside Quebec wish to preserve "national unity," or at least an "economic space" with few barriers to the movement of commodities or capital. None of these objectives, however, requires the existence of an anglophone community in Quebec. Francophone Quebec has embraced the North American way of life and its new elites are fully qualified to manage the province and conduct its relationships with the rest of the continent. The existence of an anglophone minority in Quebec might even be viewed in other parts of Canada as an unnecessary irritant and an impediment to harmonious Canada-Quebec relations.

Some Quebec anglophones, particularly those active in Alliance Quebec and its predecessors, have viewed the francophone minorities outside of Quebec as significant allies, in that francophones outside of Quebec and anglophones within Quebec have a common interest in promoting bilingualism. However, they are also competitors for the limited financial support that the federal state provides to official language minorities. Furthermore, while francophones outside of Quebec may form a tactical alliance with Quebec anglophones, they continue to regard the latter as an excessively privileged group, and their emotional sympathies are bound to be on the side of Quebec nationalism.

Whether the anglophone community can expect, or should seek, support from elements of the francophone majority within Quebec is a somewhat more difficult question to answer. In the second edition of their book *The English Fact in Quebec*, Sheila McLeod Arnopoulos and Dominique Clift suggested that "it is almost impossible to find allies among the French majority for the defence of community institutions against bureaucratic encroachment or restrictive language legislation."[5] Since those words were written, almost a decade and a half ago, the stereotype of "Westmount Rhodesians" has faded to some

extent from conscious memory, and the enthusiasm of Quebec francophones for the bureaucratic state has also probably declined. The
francophone business elite, in particular, shares some common interests with Quebec anglophones. On the other hand, there is little
evidence that significant numbers of francophones regard the existence of a quasi-autonomous anglophone community within Quebec
as an asset. Bilingualism in health, education and social services may
have some financial costs, and the existence of the minority compli-
cates Quebec's task of absorbing and integrating the increasingly
diverse immigrants on whom it relies to maintain the existing size of
its population.

Probably the most that the anglophone minority can expect from
Quebec francophones is neutrality. Even that will only be forthcoming
if anglophones, or at least some of them, collaborate with their francophone neighbours to pursue objectives unrelated to the questions
of language and federalism that have dominated Quebec politics for
the past thirty years. Municipal government provides one important
arena for this kind of collaboration, but not the only one. Like other
advanced affluent societies, Quebec has an abundance of interest
groups in which anglophones can participate in cooperation with their
francophone compatriots, at least if they are reasonably fluent in
French. These include business and professional organizations, labour
unions, charities, and groups devoted to a multitude of causes, from
feminism to the environment and from animal welfare to the promotion of culture and the arts. There are also causes that are not exclusively anglophone in nature but that should be of special interest to
Quebec anglophones, such as the protection of civil liberties, the
preservation of historic sites and monuments, and the revival of Montreal's economy. Participation in such groups and campaigns, apart
from its intrinsic merits, helps to persuade francophones that the
anglophone community is a normal, useful, and permanent part of
Quebec society, rather than a mysterious alien force or a collection of
transients.

At the same time, the community must defend its own collective
interests, since no one else has any obvious reason to do so. Preceding
chapters of this book have described the efforts of Quebec anglophones to do this in the difficult circumstances that have existed
since the end of the Quiet Revolution. Support for the Quebec Liberal Party, a protest vote for the Union Nationale, formation of the
Equality Party, the consciousness-raising of Positive Action, the quiet
lobbying of Alliance Quebec, and the more visible forms of protest
associated with Howard Galganov have all been tried in response to
various crises and events. Each tactic has produced some success and

some disappointment. What courses of action can Quebec anglophones pursue in the twenty-first century that will contribute positively to the survival and flourishing of their community? A number of suggestions can be made that are not necessarily mutually exclusive, under the general headings of party politics, pressure group politics, and less overtly political actions that would strengthen the civil society of anglophone Quebec. Before discussing these, two other possible courses of action must be described: out-migration and partition.

It is obviously in the best interests of the community to reject migration out of Quebec. Over the three decades since the issues of language and sovereignty reached a high level of intensity in the late 1960s, at least half a million Quebec anglophones have availed themselves of this option. Some, like the author of this book, left merely in search of employment, but others were motivated, at least in part, by political anxieties. Many of them may have improved their individual well-being by leaving. Whether they did or not, migration in search of new opportunities, or simply new experiences, is a normal human tendency, as well as a right entrenched since 1982 in the constitution of Canada, and it is even possible that some of the outward migration may have benefitted the anglophone community in Quebec by removing those individuals least likely to adapt to a changing Quebec and most likely to pursue extreme and counterproductive courses of action had they remained. Nonetheless, outward migration on the scale that the anglophone community of Quebec has experienced since the late 1960s must on balance be detrimental to the community's hopes of surviving as a viable entity. This is particularly so when, as seems to have been the case, a large proportion of the migrants are young people who have recently completed their formal education and are embarking on the productive part of their lives.

Anglophones cannot be prevented from leaving Quebec, if they are determined to do so, but they can be encouraged to stay. Measures to strengthen the civil society of anglophone Quebec, as discussed below, will have this effect almost by definition. Encouraging anglophones to stay in Quebec strengthens anglophone civil society, which in turn encourages more anglophones to stay in Quebec, and may encourage anglophone Canadians outside of Quebec to considering settling there.

Partition is the second course of action open to anglophones that should be rejected, although it may be superficially attractive to some elements of the community. Since the 1995 referendum, with its unexpectedly close outcome, some Quebec anglophones appear to view the partition of Quebec as their only hope of remaining within the Canadian federal state. Others may view it as the only way of retaining or restoring the status of anglophones in Quebec as an enclave distinct from the rest of the province, even if Quebec does remain a part of Canada. However, sober reflection should convince them that partition is neither realistic nor desirable as a solution to their problems. Any new successor province that would include most Quebec anglophones and allophones, as well as being geographically coherent and contiguous with Ontario, would have to include a large number of francophones, possibly amounting to almost half of its total population, whose primary loyalty would be to Quebec. This would be a recipe for repeating the tragedy of Northern Ireland, which humanity hardly needs to experience a second time.

Furthermore, the partitionists have presented no credible scenario whereby their vision could be brought about without violence on a massive scale. It is hard to imagine the partitionists successfully defending their option by force, particularly when the easier option of out-migration would be available for disgruntled federalists. People will fight when their backs are to the wall, but not when their backs are to an open road that leads to Ontario. The partitionists are also deluding themselves if they are counting on military assistance from either Canada or the United States. If Quebec should ever choose independence, neither Canada nor the United States would have any interest in supporting partition, which would embitter relations with a sovereign Quebec and produce an incurable running sore on the body of North America. Although federal ministers have raised the spectre of partition in an effort to dissuade the Québécois from voting for sovereignty, this should not be interpreted as evidence that they, or their successors, would really support partition if the Québécois chose to disregard their advice.

Short of exodus and partition, however, there are a number of less dramatic choices to be made by Quebec anglophones who are concerned about the survival of their community. How should they vote, in federal and provincial elections? How much effort should be devoted to political lobbying, of the kind associated with Alliance Quebec, and what should be the objectives of such efforts? What measures can Quebec anglophones take, individually and collectively, to strengthen their civil society?

Voting at the federal level is arguably of little importance to the community's future. This is so in part because of the federal government's limited influence on what happens in Quebec, and in part because Quebec anglophones, with an effective representation in Parliament no greater than that enjoyed by Prince Edward Island, have little influence on what happens in Ottawa. Probably the best advice that can be given in this regard is to vote in federal elections for the party that seems most likely to win a majority of seats across Canada. In this way the practice of including a Quebec anglophone in the federal cabinet is likely to be maintained for as long as possible. In addition, anglophones should take steps to ensure that persons who speak English at home (whatever their original mother tongue may have been) are nominated by the major parties to run in as many Quebec ridings as possible, or at least in those ridings where the voters are still predominantly anglophone. This means that they must maintain a certain level of activity within parties that have a serious chance of winning seats at the federal level, and must be present in large numbers at the nominating conventions where candidates are selected. The federal Liberals' increasing tendency to "parachute" candidates who are selected by the party hierarchy should also be resisted, insofar as this is possible.

Nonetheless, the most important voting choices to be made are at the provincial level. Anglophones have given overwhelming support to the Quebec Liberal Party for sixty years, except in the two elections that followed Bills 22 and 178 respectively. There is some truth to the charge that the Quebec Liberals have taken anglophone voters for granted. At the same time anglophones have been generously represented in Liberal cabinets and at least some of their representatives, such as J.A. Mathewson, George Marler, Eric Kierans, Michael Goldbloom, and Herbert Marx, have enjoyed significant influence. Particularly in recent years, anglophone voters have not always appreciated the difficulties which their representatives in the cabinet endure as they try to retain their credibility with both their anglophone voters and their francophone colleagues. Nor have they always appreciated the risks faced by the party itself in catering to its anglophone wing, when it must seek the votes of moderate nationalists in order to win or retain office.

It is interesting that anglophones gave equally strong support to the Quebec Liberal Party when it was the progressive alternative to the reactionary Union Nationale and later when it became the conservative alternative to the progressive Parti Québécois. The common thread of consistency behind this behaviour lies in the fact that the Liberal Party in each case was more individualist and less nationalist than the major alternative. This is perhaps because, as Vincent Lemieux has argued, the Liberals have always been less deeply rooted in the civil society of francophone Quebec than the other major party.[6] In the old days anglophones appeared to be left of centre because they were more distant than their francophone neighbours from the Catholic Church. Today they appear to be right of centre because they are less likely than their francophone neighbours to work in the public sector. As traditional jobs in manufacturing and the resource industries decline, employees and dependents of the public sector are becoming the social base of left-wing parties throughout the western world. Thus Quebec anglophones would probably be found disproportionately in the more conservative party even if the alternative party were not commited to sovereignty for Quebec. The fact that it is so commited, of course, makes anglophone support for the Liberals almost unanimous, except when they are temporarily disgruntled by Liberal language legislation.

It is probably rational for most anglophones to continue supporting the Quebec Liberal Party, and for many to be active within that party. Their influence, and that of the allophones who are an equally important part of the party's clientele, should be used to strengthen the party's anti-nationalist tendencies, although not to the point that it ceases to be a serious contender for office. By remaining active and supportive, anglophones can expect to be rewarded with significant representation in cabinet, and perhaps with other appointments, when the Liberals are in office. Since the Liberals are in office about half the time, this is not a negligible advantage.

Nonetheless, it might be in the community's interest if some anglophones, particularly those who do work in the public sector, supported, and even became active in, the Parti Québécois. This would lessen the Liberal Party's tendency to take anglophones for granted, would reassure francophones that anglophones are truly a part of Quebec and not a fifth column for outside interests, and might give anglophones some influence over the Quebec government when the Parti Québécois is in office. Voting for the Parti Québécois in an election, of course, does not necessarily mean voting for sovereignty in a referendum.

The other obvious alternative for Quebec anglophones is to form a new party. This has been attempted, most successfully in 1989, but the fate of the Equality Party suggests the limitations of this strategy. Unless Quebec adopts proportional representation, which would be desirable for more than one reason but is highly unlikely, a party appealing mainly to non-francophones can expect to win no more than a handful of seats. On the other hand, if such a party did manage to gain significant francophone support, it would split the federalist vote and place the Parti Québécois in office more or less permanently. Because of this dilemma, which most Quebec anglophones probably understand, forming a new party is a tactic that should be resorted to only in extreme circumstances.

Voting and elections are not the only aspects of provincial politics: interest groups are a ubiquitous feature of modern life, and Quebec is no exception to the rule. The case for participation in interest groups that are not specifically devoted to anglophone concerns has already been made. The emphasis here will be on groups, such as Alliance Quebec, that represent the anglophone community itself, or that purport to do so.

There has been much debate among Quebec anglophones about the relative merits of the "quiet diplomacy" traditionally practiced by Alliance Quebec and the more dramatic, visible, and confrontational style of activity associated with Howard Galganov and his Quebec Political Action Committee. The balance of articulate opinion seems to be moving towards the latter option, although the former has influential defenders as well.[7] The academic literature on interest groups leans towards the view that the most successful interest groups are those that work quietly behind the scenes and have a good rapport with the government and bureaucracy.[8] However, the more conspicuous and dramatic type of interest group activity can also be useful in mobilizing the supporters of what it advocates and in bringing their grievances to the attention of non-supporters.[9]

A single organization, such as Alliance Quebec, cannot play both roles simultaneously. Continuous access to policy-makers and policy-implementers, and the influence that results from it, will not normally be granted to groups or individuals with a reputation for public protest and hostility to the government, let alone civil disobedience and other forms of unlawful behaviour. On the other hand, the two forms of activity are not mutually exclusive, provided they are performed by distinct and separate organizations. Indeed the more confrontational groups can help the moderate lobbyists by making the latter look reasonable and responsible by contrast, and by implicitly warning that the government may place public order in jeopardy if it fails to give the moderates at least some of what they demand. Quebec anglophones thus need both Alliance Quebec and the Quebec Political Action Committee, or some equivalents of those two organizations.

Alliance Quebec has endured difficult times, and its future is in some doubt at the time of writing, but its difficulties do not seem to be mainly of its own making. Its foundation, following the collapse of consociational elite accommodation in Quebec, indicated the emergence of a new middle-class professional elite which had replaced the old elite of the Protestant business establishment. The new elite promised that it could win meaningful concessions for the anglophone community without seeking to turn the clock back to the days before the Quiet Revolution. Credibility and legitimacy depended on its ability to build bridges between the anglophone community and francophone political elites of both major parties. While it achieved some success at first, Alliance Quebec suffered a series of disappointments and setbacks after 1988 that made it vulnerable to attack by populist forces within the anglophone community. The populists, some of whom have francophobic tendencies, perceived Alliance Quebec as too moderate and submissive, although its reputation among francophones is if anything the reverse. The issues that Alliance Quebec has emphasized in recent years – access to English education, availability of health care in English, and jobs for young anglophones in the public and private sectors – are important but may appear mundane and are not conducive to dramatic victories in the political arena. Nonetheless, Alliance Quebec had some success in broadening its appeal beyond the British/Irish/Jewish middle class of west end Montreal. It has made serious efforts to include other ethnic groups, as well as the scattered anglophone minorities in Quebec's peripheral regions.

Another problem for Alliance Quebec has been its lack of widespread and enthusiastic support in the anglophone community as measured by the number of persons who participate in its activities or who even bother to enrol as members. While the number of card-carrying members is a closely guarded secret, few observers believe that it is anywhere near its peak level in the early to mid-1980s. This lack of support undermines the credibility of the organization and increases its dependence on federal funds, which in turn undermines its credibility even more.

The source of the problem is what students of interest groups and collective behaviour call the phenomenon of the free rider. Alliance Quebec may benefit anglophones, but the benefits that derive from its lobbying efforts are just as available to those who do not belong to the organization as to those who do so. As a result there is little or no incentive to join Alliance Quebec or to give it support, since the benefits will be available anyway. This is a problem faced by most interest groups, apart from those unions, farm organizations and professional groups that are in a position, with the help of government, to make membership compulsory for all members of their potential constituency.[10]

Another difficulty faced by Alliance Quebec is the perception that it is too closely associated with the Quebec Liberal Party, which perhaps lessens its credibility and effectiveness as a lobby group when the Parti Québécois is in office. As mentioned in previous chapters, a number of Liberal members of the National Assembly are former employees of Alliance Quebec, as was the party's former director-general, John Parisella. Even were this not the case, the perception would be difficult to avoid, given the almost unanimously federalist sympathies of the anglophone community. Between 1994 and 1998 Alliance Quebec tried to overcome this problem by concentrating on issues within Quebec rather than emphasizing "national unity" or the constitution, but the narrow federalist victory in the 1995 referendum undercut this strategy by keeping the latter issues in the limelight. Alliance Quebec's failure to take a militantly federalist position exposed it to criticism by unhappy anglophones but did not seem to win many concessions from the Parti Québécois government.

Alliance Quebec's most serious, and perhaps fatal, crisis began in October 1997 when its effective young president, Michael Hamelin, resigned to accept a federal appointment to the Immigration and Refugee Appeal Board. Constance Middleton-Hope, who had been chairperson since the May convention, was named interim president by the board, while Harold Chorney, an economist at Concordia University, assumed the chair. Middleton-Hope, although seventy years old and not widely known outside the organization, would seek a term of office in her own right at the next annual convention.

These events enabled the militant populist faction, which had run unsuccessful candidates for the presidency on several occasions, to succeed at last in May 1998. They found a credible candidate in William Johnson, a prominent journalist whose column had appeared for many years in *The Gazette,* and the author of two books highly critical of Quebec nationalism. His campaign appealed to partitionist sentiment, as well as to those who wanted freedom of choice in the language of education and recognition of English as an official language in Quebec. Johnson gained support on Montreal Island, where he was well-known and where anglophones continued to resent the Charter of the French Language, while Middleton-Hope drew support mainly from the rural areas where her more moderate approach found favour. The contest thus exposed geographical as well as ideological cleavages within Alliance Quebec. Shortly before the convention the Townshippers' Association, perhaps anticipating a Johnson presidency, announced that it was terminating its affiliation with Alliance Quebec.

The contest ended on the last weekend of May 1998, with almost twice as many delegates voting as had done so when Hamelin defeated a radical opponent a year earlier. Johnson's victory by the very narrow margin of eight votes revealed an organization that was deeply divided. Most of the board and executive members who were elected with him had supported his opponent. His strident speech of acceptance, which suggested little inclination to bind up the organization's wounds, did further damage: the Quebec Farmers' Association immediately announced plans to end its affiliation. An editorial in *The Gazette* warned Johnson to "make everyone in Alliance Quebec feel at home" so as to prevent the organization from disintegrating.[11] Premier Bouchard stated that he could not negotiate with an "extremist" like Johnson, and suggested that the federal government should reconsider its financial support for Alliance Quebec.[12] As this book went to press, the survival of the organization was very much in doubt.

Although Alliance Quebec's performance has disappointed many anglophones, its disappearance would be a serious setback for the anglophone community in Quebec. Alliance Quebec's quiet diplomacy has served a useful purpose, supplementing the efforts of anglophone representatives in the political parties. Although there may also be a place at times for more confrontational tactics, they are best left to groups outside the framework of Alliance Quebec, which is only useful if it can conduct a dialogue with Quebec governments of both major parties.

In the last analysis, however, neither party politics nor pressure group activity nor militant activism is likely to result in large numbers of significant victories for the anglophone community. As this book has emphasized, Quebec is now a majoritarian democracy rather than a consociational democracy. In a majoritarian democracy a relatively small minority cannot expect to win many victories through the political process, particularly when it is still perceived in some circles as enjoying undeserved privileges. Thus Quebec anglophones cannot rely entirely on politics, any more than they did in earlier times when political conditions were in some ways more favourable to them than is now the case. Measures to strengthen the civil society of anglophone Quebec must form part of any realistic strategy to ensure the community's future. This is not so much a new insight as a return to the wisdom of the past. Quebec anglophones commonly point out that their schools, universities, hospitals and other institutions were built through the community's own efforts rather than being given to them by the state. This is correct, and the economic resources that made those achievements possible were also accumulated through individual efforts, although the state, through its tariffs and its investments in transportation, admittedly contributed to the outcome.

What exactly is the civil society of anglophone Quebec? Two contrasting views may be discerned in the persons of Reed Scowen and Gary Caldwell, both of whom know something about the rural roots of the anglophone community as well as its present stronghold in Montreal.[13] (By coincidence Caldwell, although originally from

Ontario, has settled about twenty miles south of East Angus, the Eastern Townships community where Scowen grew up.)

Scowen defines anglophone Quebec to include anyone who speaks English, or at least anyone who uses English as his or her main language of communication. He argues that the traditional British and largely Protestant core of the community is no longer large enough or vigorous enough to survive on its own. If anglophone Quebec is defined in terms of a distinctive "culture" or "way of life," its cause is already hopeless. However, Scowen argues, the anglophone community's only distinguishing characteristic is also its greatest asset: the English language. That language is easier to learn than most, and more useful than any other because of its widespread use throughout the world. If anyone who learns it and wishes to use it in Quebec is welcomed into the community, there is no limit to the community's potential growth. However, it will be a diverse community with little common history or shared culture and mythology.

Caldwell, who has adopted the rural anglo-Quebec culture and way of life that Scowen seems to have rejected, takes a different approach. He agrees with Scowen that the British-Protestant core of the community has declined. However, he views anglophones not as a diverse collection of people who happen to share a language, but as an important cultural fragment in the Quebec mosaic. Caldwell laments the decline of the way of life which he associates with the historic roots of the community, including what he sees as a Tory collectivist political culture very different from the individualistic liberalism of the United States. Only by returning to that way of life, he suggests, can anglophone Quebec either live in harmony with francophone Quebec, which is also collectivist, or survive as an entity in any meaningful sense.

The difference of opinion between Scowen and Caldwell parallels the debate within the camp of Quebec nationalism, between those who want an inclusive Quebec that will integrate people of different backgrounds and those who see Quebec's essence in the "*pure laine*" French and Catholic culture of the original settlers and their descendants. The debate is a serious one whose participants, on both sides, deserve a respectful hearing. While the outcome of the debate is not a foregone conclusion, supporters of the inclusive vision appear to be gradually gaining the upper hand, for better or for worse. It also seems that Scowen's vision will, even more certainly, triumph over Caldwell's vision, if it has not already done so.

Caldwell's approach has a certain romantic appeal but one must conclude, with or without regret, that its time has already passed.

Caldwell himself concedes that it survives mainly in the rural areas of southern Quebec and that metropolitan Montreal, where most Quebec anglophones actually live, has already succumbed to what he views as American liberalism. The dwindling minority for whom the older vision retains any meaning might hope to survive for a generation or two more as a historical curiosity, like the few people who still speak Gaelic in Nova Scotia, but not as a significant part of twenty-first-century Quebec. Nor would the survival of British-Protestant culture in its rural strongholds be of any help to the vast majority of anglophone Quebeckers, who come from a variety of origins and are united mainly by their common desire to live in English.

To grow, or even to hold its own as a percentage of Quebec's population, the anglophone community must continue to absorb people from a variety of cultural, ethnic, and religious backgrounds. Traditionally the principal means by which it did so was by accepting the children of immigrants into English-language schools, whether Protestant or Catholic. The francophone majority for a long time encouraged this, since they wanted only "*pure laine*" children in their own schools, but belatedly they realized their mistake. The law now prohibits anglophones from accepting the children of immigrants into their schools, and the transition from denominational to linguistic school boards will not alter this fact, even though it will make the English-language school system more viable in other ways. Anglophones must find some means other than primary or secondary education to absorb persons of other languages and origins into their community.

This will not be an easy task, but it should not be abandoned as hopeless. Some institutional resources still remain: the three anglophone universities, the CEGEPs, the English-language media, the hospitals, the numerous municipalities and neighbourhoods where English is still the predominant language, and the large part of the economy that remains under anglophone control. Such institutions, some of which enjoy a national or international reputation, can serve as magnets attracting potential recruits to the anglophone community. English-language schools and the new linguistic school boards are also a significant community resource, even if access to them is limited. All of the institutions above are a source of employment for educated anglophones who would otherwise have to leave the province in search of work, and their continuing existence demonstrates that it is still possible to live a full life in Quebec while using English as one's primary language of communication.

Persons who have migrated to Quebec, and those in Canada and elsewhere who might be tempted to do so, should be encouraged to see integration into the anglophone community as an option. This is particularly important since Quebec anglophones share with their francophone neighbours the problem of a fertility rate that is too low even to maintain the existing size of the population. Alliance Quebec and its regional affiliates can play a role in this regard, as can other organizations that serve specific groups within the anglophone community, like the Quebec section of the Canadian Jewish Congress. Immigrants can be encouraged to learn English, to settle in anglophone neighbourhoods, to work in English where the law allows, to make use of the English-language media, and so forth. Quebec anglophones must accept that Quebec's primary and predominant language is French, but they should never feel apologetic about their own language or be reluctant to use it. There is a place in Quebec for both languages and no one should feel threatened by their coexistence, provided that the relative size of the two linguistic groups does not change dramatically in a short period of time.

Francophones in Quebec like to remind anglophones in Quebec that the anglophones really are a minority and should come to terms with that fact. The point is well-taken and there is no doubt that anglophones before the 1960s complacently or arrogantly assumed that they were part of a Canadian majority and could virtually forget that they lived in a French-speaking province. Those days will never return, but being a minority does not mean acquiescing in one's own disappearance. The Acadians in New Brunswick, the francophones in Ontario, the Spanish-speaking people in the southwestern United States, and the aboriginal peoples in many parts of the world, including Quebec, have demonstrated in recent years that a determined minority can make itself heard. Quebec anglophones can learn from those examples.

Ironically, they can also learn from the example of francophone Quebec, another historic entity which has shown the ability to overcome setbacks and to survive in the face of adversity. In an essay which he wrote in 1987, when Quebec nationalism seemed at the nadir of its fortunes, sociologist Hubert Guindon reflected on the failure to achieve Quebec's independence by political means and explored what he called "the other options of the national movement in Quebec."[4] He concluded that, even in defeat, Quebec nationalists could still promote their cause in three ways. The first was to maximize their occupation of Quebec's territory by invading the enclaves where anglophones still predominated. The second was to strengthen francophone-controlled sectors of the Quebec economy, particularly by investing their individual and collective savings within the province. The third was to promote the French language by insisting on using it as much as possible and by finding and reporting situations that made it difficult to do so.

In many ways this advice can be adapted, in reverse as it were, to the purpose of preserving the anglophone community in Quebec. In fact Reed Scowen's book, *A Different Vision,* which should be considered essential reading for every English-speaking Quebecker, unconsciously seems to parallel some of Guindon's advice to French-speaking Quebeckers. Scowen urges the anglophone community to promote its own language, to make use of its economic resources, and to "begin to think in terms of its territorial base within Quebec."[15] Guindon would agree with Scowen's description of the language debate in Quebec as "*a peaceful struggle for space and power.*"[16]

Scowen is not the only Quebec anglophone who understands the situation of his community in these terms. Gary Caldwell sees a possibility that anglophones can reoccupy some of their traditional strongholds in the Eastern Townships as the francophone exodus continues. He notes that anglophone farmers in recent years have on balance been more successful than their francophone counterparts and that they retain more of the traditional values associated with rural life, an ironic reversal of the old stereotypes.[17] Galganov's rally at the Fairview Shopping Centre in 1996, which resulted in the restoration of bilingual signs, also resembles the kind of action contemplated by Guindon as a means of promoting the French language.

DEMOGRAPHIC TRENDS AND THE ANGLOPHONE FUTURE

Most of those interviewed in the course of writing this book were asked, usually at the end of the interview, what future they foresaw for the anglophone community in Quebec. Nothing approaching a consensus was apparent from their answers to this question. Some were optimistic, others were pessimistic, and still others carefully hedged their bets. Optimists tended to base their views on the ability of younger anglophones to adapt to and accept a society in which French is the predominant language, the demographic strength and economic value of the English language in North America as a whole, the continuing reputation of McGill University, the apparent decline of extreme nationalism and xenophobia in Quebec, and the usefulness of a bilingual minority to a Quebec that wishes to participate fully in the continental economy. Pessimists tended to emphasize the absence of jobs in Quebec for young anglophones, the resulting exodus of the young anglophone middle class, declining enrollments in English-language schools, the pressure on immigrants to adopt French rather than English as their new language, and the perception that English-speaking Canadians are no longer moving to Quebec in significant numbers. Views on the likelihood or otherwise that Quebec will continue to be a province within the Canadian federation also influence predictions about the future of the anglophone minority.

Given the many variables and the uncertainties involved, it would be hazardous to venture forth with a categorical prediction regarding the future of the anglophone minority in Quebec. The most that can be done is to suggest a range of possibilities which in turn must depend on unverifiable assumptions about political, economic and social developments that might occur over the next several decades. Forecasting the political and economic circumstances of a generation hence would be hazardous enough, given the many sudden changes that have taken place in Quebec within living memory. Reliable predictions about migration in and out, intermarriage and assimilation, morbidity and fertility, language retention and language use, would require specialized expertise in a number of academic disciplines. Detailed and scientific forecasts, in the last analysis, must be left to the sociologists and the demographers, with the caveat that even they have not always been accurate in their predictions. The wiser among them are content to describe the present circumstances without venturing very far into the future: projecting present trends into the future has often led to dubious conclusions. An additional hazard, when a subject as politically contentious as language in Quebec is under consideration, is that the apparently scientific forecasts of scholars may be shaped, consciously or unconsciously, by their political commitments. The many forecasts by francophone scholars that Montreal would, or might, cease to be a predominantly francophone city, forecasts that are usually called upon to justify some restrictive or punitive sanction against the use of English, may be cited as evidence.

Furthermore, as discussed above, there is not even a consensus as to how the anglophone community in Quebec should be defined. If it means everyone in Quebec who can speak English, there can be no doubt that it will continue to exist, and little doubt that its numbers will increase, albeit slowly, for as long as Quebec remains geographically attached to North America. If it means those who speak English at home, the numbers will be smaller, and will be affected by intermarriage, migration, and fertility, as well as the success or otherwise of the Quebec government's efforts to encourage immigrants to adopt French. If it means those whose mother tongue is English the same variables enter into the outcome but the numbers will be smaller, excluding those who for whatever reason adopted English later in life. If the "anglophone community" is restricted to those who already spoke English in Quebec in 1977, and to their descendants, the numbers will obviously be smaller still, although how much smaller depends on variables such as out-migration. This last definition of the community may correspond to the wishes of some Quebec nationalists, who would like every Quebec resident not meeting these restrictive criteria to live in French, but it is not necessarily realistic.

However the community is defined, its future size, and other future characteristics, will also depend on a number of variables. While no effort will be made in this concluding chapter to duplicate the socio-logical and demographic studies that already exist, it may be useful to identify these variables and to refer to some of the uncertainties that surround them. This may assist readers in making their own predic-tions, or in assessing the credibility of those that have already been made. Also, since some of the variables may be influenced by actions of the anglophone community itself, this discussion may serve as background for the second part of this chapter, in which options and alternative strategies for the anglophone community are considered.

The future size of a linguistic community, or of any other aggregate of persons, is essentially the function of three variables: natural increase, migration, and the gains or losses which the community experiences through individuals either adhering to it or becoming detached from it. Migration may be understood to mean movement across a specific geographical boundary (in this case, the boundary of Quebec) while the third variable refers to changes in the affiliation of individuals which do not involve movement either into or out of Quebec.

All available evidence suggests that the rate of natural increase (or excess of births over deaths) is very low in Quebec and may soon become negative owing to a fertility rate that is not sufficient to maintain the existing size of the population over the long term.[18] Whatever its causes, this appears to be a problem shared by the anglophone and francophone communities in Quebec, both of which must rely on external reinforcement to maintain their numbers, and to maintain the population of Quebec as a whole. In the absence of any inward or outward migration, Quebec would decline in relation to the rest of Canada, and eventually in absolute terms, but the relative size of the two principal language communities in Quebec would remain fairly stable.

Migration of course cannot be ignored, and significantly compli-cates the picture. It contains two distinct elements: exchanges of population with the rest of Canada, and exchanges of population with the rest of the world. It is useful to consider these separately, as is usually done. At least until such time as Quebec becomes fully sovereign, if it ever does, the terms "immigration" and "emigration" are used only for population movements in the second category. Whether it involves the crossing of an international boundary or not, a decision to migrate is influenced both by the attractiveness of the destination and the disadvantages of remaining in the place of origin. In other words migrants must be either pushed or pulled, or both, in order to uproot themselves. Economic considerations normally determine a decision to migrate but other factors, including politics, may be influential in certain cases.

The outflow of Quebec's English-speaking population to Ontario and the West has been a constant factor in the social history of Quebec since Confederation. (Some francophones left also, as the present ethnic composition of northern and eastern Ontario attests, but they have been much more reluctant to do so, given the near impossibility of living and working in their own language in most other parts of Canada.) Historically the outflow of anglophones from Quebec was counterbalanced to some extent by the inflow of other anglophones, mainly from eastern Ontario and the Maritimes, who were attracted by the opportunities for employment in the anglophone-controlled business enterprises of Montreal. Large corporations with headquarters in Montreal also transferred their most promising managerial personnel from all over Canada to their head offices, where English of course was the language of work. In spite of this, however, the anglophone community of Quebec had a negative balance, over the years, in its exchanges of population with the rest of Canada.

As discussed in earlier chapters, restrictive language legislation and the growth of the sovereignty movement have accelerated the outward movement of anglophones from Quebec in recent years, to some extent. While it is unlikely that any more restrictive language legislation will be forthcoming, the prospects of the sovereignty movement are still uncertain. If Quebec were to become a sovereign state a large number of anglophones would undoubtedly leave, either because they would not wish to stay in the new nation-state or because the transfer of their jobs to locations in Canada would leave them with little choice. On the other hand some would remain, particularly retired persons, farmers, lawyers, anglophones with francophone spouses, and those who have fully integrated into francophone society. If the transition to sovereignty were peaceful and the two successor states parted on fairly amicable terms, the number who remained would be significantly larger than would be true otherwise, and might well comprise a majority of the anglophones living in Quebec immediately prior to independence. By way of analogy, a study of the Protestants who remained in southern Ireland after independence concludes that their population declined quite slowly between 1926 and 1971.[19] By the latter date there were even some signs of demographic revival. Despite a high rate of intermarriage with Catholics, the Protestants who remained were not assimilated into the Catholic majority.

Even in the absence of political concerns the outflow of anglophones from Quebec would probably still have accelerated in recent years for economic reasons. Since Montreal is no longer the commercial and financial centre of Canada there are simply more and better economic opportunities in Toronto, Calgary and Vancouver for persons fluent in English. It is difficult to see any reversal of this trend in the near future, given the stagnant state of Montreal's economy. Even if the city did experience a dramatic revival of its fortunes, anglophones would have to compete with francophones for any new jobs that were created. This was not the case in former times, when anglophones were better educated on average and when most white-collar jobs required fluency in English but not in French.

A common complaint of Quebec anglophones, including many of those interviewed in the course of writing this book, is that young anglophones are forced to leave the province after completing their education because they are discriminated against in the job market, and especially in the public sector, even if they are totally fluent in French. If discrimination exists in the public sector the law is being violated, since Quebec's Charter of Human Rights and Freedoms, unlike its better-known federal counterpart, explicitly prohibits discrimination on the basis of language. As far as the private sector is concerned, only anecdotal evidence is available to support the accusations of discrimination. In the public service, as opposed to the broader public sector, the number of anglophone employees is certainly remarkably low, but even here one should not jump to conclusions. Historically anglophones had little interest in the public service of Quebec, they are still often reluctant to live anywhere in the province outside of Montreal, and they are not always as fluent in French as they believe themselves to be. Thus there may be quite innocent explanations for their under-representation. Nonetheless, the perception of discrimination, whether justified or not, is probably a factor pushing young anglophones out of the province, and this does not seem likely to change in the near future.

A more recent, and perhaps more significant, phenomenon than the outflow of anglophones from Quebec is the decline in the number of Canadians from other provinces who settle there. Apprehensions about the possibility of a sovereign Quebec undoubtedly contribute to this phenomenon. In addition, Canadians in other provinces may perceive, rightly or wrongly, that life in Quebec will be inconvenient for non-francophone migrants, at least if they are not fluent in French. Non-francophone Canadians may thus be reluctant to move to Quebec for essentially the same reasons that have traditionally inhibited francophones from moving outside of Quebec. In addition to these concerns, there is the simple fact of Montreal's economic decline, which means that the traditional supply of jobs in head offices and other anglophone enterprises no longer exists. Surplus labour from the small towns and the smaller provinces of Canada, which might have gone to Montreal in the conditions of earlier times, now goes to Toronto or even to Calgary. This situation is also unlikely to change in the foreseeable future, whether Quebec becomes sovereign or not.

International population movements have also influenced the development of the anglophone community in Quebec, but the extent to which they will continue to do so is problematical. Emigration to the United States was significant at one time but is unlikely to be so in future, given the extreme difficulty of being admitted to that country on a permanent basis. It is even less likely that any foreign country, apart from the United States, would ever attract significant numbers of Quebec anglophones, or of Canadians generally.

Immigration into Quebec, from a variety of sources, traditionally reinforced the Quebec anglophone community, with unrestricted access to English schools facilitating the anglicization of the second generation even if they did not speak English on arrival. As has been described, Quebec francophones began to resent this fact after the Quiet Revolution, and took steps to end it with Bills 22 and 101. The children of immigrants must now, by law, be educated in French up to the end of high school. This does not guarantee that they will continue in French beyond high school. As late as 1994 allophone post-secondary students in Quebec were still more likely to be in an anglophone college or university than in a francophone institution.[20] Although the percentage of allophones in Quebec who could speak French increased from 47 in 1971 to 69 in 1991, the percentage who could speak English changed hardly at all. It was 69 in 1971 and 68 twenty years later.[21] The obligation to learn French in Quebec thus appears to be supplementing, rather than replacing, the tendency to learn the principal language of North America. Some at least of those immigrants who learn English will eventually adopt it as the language of work and leisure and the language which they pass on to their children. Furthermore, Quebec will continue to attract a few immigrants whose mother tongue is English. In the years 1992 through 1994 an estimated 5685 such persons immigrated to Quebec, where they comprised 4.7 per cent of all immigrants.[22] These persons, and probably their children, will retain their language, even though the children will be forced into French schools. It cannot therefore be assumed that the anglophone community will receive no reinforcements from immigration. It might continue to receive some reinforcements even in a sovereign Quebec. On the other hand, the community's ability to absorb immigrants through the school system has been significantly reduced by the deliberate policy of the Quebec state, a policy endorsed by both major political parties. When the impact of this policy is added to that of the drastic reduction in reinforcements from other parts of Canada, it is hard to foresee much growth for the anglophone community in Quebec, whether or not Quebec becomes a sovereign state.

Nonetheless, the Quebec government's interdepartmental task force on the situation of the French language predicted in its 1996 report that the percentage of Quebec residents speaking English at home would remain stable at about 11 per cent up to and including the year 2041, the latest year for which they provide a forecast.[23] This is a more optimistic forecast (from an anglophone point of view) than that which most Quebec anglophones would probably provide if asked to give an estimate. It also contrasts with Jean Chrétien's prediction that the anglophone minority would dwindle to insignificance. Who will be proved right depends, as suggested above, on many variables, including the future constitutional status of Quebec, the condition of Montreal's economy, the volume of immigration to Quebec, and the languages adopted by immigrants and their children.

LINGUISTIC SKILLS AND THE DECLINE OF SEGREGATION

Apart from the numerical size of the anglophone community, and its size in relation to the rest of Quebec, many uncertainties about its future remain. The ability of its members to communicate in French, its geographical distribution between regions, and its ethnic and religious composition are some of the variables that come to mind. As table 9.2 suggests, the extent of bilingualism among Quebec anglophones has increased significantly in recent years, and now far exceeds the extent of bilingualism among Quebec francophones. However, anglophones in Quebec are still less likely to be bilingual than francophones in other parts of Canada, or than the residents of some small European countries.[24] Particularly in Montreal and its western suburbs, where it is still possible to live mainly in English, many Quebec anglophones lack the confidence to speak French easily and have little contact with the French media or with cultural activities in the French language. One prominent anglophone interviewed for this study even

Table 9.2
Ability to Speak Both Official Languages, by Mother Tongue, in Quebec
and the Rest of Canada, 1971, 1991, and 1996

	1971	1991	1996
Quebec, anglophones	36.7	58.4	61.7
Quebec, allophones	33.1	46.5	46.7
Quebec, francophones	25.7	31.3	33.7
Rest of Canada, anglophones	3.4	6.3	6.9
Rest of Canada, allophones	3.9	5.3	5.3
Rest of Canada, francophones	77.8	81.2	83.8

Source: Calculated from data in Canada, Census, 1971, 1991, 1996.

suggested, off the record, that the retention of English-language schools is not in the best interests of the anglophone community. As an instructor in a post-secondary institution he observed that "anglophones going through our English schools here are not fully equipped to live full lives in Quebec." This fact, he concluded, contributes to the out-migration that is sapping the strength of the anglophone community.

Nonetheless, there is no doubt that the bilingualism of Quebec anglophones has improved dramatically since the Quiet Revolution, and continues to do so. In areas like the Eastern Townships, where the predominance of French is overwhelming, it probably approaches the level of bilingualism found among francophones in other provinces. As those anglophones who were educated before the Quiet Revolution become less numerous, bilingualism in the anglophone community should grow to the point where it becomes nearly universal, as it is among francophone minorities in other provinces. This will be a significant asset to the community, and to the well-being of individual anglophones in Quebec, since participation in Quebec's economy, as well as its political, social, and cultural life, more and more requires fluency in French.

Both increasing bilingualism and the rejection by francophone elites of the old consociational model of a segregated society raise the complex question of to what extent, and in what ways, will anglophones be assimilated into a predominantly French Quebec society. Francophones and other ethnic minorities in the rest of Canada and ethnic minorities in the United States are largely assimilated, and the process as it affects immigrants is not much different on either side of the border, despite the contrasting metaphors of "mosaic" and "melting pot."[25] Many francophones in Quebec have argued since the Quiet Revolution that it would be "normal" for Quebec to assimilate its minorities to the same extent as other parts of North America assimilate theirs. Assimilation is a matter of degree and usually does not imply disappearance. There are still Irish-Americans and Italian-Americans. Could Quebec anglophones become assimilated for most purposes, while retaining their language, and would this make a more peaceful and harmonious Quebec?

Assimilation is a complex phenomenon that has cultural, structural, biological and psychological aspects. Cultural assimilation means the adoption of cultural traits like those of the majority. Structural assimilation means increasing social interaction, both through primary associations like neighbourhoods and friendship and through secondary, or more formal, institutions like businesses, unions, or political parties. Biological assimilation is what takes place through intermarriage, while psychological assimilation is the process of coming to identify with the larger society: in this case, Quebec.[26]

Cultural assimilation of Quebec anglophones to the Quebec norm probably began long ago.[27] It seems to have accelerated in recent years, and it is likely that Quebec anglophones will become increasingly similar to Quebec francophones and thus increasingly distinct and socially distant from anglophones in the rest of Canada. Like other Quebeckers, Quebec anglophones live in an environment shaped by the bureaucratic state that has grown up since the Quiet Revolution, and in a political culture influenced by the issues and controversies that have attended that growth. Their experience has simply been different from that of other Canadians, just as the experience of Quebec francophones since 1960 has differed from that of francophones in other provinces. The transition from "French Canadians" to "Québécois" may be paralleled by a transition from English Canadians who happen to live in Quebec to "Anglo-Quebeckers."

Although Quebec anglophones have always lived in rather unique circumstances, their differences from other anglophone Canadians have traditionally been lessened by the movement of Canadians from other provinces into Montreal. If, as predicted, few Canadians move to Quebec over the next few decades, the anglophone community in Quebec will be much less influenced than before by trends and fashions and attitudes in the rest of Canada. At the same time continental free trade is tending to accentuate north/south interaction and interdependence at the expense of ties with neighbouring provinces. Thus over time anglophones in Quebec may become as different from Canadians as Canadians are different from the people of the United States.

One area in which this difference is already apparent is that of language. This is true not only in the obvious sense that a majority of Quebec anglophones are bilingual, while the vast majority of other anglophone Canadians are not. It is also true in the sense that the English spoken in Quebec differs from that spoken elsewhere, and that this is a fairly recent phenomenon. A study of Quebec and Ontario English in 1958 found some differences in vocabulary, but all of the words found in one province but not the other appeared to be of British or American origin.[28] The *Oxford Companion to the English Language,* published in 1992, found a significant influence of Quebec French on Quebec English,[29] while five years later another reference book, the *Guide to Canadian English Usage,* described Quebec English as a "new Canadian regional dialect."[30]

The English language of Quebec is distinctive in several ways. Quebec French words are borrowed where there is no obvious English equivalent, as for example "dépanneur" meaning a small grocery store, "poutine" meaning cheese-covered French fried potatoes (a concoction invented in 1957), "allophone" meaning someone of neither French nor English mother tongue, or "CEGEP" meaning a junior college. In addition standard French words are often used by Quebec anglophones when speaking English even though there is an English equivalent that is used elsewhere in North America. Examples might include autoroute (limited access highway), colloque (conference), or sondage (public opinion poll). Lastly, some words which exist in standard English are used with a distinctive meaning that corresponds to that of a similar word in the French language. Thus an animator in Quebec English means a discussion leader, not a cartoonist, a conference may mean a lecture, rather than a series of meetings, and a congress may mean a convention, rather than a legislative institution.

Structural assimilation of Quebec anglophones into Quebec society is a large topic that has been touched upon at several points in this study. In the primary and informal sense it seems to be gradually increasing, most noticeably in rural areas like the Eastern Townships, to some extent in downtown Montreal, and perhaps least in the Montreal suburbs, although even there it has been encouraged by the influx of francophones and by increasing bilingualism among anglophones. Residential segregation in metropolitan Montreal has noticeably declined since the Quiet Revolution, mainly because the disparity of average income and wealth between the two lingusitic communities has disappeared.

Secondary structural assimilation, involving participation by anglophones and francophones in formal institutions, has taken place to a limited extent since the old consociational barriers broke down. For example, the traditionally "English" hospitals are now required to serve francophone patients and there is more mingling than before in the offices of large private corporations. On the other hand separateness continues in education (which will be reinforced by the new linguistic boards) and anglophones are under-represented in the public service, in state enterprises, and in labour unions.

Biological assimilation is not an entirely new phenomenon, as suggested by the number of prominent francophones who have English, Irish or Scottish ancestors or family names. It seems to be accelerating, however, as more structural assimilation takes place. More social interaction leads to more intermarriage, and a large proportion of Quebec anglophones who have married in recent years have chosen a francophone spouse. Presumably the children of such marriages will be bilingual, although the extent to which they will identify with the anglophone community remains to be seen.

Finally, psychological assimilation may be roughly measured by the extent to which Quebec anglophones identify as Quebeckers and give priority to that identity over other identities, including their Canadian identity. If Quebec anglophones become more assimilated into Quebec and more distinct from other Canadians, will their Quebec identity eventually take precedence over their Canadian identity, as it does for most francophones in Quebec? Will some of them discard their Canadian identity entirely? For this to happen Quebec anglophones would have to feel much more secure in Quebec than most of them do at present. Insecurity is largely the product of the controversies over language policy that have afflicted Quebec since 1968, and the perception that the rights of anglophones have been curtailed. The political controversies over language were in part created deliberately by francophone politicians, but they were also the result of genuine anxiety and resentment among the francophone population. Since the anxiety and resentment appear to be subsiding, the controversies may disappear or at least remain dormant, and the anglophones who have remained in Quebec may feel more at home there. If that occurs, it is possible that significant numbers of them might follow the example of Kevin Drummond and Richard Holden by transferring their primary, or even exclusive, loyalty to Quebec. However, this will not happen quickly or on a massive scale. It is natural for minority groups to be wary of even the most benign forms of nationalism. There is even some evidence that the Loyalists who wished the American colonies to remain under British rule, and who migrated to Canada after independence was achieved, were disproportionately drawn from ethnic minorities.[31]

IN CONCLUSION

Great changes have taken place in Quebec over the last four decades. Apart from the technological, economic, social, and cultural changes that have transformed everyday life in all of North America, Quebec has undergone a revolutionary, but remarkably peaceful, transformation in the relations between church and state and in the relations between its two principal linguistic communities. The francophone majority has gained control of the economic life of the province, as nearly as is possible in a small province that participates in a global economy. Income differentials between francophones and anglophones have disappeared. French has become the dominant language in all spheres of Quebec life. The provincial state now serves the entire population directly, rather than delegating many of its functions to quasi-private institutions serving particular ethnic or religious groups. These changes have made Quebec more "normal," to use a word much favoured by Quebec nationalists, although they have imposed considerable stresses and strains on the Canadian federation. The changes have also imposed considerable inconvenience and psychological discomfort on Quebec anglophones, and caused inevitable resentment. However, the resentment has not taken violent forms, mainly because the safety valve of unhindered migration to other parts of Canada has been available for the seriously discontented. Those who have remained seem to have adapted reasonably well to the new order.

The extent of the transformation in Quebec, and the fact that the province has never been as French as it is now since before the battle on the Plains of Abraham, has not been sufficiently appreciated. In particular, it is sad to relate that a few Quebec nationalists continue to allege that the French language is in danger in Quebec, or at least in Montreal. Whatever their motivation may be, such allegations can only stir the pot of intercommunal animosity and damage the economic and social fabric of Quebec. All errors contain some truth, as Pope Pius XI asserted in his encyclical, *Quadrigesimo Anno,* and the kernel of truth in this error consists of the following facts: most immigrants to Quebec settle initially on Montreal Island, the majority of Quebeckers who speak English at home live on Montreal Island, and francophones are gradually leaving Montreal Island to settle in more distant suburbs.

Because of these facts, particularly the last, Montreal Island appears likely to lose its *"pure laine"* majority early in the next century, about half a century after Toronto ceased to be a city of predominantly British and Irish ethnicity. Assuming relatively large and continuing volumes of immigration, which incidentally cannot be taken for granted, it is even possible that a majority of Montreal Island's residents may at some future date speak languages other than French at home. No responsible study predicts, however, that more residents of Montreal Island will speak English than French at home. The Quebec government's interdepartmental task force on the French language predicted in its 1996 report that by the year 2041 French will be the home language of 40.4 per cent of the people of Montreal Island, and English will be the home language of 23.7 per cent.[32] Thus the ratio of French to English speakers will be about five to three. For what it is worth, the ratio between French and English speakers on Montreal Island was almost the same in the first census after Confederation. The third-ranking language will presumably be Spanish, a language quite similar to French. Hispanophones in Quebec are almost three times as likely to adopt French as their second language as they are to adopt English.[33]

In any event, no reasonable purpose is served by adopting the island as a working definition of "Montreal," apart from the fact that this procedure presents the future of the French language in the worst possible light. By 2041 the off-island suburbs, according to the same projection, will have a total population of two million persons, about the same as the predicted population of the island, and they will be overwhelmingly French, as they are at present. Whether or not it becomes, as the former regional municipality of Metropolitan Toronto has already become, a single city, Montreal Island will by then be no more than the inner core of a vast urban agglomeration. It should come as no surprise that minority groups will be concentrated in the core while the dominant ethnic group will live mainly in the suburbs. This has long been the pattern in every other major North American city, and is increasingly the pattern in European cities as well. In fact the movement of francophones from Montreal Island to the outer suburbs, the consequences of which are so often deplored by Quebec nationalists, is the logical consequence of the social and economic emancipation which francophones have achieved since the Quiet Revolution.

J. Arthur Mathewson, the last anglophone to serve as provincial treasurer of Quebec, predicted in 1941 that Quebec would remain French "until the Laurentian mountains were flattened" or, for all practical purposes, forever.[34] All available evidence suggests that Mathewson was correct. It is probably equally safe to predict, however, that an English-speaking minority will also exist in Quebec for the foreseeable future. Recent developments provide some reason to hope that its continuation will be accepted, although perhaps not enthusiastically welcomed, by the francophone majority, whether or not Quebec continues to be part of the Canadian federation. One may also hope that the anglophone minority in Quebec will strike a reasonable balance between defending its own collective interests, insofar as that is necessary, and contributing positively to the progress of Quebec, as it has done for more than two hundred years.

Appendix:
List of Persons Interviewed

Warren Allmand
Gordon Atkinson
Nick auf der Maur
David Berger
Lawrence Bergman
Peter Blaikie
Rod Blaker
Harry Blank
Casper Bloom
Gary Caldwell
Neil Cameron
Geoffrey Chambers
John Ciaccia
Russell Copeman
William Cosgrove
Joan Dougherty
Vaughan Dowie
Kevin Drummond
Sam Elkas
Sheila Finestone
Kenneth Fraser
Richard French
Howard Galganov
Michael Goldbloom
Victor Goldbloom
Heward Grafftey
Julius Grey
Michael Hamelin
Frank Hanley
Keith Henderson
Harold Herbert

Richard Holden
Donald Johnston
Robert Keaton
Geoffrey Kelley
Eric Kierans
Maurice King
Robert Libman
Clifford Lincoln
John Lynch-Staunton
Bryce Mackasey
Eric Maldoff
Herbert Marx
Storrs McCall
Alan McNaughton
Robert Middlemiss
Henry Milner
John O'Gallagher
Royal Orr
John Parisella
Alex Paterson
Maximilien Polak
Raymond Rock
Reed Scowen
William Shaw
Christos Sirros
William Tetley
Harold Thuringer
John Trent
John Turner
Gerry Weiner
Russell Williams

Notes

CHAPTER ONE

1 McRae, "The Plural Society and the Western Political Tradition," 685.
2 Mill, *Considerations on Representative Government*, 309.
3 Lord Acton, "Nationality," 160–1.
4 The words in quotation marks would have been added to the Canadian constitution under the terms of Section 1 of the constitutional amendment bill contained in the Meech Lake Accord (1987).
5 Hamilton, Madison, and Jay, *The Federalist Papers*.
6 The similarities and differences between federalism and consociationalism, as well as the possibility that both may appear simultaneously, are discussed in Arend Lijphart, "Consociation and Federation: Conceptual and Empirical Links."
7 The thesis that Quebec has a strong corporatist tradition is presented by Clinton Archibald, *Un Québec corporatiste?* The influence of the Church in promoting corporatism is discussed at 55–82.
8 Lijphart, *The Politics of Accommodation: Pluralism and Democracy in the Netherlands*, 1.
9 Lijphart, "Consociational Democracy," 216.
10 Lijphart, *The Politics of Accommodation*, 122–38.
11 Ibid., 200–2.
12 Lijphart, "Self-Determination versus Pre-Determination of Ethnic Minorities in Power-Sharing Systems," 277–8.
13 Nordlinger, *Conflict Regulation in Divided Societies*, 117–19.

14 Pappalardo, "The Conditions for Consociational Democracy: a Logical and Empirical Critique."
15 Lijphart, "Typologies of Democratic Systems," 21.
16 Daalder, "The Consociational Democracy Theme," 616.
17 Lorwin, "Segmented Pluralism: Ideological Cleavages and Political Cohesion in the Smaller European Democracies," 37n5.
18 Lustick, "Stability in Deeply Divided Societies: Consociationalism versus Control."
19 Marger, *Race and Ethnic Relations: American and Global Perspectives*, 144.
20 Ibid., 147.
21 Lijphart, "Cultural Diversity and Theories of Political Integration."
22 Noel, "Consociational Democracy and Canadian Federalism."
23 Porter, *The Vertical Mosaic: An Analysis of Social Class and Power in Canada*, 382.
24 McRae, "Consociationalism and the Canadian Political System."
25 Ibid., 259.
26 Smiley, "French-English Relations in Canada and Consociational Democracy," 180.
27 Ibid., 202.
28 Fournier, *The Quebec Establishment: The Ruling Class and The State*.
29 McRoberts, *Quebec: Social Change and Political Crisis*, 35–6.
30 Esman, *Ethnic Politics*, 147–75.
31 Ibid., 170.
32 Ibid., 171.
33 O'Donnell, "Consociationalism, English Quebec, and the Chauveau Ministry."
34 Cooper, "French-English subcultural segmentation: an analysis of consociational politics in Quebec."
35 Aunger, *In Search of Political Stability: A Comparative Study of New Brunswick and Northern Ireland*, 183–6.
36 Heintzman, "The Political Culture of Quebec, 1840–1960."
37 *The Statesman's Yearbook 1976–77*, 459.
38 Scowen, *A Different Vision*, 99.

CHAPTER TWO

1 For a fuller account of the origins of the anglophone minority in Quebec see Rudin, *The Forgotten Quebecers: A History of English-Speaking Quebec 1759–1980*, 43–66. This book is the best introduction to the history of anglophones in the province.
2 Earl of Durham, *The Report of the Earl of Durham, Her Majesty's High Commissioner and Governor-General of British North America*, 8.
3 Ibid., 43–4.

4 Ibid., 47.

5 Monet, *The Last Cannon Shot: A Study of French Canadian Nationalism 1837–1850*, 327–8.

6 Careless, *The Union of the Canadas 1841–1857*, 129.

7 Bawden, "The English-Speaking Community of Montreal 1850–1867," 164–6.

8 Cross, "The Irish in Montreal 1867–1896," 122.

9 Noel, *Patrons, Clients, Brokers: Ontario Society and Politics 1791–1896*, 164–75.

10 Rudin, *The Forgotten Quebecers*, 28, table 1.1.

11 Corbeil, "Les députés anglophones et le premier gouvernement du Québec de 1867 à 1871," 46.

12 Ibid., 55.

13 Ibid., 313, 321–5.

14 Canada, *Parliamentary Debates on the Subject of the Confederation of the British North American Provinces*, 510–11.

15 Corbeil, "Les députés anglophones," 308.

16 Skelton, *The Life and Times of Sir Alexander Tilloch Galt*, 401–5.

17 O'Donnell, "Consociationalism, English Quebec, and the Chauveau Ministry," 58–9.

18 This belief is discussed in Arnopoulos and Clift, *The English Fact in Quebec*, 35–50.

19 Stevenson, *Ex Uno Plures: Federal-Provincial Relations in Canada, 1867–1896*, 230–52.

20 O'Donnell, "Consociationalism, English Quebec," 60–1, 120.

21 Ibid., 63–6.

22 Ibid., 27–8.

23 Galt, *Civil Liberty in Lower Canada*, 7.

24 White Jr., *The Protestant Minority in Quebec in its Political Relations with the Roman Catholic Majority: A Letter Addressed to Sir Alexander Tilloch Galt*.

25 Heintzman, "The Political Culture of Quebec, 1840–1960."

26 Quebec, *Legislative Debates*, 12 November 1912, 36; 26 November 1912, 161–75; 28 November 1912, 199–210.

27 Rudin, *The Forgotten Quebecers*, 155, table 6.1.

28 e.g. Felix Carbray (Quebec West) in *Legislative Debates*, 28 March 1883, 1315–22.

29 *Legislative Debates*, 6 February 1878, 139–44.

30 Legislative Assembly, *Debates*, 28 November 1968, 4372–3.

31 Skelton, *The Life and Times of Sir Alexander Tilloch Galt*, 490.

32 This episode is described in Stevenson, *Ex Uno Plures*, 101.

33 Quoted in Hamelin and Beaudoin, "Les cabinets provinciaux, 1867–1967," 99.

34 Black, *Duplessis*, 132.
35 Details of Mathewson's background are taken from Genest, *Godbout,* 128–9.
36 Stevenson, *Ex Uno Plures*, 249, 251.
37 Cox, "The Quebec Provincial Election of 1886," 112–14.
38 Ibid., 114–18.
39 Hill, "Robert Sellar and the Huntingdon Gleaner," 429.
40 Ibid., 486–7.
41 Miller, *Equal Rights: The Jesuits' Estates Act Controversy*, 69, 115–18.
42 Hill, "Robert Sellar and the Huntingdon Gleaner," 493.
43 Angell, "Quebec Provincial Politics in the 1920s," 174–6.
44 Rudin, *The Forgotten Quebecers*, 175–99.
45 Hill, "Robert Sellar and the Huntingdon Gleaner," 426.
46 Sellar, *The Tragedy of Quebec*, 374.
47 Hunter, "The French Invasion of the Eastern Townships: A Regional Study," 174.
48 Westley, *Remembrance of Grandeur*, 213.
49 Ames, *The City Below the Hill*, 68, 105.
50 Copp, *The Anatomy of Poverty: The Condition of the Working Class in Montreal 1897–1929*, 114–21.
51 Reynolds, *The British Immigrant: His Social and Economic Adjustment in Canada*, 99.
52 Ibid., 102.
53 Peate, *Girl in a Red River Coat*, 15.
54 MacLennan, *The Watch That Ends the Night*, 112.
55 Westley, *Remembrance of Grandeur*, 211.
56 Jamieson, "French and English in the Institutional Structure of Montreal," 141a.
57 Tulchinsky, "The Third Solitude: A.M. Klein's Jewish Montreal, 1910–1950."
58 Bourassa, *Les Relations ethniques dans la vie politique montréalaise*, 35.
59 Ibid., 73.
60 Ibid., 41.
61 Westley, *Remembrance of Grandeur*, 265.
62 Richard Holden, interview with author, 6 June 1995.
63 Trudeau's essay, first published in 1958, is reprinted in his *Federalism and the French Canadians*.
64 Laurendeau, "The Astonishing Attitude of the English in Quebec."
65 Black, *Duplessis*, 46–7.
66 Jedwab, "The Political Behaviour of Two Montreal Anglophone Constituencies during the Duplessis Era, 1935–1956," 23–4.
67 Black, *Duplessis*, 104. The story is widely told in English-speaking Montreal, with numerous embellishments.

68 Ibid., 147.

69 *Statutes of Quebec,* 1937, ch. 13.

70 The quote is from the text of the repeal measure, *Statutes of Quebec,* 1938, ch. 22.

71 Power, *A Party Politician: The Memoirs of Chubby Power,* 347.

72 Jedwab, "Political Behaviour of Two Montreal Anglophone Constituencies," 41.

73 Quinn, "The Quebec Provincial Election of 1944," 33–7.

74 le Terreur, *Les tribulations des conservateurs au Québec,* 172.

75 Trépanier, "L'opinion publique anglo-québécoise et l'autonomie provinciale (1945–46)."

76 Duplessis' relations with the English media and their owners are discussed in Black, *Duplessis,* 603–11 and 639–44.

77 Jedwab, "Political Behaviour of Two Montreal Anglophone Constituencies," 69.

78 John Turner, interview with author, 31 March 1995.

79 Jedwab, "Political Behaviour of Two Montreal Anglophone Constituencies," 84–5.

80 Eric Kierans, interview with author, 1 August 1994.

81 Frank Hanley, interview with author, 26 August 1994.

82 Globensky, "Voting Behaviour in Three Provincial Elections in Quebec." 135–8.

83 Westley, *Remembrance of Grandeur,* 218.

84 Creighton, *John A. Macdonald: The Young Politician,* 473–4.

85 Hill, "Robert Sellar and the Huntingdon Gleaner," 116–17.

86 National Archives of Canada, George Perley Papers, vol. 9, file 3, Borden to Perley, 23 September 1917.

87 Jedwab, "Political Behaviour of Two Montreal Anglophone Constituencies," 47.

88 House of Commons, *Debates,* 25 November 1953, 345–6.

89 Heward Grafftey, interview with author, 12 May 1995.

CHAPTER THREE

1 Black, *Duplessis,* 307.

2 Lieberson, "Bilingualism in Montreal: A Demographic Analysis."

3 Thomson, *Jean Lesage and the Quiet Revolution,* 87.

4 "A close race; Mr Barrette holds his seat in Joliette," *Montréal-Matin,* 23 June 1960, 1.

5 The comment appears in Goldwin Smith, *Canada and the Canadian Question,* 8.

6 Three of the main theories are summarized in Coleman, *The Independence Movement in Quebec 1945–1980,* 4–16.

318 Notes to pages 64–77

7 Guindon, "The social evolution of Quebec reconsidered" in his *Quebec Society: Tradition, Modernity, and Nationhood*. The paper was originally published in 1960. This book of collected essays is the best introduction to the Quiet Revolution.

8 Guindon, "The crown, the Catholic church, and the French Canadian people: the historical roots of Quebec nationalism." Perhaps the most brilliant of Guindon's essays, this one was written in 1978.

9 Latouche, "La vraie nature de … la révolution tranquille," tableau I, 529, tableau V, 534.

10 Guindon, "The social evolution of Quebec reconsidered," 23.

11 Oliver, *The Passionate Debate: The Social and Political Ideas of Quebec Nationalism, 1920–1945*, 105–79.

12 The development of these two currents of opposition in the Duplessis era is described and explained in Behiels, *Prelude to Quebec's Quiet Revolution: Liberalism versus Neo-Nationalism, 1945–1960*.

13 See note 11, above.

14 Tocqueville, *The Old Regime and the French Revolution*, 22–32.

15 *Report of the Royal Commission on Bilingualism and Biculturalism, Book III, The Work World*, 56.

16 Ibid., 54.

17 Ibid., 18–19.

18 Ibid., 21.

19 Data on the urban ridings are from Bernier, "La structure socio-économique de l'électorat montréalais et les partis politiques québécois," 129. Data on the rural ridings are from Globensky, "Voting Behaviour in Three Provincial Elections in Quebec," 169, 173.

20 Globensky, "Voting Behaviour," 135, 169.

21 Harry Blank, interview with author, 23 August 1994.

22 Quinn, *The Union Nationale: Quebec Nationalism from Duplessis to Lévesque*, 207.

23 Data on the ethnic composition of ridings are from Bernier, "La structure socio-économique," 146–7.

24 Ken Fraser, interview with author, 8 May 1995.

25 Lapalme, *Le vent de l'oubli*, 62.

26 Hamelin and Beaudoin, "Les cabinets provinciaux, 1867–1967," 113.

27 Black, *Duplessis*, 343.

28 Lapalme, *Le vent de l'oubli*, 53–4.

29 Thomson, *Jean Lesage and the Quiet Revolution*, 97, 180.

30 Gallichan, "De la Montreal Light, Heat and Power à Hydro-Québec," 69.

31 Thomson, *Jean Lesage and the Quiet Revolution*, 114.

32 Ibid., 182, 213.

33 Eric Kierans, interview with author, 1 August 1994.

34 Kierans, interview. Marler's reservations are noted in Thomson, *Jean Lesage and the Quiet Revolution*, 138.

35 Kierans, interview.
36 McDougall, *The Politics and Economics of Eric Kierans: A Man for all Canadas*, 40.
37 Ibid., 50.
38 Kierans, interview.
39 Newman, *The Distemper of Our Times, Canadian Politics in Transition: 1963–1968*, 410–12.
40 Richard French, interview with author, 9 May 1995.
41 Richard Holden, interview with author, 6 June 1995.
42 Citrin, "The Quebec General Election of 1962," 111.
43 Ferguson, "Quebec's English few bid for a backlash," 1.
44 Quebec, Legislative Assembly, *Debates*, 31 January 1964, 518–19, 604–5.
45 Ibid., 23 January 1964, 273–5.
46 Ibid., 28 January 1964, 374–5.
47 Cahill, "A Study of Political Attitudes in Pontiac County"; Zinman, "Lachute, Quebec, French-English Frontier: A Case Study in Language and Community."
48 Cahill, "Study of Political Attitudes," 104–5.
49 Legislative Assembly, *Debates*, 10 February 1966, 541.
50 Legislative Assembly, *Debates*, 14 February 1967, 1179–80.
51 This issue is discussed in Keough, "The Quebec Department of Education, Cultural Pluralism, and the Anglophone Catholic Minority," 91–113.
52 Ibid., 80–2.
53 Price, "The Social Construction of Ethnicity: The Case of English Montrealers," 354–5.
54 Keough, "The Quebec Department of Education," 86–90.
55 John Turner, interview with author, 31 March 1995.
56 Chaput, *Pourquoi je suis séparatiste.*
57 Guy Bourassa, *Les relations ethniques dans la vie politique montréalaise*, 42.
58 Caldwell, *A Demographic Profile of the English-Speaking Population of Quebec 1921–1971*, 74.
59 Rudin, *The Forgotten Quebecers: A History of English-Speaking Quebec 1759–1980*, 235.
60 Laczko, "English Canadians and Quebecois Nationalism," 47.
61 Reilly, "Political Attitudes among Law Students in Quebec."
62 Cahill, "Study of Political Attitudes," 155–6, 161.
63 Price, "The Social Construction of Ethnicity," 338.
64 Ibid., 350.
65 Romalis, "The Attitudes of the Montreal Jewish Community Toward French Canadian Nationalism and Separatism," 15–23.
66 Mallory, "English-Speaking Quebeckers in a Separate Quebec," 138.
67 Scott and Oliver, eds., *Quebec States Her Case.*
68 Legislative Assembly, *Debates*, 30 March 1967, 1898.

69 For an interesting retrospective account of the de Gaulle visit, see Michael Goldbloom, "That infamous cry," *The Gazette,* 20 July 1997, C1–C3.
70 Mallory, "English-Speaking Quebeckers in a Separate Quebec," 125.
71 Cahill, "Study of Political Attitudes," 157–60.
72 Heward Grafftey, interview with author, 12 May 1995. Grafftey believes that Bill Hamilton's physical handicap made Diefenbaker uncomfortable. Generally, however, Diefenbaker was suspicious of the ministers who had not supported him in the leadership contest of 1956, a category that included Hamilton. See Peter C. Newman, *Renegade in Power: The Diefenbaker Years,* 95.
73 Sévigny, *This Game of Politics,* 23, 76.
74 Newman, *Renegade in Power,* 99.
75 Grafftey, interview.
76 Sévigny, *This Game of Politics,* 23.
77 House of Commons, *Debates,* 25 November 1957, 1467–8.
78 Ibid., 1492–3.
79 Turner, interview.
80 Pelletier, *L'aventure du pouvoir 1968–1975,* 79–80.
81 Alan McNaughton, interview with author, 24 August 1994.
82 Victor Goldbloom, interview with author, 30 August 1995.
83 Warren Allmand, interview with author, 9 May 1996.
84 William Tetley, interview with author, 24 August 1994.
85 Turner, interview.
86 Kierans, interview.
87 Canada, *Twenty-Eighth General Election 1968: Report of the Chief Electoral Officer,* xiv–xvi.

CHAPTER FOUR

1 See the list of incidents in Pelletier, *The October Crisis,* 197–205.
2 Chodos and auf der Maur, eds., *Quebec: A Chronicle 1968–1972,* 27–9.
3 Canada, *Census,* 1951, vol. I, table 32; 1961, vol. I, part 2, table 35; 1971, vol. I, part 3, table 2.
4 Quebec, *Report of the Commission of Inquiry on the Position of the French Language and on Language Rights in Quebec* (Quebec: 1972), book III, table A-11, 473–9.
5 Boissevain, *The Italians of Montreal: Social Adjustment in a Plural Society,* 2, 37–40, 45–7, 60, 64, 65.
6 Cappon, *Conflit entre les Néo-Canadiens et les francophones de Montréal,* 135–6.
7 Parisella, "Pressure Group Politics: Case Study of the St Léonard Schools Crisis," 46–7.

8 Ibid., 49.

9 This paragraph is based on Parisella, "Pressure Group Politics," 47–53.

10 Ibid., 121.

11 Ibid., 136.

12 Ibid., 130–1.

13 Ibid., 147–8.

14 Quebec, Legislative Assembly, *Debates*, 16 December 1968, 4970–1.

15 Parisella, "Pressure Group Politics," 152–5.

16 Ibid., 157.

17 Holden, *1970 Election Quebec Crucible*, 22.

18 Quinn, *The Union Nationale: Quebec Nationalism from Duplessis to Lévesque*, 253.

19 *Statutes of Quebec*, 1969, ch. 9.

20 Quinn, *The Union Nationale*, 255–6.

21 *The Gazette*, 24 October 1969.

22 *Statutes of Quebec*, 1965, ch. 87.

23 See the briefs by the Protestant School Board of Greater Montreal, the Canadian Jewish Congress, and the Montreal Board of Trade, in Legislative Assembly, *Debates*, Standing Committee on Education, B24–B25, B111–B115, and B13–B15.

24 Fournier, "A Political Analysis of School Reorganization in Montreal," 100.

25 Ibid., 86–7.

26 Keough, "The Quebec Department of Education, Cultural Pluralism, and the Anglophone Catholic Minority," 86–7.

27 See for example Milner, *The Long Road to Reform: Restructuring Public Education in Quebec*, 27.

28 Tetley, "Language and Education Rights in Quebec and Canada," 192.

29 William Tetley, interview with author, 25 August 1994.

30 Legislative Assembly, *Debates*, 28 November 1968, 4370–2.

31 The amalgamation is discussed in Sancton, *Governing the Island of Montreal: Language Differences and Metropolitan Politics*, 93–119.

32 Legislative Assembly, *Debates*, 15 December 1969, 4927–8 (speech by Victor Goldbloom) and 4931 (vote on second reading).

33 Hubert Bauch, "The Numbers Game: nationalists no longer count on Jacques Henripin," *The Gazette*, 16 February 1991.

34 Parisella, "Pressure Group Politics," 175.

35 Smith, *Les élections 1970 au Québec: Le coup d'État du 29 avril*, 84.

36 Frank Hanley, interview with author, 26 August 1994.

37 Holden, *1970 Election Quebec Crucible*, 122.

38 Tetley, interview.

39 Victor Goldbloom, interview with author, 30 August 1995.

40 Kevin Drummond, interview with author, 26 April 1996.

41 For a brief historical and descriptive account of the protected ridings see Bonenfant, "Les douze circonscriptions électorales privilégiées du Québec."

42 Ken Fraser, interview with author, 8 May 1995.

43 Quebec, National Assembly, *Debates*, 19 December 1970, 2610–14. See also the speech by Ken Fraser at 2617–18.

44 National Assembly, *Debates*, Standing Committee on Institutions, 21 June 1972, B3804–B3807.

45 Harry Blank, interview with author, 23 August 1994.

46 *The Gazette*, 19 February 1971, p. 1; 22 February 1971, p. 1; and 10 March 1971, p. 1.

47 Sancton, *Governing the Island of Montreal*, 132–7.

48 Robert Keaton, interview with author, 21 February 1996.

49 Drummond, interview.

50 National Assembly, *Debates*, 6 July 1971, 3059.

51 Fournier, "A Political Analysis of School Reorganization in Montreal," 106.

52 For Goldbloom's speech see National Assembly, *Debates*, 3 December 1971, 4660–2.

53 *Statutes of Quebec*, 1971, ch. 60. See the speech by William Tetley on Bill 71 in National Assembly, *Debates*, 7 December 1972, 3035–7.

54 *Statutes of Quebec*, 1971, ch. 48. The introduction and adoption of the bill are described in Sancton, *Governing the Island of Montreal*, 174–6.

55 Sancton, *Governing the Island of Montreal*, 180–4.

56 National Assembly, *Debates*, 25 November 1971, 4439–40.

57 John Ciaccia, interview with author, 22 May 1996.

58 *The Montreal Star*, 28 February 1973.

59 Quebec, *Report of the Commission of Inquiry on the Position of the French Language and on Language Rights in Quebec* 1972, Book I: *Language of Work*, Book II: *Language Rights*, Book III: *The Ethnic Groups*.

60 Quebec, *Report of the Commission of Inquiry*, Book I, 48, table I. 24.

61 The 92 recommendations are listed in *Report of the Commission of Inquiry*, Book I, 291–305.

62 They are listed in *Report of the Commission of Inquiry*, Book III, 445–57.

63 Ibid., 273.

64 Tetley, "Language and Education Rights in Quebec and Canada," 193.

65 Tetley, interview.

66 Saywell, ed., *Canadian Annual Review of Politics and Public Affairs 1973*, 130.

67 Goldbloom, interview.

68 Ciaccia, interview.

69 National Assembly, *Debates,* 20 March 1974, 84–7, and 21 March 1974, 113–16.

70 *Statutes of Quebec,* 1974, ch. 6.

71 Robert Bourassa, *Gouverner le Québec,* 111–12. The book is based on a series of seminars given by Mr Bourassa at the University of Montreal.

72 Tetley, interview.

73 Drummond, interview.

74 Goldbloom, interview.

75 Tetley, interview.

76 Drummond, interview.

77 Taddeo and Taras, *Le débat linguistique au Québec: La communauté italienne et la langue d'enseignement,* 98, 148.

78 Bourassa, *Gouverner le Québec,* 124.

79 Goldbloom, interview.

80 Their briefs can be found in National Assembly, *Debates,* Standing Committee on Education, B3339–B5335.

81 Ibid., B4258.

82 National Assembly, *Debates,* 13 July 1974, 1837–9.

83 Ibid., 15 July 1974, 1863–4. In fact Drummond had been quoted in *The Gazette* of 23 May 1974 as saying that he preferred Bill 63 to Bill 22 which "doesn't seem to please anyone."

84 Ibid., 1859–61.

85 Ibid., 12 July 1974, 1726–8.

86 Ibid., 13 July 1974, 1798–1801.

87 Ibid., 15 July 1974, 1854–5.

88 Ibid., 1888–91.

89 Ibid., 1891–2.

90 *The Montreal Star,* 22 May 1974.

91 *The Gazette,* 23 May 1974 and *The Montreal Star,* 17 June 1974. In the later interview Scott had a much longer list of objections than in the earlier one.

92 Tetley, interview.

93 Ken Fraser, interview with author, 8 May 1995.

94 The two roll calls are recorded in National Assembly, *Debates,* 15 July 1974, 1905 and 30 July 1974, 2269.

95 Goldbloom, interview.

96 Tetley, interview.

97 Fraser, interview.

98 *Statutes of Quebec,* 1975, ch. 6.

99 Taddeo and Taras, *Le débat linguistique au Québec,* 149–53, 169.

100 Breton, "The Production and Allocation of Symbolic Resources: An Analysis of the Linguistic and Ethnocultural Fields in Canada," 125–6.

101 Kenneth A. Price, "The Social Construction of Ethnicity: The Case of English Montrealers," 347.

102 Ibid., 358.

103 Laczko, "English Canadians and Quebecois Nationalism," 19, 68, 79–81, 84–6, 100–5.

104 Arnopoulos, "Integration of English Into French Quebec Society: Some New Directions," 92–6, 100–4, 119–22.

105 Ibid., 135.

106 Vaughan Dowie, interview with author, 24 May 1996.

107 Keaton, interview.

108 auf der Maur, "I Was the October Crisis."

109 *The Gazette*, 12 November 1974, 4.

110 McKenna and Purcell, *Drapeau*, 327–8.

111 Ibid., 339.

112 William Shaw, interview with author, 23 August 1994.

113 Shaw, interview.

114 Keaton, interview.

115 Nick auf der Maur, interview with author, 22 February 1996.

116 Bernard, *Québec: élections 1976*, 111. Percentages of anglophones for each of the island ridings are shown on 136.

117 Goldbloom, interview.

118 Saywell, *Canadian Annual Review of Politics and Public Affairs 1976*, 120.

119 John O'Gallagher, interview with author, 12 May 1995.

CHAPTER FIVE

1 Leslie, "Ethnic Hierarchies and Minority Consciousness in Quebec," 129.

2 Eric Maldoff, interview with author, 8 June 1995. This account of the founding of Participation Québec is also based on an interview with Michael Goldbloom, 7 June 1995.

3 This account of the founding of Positive Action is based on interviews with Storrs McCall, 12 May 1995 and with Alex Paterson, 7 June 1995, as well as documents provided by Professor McCall.

4 McCall, interview.

5 Paterson, interview.

6 Peter Blaikie, interview with author, 11 May 1995.

7 The estimate is in the Positive Action brief concerning Bill 1, in Quebec, National Assembly, *Debates*, Standing Committee on Education, Cultural Affairs, and Communications, 28 June 1977, CLF961–70.

8 Henry Milner supplied the estimate when questioned during their presentation to a legislative committee. Ibid., CLF919.

9 McCall and Paterson, interviews.

10 Maldoff, interview.

11 The results were collected in Schacter, "Working Papers on English Language Institutions in Quebec," of which several photocopies survive. It was never published.

12 *Statutes of Quebec*, 1977, ch. 5.

13 Montalembert is quoted in Heather Lysons, "The Language Question and Quebec Education," 328. Laurin may have taken the quote from this source. For his version, see National Assembly, *Debates*, 19 July 1977, 2188.

14 Their brief is printed in National Assembly, *Debates*, Standing Committee on Education, Cultural Affairs, and Communications, 22 June 1977, CLF648–55.

15 Ibid., 28 June 1977, CLF961–70.

16 Ibid., 4 July 1977, CLF1282–92.

17 Ibid., 7 July 1977, CLF1616–26.

18 National Assembly, *Debates*, 1 August 1977, 2560–3.

19 Ibid., 25 July 1977, 2344 and 1 August 1977, 2567.

20 Ibid., 26 July 1977, 2392–4.

21 Ibid., 1 August 1977, 2577–80.

22 Ibid., 2571–3.

23 John O'Gallagher, interview with author, 12 May 1995.

24 Maldoff, interview.

25 *Protestant School Board of Greater Montreal* v *Minister of Education of Quebec* [1976] 83 D.L.R. 93d 645 (Quebec Superior Court).

26 Blaikie, interview.

27 Ibid.

28 *A.G. Quebec* v *Blaikie* [1979] 2 S.C.R. 1016.

29 *A.G. Manitoba* v *Forest* [1979] 2 S.C.R. 1032.

30 Jedwab, *English in Montreal: A Layman's Look at the Current Situation*, 87.

31 Joan Dougherty, interview with author, 24 August 1994.

32 Royal Orr, interview with author, 22 February 1996.

33 Fraser, *PQ: René Lévesque and the Parti Québécois in Power*, 342.

34 Canada, *Census*, 1976, catalogue no. 92-821; and 1981, catalogue no. 92-902.

35 Maheu, "L'émigration des anglophones québécois."

36 A useful account of the Sun Life episode appears in Clark, *Montreal The New Cité*, 56–65.

37 Scowen, *La réalité du transfert des entreprises en dehors du Québec*. A list of the enterprises relocated is reproduced in Benjamin Higgins: *The Rise – and Fall? Of Montreal*, 66–9.

38 Caldwell, "Itinéraire migratoire des jeunes qui ont quitté l'école secondaire anglaise au Québec en 1971."

39 Lange, "Montreal Anglophones: Social Distance and Emigration."

40 Ibid., 108–15.

41 Ibid., 129–30.

42 Ibid., 146.

43 Locher, *Les anglophones de Montréal: émigration et évolution des attitudes 1978–1983.*

44 Ibid., 37.

45 Ibid., 79.

46 Ibid., 83.

47 Ibid., 79–86.

48 Ibid., 140.

49 Hirschman, *Exit, Voice and Loyalty: Responses to Decline in Firms, Organizations, and States.*

50 Ibid., 43.

51 Robert Keaton, interview with author, 21 February 1996.

52 National Assembly, *Debates,* 10 April 1980, 5820–2.

53 Ibid., 11 December 1979, 4270.

54 Shaw and Albert, *Partition: The Price of Quebec's Independence.*

55 Ryan's promises are summarized in Scowen, *A Different Vision: The English in Quebec in the 1990s,* 27.

56 Victor Goldbloom, interview with author, 30 August 1995.

57 Reed Scowen, interview with author, 2 September 1994.

58 Herbert Marx, interview with author, 9 June 1995.

59 Maximilien Polak, interview with author, 21 February 1996.

60 National Assembly, *Debates,* 14 December 1979, 4499.

61 Quebec Liberal Party, *A New Canadian Federation.*

62 John Parisella, interview with author, 6 June 1995.

63 Dougherty, interview.

64 William Shaw, interview with author, 23 August 1994.

65 Parisella, interview.

66 Clifford Lincoln, interview with author, 15 August 1996.

67 John Trent, interview with author, 9 May 1996.

68 Robert Middlemiss, interview with author, 21 May 1996.

69 Parisella, interview.

70 Polak, interview.

71 Christos Sirros, interview with author, 19 August 1996.

72 Dougherty, interview.

73 National Assembly, *Debates,* Standing Committee on Cultural Communities and Immigration, 5 June 1981, B545–B546.

74 Fraser, *PQ,* 95.

75 Henry Milner, interview with author, 13 February 1995.

76 Photocopies of both advertisements were supplied to the author by Henry Milner.

77 "Address by Prime Minister René Lévesque to the English Community on Sovereignty-Association," Montreal: 23 March 1980. Text supplied to the author by Henry Milner.

78 Milner, interview.

79 Kevin Drummond, interview with author, 26 April 1996.

80 Parti Québécois, "Document de consultation préparé par les membres de la commission nationale des anglophones, à l'intention des militants du parti," November 1980.

81 National Assembly, *Debates*, 22 June 1982, 5368.

82 Dougherty, interview; and Richard French, interview with author, 9 May 1995.

83 Dominique Clift, a francophone journalist who had worked for *The Montreal Star*, also underestimated the prospects of Quebec nationalism in a book published just before the 1981 election. See Clift, *Le déclin du nationalisme au Québec*.

84 Data on federal funding are from Prosperi, "The Dynamics of Ethno-Linguistic Mobilization in Canada: A Case Study of Alliance Quebec," 50–2.

85 Casper Bloom, interview with author, 22 February 1996.

86 Maldoff, interview.

87 Sheila Finestone, interview with author, 7 May 1996.

88 Michael Goldbloom, interview with author, 7 June 1995.

89 The formal structures are described in Prosperi, "The Dynamics of Ethno-Linguistic Mobilization in Canada," 60–3.

90 Michael Goldbloom, interview.

91 Paterson, interview.

92 Prosperi, "The Dynamics of Ethno-Linguistic Mobilization in Canada," 50–1.

93 Maldoff, interview. Maldoff's letter to Lévesque is reproduced in Prosperi, "The Dynamics of Ethno-Linguistic Mobilization in Canada," 112–15.

94 *The Gazette*, 3 November 1982. At least eight pages of the newspaper were devoted, in whole or in part, to the story.

95 Vaughan Dowie, interview with author, 24 May 1996.

96 Maldoff, interview.

97 National Assembly, *Debates*, 7 December 1983, 3985–8.

98 *Statutes of Quebec*, 1983, ch. 56.

99 The document is summarized in Milner, *The Long Road to Reform: Restructuring Public Education in Quebec*, 79–86.

100 The concepts of legitimacy and mandate are discussed in Kwavnick, *Organized Labour and Pressure Politics: The Canadian Labour Congress 1956–1968*, 1–32.

CHAPTER SIX

1 Fraser, *PQ: René Lévesque and the Parti Québécois in Power,* 341.
2 MacDonald, *From Bourassa to Bourassa: A Pivotal Decade in Canadian History,* 309.
3 Richard French, interview with author, 9 May 1995.
4 Herbert Marx, interview with author, 9 June 1995.
5 Harry Blank, interview with author, 23 August 1994.
6 National Assembly, *Debates,* 19 June 1985, 4896–7.
7 *The Gazette,* 3 December 1985.
8 Reed Scowen, interview with author, 2 September 1994.
9 Scowen, interview.
10 Clifford Lincoln, interview with author, 15 August 1996.
11 *A.G. Quebec* v *Quebec Association of Protestant School Boards* et al., [1984] 2 S.C.R., 66.
12 *Statutes of Quebec,* 1986, ch. 46.
13 Quebec Liberal Party, Resolution no. 5, "Services gouvernementaux," June 1985. Copy supplied to the author by Herbert Marx.
14 *Statutes of Quebec,* 1986, ch. 106.
15 Christos Sirros, interview with author, 19 August 1996, and Russell Williams, interview with author, 22 May 1996.
16 National Assembly, *Debates,* 8 December 1986, 4943–6.
17 Ibid., 4963–6.
18 Ibid., 9 December 1986, 5070–3.
19 *Statutes of Quebec,* 1988, ch. 84.
20 *Reference re Education Act (Quebec),* [1993] 2 S.C.R., 511.
21 See Dougherty's speech in National Assembly, *Debates,* 25 October 1988, 2714–17.
22 Joan Dougherty, interview with author, 24 August 1994.
23 National Assembly, *Debates,* 17 May 1988, CE526–CE536.
24 Ibid., Standing Committee on Cultural Communities and Immigration, 2 November 1983, B8856–B8860.
25 French, interview.
26 National Assembly, *Debates,* 16 April 1986, 927–9.
27 Ibid., 17 April 1986, 947–8, and 22 April 1986, 961–3.
28 Quebec Liberal Party, resolution no. 6, "Politique linguistique," June 1986. Copy supplied to the author by Herbert Marx.
29 National Assembly, *Debates,* 23 October 1986, 3484–5.
30 Ibid., 19 December 1986, 5837.
31 Marx, interview.
32 Canada, Commissioner of Official Languages, *Annual Report 1987,* 9. The phrase used in the French version was "l'humiliation de son rival."

33 National Assembly, *Debates*, 23 March 1988, 367–8.

34 *Ford* v *Quebec*, [1988] 2 S.C.R., 712.

35 *The Gazette*, 16 December 1988. Perhaps the audience who applauded Rose at CEGEP St-Laurent did not know that Laporte had been one of the first politicians to take a serious interest in protecting the French language.

36 *Statutes of Quebec*, 1988, ch. 54.

37 Dougherty, interview.

38 William Cosgrove, interview with author, 20 February 1996.

39 Dougherty, interview.

40 Lincoln, interview. Lincoln, French and Marx all say that French and Marx did not participate in this effort, despite some published accounts to the contrary.

41 Robert Bourassa, *Gouverner le Québec*, 171–3.

42 Lincoln, interview.

43 National Assembly, *Debates*, 20 December 1988, 4417.

44 French and Marx interviews.

45 John Ciaccia, interview with author, 22 May 1996.

46 National Assembly, *Debates*, 20 December 1988, 4411–12.

47 Ibid., 4473–5.

48 King, *The First Step*, 214.

49 Libman, *Riding the Rapids: The White-Water Rise and Fall of Quebec's Anglo Protest*, 26.

50 Robert Libman, interview with author, 10 May 1995.

51 Libman, *Riding the Rapids*, 28.

52 Shaw and Albert, *Partition: The Price of Quebec's Independence*.

53 Libman, *Riding the Rapids*, 11–13.

54 Libman, interview.

55 David Berger, interview with author, 9 October 1997.

56 Bernstein's description of his candidacy is quoted in Libman, *Riding the Rapids*, 73.

57 Richard Holden, interview with author, 6 June 1995.

58 Neil Cameron, interview with author, 11 May 1995.

59 Russell Copeman, interview with author, 22 May 1996.

60 Richard French, interview.

61 Maximilien Polak, interview with author, 21 February 1996.

62 Sam Elkas, interview with author, 16 August 1996.

63 Cosgrove, interview.

64 Holden, interview.

65 Pierre Drouilly, "Le succès des partis Égalité et Unité," *Le Devoir*, 4 October 1989.

66 King, *The First Step*, 216–17.

67 *The Gazette*, 27 September 1989.

68 Michael Goldbloom, interview with author, 7 June 1995.

69 Peter Blaikie, interview with author, 11 May 1995.

70 Royal Orr, interview with author, 22 February 1996.

71 Blaikie, interview.

72 Peter Blaikie, "Dispelling the Misconceptions," *The Globe and Mail,* 14 September 1989, A7.

73 Robert Keaton, interview with author, 21 February 1996.

74 National Assembly, *Debates,* 27 August 1991, 9775–6.

75 Scowen, *A Different Vision: The English in Quebec in the 1990s,* 49–56.

76 Ibid., 148–9.

77 Ibid., 72.

78 Ibid., 61.

79 Scowen, interview. See also his undated document, "For the Directors of Alliance Quebec: A New Approach for Alliance Quebec" (copy provided to the author by Reed Scowen).

80 Scowen, interview.

81 See Alliance Quebec's report: *Task Force on Job Opportunities for English-Speaking Youth in Quebec.*

82 Maurice King, interview with author, 19 August 1996.

83 Keaton, interview.

84 This paragraph and the four that follow are based on interviews with Gordon Atkinson, 9 May 1995, and with Robert Libman, Neil Cameron, and Richard Holden.

85 Libman, *Riding the Rapids,* 55.

86 Libman, interview.

87 Libman, *Riding the Rapids,* 157.

88 Keith Henderson, interview with author, 20 February 1996.

89 Libman, *Riding the Rapids,* 160.

90 Libman and Cosgrove interviews.

91 National Assembly, *Debates,* 14 June 1990, 3310.

92 John Parisella, interview with author, 6 June 1995; Cosgrove and Williams, interviews.

93 National Assembly, *Debates,* 2 April 1992, 337–9.

94 *Greater Montreal Protestant School Board* v *Quebec,* [1989] 1 S.C.R. 377.

95 Gretta Chambers, Chairperson, Task Force on English Education, *Report to the Minister of Education of Quebec* (Montreal, January 1992).

96 National Assembly, *Debates,* 14 May 1992, 860–1.

97 Mordecai Richler, "A Reporter at Large" and *Oh Canada! Oh Quebec! Requiem for a Divided Country.*

98 National Assembly, *Debates,* 31 March 1993, 5779–80.

99 The full decision appears in King, *The First Step,* 245–68.

100 Canada, Commissioner of Official Languages, *Annual Report 1993,* 126.

101 National Assembly, *Debates*, 25 May 1993, CC993–CC994 and CC1002–CC1014.
102 Keaton, interview.
103 *Statutes of Quebec*, 1993, ch. 40.
104 National Assembly, *Debates*, 17 June 1993, 7960.
105 Gordon Atkinson, interview with author, 9 May 1995.
106 *The Economist*, 12 October 1996, 95.

CHAPTER SEVEN

1 National Assembly, *Debates*, 23 March 1994, 85–6.
2 Libman, *Riding the Rapids: The White-Water Rise and Fall of Quebec's Anglo Protest*, 196–200.
3 Ibid., 196.
4 Russell Copeman, interview with author, 22 May 1996.
5 Robert Keaton, interview with author, 21 February 1996.
6 William Cosgrove, interview with author, 20 February 1996.
7 National Assembly, *Debates*, 30 November 1994, 39.
8 *The Globe and Mail*, 5 August 1994, A5.
9 *The Gazette*, 14 September 1994, A8.
10 Parti Québécois, *The English-Speaking Community: An Integral Part of a Sovereign Quebec*, 19, 26–7.
11 *The Gazette*, 16 June 1994, A1.
12 Parti Québécois, *Le Québec dans un monde nouveau*, 58, 67.
13 Richard, *Jacques Parizeau: Un bâtisseur*, 222.
14 Gary Caldwell, interview with author, 20 August 1996.
15 Keith Henderson, interview with author, 20 February 1996.
16 *The Gazette*, 4 April 1996, A8. As discussed in chapter 8 of this book, Robert Libman and the Equality Party had challenged aspects of Quebec's referendum law pertaining to the regulation of expenses after the referendum of 1992, but the Supreme Court of Canada's decision on the *Libman* case was not handed down until 1997.
17 Charron, *La partition du Québec: De Lord Durham à Stéphane Dion*.
18 Bercuson and Cooper, *Deconfederation: Canada without Quebec*.
19 Ibid., 162.
20 Reid, *Canada Remapped: How the Partition of Quebec will Reshape the Nation*.
21 Scott, "Issues Relating to Quebec Independence: Remarks prepared for delivery as a guest speaker at a public meeting" (Montreal, October 1992), 21.
22 Ibid., 28.
23 The texts of both the March and November resolutions are reproduced in a party document entitled *Territorial Rights: The Partition of Quebec* (Revision 1, Montreal, January 1996), 1.

24 Henderson, interview.
25 *The Globe and Mail,* 5 February 1996, A4.
26 *The Globe and Mail,* 30 January 1996, A1.
27 *The Globe and Mail,* 19 March 1996, A8.
28 *The Toronto Star,* 11 October 1997, B5.
29 Howard Galganov, interview with author, 25 February 1997.
30 *The Gazette,* 26 April 1996, A1.
31 Galganov, interview.
32 The comments from Serge Ménard and Michael Hamelin are quoted in *The Gazette,* 17 August 1996, A12.
33 *The Globe and Mail,* 13 September 1996, A12.
34 Galganov, interview.
35 Galganov, interview.
36 Michael Hamelin, interview with author, 23 February 1996.
37 *The Gazette,* 17 February 1996, A11.
38 *The Gazette,* 20 February 1996, A10.
39 *The Gazette,* 24 February 1996, B6. The entire page was devoted to excerpts from the report.
40 *The Gazette,* 22 February 1996, A1, A2.
41 *The Gazette,* 9 March 1996, B5.
42 *The Gazette,* 12 March 1996, A8. The entire page was devoted to excerpts from the speech.
43 Ibid., A9.
44 Quebec, *Le Français langue commune: Enjeu de la société québécoise.*
45 *The Gazette,* 23 March 1996, B4.
46 *The Gazette,* 4 April 1996, A1.
47 Alex Paterson, interview with author, 7 June 1995. See also Sloan, "Quebec: Progress and Problems."
48 *The Gazette,* 14 September 1995, A1.
49 *The Gazette,* 2 May 1996, B3. Almost the entire page was devoted to excerpts from the letter.
50 Barker, "Bills 142 and 101."
51 *The Gazette,* 17 August 1996, A3.
52 National Assembly, *Debates,* Standing Committe on Culture, 28 August 1996, CC10, 22.
53 Ibid., 29 August 1996, CC11, 75.
54 Ibid., 3 September 1996, CC12, 39–40.
55 National Assembly, *Debates,* 12 December 1996, 4325–6.
56 *Statutes of Quebec,* 1997, ch. 24.
57 *The Gazette,* 23 November 1996, A1.
58 *The Gazette,* 24 November 1996, A1.
59 *The Gazette,* 25 November 1996, A1.
60 *The Gazette,* 23 January 1997, A7.

61 *Le Devoir,* 27 January 1997, A1.

62 *The Gazette,* 4 February 1997, A1.

63 *Statutes of Quebec,* 1988, ch. 84.

64 National Assembly, *Debates,* 25 March 1996, 6.

65 Ibid., Standing Committee on Education, 24 May 1996, CE6, 3.

66 Ibid., 16.

67 *The Gazette,* 17 August 1996, A1 and A13.

68 *The Gazette,* 20 August 1996, B3.

69 *The Gazette,* 23 January 1997, A1.

70 Michael J. Hamelin, "Use Bill 107," *The Gazette,* 15 February 1997, B5.

71 *Mahe v Alberta,* [1990] 1 S.C.R. 342.

72 *The Globe and Mail,* 12 February 1997, A12.

73 *The Gazette,* 11 February 1997, A1.

74 House of Commons, *Debates,* 12 February 1997, 8011.

75 *The Gazette,* 18 February 1997, A1.

76 *Le Devoir,* 25 February 1997, A1.

77 *The Gazette,* 16 April 1997, A1-A2.

78 *The Gazette,* 29 May 1997, A9.

79 *Statutes of Quebec,* 1997, ch. 47.

80 *The Globe and Mail,* 19 November 1997, A4, and 16 December 1997, A7.

CHAPTER EIGHT

1 The centrifugal tendencies during the Trudeau years are discussed in Gwyn, *The Northern Magus: Pierre Trudeau and Canadians,* 253–64.

2 Johnston, *Up the Hill,* 31–2.

3 Donald Johnston, interview with author, 23 August 1994.

4 Sheila Finestone, interview with author, 7 May 1996.

5 Rod Blaker, interview with author, 30 August 1995.

6 Peter Blaikie, interview with author, 11 May 1995.

7 Blaker, interview, and Hal Herbert, interview with author, 15 August 1996.

8 Gerry Weiner, interview with author, 10 April 1995.

9 Nick auf der Maur, interview with author, 22 February 1996.

10 This paragraph is based on data from the reports of the Chief Electoral Officer on various federal general elections.

11 Eric Kierans, interview with author, 1 August 1994.

12 Trudeau, *Memoirs,* 160.

13 A copy of the unpublished manuscript, entitled *Reminiscences of a Trained Seal,* was given to the author by Mr Herbert. The quote is from p. 296.

14 Snell and Vaughan, *The Supreme Court of Canada: History of the Institution,* 225.

15 Ibid., 198.

16 *Revised Statutes of Canada*, 1985, ch. S-26, sec. 6.

17 Josée Legault, *L'invention d'une minorité: les Anglo-Québécois*, 67.

18 Warren Allmand, interview with author, 9 May 1996.

19 House of Commons, *Debates*, 21 December 1988, 525.

20 The reference is to an interview with the then Minister of Justice, reported in *La Presse*, 26 April 1982, A5.

21 Raymond Rock, interview with author, 8 May 1996.

22 Libman, *Riding the Rapids*, 61.

23 *Statutes of Canada*, 1968–69, ch. 54.

24 Canada, Commissioner of Official Languages, *Annual Report 1972–73* (Ottawa: Information Canada 1974), 67.

25 Ibid., *Annual Report 1977* (Ottawa: Minister of Supply and Services 1978), 25.

26 Ibid., *Annual Report 1978* (Ottawa: Minister of Supply and Services 1979), 31.

27 Ibid., *Annual Report 1979* (Ottawa: Minister of Supply and Services 1980), 24–6.

28 Ibid., *Annual Report 1980* (Ottawa: Minister of Supply and Services 1981), 24.

29 Ibid., *Annual Report 1981* (Ottawa: Minister of Supply and Services 1982), 31.

30 Ibid., *Annual Report 1982* (Ottawa: Minister of Supply and Services 1983), 24–6.

31 Ibid., *Annual Report 1983* (Ottawa: Minister of Supply and Services 1984), 19–20.

32 Ibid., *Annual Report 1986* (Ottawa: Minister of Supply and Services 1987), 157.

33 Ibid., *Annual Report 1988* (Ottawa: Minister of Supply and Services 1989), 230.

34 Ibid., *Annual Report 1991* (Ottawa: Minister of Supply and Services 1992), 131–2, and *Annual Report 1992* (Ottawa: Minister of Supply and Services 1993), 113.

35 Ibid., *Annual Report 1995* (Ottawa: Minister of Supply and Services 1996), 80, and *Annual Report 1996* (Ottawa: Minister of Supply and Services 1997), 75.

36 Sharon McCully, "Quebec's Eastern Townships: English-speakers and the Federal Public Service," 14–15.

37 Canada, Commissioner of Official Languages, *Annual Report 1987* (Ottawa: Minister of Supply and Services 1988), 61.

38 Ibid., *Annual Report 1988* (Ottawa: Minister of Supply and Services 1989), 100.

39 Ibid., *Annual Report 1996* (Ottawa: Minister of Supply and Services 1997), 78–9.

40 *Statutes of Canada*, 1987–88, ch. 38, sec. 2(b).

41 Ibid., sec. 43:1(a).

42 Ibid., sec. 43:1(d).

43 Cited by Jacques Brassard in National Assembly, *Debates*, 4 May 1988, 773–4.

44 National Assembly, *Debates*, 16 June 1988, 2353–7.

45 Canada, Privy Council Office, *Federal-Provincial Programs and Activities, A Descriptive Inventory 1992–1993* (Ottawa: Minister of Public Works and Government Services 1993), 25–2.

46 Ibid., *Federal Programs and Activities, A Descriptive Inventory 1994–1995* (Ottawa: Minister of Public Works and Government Services 1995), 5–9, 5–10.

47 Prosperi, "The Dynamics of Ethno-Linguistic Mobilization in Canada," 52.

48 Ibid., 98.

49 Michael Hamelin, interview with author, 23 February 1996. See also Canada, Commissioner of Official Languages, *Annual Report 1982* (Ottawa: Minister of Supply and Services 1983), 25.

50 The history and description of the program are taken from Canada, Court Challenges Program, *Annual Report 1994–1995* (Winnipeg: Court Challenges Program 1995), 7–14.

51 Ibid., 16, 18.

52 Canada, Commissioner of Official Languages, *Language Rights and the Court Challenges Program.*

53 *A.G. Quebec v Blaikie* (No. 2) [1981] 1 S.C.R. 312.

54 *A.G. Quebec v Association of Quebec Protestant School Boards* [1984] 2 S.C.R. 66.

55 Alex Paterson, interview with author, 7 June 1995.

56 *MacDonald v City of Montreal* [1986] 1 S.C.R. 460.

57 *Regina v Cross* [1993] 76 C.C.C. (3rd) 445.

58 Canada, Commissioner of Official Languages, *Annual Report 1989* (Ottawa: Minister of Supply and Services 1990), 203.

59 Sawatsky, *Mulroney: The Politics of Ambition*, 14.

60 Ibid., 382.

61 House of Commons, *Debates*, 19 December 1988, 297, and 21 December 1988, 522–3.

62 Trudeau, *Federalism and the French Canadians*, 31.

63 Alex Paterson, interview.

64 William Tetley, interview with author, 25 August 1994.

65 A useful collection of Scott's writings is *Essays on the Constitution, Aspects of Canadian Law and Politics.* See especially "The Special Nature of Canadian Federalism," 175–89, and "Centralization and Decentralization in Canadian Federalism," 251–79.

66 Parliament, Special Joint Committee on the Constitution, *Minutes of Proceedings and Evidence*, 19 November 1980, 8:31.

67 Ibid., 18 November 1980, 7:53–7:54.

68 Ibid., 24 November 1980, 11:12.

69 Ibid., 18 November 1980, 7:55–7:56.

70 Ibid., 18 November 1980, 7:73–7:74.

71 Quebec Liberal Party, *A New Canadian Federation.*

72 Fraser, *PQ: René Lévesque and the Parti Québécois in Power,* 290, 291.

73 John Ciaccia, interview with author, 22 May 1996.

74 National Assembly, *Debates,* 2 October 1981, 133–4.

75 Interviews with author: Joan Dougherty, 24 August 1994; Richard French, 9 May 1995; John O'Gallagher, 12 May 1995.

76 Interviews with author: Herbert Marx, 9 June 1995; Reed Scowen, 2 September 1994; Christos Sirros, 19 August 1996.

77 House of Commons, *Debates,* 23 October 1981, 12115.

78 Ibid., 9 November 1981, 12681–2.

79 Johnston, interview.

80 House of Commons, *Debates,* 1 December 1981, 13593.

81 *Statutes of Quebec,* 1975, ch. 6.

82 Legault, *L'invention d'une minorité,* 147.

83 National Assembly, *Debates,* Standing Committee on Institutions, 20 May 1987, CI2359–CI2370.

84 Royal Orr, interview with author, 22 February 1996.

85 Parliament, Special Joint Committee on the 1987 Constitutional Accord, *Minutes of Proceedings and Evidence,* 18 August 1987. The complete text of the brief is at 8A:1–8A:15. The quote is from 8A:14.

86 Ibid., 8:80.

87 Ibid., 19 August 1987, 9:11.

88 Parliament, Senate Submissions Group on the Meech Lake Constitutional Accord, *Proceedings,* 4 March 1988, 3:36.

89 Ibid., 3:64.

90 Ibid., 29 February 1988, 1:65–1:69.

91 House of Commons, *Debates,* 26 June 1987, 7671–2.

92 Ibid., 5 October 1987, 9671–2.

93 Ibid., 6 October 1987, 9735.

94 Ibid., 21 October 1987, 10254.

95 David Berger, interview with author, 9 October 1997.

96 House of Commons, *Debates,* 22 June 1988, 16728–9.

97 Finestone, interview.

98 National Assembly, *Debates,* 28 March 1990, 1441–3.

99 Geoffrey Chambers, interview with author, 19 February 1996.

100 A detailed but unsympathetic account of Bourassa's handling of the constitutional issue after 1990 may be found in two massive volumes by J.-F. Lisée, *Le Tricheur: Robert Bourassa et les Québécois 1990–1991* and *Le Naufrageur: Robert Bourassa et les Québécois 1991–1992.* Lisée, who later

worked for the Parizeau and Bouchard governments, blames Bourassa for preventing Quebec from gaining its independence after the collapse of Meech Lake.

101 William Cosgrove, interview with author, 20 February 1996.

102 Lisée, *Le Tricheur*, 271.

103 Cosgrove, interview.

104 Lisée, *Le Tricheur*, 334.

105 Cosgrove, interview. Cosgrove was also interviewed by Jean-François Lisée, and the account of his actions in *Le Tricheur* agrees with his recollections.

106 Richard Holden, interview with author, 6 June 1995. The text of the statement is in National Assembly, *Report of the Commission on the Political and Constitutional Future of Quebec*, March 1991, 120–4.

107 The roll call vote is recorded in National Assembly, *Debates*, 20 June 1991, 9737.

108 Parliament, Special Joint Committee on a Renewed Canada, *Minutes of Proceedings and Evidence*, 11 December 1991, 29:30–2.

109 Ibid., 3 February 1992, 58:47–8.

110 Ibid., 58:24–7.

111 Ibid., 17 December 1991, 32:31–5.

112 National Assembly, *Debates*, 11 March 1992, 11897, and 18 March 1992, 12047.

113 Ibid., 2nd session, 16 September 1992, 3668–9.

114 Ibid., 10 September 1992, 3374–9, and 9 September 1992, 3331–2.

115 Neil Cameron, interview with author, 11 May 1995.

116 National Assembly, *Debates*, 16 September 1992, 3638.

117 *Revised Statutes of Quebec*, ch. C-64.

118 *Libman v A.G. Quebec* (Unreported).

119 Robert Keaton, interview with author, 21 February 1996.

120 Percentages calculated from the vote for each Quebec riding as reported in *The Gazette*, 27 October 1992, B-10.

121 Le Duc and Pammett, "Referendum Voting: Attitudes and Behaviour in the 1992 Constitutional Referendum," 21.

122 For a useful discussion of these tendencies, see McBride and Shields, *Dismantling a Nation: The Transition to Corporate Rule in Canada*, 101–40.

123 Stéphane Dion, "Explaining Quebec Nationalism," 120.

CHAPTER NINE

1 Joy, *Languages in Conflict: The Canadian Experience*, 135. This edition is a reprint of the book that was privately published in 1967.

2 Ibid., 136.

3 *La Presse*, 26 April 1982, A5.

4 McCall's response is in *The Gazette,* 4 May 1982, B3.

5 Arnopoulos and Clift, *The English Fact in Quebec,* 194.

6 Lemieux, *Le Parti libéral du Québec: Alliances, rivalités et neutralités,* 202–3.

7 The case for a non-confrontational approach is ably presented by Julius Grey, "Building Bridges," *The Gazette,* 16 July 1997, B3.

8 See for example Pross, *Group Politics and Public Policy,* 110–13.

9 Ibid., 117–19.

10 The classic statement of the problem is Olson, *The Logic of Collective Action: Public Goods and the Theory of Groups.*

11 *The Gazette,* 2 June 1998, B2.

12 Ibid., A8.

13 The essential sources are Scowen, *A Different Vision: The English in Quebec in the 1990s* and Gary Caldwell, *La question du Québec anglais.* The paragraphs that follow are based on these two books and on interviews by the author with Reed Scowen, 2 September 1994, and with Gary Caldwell, 20 August 1996.

14 Guindon, "The other options of the national movement in Quebec," 163–70.

15 Scowen, *A Different Vision,* 110.

16 Ibid., 99. Emphasis in the original.

17 Caldwell, interview.

18 Henripin, "Population Trends and Policies in Quebec," 304–18.

19 Bowen, *Protestants in a Catholic State: Ireland's Privileged Minority,* 21.

20 Jedwab, *English in Montreal: A Layman's Look at the Current Situation,* 112, 114.

21 Ibid., 120.

22 Ibid., 31.

23 Quebec, *Le français langue commune: Enjeu de la société québécoise,* 276.

24 More than half of people surveyed in the European Union claim the ability to speak at least one European language other than their own, with overwhelming majorities in Luxembourg, the Netherlands, Denmark and Sweden claiming this ability. A quarter of the people in the United Kingdom claim the ability to speak French – a significantly higher proportion than do so in Ontario. See "Euro-tongues wag in English," *The Economist,* 25 October 1997, 60.

25 The similarities are discussed in Reitz and Breton, *The Illusion of Difference: Realities of Ethnicity in Canada and the United States.*

26 For a fuller discussion see Marger, *Race and Ethnic Relations: American and Global Perspectives,* 116–21.

27 Margaret Westley cites the example of a former Quebec anglophone who shocked a Toronto gathering with a joke that reflected the cynical view of electoral politics in the Quebec of the Duplessis era. Westley, *Remembrance of Grandeur,* 290.

28 Hamilton, "Notes on Montreal English."

29 See Ingrid Peritz, "The world 'remarks' our French-influenced English," *The Gazette*, 11 July 1992, B1.

30 See Ingrid Peritz, "Quebec English elevated to dialect," *The Gazette*, 20 August 1997, A1.

31 Bell, *The Roots of Disunity: A Study of Canadian Political Culture*, 72–3.

32 *Le français langue commune*, 276.

33 Jedwab, *English in Montreal*, 69.

34 Quoted in Genest, *Godbout*, 183.

Bibliography

GOVERNMENT PUBLICATIONS

Canada

Census, 1951, 1961, 1971, 1976, 1981, 1991, 1996
Commissioner of Official Languages. *Annual Report* 1972–73 to 1983, 1986,
   1987, 1988, 1991, 1992, 1993, 1995, 1996
Court Challenges Program, *Annual Report 1994–95*
House of Commons, *Debates*
Privy Council Office. *Federal-Provincial Programs and Activities, A Descriptive
   Inventory, 1992–1993, 1994–1995*
Revised Statutes of Canada
Senate Submissions Group on the Meech Lake Constitutional Accord.
   Proceedings
Statutes of Canada
Special Joint Committee on a Renewed Canada, *Minutes of Proceedings and
   Evidence*
Special Joint Committee on the Constitution. *Minutes of Proceedings and Evidence*
Special Joint Committee on the 1987 Constitutional Accord. *Minutes of Pro-
   ceedings and Evidence*
Twenty-Eighth General Election 1968: Report of the Chief Electoral Officer

Quebec

Legislative Assembly, *Debates*

National Assembly, *Debates*
Statutes of Quebec

LEGAL CASES

A.G. Quebec v Blaikie
A.G. Manitoba v Forest
A.G. Quebec v Quebec Association of Protestant School Boards et al.
Ford v Quebec
Greater Montreal Protestant School Board v Quebec
Libman v A.G. Quebec
MacDonald v City of Montreal
Mahe v Alberta
Protestant School Board of Greater Montreal v Minister of Education of Quebec
Regina v Cross
Reference re Education Act (Quebec)

PARTY RESOLUTIONS

Quebec Liberal Party. Resolution no. 5, June 1985.
– Resolution no. 6, June 1986.

NEWSPAPERS AND MAGAZINES

Le Devoir
The Economist
The Gazette
The Globe and Mail
The Montreal Star
Montréal-Matin
La Presse
Saturday Night
The Toronto Star

BOOKS AND ARTICLES

Lord Acton, "Nationality." In *Essays on Freedom and Power*. Cleveland: World Publishing 1955. 160–1.
Alliance Quebec, *Report of Task Force on Job Opportunities for English-Speaking Youth in Quebec*. Montreal: Alliance Quebec 1992
Ames, Herbert Brown. *The City Below the Hill*. Toronto: University of Toronto Press 1972; reprint of the 1897 edition.

Amit-Talai, Vered. "Will They Go?: A Study of Intentions Regarding Migration Among Secondary V Students in Quebec." *Canadian Ethnic Studies* 25 (1993): 50–61.

Anctil, Pierre. "Double majorité et multiplicité ethnoculturelle à Montréal." *Recherches sociographiques* 25 (1984): 441–56.

Angell, Harold M. "Quebec Provincial Politics in the 1920s." M.A. thesis, McGill University, 1960.

Archibald, Clinton. *Un Québec corporatiste?* Hull: Éditions Asticou 1983.

Arnopoulos, Sheila McLeod. "Integration of English into French Quebec Society: Some New Directions." M.A. thesis, Concordia University, 1978.

Arnopoulos, Sheila McLeod, and Dominique Clift. *The English Fact in Quebec.* 2nd edition. Montreal and Kingston: McGill-Queen's University Press 1984.

auf der Maur, Nick. "I Was the October Crisis." *Saturday Night* 110, no. 9 (1995): 93–4.

Aunger, Edmund A. *In Search of Political Stability: A Comparative Study of New Brunswick and Northern Ireland.* Montreal and Kingston: McGill-Queen's University Press 1981.

Barker, Charles. "Bills 142 and 101." *Language and Society* 46 (summer 1994): 22–3.

Bauer, Julien. *Les Minorités au Québec.* Montréal: Boréal 1994

Bawden, James E.A. "The English-Speaking Community of Montreal 1850–1867." M.A. thesis, Wilfrid Laurier University, 1975.

Behiels, Michael D. *Prelude to Quebec's Quiet Revolution: Liberalism versus Neo-Nationalism, 1945–1960.* Montreal and Kingston: McGill-Queen's University Press 1985.

Bell, David V.J. *The Roots of Disunity: A Study of Canadian Political Culture.* Revised edition. Toronto: Oxford University Press 1992.

Bercuson, David J. *True Patriot: The Life of Brooke Claxton.* Toronto: University of Toronto Press 1993.

Bercuson, David J., and Barry Cooper. *Deconfederation: Canada without Quebec.* Toronto: Key Porter Books 1991.

Bernard, André. *Québec: élections 1976.* Montréal: Éditions Hurtubise HMH 1976.

Bernier, Gérald. "La structure socio-économique de l'éléctorat montréalais et les partis politiques québécois: 1956–1966." M.A. thesis, Université de Montréal, 1969.

Black, Conrad. *Duplessis.* Toronto: McClelland and Stewart 1977.

Boissevain, Jeremy. *The Italians of Montreal: Social Adjustment in a Plural Society.* Studies of the Royal Commission on Bilingualism and Biculturalism, no. 7. Ottawa: Information Canada 1970.

Bolduc, Denis, and Pierre Fortin. "Les Francophones sont-ils plus 'xénophobes' que les Anglophones au Québec? Une analyse quantitative exploratoire." *Canadian Ethnic Studies* 22 (1990): 54–77.

Bonenfant, Jean-Charles. "Les douze circonscriptions électorales privilegiées du Québec." *Cahiers de Géographie* no. 12 (1962): 161–6.

Bothwell, Robert. "Out, Damned Spot: English Rights in Quebec." In J.L. Granatstein and Kenneth McNaught, eds., *"English Canada" Speaks Out.* Toronto: Doubleday 1991.

Bourassa, Guy. *Les Relations ethniques dans la vie politique montréalaise.* Studies of the Royal Commission on Bilingualism and Biculturalism, no. 10. Ottawa: Information Canada 1971.

Bourassa, Robert. *Gouverner le Québec.* Montréal: Fides 1995.

Bourhis, Richard Y. "The Charter of the French Language and Cross-Cultural Communication in Montreal." In *Conflict and Language Planning in Quebec.* Clevedon, England: Multilingual Matters Ltd. 1984.

– "Ethnic and Language Attitudes in Quebec." In J.W. Berry and J.A. Laponce, eds., *Ethnicity and Culture in Canada: The Research Landscape.* Toronto: University of Toronto Press 1994.

Bowen, Kurt. *Protestants in a Catholic State: Ireland's Privileged Minority.* Montreal and Kingston: McGill-Queen's University Press 1983.

Breton, Raymond. "The Production and Allocation of Symbolic Resources: An Analysis of the Linguistic and Ethnocultural Fields in Canada." *Canadian Review of Sociology and Anthropology* 21, no. 2 (1984): 123–44.

Cahill, Elizabeth. "A Study of Political Attitudes in Pontiac County." Ph.D. diss., McGill University, 1971.

Caldwell, Gary. *A Demographic Profile of the English-Speaking Population of Quebec 1921–1971.* Quebec: International Centre for Research on Bilingualism 1974.

– "English-Speaking Quebec in the Light of its Reaction to Bill 22." *American Review of Canadian Studies* 6 (1976): 42–56.

– "Itinéraire migratoire des jeunes qui ont quitté l'école secondaire anglaise au Québec en 1971." *Cahiers québécois de démographie* 12, no. 2 (1983): 281–94.

– "Anglo-Quebec: Demographic Realities and Options for the Future." In Richard Y. Bourhis, ed., *Conflict and Language Planning in Quebec.* Clevedon, England: Multilingual Matters Ltd. 1984.

– "Discovering and Developing English-Canadian Nationalism in Quebec." *Canadian Review of Studies in Nationalism* 11 (1984): 245–56.

– *La question du Québec anglais.* Québec: Institut québécois de recherche sur la culture 1994.

Caldwell, Gary, and Eric Waddell. *The English of Quebec: From Majority to Minority Status.* Québec: Institut québécois de recherche sur la culture 1982.

Canada. *Parliamentary Debates on the Subject of the Confederation of the British North American Provinces.* Quebec: Hunter, Rose and Co. 1865.

– *Report of the Royal Commission on Bilingualism and Biculturalism, Book III. The Work World.* Ottawa: Queen's Printer 1969.

- *Twenty-Eighth General Election 1968: Report of the Chief Electoral Officer.* Ottawa: Queen's Printer 1969.
- Commissioner of Official Languages, *Language Rights and the Court Challenges Program: A Review of Its Accomplishments and the Impact of Its Abolition.* Ottawa: Minister of Supplies and Services 1992.

Cappon, Paul. *Conflit entre les Néo-Canadiens et les francophones de Montréal.* Québec: Presses de l'Université Laval 1974.

Careless, J.M.S. *The Union of the Canadas 1841–1857.* Toronto: McClelland and Stewart 1967.

Chaput, Marcel. *Pourquoi je suis séparatiste.* Montréal: Éditions du Jour 1961.

Charron, Claude G. *La partition du Québec: De Lord Durham à Stéphane Dion.* Montréal: VLB Éditeur 1996.

Chodos, Robert, and Nick auf der Maur, eds. *Quebec: A Chronicle 1968–1972.* Toronto: James Lewis and Samuel 1972.

Citrin, Jacob. "The Quebec General Election of 1962." M.A. thesis, McGill University, 1963.

Clark, Gerald. *Montreal the New Cité.* Toronto: McClelland and Stewart 1982.

Clift, Dominique. *Le déclin du nationalisme au Québec.* Montréal: Libre Expression 1981.

Coleman, William D. *The Independence Movement in Quebec 1945–1980.* Toronto: University of Toronto Press 1984.

Cooper, Christopher C. "French-English Subcultural Segmentation: An Analysis of Consociational Politics in Quebec." M.A. thesis, University of Alberta, 1987.

Copp, Terry. *The Anatomy of Poverty: The Condition of the Working Class in Montreal 1897–1929.* Toronto: McClelland and Stewart 1974.

Corbeil, Pierre. "Les députés anglophones et le premier gouvernement du Québec de 1867 à 1871." Ph.D. diss., Université de Montréal, 1978.

Coulombe, Pierre A. *Language Rights in French Canada.* New York: Peter Lang 1995.

Cox, Robert W. "The Quebec Provincial Election of 1886." M.A. thesis, McGill University, 1948.

Creighton, Donald. *John A. Macdonald: The Young Politician.* Toronto: Macmillan 1952.

Cross, Dorothy Suzanne. "The Irish in Montreal 1867–1896." M.A. thesis, McGill University, 1968.

Daalder, Hans. "The Consociational Democracy Theme." *World Politics* 26, no. 4 (1974): 604–21.

Dion, Stéphane. "Understanding Quebec Nationalism." In R. Kent Weaver, ed., *The Collapse of Canada?* Washington: The Brookings Institution 1992.

Earl of Durham. *The Report of the Earl of Durham, Her Majesty's High Commissioner and Governor-General of British North America.* London: Methuen 1902.

Edwards, Reginald. "Historical Background of the English-Language CEGEPs of Quebec." McGill Journal of Education 25 (1990): 147–74.

Esman, Milton J. *Ethnic Politics.* Ithaca and London: Cornell University Press 1994.

Ferguson, Ted. "Quebec's English Few Bid For a Backlash." *Maclean's Magazine* 79, no. 12 (4 June 1966).

Fournier, Pierre. "A Political Analysis of School Reorganization in Montreal." M.A. thesis, McGill University, 1971.

– *The Quebec Establishment: The Ruling Class and the State.* Montreal: Black Rose Books 1976.

Fraser, Graham. *PQ: René Lévesque and the Parti Québécois in Power.* Toronto: Macmillan 1984.

Gallichan, Gilles. "De la Montreal Light, Heat and Power à Hydro-Québec." In Yves Bélanger and Robert Comeau, eds., *Hydro-Québec: Autres temps, autres défis.* Montréal: Presses de l'Université du Québec 1995.

Galt, Sir Alexander T. *Civil Liberty in Lower Canada.* Montreal: D. Bentley and Co. 1876.

Genest, Jean-Guy. *Godbout.* Sillery: Septentrion 1996.

Globensky, Peter Andre. "Voting Behaviour in Three Provincial Elections in Quebec: An Aggregate Data Analysis of the Voting Behaviour Patterns of the Quebec Provincial Electorate in the Elections of 1952, 1960, and 1962." M.A. thesis, McMaster University, 1973.

Grace, Robert J. *The Irish in Quebec: An Introduction to the Historiography.* Québec: Institut québécois de recherche sur la culture 1993.

Guardia, Raymond, and David Schulze. *Community Activism in Notre Dame de Grace Since World War II: An Analysis Based on Oral History.* Montreal: Third Image Oral History Project 1984.

Guindon, Hubert. "The crown, the Catholic church, and the French Canadian people: the historical roots of Quebec nationalism." In *Quebec Society: Tradition, Modernity and Nationhood.* Toronto: University of Toronto Press 1988.

– "The other options of the national movement in Quebec." In *Quebec Society: Tradition, Modernity and Nationhood.* Toronto: University of Toronto Press 1988.

– "The social evolution of Quebec reconsidered." In *Quebec Society: Tradition, Modernity and Nationhood.* Toronto: University of Toronto Press 1988.

Gwyn, Richard. *The Northern Magus: Pierre Trudeau and Canadians.* Toronto: McClelland and Stewart 1980.

Hamelin, Jean, and Louise Beaudoin. "Les cabinets provinciaux, 1867–1967." In Richard Desrosiers, ed., *Le personnel politique québécois.* Montréal: Boréal 1972.

Hamilton, Alexander, James Madison, and John Jay. *The Federalist Papers.* New York: Mentor Books 1961.

Hamilton, Donald E. "Notes on Montreal English." *Journal of the Canadian Linguistics Association* 4, no. 2 (1958): 70–9.

Heintzman, Ralph. "The Political Culture of Quebec, 1840–1960." *Canadian Journal of Political Science* 16, no. 1 (1983): 3–59.

Helly, Denise. "Politique québécoise face au 'pluralisme culturel' et pistes de recherche: 1977–1990." In J.W. Berry and J.A. Laponce, eds., *Ethnicity and Culture in Canada: The Research Landscape*. Toronto: University of Toronto Press 1994.

Henchey, Norman. "Quebec Education: The Unfinished Revolution." In Terence Morrison and Anthony Burton, eds., *Options, Reforms and Alternatives for Canadian Education*. Toronto: Holt, Rinehart and Winston 1973.

Henchey, Norman, and Donald Burgess. *Between Past and Future: Quebec Education in Transition*. Calgary: Detselig Enterprises 1987.

Henripin, Jacques. "Population Trends and Policies in Quebec." In Alain Gagnon, ed., *Quebec State and Society*, 2nd edition. Scarborough: Nelson Canada 1993.

Herbert, Harold. *Reminiscences of a Trained Seal* (unpublished).

Herzeg, Lynn. "The New Quiet Revolution." *Canadian Forum* (August/September 1984): 6–11.

Higgins, Benjamin. *The Rise – and Fall? of Montreal*. Moncton: Canadian Institute for Research on Regional Development 1985.

Hill, Robert Andrew. "Robert Sellar and the Huntingdon Gleaner: The Conscience of Rural Protestant Quebec." Ph.D. diss., McGill University, 1970.

Hirschman, Albert O. *Exit, Voice, and Loyalty: Responses to Decline in Firms, Organizations, and States*. Cambridge: Harvard University Press 1970.

Holden, Richard B. *1970 Election Quebec Crucible*. Montréal: Éditions Ariès 1970.

Hunter, Jean I. "The French Invasion of the Eastern Townships: A Regional Study." M.A. thesis, McGill University, 1939.

Jamieson, Stuart M. "French and English in the Institutional Structure of Montreal: A Study of the Social and Economic Division of Labour." M.A. thesis, McGill University, 1938.

Jedwab, Jack. "The Political Behaviour of Two Montreal Anglophone Constituencies During the Duplessis Era, 1935–1956: The Case of Westmount and Notre Dame de Grace." M.A. thesis, Concordia University, 1982.

– "Montreal Anglophones and the Quiet Revolution: Interest or Indifference?" Paper presented at the annual meeting of the Canadian Political Science Association, June 1984.

– "Uniting Uptowners and Downtowners: The Jewish Electorate and Quebec Provincial Politics 1927–39." *Canadian Ethnic Studies* 18 (1986): 7–19.

– "Les minorités du Québec et la question de l'unité nationale: étude du comportement électoral des québécois non-francophones 1992–94." Paper presented at the annual meeting of L'association canadienne-française pour l'avancement des sciences, 1995.

‒ *English in Montreal: A Layman's Look at the Current Situation*. Montréal: Éditions Images 1996.

Johnston, Donald. *Up the Hill*. Montreal and Toronto: Optimum Publishing 1986.

Joy, Richard J. *Languages in Conflict: The Canadian Experience*. Toronto: McClelland and Stewart 1972.

Keough, Brian Arthur. "The Quebec Department of Education, Cultural Pluralism, and the Anglophone Catholic Minority." M.A. thesis, McGill University, 1974.

Khouri, Nadia. *Qui a peur de Mordecai Richler?* Montréal: Éditions Balzac 1995.

King, Maurice J., *The First Step*. Huntingdon: Southwest Quebec Publishing 1993.

Kwavnick, David. *Organized Labour and Pressure Politics: The Canadian Labour Congress 1956–1968*. Montreal and London: McGill-Queen's University Press 1972.

Laczko, Leslie S. "English Canadians and Quebecois Nationalism." M.A. thesis, McGill University, 1974.

‒ "English Canadians and Quebecois Nationalism: An Empirical Analysis." *Canadian Review of Sociology and Anthropology* 15 (1978): 206–17.

‒ "Feelings of Threat among English-Speaking Quebeckers." In Hubert Guindon, Daniel Glenday and A. Turowetz, eds., *Modernization and the Canadian State*. Toronto: Macmillan 1978.

‒ *Pluralism and Inequality in Quebec*. Toronto: University of Toronto Press 1995.

Lange, Melanie Jane. "Montreal Anglophones: Social Distance and Emigration." M.A. thesis, McGill University, 1985.

Lapalme, Georges-Émile. *Le vent de l'oubli*. Montréal: Leméac 1970.

Latouche, Daniel. "La vraie nature de... la révolution tranquille." *Canadian Journal of Political Science* 7 (1974): 525–36.

Laurendeau, André. "The Astonishing Attitude of the English in Quebec." *Maclean's Magazine* 72, no. 10 (9 May 1959).

Le Duc, Lawrence, and Jon H. Pammett. "Referendum Voting: Attitudes and Behaviour in the 1992 Constitutional Referendum." *Canadian Journal of Political Science* 28, no. 1 (1995): 3–33.

Legault, Josée. *L' invention d'une minorité: les anglo-québécois*. Montréal: Boréal 1992.

‒ "La minorité anglo-québécoise et le référendum." *Choix* 1, no. 9 (1995): 4–15.

Lemieux, Vincent. *Le Parti libéral du Québec: Alliances, rivalités et neutralités*. Sainte-Foy: Presses de l'Université Laval 1993.

Leslie, Peter. "Ethnic Hierarchies and Minority Consciousness in Quebec." In Richard Simeon, ed., *Must Canada Fail?* Montreal and London: McGill-Queen's University Press 1977.

le Terreur, Marc. *Les tribulations des conservateurs au Québec.* Québec: Presses de l'Université Laval 1973.

Levine, Marc V. *The Reconquest of Montreal: Language Policy and Social Change in a Bilingual City.* Philadelphia: Temple University Press 1990.

Libman, Robert. *Riding the Rapids: The White-Water Rise and Fall of Quebec's Anglo Protest.* Montreal: Robert Davies Publishing 1995.

Lieberson, Stanley. "Bilingualism in Montreal: A Demographic Analysis." *American Journal of Sociology* 71, no. 1 (1965): 10–25.

Lijphart, Arend. *The Politics of Accommodation: Pluralism and Democracy in the Netherlands.* Berkeley and Los Angeles: University of California Press 1968.

– "Typologies of Democratic Systems." *Comparative Political Studies* 1 (1968): 3–44.

– "Consociational Democracy." *World Politics* 21, no. 2 (1969): 207–25.

– "Cultural Diversity and Theories of Political Integration." *Canadian Journal of Political Science* 4, no. 4 (1971): 1–14.

– "Consociation and Federation: Conceptual and Empirical Links." *Canadian Journal of Political Science* 12, no. 3 (1979): 499–515.

– "Self-Determination versus Pre-Determination of Ethnic Minorities in Power-Sharing Systems." In Will Kymlicka, ed., *The Rights of Minority Cultures.* New York: Oxford University Press 1995.

Lisée, Jean-François. *Le Tricheur: Robert Bourassa et les Québécois, 1990–1991.* Montréal: Boréal 1994.

– *Le Naufrageur: Robert Bourassa et les Québécois 1991–1992.* Montréal: Boréal 1994.

Little, J.I. "Watching the Frontier Disappear: English-Speaking Reaction to French-Canadian Colonization in the Eastern Townships, 1844–90." *Journal of Canadian Studies* 15 (1980): 93–111.

Locher, Uli. *Les anglophones de Montréal: émigration et évolution des attitudes 1978–1983.* Québec: Conseil de la langue française 1988.

Lorwin, Val R. "Segmented Pluralism: Ideological Cleavages and Political Cohesion in the Smaller European Democracies." In Kenneth D. McRae, ed., *Consociational Democracy: Political Accommodation in Segmented Societies.* Toronto: McClelland and Stewart 1974.

Lubin, Martin. "Quebec Nonfrancophones and the United States." In Alfred O. Hero Jr and Marcel Daneau, eds., *Problems and Opportunities in U.S.-Quebec Relations.* Boulder: Westview 1984.

Lustick, Ian. "Stability in Deeply Divided Societies: Consociationalism versus Control." *World Politics* 31, no. 3 (1979): 325–44.

Lysons, Heather. "The Language Question and Quebec Education." In Terence Morrison and Anthony Burton, eds., *Options: Reforms and Alternatives for Canadian Education.* Toronto: Holt, Rinehart and Winston 1973.

MacDonald, L. Ian. *From Bourassa to Bourassa, A Pivotal Decade in Canadian History.* Montreal: Harvest House 1984.

MacLennan, Hugh. *The Watch That Ends the Night.* Toronto: Macmillan 1959.

Maheu, Robert. "L'émigration des anglophones québécois." *Cahiers québécois de démographie* 12, no. 2 (1983): 271–80.

Mallory, J.R. "English-Speaking Quebeckers in a Separate Quebec." In R.M. Burns, ed., *One Country or Two?* Montreal and Kingston: McGill-Queen's University Press 1971.

Marger, Martin N. *Race and Ethnic Relations: American and Global Perspectives,* 3rd edition. Belmont: Wadsworth 1994.

Marshall, Joan. *A Solitary Pillar: Montreal's Anglican Church and the Quiet Revolution.* Montreal and Kingston: McGill-Queen's University Press 1995.

McBride, Stephen, and John Shields. *Dismantling a Nation: The Transition to Corporate Rule in Canada.* 2nd edition. Halifax: Fernwood Publishing 1997.

McCully, Sharon. "Quebec's Eastern Townships: English-Speakers and the Federal Public Service." *Language and Society* 43 (summer 1993): 14–15.

McDougall, John N. *The Politics and Economics of Eric Kierans: A Man for All Canadas.* Montreal and Kingston: McGill-Queen's University Press 1993.

McKenna, Brian, and Susan Purcell. *Drapeau.* Toronto: Clarke, Irwin 1980.

McRae, Kenneth D. "Consociationalism and the Canadian Political System." In *Consociational Democracy: Political Accommodation in Segmented Societies.* Toronto: McClelland and Stewart 1974.

– "The Plural Society and the Western Political Tradition." *Canadian Journal of Political Science* 12, no. 4 (1979): 675–88.

McRoberts, Kenneth. *Quebec: Social Change and Political Crisis,* 3rd edition. Toronto: McClelland and Stewart 1988.

Mellos, Koula. "The Quebec General Election of 1966." M.A. thesis, McGill University, 1967.

Mill, John Stuart. *Considerations on Representative Government.* Chicago: Henry Regnery 1962.

Miller, J.R. *Equal Rights: The Jesuits' Estates Act Controversy.* Montreal and Kingston: McGill-Queen's University Press 1979.

Milner, Henry. *The Long Road to Reform: Restructuring Public Education in Quebec.* Montreal and Kingston: McGill-Queen's University Press 1986.

Monet, S.J. Jacques. *The Last Cannon Shot: A Study of French Canadian Nationalism 1837–1850.* Toronto: University of Toronto Press 1969.

Newman, Peter C. *Renegade in Power: The Diefenbaker Years.* Toronto: McClelland and Stewart 1963.

– *The Distemper of Our Times, Canadian Politics in Transition: 1963–1968.* Toronto: McClelland and Stewart 1968.

Noel, S.J.R. "Consociational Democracy and Canadian Federalism." *Canadian Journal of Political Science* 4, no. 1 (1971): 15–18.

– *Patrons, Clients, Brokers: Ontario Society and Politics 1791–1896.* Toronto: University of Toronto Press 1990.

Nordlinger, Eric A. *Conflict Regulation in Divided Societies*. Cambridge: Center for International Affairs, Harvard University 1972.

O'Donnell, Brendan P. "Consociationalism, English Quebec, and the Chauveau Ministry, 1867–1872: A Study of Political Accommodation." M.A. thesis, Wilfrid Laurier University, 1980.

Oliver, Michael. *The Passionate Debate: The Social and Political Ideas of Quebec Nationalism 1920–1945*. Montreal: Véhicule Press 1991.

Olson, Mancur. *The Logic of Collective Action: Public Goods and the Theory of Groups*. Cambridge and London: Harvard University Press 1965.

Pal, Leslie A. "Official Language Minorities and the State." In William D. Coleman and Grace Skogstad, *Policy Communities and Public Policy in Canada*. Mississauga: Copp Clark Pitman 1995.

Pappalardo, Adriano. "The Conditions for Consociational Democracy: A Logical and Empirical Critique." *European Journal of Political Research* 9 (1981): 365–90.

Parisella, John. "Pressure Group Politics: Case Study of the St. Léonard Schools Crisis." M.A. thesis, McGill University, 1971.

Parti Québécois. *The English-Speaking Community: An Integral Part of a Sovereign Quebec*. Montréal: Parti Québécois 1993.

– *Le Québec dans un monde nouveau*. Montréal: VLB Éditeur 1993.

Peate, Mary. *Girl in a Red River Coat*. Toronto: Clarke Irwin 1970.

Pelletier, Gérard. *The October Crisis*. Toronto: McClelland and Stewart 1971.

– *L'aventure du pouvoir 1968–1975*. Montréal: Stanké 1992.

Porter, John. *The Vertical Mosaic: An Analysis of Social Class and Power in Canada*. Toronto: University of Toronto Press 1965.

Power, Charles G. *A Party Politician: The Memoirs of Chubby Power*. Norman Ward, ed. Toronto: Macmillan 1966.

Price, Kenneth A. "The Social Construction of Ethnicity: The Case of English Montrealers." Ph.D. diss., York University, 1980.

Prosperi, Paul. "The Dynamics of Ethno-Linguistic Mobilization in Canada: A Case Study of Alliance Quebec." M.A. thesis, University of Ottawa, 1996.

Pross, A. Paul. *Group Politics and Public Policy*. Toronto: Oxford University Press 1986.

Quebec. *Report of the Commission of Inquiry on the Position of the French Language and on Language Rights in Quebec*. Quebec: 1972.

– *Report of the Commission on the Political and Constitutional Future of Quebec*. Quebec: 1994.

– Task Force on English Education. *Report to the Minister of Education of Quebec*. Montreal: 1992.

– Comité interministériel sur la situation de la langue française. *Le Français langue commune: Enjeu de la société québécoise*. Québec: Ministère de la Culture et des Communications 1996.

Quebec Liberal Party. *A New Canadian Federation.* Montreal: Quebec Liberal Party 1980.

Quinn, Herbert F. "The Quebec Provincial Election of 1944: An Analysis of the Role of the Election in the Democratic Process." M.A. thesis, McGill University, 1946.

– *The Union Nationale: Quebec Nationalism from Duplessis to Lévesque,* 2nd edition. Toronto: University of Toronto Press 1979.

Reid, Scott. *Canada Remapped: How the Partition of Quebec will Reshape the Nation.* Vancouver: Pulp Press 1992.

Reilly, Wayne G. "Political Attitudes among Law Students in Quebec." *Canadian Journal of Political Science* 4, no. 1 (1971): 122–31.

Reitz, Jeffrey G., and Raymond Breton. *The Illusion of Difference: Realities of Ethnicity in Canada and the United States.* Toronto: C.D. Howe Institute 1994.

Reynolds, Lloyd G. *The British Immigrant: His Social and Economic Adjustment in Canada.* Toronto: Oxford University Press 1935.

Richard, Laurence. *Jacques Parizeau: Un bâtisseur.* Montréal: Les Éditions de l'Homme 1992.

Richler, Mordecai. "A Reporter at Large." *The New Yorker,* 23 September 1991: 40–92.

– *Oh Canada! Oh Quebec! Requiem for a Divided Country.* Toronto: Penguin Books 1992.

Romalis, Coleman. "The Attitudes of the Montreal Jewish Community Toward French Canadian Nationalism and Separatism." M.A. thesis, McGill University, 1967.

Rose, Courtice, "The Concept of Reach and the Anglophone Minority in Quebec." *Canadian Ethnic Studies* 17 (1985): 1–16.

Rosenberg, M. Michael, and Jack Jedwab. "Institutional Completeness, Ethnic Organizational Style and the Role of the State: The Jewish, Italian and Greek Communities of Montreal." *Canadian Review of Sociology and Anthropology* 29 (1992): 266–87.

Ross, Aileen D. "The Cultural Effects of Population Changes in the Eastern Townships." *Canadian Journal of Economics* 9 (1943): 447–62.

Rudin, Ronald. *The Forgotten Quebecers: A History of English-Speaking Quebec 1759–1980.* Québec: Institut québécois de recherche sur la culture 1985.

Sancton, Andrew. *Governing the Island of Montreal: Language Differences and Metropolitan Politics.* Berkeley and Los Angeles: University of California Press 1985.

Sawatsky, John. *Mulroney: The Politics of Ambition.* Toronto: Macfarlane, Walter and Ross 1991.

Saywell, John. *Canadian Annual Review of Politics and Public Affairs 1973.* Toronto: University of Toronto Press 1974.

– *Canadian Annual Review of Politics and Public Affairs 1976.* Toronto: University of Toronto Press 1977.

Schacter, Susan. "Working Papers on English Language Institutions in Quebec." Montreal: Alliance Quebec 1982 (unpublished).

Scott, Frank, and Michael Oliver, eds. *Quebec States Her Case*. Toronto: Macmillan 1964.

Scott, Frank R. *Essays on the Constitution, Aspects of Canadian Law and Politics*. Toronto: University of Toronto Press 1977.

Scowen, Reed. *La réalité du transfert des entreprises en dehors du Québec*. Montréal: November 1978.

– *A Different Vision: The English in Quebec in the 1990s*. Don Mills: Maxwell Macmillan 1991.

Sellar, Robert. *The Tragedy of Quebec*. Toronto: University of Toronto Press 1974.

Sévigny, Pierre. *This Game of Politics*. Toronto: McClelland and Stewart 1965.

Shaw, William F., and Lionel Albert. *Partition: The Price of Quebec's Independence*. Montreal: Thornhill Publishing 1980.

Skelton, O.D. *The Life and Times of Sir Alexander Tilloch Galt*. Toronto: Oxford University Press 1920.

Sloan, Tom. "Quebec: Progress and Problems." *Language and Society* 46 (summer 1994): 19–21.

Smiley, Donald V. "French-English Relations in Canada and Consociational Democracy." In Milton V. Esman, ed., *Ethnic Conflict in the Western World*. Ithaca: Cornell University Press 1977.

Smith, Bernard. *Les élections 1970 au Québec, Le coup d'état du 29 avril*. Montréal: Éditions Actualité 1970.

Smith, Goldwin. *Canada and the Canadian Question*. Toronto: University of Toronto Press 1971; first published 1891.

Smith, Richard. "Goodbye Noblesse Oblige: Quebec Anglos in Crisis." In J.L. Granatstein and Kenneth McNaught, eds., *"English Canada" Speaks Out*. Toronto: Doubleday 1991.

Snell, James G., and Frederick Vaughan. *The Supreme Court of Canada: History of the Institution*. Toronto: University of Toronto Press 1985.

Stevenson, Garth. *Ex Uno Plures: Federal-Provincial Relations in Canada, 1867–1896*. Montreal and Kingston: McGill-Queen's University Press 1993.

Taddeo, Donat J., and Raymond C. Taras. *Le débat linguistique au Québec: La communauté italienne et la langue d'enseignement*. Montréal: Presses de l'Université de Montréal 1987.

Taylor, Donald M., and Lise Dubé-Simard. "Language Planning and Intergroup Relations: Anglophone and Francophone Attitudes Toward the Charter of the French Language." In Richard Y. Bourhis, ed., *Conflict and Language Planning in Quebec*. Clevedon, England: Multilingual Matters Ltd. 1984.

Tetley, William. "Language and Education Rights in Quebec and Canada." *Law and Contemporary Problems* 45, no. 4 (1982): 177–219.

Thomson, Dale C. *Jean Lesage and the Quiet Revolution.* Toronto: Macmillan 1984.

Tocqueville, Alexis de. *The Old Regime and the French Revolution.* New York: Doubleday Anchor 1955.

Trépanier, Pierre. "L'opinion publique anglo-québécoise et l'autonomie provinciale (1945–46)." *L'action nationale* 67 (1977): 34–55.

Trudeau, Pierre Elliott. *Federalism and the French Canadians.* Toronto: Macmillan 1968.

– *Memoirs.* Toronto: McClelland and Stewart 1993.

Tulchinsky, Gerald. "The Third Solitude: A.M. Klein's Jewish Montreal, 1910–1950." *Journal of Canadian Studies* 19, no. 2 (1984): 96–112.

van Nus, Walter. "The Role of Suburban Government in the City-Building Process: The Case of Notre Dame de Graces, (*sic*) Quebec, 1876–1910." *Urban History Review* 13 (1984): 91–103.

Veltman, Calvin. "L'évolution de la ségrégation linguistique à Montréal, 1961–1981." *Recherches sociographiques* 24 (1983): 379–90.

Webber, Jeremy. "Le réferendum et l'avenir des anglophones du Québec." *Choix* 1, no. 9 (1995): 16–28.

Westley, Margaret. *Remembrance of Grandeur: The Anglo-Protestant Elite of Montreal, 1900–1950.* Montréal: Libre Expression 1990.

White, Thomas Jr. *The Protestant Minority in Quebec in its Political Relations with the Roman Catholic Majority: A Letter Addressed to Sir Alexander Tilloch Galt.* Montreal: Dawson Brothers 1876.

Zinman, Rosalind. "Lachute, Quebec, French-English Frontier: A Case Study in Language and Community." M.A. thesis, Concordia University, 1975.

Index